Nandris, Grigore, 1895-1968.

Colloquial Rumanian: grammar, exercises, reader vocabulary

COLLOQUIAL
RUMANIAN

Uniform with this volume

COLLOQUIAL FRENCH
COLLOQUIAL GERMAN
COLLOQUIAL ITALIAN
COLLOQUIAL JAPANESE
COLLOQUIAL ARABIC
COLLOQUIAL PERSIAN
COLLOQUIAL SPANISH
COLLOQUIAL CHINESE
COLLOQUIAL ENGLISH
COLLOQUIAL HINDUSTANI
COLLOQUIAL HUNGARIAN
COLLOQUIAL MALAY
COLLOQUIAL RUSSIAN

London
Kegan Paul, Trench, Trubner
& Co. Ltd.

COLLOQUIAL RUMANIAN

Grammar, Exercises, Reader Vocabulary

By

GRIGORE NANDRIȘ, M.A., Ph.D.

Professor of Slavonic Philology at the University of Bucharest, Visiting Lecturer in Rumanian at the School for Slavonic and East European Studies at London University

LONDON

KEGAN PAUL, TRENCH, TRUBNER & CO. LTD.

BROADWAY HOUSE: 68–74 CARTER LANE, E.C.

First published August 1945

Printed in Great Britain by T. and A. Constable Ltd.
at the University Press, Edinburgh

CONTENTS

Verbs

Adverbs

Prepositions and Conjunctions

Interjections

PART III—Word Formation

Composition

Derivation

PART IV—Syntax

Word-Order

THE PRONOUN

THE VERB

ADVERBIAL CLAUSES

INTRODUCTORY NOTE

As Director of the University of London School of Slavonic and East European Studies, I am very glad to introduce this Grammar to the public. Its author, Dr. G. Nandriş, is a member of the School's staff.

The School in its work had long felt the need for a Grammar of the Rumanian language, and Dr. G. Nandriş worked out the plan of his book in courses which he held in the School. It is therefore with special pleasure that I take this opportunity to introduce his book, and I hope that the volume will meet with general approval and fill a real need in the provision of books for language studies.

WILLIAM J. ROSE.

15 Gordon Square,
London, W.C. 1.
January 1945.

PREFACE

Rumanian is a Latin (Romance) language spoken by some fifteen million Rumanians inhabiting the territory situated on the Lower Danube between the Black Sea and the River Dniester (Nistru) in the east, the borders (1939) of Poland and Czechoslovakia in the north, and the plain of the River Tisa (Theiss) in the west. About two million Rumanians, including the Rumanians in America, live outside this territory.[1]

Among the 120 languages spoken in Europe, Rumanian has the ninth place, coming after Spanish—spoken by some sixteen millions—and before Dutch—with some twelve millions.

In the Latin linguistic family, composed of nine languages, Rumanian has the fourth numerical place, after Italian, French, Spanish and before Portuguese, Catalan, Frioulan, Roumansh and Ladin. Like the Roumansh of Switzerland, Rumanian preserved the name of *Rome* in its denomination.[2]

All other Latin languages are offspring of the Latin of the Western Roman Empire, and are called West Romance languages. Rumanian is the only survivor of the Latin language spoken in the Eastern Roman Empire. In linguistic terms we may define Rumanian as an evolved form of East Latin with the changes and influences it has experienced during twenty centuries.

Being cut off from the Western Latin area, through the

[1] Other names given to the Rumanians :

Moldavians—the inhabitants of the north-eastern province of Rumania (Moldova), and the Rumanians of Russia, east of the River Dniester.

Walachians—the inhabitants of the southern province of Rumania, between the Carpathians and the Danube (Walachia, Muntenia or Țara Românească), and the Rumanians in the neighbouring areas of Bulgaria and Serbia.

In the same way, Rumanians are named after the provinces they inhabit : Transylvanians, Oltenians, Bessarabians, Bucovinians, Dobrudzhians.

[2] The modern Rumanian terms are : Român (*n.*) ; *român, românesc* (*adj.*) ; România (*n.*)=Rumania. The old and popular term, however, is, according to the phonetical rules of the Rumanian language, *Rumân* (*n.*).

settlement of the Slavs in South-Eastern Europe in the seventh century, and through the settlement of the Magyars in Central Europe in the ninth century, the Rumanian language has had an evolution independent of the other Romance languages. Because this evolution did not continue to be influenced by medieval Latin, like the evolution of the Western Romance languages, the Rumanian language is in some ways more conservative than the Western Romance languages, i.e. it is nearer to Latin.

Instead it was influenced by the languages of Eastern Europe with which it came in contact; especially by the Slavonic languages, in their older form of the seventh century and later. This influence affected principally the vocabulary. On the other hand, Rumanian has had a common evolution with the Balkan languages of to-day which are built on the same ethnographical substratum.

The consequence of the first influence is a multitude of foreign words in the Rumanian of to-day. The consequence of the second fact is a number of conformities to the other Balkan languages—Albanian, Bulgarian, Greek and Serbian. These conformities are so peculiar to the Balkan languages that, although they belong genealogically to four different linguistic families—Romance, Slav, Greek and Thraco-Illyrian, they form together a Balkan linguistic group.

The importance of the foreign elements in the Rumanian language has been exaggerated. On the basis of the dry statistics of the dictionaries these elements are numerous. According to the very imperfect etymological dictionary of Cihac (*Dictionnaire d'étymologie daco-roumaine*, Frankfort, 1870-79) the proportion between different elements in Rumanian is this: Latin elements 1165, i.e. one-fifth; Slavonic elements 2361, i.e. two-fifths; Turkish 965, New Greek 695, Hungarian 689, Albanian 50. But on the basis of their currency, the actual Rumanian language works with 85-90 per cent. Latin elements in its composition. You cannot express the simplest idea without Latin elements; there exist, however, entire poems or prose pages almost without any foreign elements, and these are not literary products of a spurious patriotism. On the other hand, there are foreign elements which occur only once in some old text. The law of expression alone decides the destiny of words in a language.

The existence of foreign elements in a language has nothing to do with the racial composition of the people. Linguistic facts must be kept apart from anthropological facts ; e.g. the Latin and Greek elements of the English language do not indicate the part the Romans or the Greeks took in the forming of the English people.

Anthropologically speaking, the Rumanian people represent the romanized Thracians of South-Eastern Europe, with an admixture of Slavs and other elements which entered the Thraco-Roman composition during nearly two thousand years of the history of the Rumanian people. However, this problem does not constitute a part of linguistic studies.

The process of Romanization in the Eastern Roman Empire was a similar one to that in the Western. Everywhere Roman administration and Latin culture caused the autochthonous languages to be superseded by Latin. The breaking up of the unity of Roman civilization—a consequence of the splitting of the Roman Empire—made it possible for different provinces to develop the Latin language along their own lines. The Rumanian language represents the evolution of Eastern, i.e. Balkan Latin.

The Dialects of the Rumanian language.

The Rumanian language of to-day has four main dialects:

1. The *Daco-Rumanian* dialect is the language spoken in the ancient Dacia, north of the Danube, conquered by the Emperor Trajan in 102-106 A.D. This dialect, especially the Southern (Walachian) form, is to-day the cultural and literary language of the Rumanian people.

In spite of small differences existing between the subdialects in various Daco-Rumanian regions to-day, this North-Danubian dialect is so uniform that Rumanians from all extremities of the country can understand and speak with each other without any difficulty. Daco-Rumanian is also spoken by the Rumanians in the neighbouring areas of Russia, Czechoslovakia, Yugoslavia and Bulgaria, as well as by those in America.

2. The *Aroumanian* or *Macedo-Rumanian* dialect is spoken by Rumanians in the Balkans (Greece, Macedonia, Albania, Yugoslavia, Bulgaria). These people are also called *Cutsovlachs, Vlachs, Tsintsars.* They inhabit the towns and villages and are renowned as tradesmen and skilled artisans everywhere in the Balkans and even in Central Europe. In the Middle Ages they had important cultural centres like that of Moscopolis. Many of the Macedo-Rumanians live a half-nomad life as shepherds in the mountains and on the plains of the Balkans (Epirus, Pindus, Thessaly, Macedonia). After the First World War many of them were settled in the kingdom of Rumania, in Southern Dobrudzha.

3. The *Megleno-Rumanians* or *Meglenites* speak another dialect. They inhabit some (about seven) villages in the Moglen region, north-east of Salonika. In the First World War their villages were in the front line and most of them were destroyed.

4. The *Istro-Rumanians*, a branch of the Rumanian race pushed towards the West from the Rumanian trunk, speak another Rumanian dialect. They inhabit some villages in the Istria peninsula, south-east of Trieste, near Monte Maggiore. They number only some thousands.

The last three dialects are hardly to be understood by the Daco-Rumanians without being studied.

The earliest evidence of the Rumanian language is a phrase mentioned by the Byzantine chroniclers, *Theophylactos Simocathes* of the seventh century and *Theophanes Confessor* of the eighth century. Both these writers had apparently a common older source where they found the fact that during a panic in the army of the Byzantine general Comentiolus, who fought against the Avars (587 A.D.), a soldier shouted in his native language: "*retorna* or *torna, torna fratre*"= (return, brother)!

If, however, we ignore these few words which are differentiated from Latin, and mention only that Latin and Slav documents of the twelfth to the fourteenth centuries contain Rumanian words which disclose the ancient aspect of the Rumanian language, we can say that the first written samples of Rumanian are found in glosses of the fifteenth century and in a Rumanian letter written in 1521 by a certain Neacşu of Câmpulung (Walachia) to his friend Hans Bengner of Braşov (Transylvania) to inform him about the approach of the Turks.

Beginning with the fourteenth century, when the Rumanians created their first greater political organizations north of the Danube,[1] they used in the Church and in their political affairs the Middle Slavonic language, a form of the Old Church Slavonic of the ninth to the eleventh centuries, with local variations. It is through this language, which played in the life of the Orthodox people of Eastern Europe a similar rôle to that of Latin in the West, that the Rumanians were in touch with Byzantine culture. A rich Slavonic literature of religious writings, annals, and pseudo-religious books was created in this language in the Rumanian countries.

The first Rumanian texts were written in the sixteenth century in Northern Transylvania (Maramureş). They are reproductions of older manuscripts of the fifteenth century and are translations of parts of the Bible made under the influence of Hussitism or the Reformation. The Acts (*Codex of Voroneț*), the Psalms (*Psalter of Șcheia*, *Psalter of Voroneț*, *Psalter Hurmuzachi*), the Old Testament—Genesis and Exodus (*Palia of Orăștie*), religious and pseudo-religious writing (*Codex Sturdzanus*) are among them.

The first books printed on Rumanian soil were in Slavonic —a Missal in 1508, the Gospels in 1512—on a printing press brought from Venice, after it had printed the first Slav books in Cetinje (Montenegro).

[1] Chaucer in his poem *The Book of the Duchesse*, written in 1369, mentions one of the Rumanian political organizations :

Ne sende men in-to Walakaye.
To Prusye and in-to Tartarye.
(Verses 1024-1025.)

The first Rumanian book, the Gospels, was printed in 1560-61, by the Deacon Coresi. Of an earlier Catechism, printed in 1544 in Sibiu under the influence of the Reformation, no copy has yet been found.

The seventeenth century was the golden epoch of Old Rumanian culture, ecclesiastical as well as secular. The Bible is translated from Greek and printed in a monumental edition (1688). The chroniclers affirmed the Roman descent of the Rumanians and awakened national consciousness. "*Dela Râm ne tragem și cu a lor cuvinte ni-e amestecat graiul,*"=(From the Romans we have our origins, and with their words our language is mixed), states the Moldavian chronicler Miron Costîn (1633-91).

But now another language as well as the Slavonic and the Rumanian, entered into competition. This was the Greek of the Phanariots, who, beginning from about 1710, occupied the thrones of the two Principalities, buying them from the Turks.

The end of the eighteenth century marks a reaction against foreign influences and oppressive domination, and an emphasis upon Latin origins. Philologists and historians preach the rights of the people before even the French Revolution affirms them and Romanticism justifies them.

The spiritual result of Romanticism was a return to national tradition in the nineteenth century; the political result was the return of native-born rulers at the beginning of the nineteenth century and the union of the two Principalities (1859) in one state.

The nineteenth century brought both increased contact with the West and assimilation of Western ideas and also the manifestation of Rumanian originality. The old autochthonous culture, enriched by Byzantine elements, began to grow into a new unity. In the twentieth century, after the First World War, the Rumanian people was united in one state—the first union in the sixteenth century, under the Voevod Michael the Brave (1593-1601), was a short one—and gathered after centuries its spiritual and material forces into one political and cultural unit.

ACKNOWLEDGMENTS

THE author wishes to express his thanks for the willing help given to him by different people.

Professor W. J. Rose, Director of the School of Slavonic and East European Studies, went through the manuscript with me and suggested some improvements in the style.

The keen interest in some problems of the language shown by students in Rumanian in the School of Slavonic and East European Studies has been a valuable stimulant in the making of this book. In particular I want to thank Mr. N. W. Newcombe for his translation of a very difficult folk-poem included in the texts.

Last but not least, I must thank my wife for her help throughout the whole of my work.

I owe much to other authors in this field. Many examples of Rumanian Syntax are at least suggested by the excellent work of Kr. Sandfeld and Hedvig Olsen, *Syntaxe Roumaine*, Paris, 1936.

If this book succeeds in guiding the first steps of the student desiring to enter the field of the Rumanian language and culture it will have fulfilled its purpose.

G. NANDRIŞ.

ABBREVIATIONS

A., *acc.*, accusative.
a., *adj.*, adjective.
acc., accusative.
adv., adverb.
art., article.
cf., see.
comp., comparative.
conj., conjunction.
conjug., conjugation.
cp., see.
D., *dat.*, dative.
dial., dialectal.
dim., diminutive.
e.g., for example.
f., *fem.*, feminine.
G., *gen.*, genitive.
imp., imperative.
impf., imperfect.
ind., indicative.
indef., indefinite.
inf., infinitive.
intr., intransitive.
lit., literally.
m., *masc.*, masculine.
mix., mixed, neuter gender.
n., noun.
N., *nom.*, nominative.
num., numeral.
obj., object.
part., participle.
pass., passive.
pers., person.
pl., *plur.*, plural.
poss., possessive.
p. part., past participle.
pr. part., present participle.
pr., pronounced.
pred., predicate.
pref., prefix.
prep., preposition.
pres., present.
pron., pronoun.
prop., proper (noun).
prov., proverb.
refl., reflexive.
sg., *sing.*, singular.
subj., subject, subjunctive.
suf., suffix.
sup., superlative.
tr., transitive.
v., verb.
vbl., verbal.
vide, see.
voc., vocative.

SYMBOLS

The graphic symbols for the transcription of Rumanian sounds are explained in the text under every sound. (See **1.** 2–**1.** 5.)

References are to the number of the sections.

>placed after a word or a sound means that the word or the sound after this sign is an evolution of that before: e.g. **a înnopta> a înopta;** <placed after a word or a sound means that the word or the sound before the sign is derived from that following it: e.g. **a înota<a înnota.**

ˈ indicates that the following syllable is stressed: **negru** "black" [ˈne-groo], **perete** "wall" [pe-ˈre-te].

̯ placed under a vowel means that it is a semivowel: **el** "he" [i̯el].

\- marks syllable-division.

[ ] include phonetical transcriptions.

( ) include secondary or alternative forms and abbreviations.

PART I

PRONUNCIATION AND SPELLING

1. 1. The Rumanian Alphabet

THE Rumanian alphabet consists of 26 letters of the Roman alphabet. Till the middle of the nineteenth century it used a mixed alphabet composed of Latin and Cyrillic (Slavonic) letters, which evolved from an older pure Cyrillic alphabet in use for the writing of Rumanian from the sixteenth to the eighteenth century.

As a rule the 26 letters correspond to 25 sounds. The number of other sounds, obtained by combined letters, is small. The inconsistencies in the use of the letters, i.e. the writing of letters where they are not required, or the omission of letters where some sounds exist, are reduced to a minimum. We can say that the overwhelming tendency in Rumanian is to reproduce every sound with a letter.

Here are the 26 letters; five are formed with diacritical marks:

A a [Ah][1]   **Ă ă** [ă]; **Â â** = **Î î** [î]
B b [be]
C c [che]
D d [de]
E e [e]
F f [fe]
G g [dzhe]
H h [hah]
I i [ee]   **Î î** = **â**
J j [zhe]
L l [le]
M m [me]
N n [ne]
O o [o]

[1] In brackets are given the names of the letters transcribed with the symbols used in the Pronunciation (cp. 1. 2).

P p	[pe]		
R r	[re]		
S s	[se]	**Ş ş**	[she]
T t	[te]	**Ţ ţ**	[tse]
U u	[oo]		
V v	[ve]		
Z z	[ze]		

To these letters should be added the following, which occur only in foreign words and in a few family names:

K k [kah]
Q q [kve]
X x [eeks]
Y y [ee-ˈpsee-lon] or [ee grec]
W w [ve ˈdoo-bloo]

1. 2. The Pronunciation

There is no identity between any Rumanian and any English sound. Consequently the description and comparison of sounds will be only approximate and will try to be helpful in the study of the language. Good pronunciation can only be learned by hearing a good pronunciation, and by practising it. For the same reasons a transcription is of very relative value and help.

Vowel-sounds

For practical purposes we will try to give a summary description of the Rumanian sounds. Here are the Rumanian vowels grouped in a scheme corresponding to their position in the mouth:

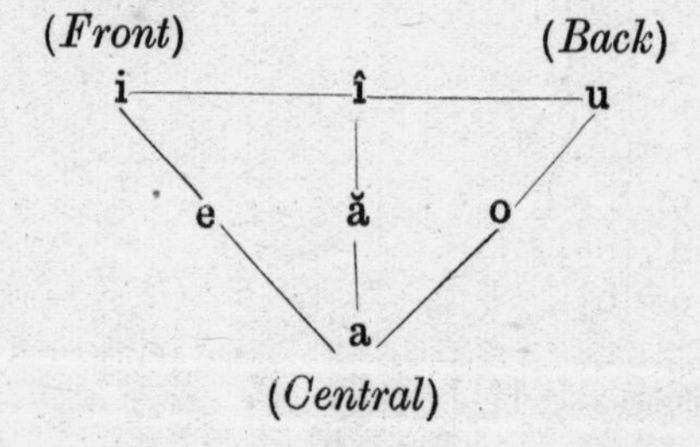

a) **i** is a not-rounded, close vowel. It is produced in the same way as the English vowel in *reed*, to *feel*, but it is not long like the English vowel. Yet the Rumanian **i** is not broad like the English *i* in *bit*, *fish*, *print*. The phonetic transcription of this Rumanian vowel for an English-speaking person would be [*ee*]:

din (*prep.*)	[deen]	from, out, of
lin (*a.*)	[leen]	mild

Note 1.—At the end of a word, when unstressed, **i** is a reduced sound, which softens the foregoing consonant. In diphthongs (cp. 1. 3 **a**) **i** sounds like the English semi-vowel *y* in *year*. We shall transcribe this sound with i̯. The graphic notation of these two sounds, full **i** and semi-vowel **i**, is in Rumanian the same and therefore may be confusing:

păreţi (*n. pl.*)	[pă-ˈretsi̯]	walls
ţii (2*nd pers. sing.*)	[tseei̯]	thou holdest, you hold
veri (*n. pl.*)	[veri̯]	summers; cousins (*m.*)
vecini (*n. pl.*)	[ve-ˈtcheeni̯]	neighbours

Note 2.—Final stressed **i**, or final **i** preceded by a consonant (b, c, d, g, p, s, t, v) plus **r** is pronounced as a full vowel:

a veni (*inf.*)	[ah ve-ˈnee]	to come
tigri (*n. pl.*)	[ˈtee-gree]	tigers
litri (*n. pl.*)	[ˈlee-tree]	litres, capacity measures of 1 kg.

After a consonant plus **l**, final **i** is ambiguous:

sufli (2*nd sing.*)	[ˈsoo-flee *or* soofli̯]	you blow
umbli (2*nd sing.*)	[ˈoom-blee *or* oombli̯]	you walk

b) **e** is a not-rounded, half-close vowel. It sounds closer than *e* in English *get*, and is more open than French *é* in *été*:

sete (*n.*)	[ˈse-te]	thirst
lege (*n.*)	[ˈle-dzhe]	law
tren (*n.*)	[tren]	train

Note.—The vowels **e** and **i** at the beginning of a word or of a syllable, except in recently imported words, are pronounced with a preceding semivowel i̯ (cp. 1. 3 **a**):

	el este (*3rd sing.*)	[i̯el ˈi̯es-te]	he is
	prieten (*n.*)	[pree-ˈi̯e-ten]	friend
but:	**energie** (*n.*)	[e-ner-ˈdzhee-i̯e]	energy
	eră (*n.*)	[ˈe-ră]	era

c) î, â is a middle vowel, close, not-rounded. The tip of the tongue touches the interior part of the lower teeth. The middle part of the tongue is lower than when pronouncing **i**. The resonance is produced in the central region, not in the frontal as in the case of **i**. By pronouncing a back **u** without rounded lips one approaches the formation of **î**.

For the transcription of this sound will be used the symbol **î**:

în (*prep.*)	[în]	in
sânge (*n.*)	[ˈsîn-dzhe]	blood
cât (*adv.*)	[kît]	how much

Note.—In Rumanian orthography the letter **î** is used: (1) at the beginning of words: **în**=in; (2) at the end of the verbs of the 4th conjugation ending in **-rî**, as well as in words derived from these verbs: **a urî** [ah ooˈrî], to hate, **urît** [ooˈrît], hated.

d) ă is a middle vowel; in comparison with **î** it is pronounced more backwards, with not-rounded lips, half open. The back part of the tongue is lifted towards the soft palate. **ă** sounds opener than **î**, and a little deeper than the English indefinite vowel in words like *tur*n, *bur*n, *suff*er, *fath*er, without being as deep as the English vowels in *but*, *cut*. Both these Rumanian sounds constitute a difficulty for the foreigner and make an impression of obscure vowels, similar to the frequent obscure vowels of English.

We shall transcribe this sound by **ă**:

văd (*v.*)	[văd]	I see
casă (*n.*)	[ˈka-să]	house
pământ (*n.*)	[pă-ˈmînt]	earth

e) **a** is a middle vowel pronounced with not-rounded lips. It is of the category of English *a* in *far*, *father*, *path*, but it is not long and open like the English vowel. We will transcribe it by **ah** (in which **h** should never be pronounced):

mama (*n.*)	[ˈmah-mah]	the mother
apa (*n.*)	[ˈah-pah]	the water

f) **u** is a back vowel, close, pronounced with slightly rounded lips. It sounds like the English *u* in *rule*, or *oo* in *soon*. The phonetic transcription would be **oo**:

bun (*adj.*)	[boon]	good
lucru (*n.*)	[ˈloo-kroo]	thing, work

g) **o** is a close back vowel pronounced with rounded lips. In comparison with English *o* in *not*, the Rumanian is very close. The transcription will be **o**:

sora (*n.*)	[ˈso-rah]	the sister
domnul (*n.*)	[ˈdom-nool]	the gentleman
pom (*n.*)	[pom]	tree
om (*n.*)	[u̯om]	man

Note.—The order of the vowels, from the point of view of their opening, i.e. the distance between the jaws, is the following, starting with the least open, i.e. the vowel pronounced with the smallest distance between the jaws:

î, i, u, e, o, ă, a.

Reading Exercise No. 1

(Final -i)

bun (*adj. m.*) [boon], good; **buni** (*adj. m. pl.*) [booni̯]; **a înnebuni** (*inf.*) [ah în-ne-boo-ˈnee], to get mad.

vecin (*n.*) [ve-ˈtcheen], neighbour; **vecini** (*n. pl.*) [ve-ˈtcheeni̯]; **a veni** (*inf.*) [ah ve-ˈnee], to come.

lup (*n.*) [loop], wolf; **lupi** (*n. pl.*) [loopi̯]; **a topi** (*inf.*) [ah to-ˈpee], to melt.

sur (*adj. m.*) [soor], grey; **suri** (*adj. m. pl.*) [soori̯]; **a însuri** (*inf.*) [ah în-soo-ˈree], to become grey.

sfânt (*n.*, *adj. m.*) [sfînt], saint, holy ; **sfinţi** (*n.*, *adj. m. pl.*) [sfeentsi̯] ; **a sfinţi** (*inf.*) [ah sfeen-ˈtsee], to consecrate.
rob (*n.*) [rob], slave ; **robi** (*n. pl.*) [robi̯] ; **a robi** (*inf.*) [ah ro-ˈbee], to enslave.
urez (1*st sing.*) [oo-ˈrez], I wish luck, I congratulate ; **urezi** (2*nd sing.*) [oo-ˈrezi̯] ; **a înverzi** (*inf.*) [ah în-ver-ˈzee], to become green.
treaz (*adj. m.*) [tre̯ahz], awake, sober ; **treji** (*adj. m. pl.*) [trezhi̯] ; **a trezi** (*inf.*) [ah tre-ˈzee], to awake (*tr.*).
mănânc (1*st sing.*) [mă-ˈnîŋk] (cf. 1. 4 **e**), I eat ; **mănânci** (2*nd sing.*) [mă-ˈnîntchi̯] ; **a munci** (*inf.*) [ah moon-ˈtchee], to toil.
merg (1*st sing.*) [merg], I go ; **mergi** (2*nd sing.*) [merdzhi̯] ; **a fugi** (*inf.*) [ah foo-ˈdzhee], to run away, flee.
urs (*n.*) [oors], bear ; **urşi** (*n. pl.*) [oorshi̯] ; **a tuşi** (*inf.*) [ah too-ˈshee], to cough.
veche (*adj. f.*) [ˈve-ke], old ; **vechi** (*adj. pl.*) [veki̯] ; **a se învechi** (*inf.*) [ah se în-ve-ˈkee], to become old.

1. 3. Semivowels and Diphthongs

There are three semivowels in Rumanian : i̯, e̯ and u̯. When **o** is part of a diphthong, and so becomes semivowel, it is pronounced like a semivowel u̯. The orthography notes these semivowels with the letters **i**, **e**, **u** and **o**. Sometimes the semivowels are not written at all, e.g. **om** [u̯om], man, human being.

a) The unstressed **i**, in final position, is a semivowel and softens the foregoing consonant (cp. 1. 2 **a**, Note 1). Combined with full vowels, this i̯ forms diphthongs :

piatră (*n.*)	[ˈpi̯ah-tră]	stone
mai (*adv.*)	[mahi̯]	more
iepure, epure (*n.*)	[ˈi̯e-poo-re]	hare
tei (*n. pl.*)	[tei̯]	lime-trees
iute (*adj.*)	[ˈi̯oo-te]	quick
cuib (*n.*)	[kooi̯b]	nest
voios (*adj.*)	[vo-ˈi̯os]	gay, glad

boi (*n. pl.*)	[boi̯]	oxen
inimă (*n.*)	[ˈi̯ee-nee-mă]	heart
fii (*n. pl.*)	[feei̯]	sons
întâi (*adv.*)	[în-ˈtîi̯]	first

The semivowel i̯ corresponds to the English sound represented by *y*, or by other letters in words like *year* [i̯iə(r)], *ewe* [i̯ū], *Europe* [ˈi̯uə-rəp], *huge* [hi̯ūdzh], *genius* [ˈdzhī-ni̯əs).

b) The semivowel u̯ combined with a full vowel forms a series of falling and rising diphthongs :

dau (*v.*)	[dahu̯]	I give
ziua (*n.*)	[ˈzee-u̯ah]	the day
bou (*n.*)	[bou̯]	ox
ou (*n.*)	[u̯ou̯]	egg
râu (*n.*)	[rîu̯]	river
leu (*n.*)	[leu̯]	lion
viu (*adj.*)	[veeu̯]	alive
său (*n.*)	[său]	tallow
piuă (*n.*)	[ˈpee-u̯ă]	fulling-mill, mortar

The semivowel u̯ sounds like the English *w* or *u* in : *what, water, quality, house.*

c) Diphthongs with e̯ and o̯ are rising diphthongs: **ea** [e̯ah], **oa** [o̯ah], **eo** [e̯o] :

seara (*n.*)	[ˈse̯ah-rah]	the evening
moară (*n.*)	[ˈmo̯ah-ră]	mill
deodată (*n.*)	[de̯o-ˈdah-tă]	suddenly

d) The orthography may be misleading. Words written the same way are read differently, depending upon syllabic division and upon other factors ; for instance, words recently imported into the language preserve a pronunciation near to that of the language which they come from :

	coadă (*n.*)	[ˈko̯ah-dă]	tail
but :	**oază** (*n.*)	[o-ˈah-ză]	oasis
	aud (*v.*)	[ah-ˈood]	I hear
but :	**auditiv** (*adj.*)	[ahu̯-dee-ˈteev]	audịtive

	era (*v.*)	[i̯e-ˈrah]	he was (being)
but :	**era** (*n.*)	[ˈe-rah]	the era, the epoch
	prieten (*n.*)	[pree-ˈi̯e-ten]	friend
but :	**client** (*n.*)	[klee-ˈent]	customer, client
	ai (*v.*)	[ahi̯]	thou hast, you have
but :	**aici** (*adv.*)	[ah-ˈi̯eechi̯]	here

e) In the preceding examples the semivowels in combination with full vowels formed diphthongs ; that is, there arose combined sounds with one single stress which formed a syllable.

Some of these diphthongs are *rising* when the first part is a semivowel, others are *falling* when the first part is a full vowel :

iar (*adv.*)	[i̯ahr]	again
haină (*n.*)	[ˈhahi̯-nă]	coat, clothes
iute (*adv.*)	[ˈi̯oo-te]	quickly
cui (*n.*)	[kooi̯]	nail
el (*pron.*)	[i̯el]	he
trei (*num.*)	[trei̯]	three
in (*n.*)	[i̯een]	flax
fii (*n. pl.*)	[feei̯]	sons

f) In the light of the preceding examples we have the following two diphthong-series :

Rising diphthongs : **ia, ie, ii, io, iu, ea, oa, eo, ua, uă.**
(Transcribed : i̯ah, i̯e, i̯ee, i̯o, i̯oo, e̯ah, o̯ah, e̯o, u̯ah, u̯ă.)

Falling diphthongs : **ai, au, ăi, ău, îu, ei, eu, îi, oi, ou, ui, ii, iu.**
(Transcribed : ahi̯, ahu̯, ăi̯, ău̯, îu̯, ei̯, eu̯, îi̯, oi̯, ou̯, ooi̯, eei̯, eeu̯.)

g) A diphthong in combination with a semivowel may form a triphthong :

(eu) iau (*v.*)	[(i̯eu̯) i̯ahu̯]	I take
(eu) beau (*v.*)	[(i̯eu̯) be̯ahu̯]	I drink
fiii (*n. pl.*)	[ˈfee-i̯eei̯]	the sons

Note.—The semivowels i̯, e̯ and u̯ (o̯) could be roughly transcribed by the English letters *y* and *w*:

eu	[yew=i̯eu]	I
leu	[lew=leu̯]	lion
in	[yeen=i̯een]	flax
noapte	[ˈnwahp-te=ˈno̯ahp-te]	night
seara	[ˈsyah-rah=ˈse̯ah-rah]	evening

However, this transcription could be ambiguous and misleading; so we shall use the letters: i̯, e̯, u̯ (o̯) for the transcription of the Rumanian semivowels.

Reading Exercise No. 2

(Diphthongs and vowels in hiatus)

(*a*)

iarbă (*n.*) [ˈi̯ahr-bă], grass; **taină** (*n.*) [ˈtahi̯-nă], secret; **laic** (*n.*) [ˈlah-i̯eek], layman; **hiat** (*n.*) [hee-ˈaht], hiatus.

iepure (*n.*) [ˈi̯e-poo-re], hare; **tei** (*n.*) [tei̯], lime-tree; **întreit** (*adj.*) [în-tre-ˈi̯eet], threefold; **client** (*n.*) [klee-ˈent], customer.

prieten (*n.*) [pree-ˈi̯e-ten], friend; **trei** (*num.*) [trei̯], three; **cheile** (*n. pl.*) [ˈke-i̯ee-le], the keys; **pietate** (*n.*) [pee-e-ˈtah-te], piety.

Iordan (*n.*) [i̯or-ˈdahn], Jordan; **boi** (*n. pl.*) [boi̯], oxen; **îndoit** (*adj.*) [în-ˈdo-i̯eet], twofold; **mioriţă** (*n.*) [mee-o-ˈree-tsă], young sheep.

iute (*adv.*) [ˈi̯oo-te], quickly; **cui** (*n.*) [kooi̯], nail; **ruină** (*n.*) [roo-ˈi̯ee-nă], ruin; **triumf** (*n.*) [tree-ˈoomf], triumph.

mireasă (*n.*) [mee-ˈre̯ah-să], bride; **reacţie** (*n.*) [re-ˈahk-tsee-i̯e], reaction; **aerisit** (*adj.*) [ah-e-ree-seet], aerated.

boală (*n.*) [bo̯ah-lă], illness; **coaliţie** (*n.*) [ko-ah-ˈlee-tsee-i̯e], coalition; **aortă** (*n.*) [ah-ˈor-tă], aorta.

deodată (*adv.*) [de̯o-ˈdah-tă *or* de-o-ˈdah-tă], suddenly; **leopard** (*n.*) [le-o-ˈpahrd], leopard; **poet** (*n.*) [po-ˈet], poet.

(*b*)

cai (*n. pl.*) [kahi̯], horses ; **piatră** (*n.*) [ˈpi̯ah-tră], stone ; **caisă** (*n.*) [kah-ˈi̯ee-să], apricot ; **cianură** (*n.*) [tchee-ah-ˈnoo-ră], cyanide.

stau (1*st sing.*) [stahu̯], I stay ; **aud** (1*st sing.*) [ah-ˈood], I hear ; **aluat** (*n.*) [ah-loo-ˈaht], dough, paste.

flăcăi (*n. pl.*) [flă-kăi̯], lads ; **făină** (*n.*) [fă-i̯ee-nă], flour.

tău (*poss. pron.*) [tău̯], thine ; **două** (*num. fem.*) [ˈdo-u̯ă], two ; **răutate** (*n.*) [ră-oo-ˈtah-te], wickedness.

grâu (*n.*) [grîu̯], wheat ; **râuleţ** (*n.*) [rî-oo-ˈlets], brook, stream.

leu (*n.*) [leu̯], lion ; **zmeură** (*n.*) [ˈzme-oo-ră], raspberry.

instruesc (1*st sing.*) [i̯een-stroo-ˈi̯esk], I instruct.

câine (*n.*) [ˈkîi-ne], dog ; **tămâind** (*pres. part.*) [tă-mî-ˈi̯eend], burning incense.

bou (*n.*) [bou̯], ox ; **bouleţ** (*n.*) [bo-oo-ˈlets], bullock ; **vouă** (*pers. pron.*) [ˈvo-u̯ă], to you.

pui (*n.*) [pooi̯], chicken ; **ciumă** (*n.*) [ˈtchi̯oo-mă], plague ; **a se sui** (*inf.*) [ah se soo-ˈi̯ee], to climb.

(*c*)

eu (*pers. pron.*) [i̯eu̯], I ; **eufonie** (*n.*) [eu̯-fo-ˈnee-i̯e], euphony.

iau (1*st sing.*) [i̯ahu̯], I take ; **iaurt** (*n.*) [i̯ah-ˈoort], yoghourt.

inimă (*n.*) [ˈi̯ee-nee-mă], heart ; **copii** (*n. pl.*) [ko-ˈpeei̯], children ; **copiii** (*n. pl.*) [ko-ˈpee-i̯eei̯], the children.

ou (*n.*) [u̯ou̯], egg.

ei (*pers. pron.*) [i̯ei̯], they.

1. 4. The Consonants

If we arrange the consonants in accordance with the place where they are articulated and the way they are pronounced, we obtain the following scheme of Rumanian consonants :

	Labial	*Labio-dental*	*Dental*	*Palatal*	*Velar*
Plosives (stops)	**p, b**		**t, d**	**chi** [kee], **ghi** [gee] **che** [ke], **ghe** [ge]	**c** [k], **g**
Fricatives		**f, v**	**s, z**	**ş** [sh], **j** [zh]	**h**
Nasals	**m**		**n**		
Lateral			**l**		
Rolled			**r**		
Compound consonants (affricates)			**ţ** [ts]	**ci** [tchee], **gi** [dzhee] **ce** [tche], **ge** [dzhe]	

a) From the first series of consonants, the voiceless plosives **p, t, c** are pronounced without the aspiration they have in standard English; the voiced plosives **b, d, g** are pronounced nearly like the English consonants:

Când (*adv.*)	[kînd]	when
te (*acc. pron.*)	[te]	(at) you
latră (3*rd pers. sing. pres.*)	[ˈlah-tră]	barks
un (*indef. art.*)	[oon]	a
câine (*n.*)	[ˈkîi-ne]	dog
astupă-i (*imp. pres.+dat. pron.*)	[ah-ˈstoo-păi̯]	fill him
gura (*n.*)	[ˈgoo-rah]	the mouth
cu (*prep.*)	[koo]	with
pâine (*n.*)	[ˈpîi̯-ne]	bread

b) The consonants **c** and **g** followed by **e** or **i** are pronounced like English *ch, tch* and *dzh* (cp. 1. 6 l):

ce (*pron.*)	[tche]	what
pace (*n.*)	[ˈpah-tche]	peace
cinci (*num.*)	[tcheentchi̯]	five
rege (*n.*)	[ˈre-dzhe]	king
ginere (*n.*)	[ˈdzhee̯-ne̯-re]	son-in-law

c) When **c** and **g** are palatalized (softened), the letter **h** is inserted between them and the following front vowel and they are pronounced like English *k* and *g* in *kin*, *get*:

chem (*v.*)	[ki̯em]	I call
lichid (*adj.*)	[lee-ˈkeed]	liquid
ghiaţă (*n.*)	[ˈgi̯ah-tsă]	ice
Gheorghe (*n.*)	[ˈgeor-ge]	George

d) The letter **ş** notes a consonant similar to that transcribed by *sh* in English, or by *si*, *ti* in words like *mission*, *nation*. The letter **j** notes a consonant similar to that written in English by *z* in *azure*, by *s* in *vision*, *measure*:

şapte (*num.*)	[shahp-te]	seven
cleşte (*n.*)	[ˈklesh-te]	pincers
jug (*n.*)	[zhoog]	yoke
primejdie (*n.*)	[pree-ˈmezh-dee-i̯e]	danger

e) **n** followed by **c** or **g** is a back sound, i.e. it is articulated in the back region of **c** and **g**; to mark that, **n** is transcribed with ŋ:

bancă (*n.*)	[ˈbahŋ-kă]	bank; seat, bench
stâncă (*n.*)	[ˈstîŋ-kă]	rock
lung (*adj.*)	[looŋ]	long
îngust (*adj.*)	[îŋ-ˈgoost]	narrow

f) The lateral **l** is clear. It is produced, in the frontal region, with the tip of the tongue fixed behind the upper teeth. It is not dark (velar and deep) like the standard English *l*. Practically there is a single **l** in Rumanian, though it is sounded differently according to the neighbouring vowels.

The rolled **r** is always pronounced with vibrations produced by the tip of the tongue behind the upper teeth:

limbă (*n.*)	[ˈleem-bă]	tongue
alb (*adj.*)	[ahlb]	white
culme (*n.*)	[ˈkool-me]	summit, peak

popor (*n.*) [po-ˈpor] people
scriu (*v.*) [skreeu̯] I am writing
hârtie (*n.*) [hîr-ˈtee-i̯e] paper

g) The velar **h** is not identical with the English glottal fricative **h**. Generally the Rumanian **h** is pronounced in the velar region with a friction caused by the emitted air on the palate :

mâhnit (*adj.*) [mîh-ˈneet] sad
odihnă (*n.*) [o-ˈdeeh-nă] rest
heruvim (*n.*) [he-roo-ˈveem] cherub
Prahova (*prop. n.*) [ˈprah-ho-vah]

Therefore the spelling of Christ may be :

Christos [hrees-ˈtos] or **Hristos** [hrees-ˈtos]

However it must be remembered that this pronunciation is not general. It is peculiar to the South. In the North, **h** is pronounced with less friction or without friction :

hotar (*n.*) [ho-ˈtahr] frontier
hat (*n.*) [haht] separating line between two fields

h) The compound consonant **ţ** sounds like *ts* in English *hats* :

ţap (*n.*) [tsahp] he-goat
ţinţar (*n.*) [tseen-ˈtsahr] mosquito

i) The voiceless labio-dental **f** is pronounced like the English *f* :

formă (*n.*) [ˈfor-mă] form
triumf (*n.*) [tree-ˈoomf] triumph
afacere (*n.*) [ah-ˈfah-tche-re] business

The voiced labio-dental **v** is pronounced like the English *v* :

convorbire (*n.*) [kon-vor-ˈbee-re] conversation
venin (*n.*) [ve-ˈneen] poison

j) The postdental voiceless **s** and voiced **z** are pronounced nearly as the corresponding English sounds :

soare (*n.*)	[ˈso̯ah-re]	sun
apus (*n.*)	[ah-ˈpoos]	sunset
zori (*n. pl.*)	[ˈzori̯]	dawn
acuz (*v.*)	[ah-ˈkooz]	I accuse

k) The voiceless consonant **s** is pronounced **z** before the voiced **b**, **d**, **g**, **v**, and sometimes in new borrowed words between two vowels. Generally good pronunciation avoids the voiced **z**, the tendency being to pronounce **s** even before voiced consonants. The spelling is uncertain in these cases :

(eu) sbor, zbor	[sbor]	I am flying
sgomot, zgomot	[ˈsgo-mot]	noise
visită, vizită	[ˈvee-see-tă]	visit, call

l) The letters **k**, **ph**, **q**, **x**, **y**, **w**, used only in foreign words (and in some surnames), reproduce the respective sounds of foreign languages. Rumanian spelling respects the original form of foreign proper names :

Kogălniceanu [Ko-găl-nee-ˈtche̯ah-noo]
Shakespeare
Xenopol [Kse-ˈno-pol]
Waterloo

m) Double consonants are used when they exist in the pronunciation :

accept (*v.*)	[ahk-ˈtchept]	I accept
accelerat (*adj.*)	[ahk-tche-le-ˈraht]	accelerated

Or when they are formed by juxtaposition :

a înnota [ah în-no-ˈtah]<**în**+**nota**, to swim
innavigabil [ee-nah-vee-ˈgah-beel]<**in**+**navigabil**, unnavigable
cellalt [ˈtchel-lahlt]<**cel**+**lalt**, the other

There is, however, a tendency to write : **a înota**, **inavigabil** and even **celalt**.

Only one consonant is used in :

sugestie [soo-ˈdzhes-tee-i̯e], suggestion
bacil [bah-ˈtcheel], bacillus
a colabora [ah ko-lah-bo-ˈrah], to collaborate

Even in homophones the tendency is not to differentiate between :

masă (*n.*) [ˈmah-să], table : **masă** (*n.*), mass
casă (*n.*) [ˈkah-să], house : **casă** (*n.*), safe

Reading Exercise No. 3

Unde-i uşa [ˈoon-dei̯ ˈoo-shah] ? Where is the door ?
Cine-i în casă [ˈtchee-nei̯ în ˈka-să] ? Who is in the house ?
Cine-s domnii din stradă [ˈtchee-nes ˈdom-neei̯ deen ˈstrah-dă] ?
Who are the gentlemen in the street ?
Unde-s cărţile [ˈoon-des ˈkăr-tsee-le] ? Where are the books ?
Cărţile-s pe masă [ˈkăr-tsee-les pe ˈmah-să].
The books are on the table.

Tinerii	[ˈtee-ne-reei̯]	(The) youth
trebuie	[ˈtre-boo-i̯e]	should
să respecte	[să res-ˈpek-te]	respect
pe bătrâni.	[pe bă-ˈtrîni̯].	old people.
Te întreb	[te în-ˈtreb]	I ask you (thee)
de sănătate.	[de să-nă-ˈtah-te].	about (your) health.
Vorba dulce	[ˈvor-bah ˈdool-tche]	The sweet word
mult aduce.	[ˈmoolt ah-ˈdoo-tche].	brings much (good).
Paserile	[ˈpah-se-ree-le]	The birds
cântă	[ˈkîn-tă]	are singing
primăvara.	[ˈpree-mă-ˈvah-rah]	(in) spring.
Viaţa-i	[ˈvi̯ah-tsah-i̯]	(The) life is
datorie	[dah-to-ˈree-i̯e]	a duty
grea	[ˈgreah]	hard (difficult)
şi laşii	[shee ˈlah-shee-i̯]	and (the) cowards
se'ngrozesc	[se'n-gro-ˈzesk]	are afraid
de ea. (G. Coşbuc)	[de i̯ah].	of it.

Unde-i unul nu-i putere
[ˈoon-dei̯ ˈoo-nool nooi̯ poo-ˈte-re]
Where (there) is (only) one (there) is no strength
La nevoi şi la durere
[lah ne-ˈvoi̯ shee lah doo-ˈre-re]
In need and in sorrow
Unde-s doi puterea creşte
[ˈoon-des doi̯ poo-ˈte-re̯a ˈkresh-te]
Where (there) are two the power increases
Şi duşmanul nu sporeşte.
[shee doosh-ˈmah-nool noo spo-ˈresh-te].
And the enemy has no success. (**Hora Unirii.**)

1. 5. The Accent

The accent of Rumanian words is a dynamic one, i.e. the stressed syllable is pronounced with more breath force.

a) As a general rule words of several syllables are stressed on the last syllable but one. But there are many cases where the accent is on the first, third, fourth, or even fifth syllable from the end :

(1)	**pământ** (*n.*)	[pă-ˈmînt]	earth
	frumos (*adj.*)	[froo-ˈmos]	beautiful
(2)	**carte** (*n.*)	[ˈkahr-te]	book
	albină (*n.*)	[ahl-ˈbeen-nă]	bee
(3)	**cântece** (*n. pl.*)	[ˈkîn-te-tche]	songs
	surzenie (*n.*)	[soor-ˈze-nee-i̯e]	deafness
(4)	**cântecele** (*n. pl.*)	[ˈkîn-te-tche-le]	the songs
	prepeliţa (*n.*)	[ˈpre-pe-lee-tsah]	the partridge
	but also :	[pre-pe-ˈlee-tsah]	
(5)	**prepeliţelor**	[ˈpre-pe-lee-tse-lor]	of the partridges
	but also :	[prepe-ˈlee-tse-lor]	

There is no fixed rule as to the place of the accent in a word. However, if we analyse the different groups, we see that category (1) comprises words ending with a consonant. To this rule words in which the final syllable is a former suffix form exceptions :

singuratec (*adj.*)	[seen-goo-ˈrah-tek]	lonely
strigăt (*n.*)	[ˈstree-găt]	shout
putred (*adj.*	[ˈpoo-tred]	rotten
sunet (*n.*)	[ˈsoo-net]	sound

but : **brădet** (*n.*) [bră-ˈdet], thicket of fir-trees, from **brad** [brahd], fir-tree

Category (2) comprises words ending with a vowel. Exceptions to this rule are words ending with diphthongs ; those are stressed on the first part of the diphthong :

Dumnezeu (*n.*)	[doom-ne-ˈzeu̯]	God
femei (*n. pl.*)	[fe-ˈmei̯]	women

Other exceptions to this category are words of Turkish origin ending with **a**, which are stressed on the last syllable :

para (*n.*)	[pa-ˈrah]	coin, money
basma (*n.*)	[bahs-ˈmah]	kerchief

Verbal forms of the third person simple past (preterite) and imperfect are stressed on the last syllable :

(el) avu (*v.*)	[i̯el ah-ˈvoo]	he had
(el) vedea (*v.*)	[iel ve-ˈdea]	he was seeing

The categories (3), (4) and (5) comprise morphological forms of Latin words and words of Slav origin.

b) The accent remains fixed on the same syllable in the various flexional forms of the noun, but it is mobile in the conjugation forms of the verb :

un cântec (*n.*)	[ˈkîn-tek]	a song
două cântece (*n. pl.*)	[ˈdo-u̯ă ˈkîn-te-tche]	two songs
cântecelor (*n. gen. pl.*)	[ˈkîn-te-tche-lor]	of the songs

but :

mor (*v.*)	[mor]	I am dying
noi murim (1*st pl.*)	[noi̯ moo-ˈreem]	we are dying

c) The accent changes its place in derived noun or adjectival forms :

scaun (*n.*)	[ˈskah-oon]	chair
scăunel (*n.*)	[skă-oo-ˈnel]	little chair
rege (*n.*)	[ˈre-dzhe]	king
regină (*n.*)	[re-ˈdzhee-nă]	queen
regal (*adj.*)	[re-ˈgahl]	kingly
regesc (*adj.*)	[re-ˈdzhesk]	kingly
carte (*n.*)	[ˈkahr-te]	book
cărticică (*n.*)	[kăr-tee-ˈtchee-kă]	little book
cărturar (*n.*)	[kăr-too-ˈrahr]	scholar

Note.—As a rule the accent is not marked ; sometimes it is marked with a grave on the last syllable ; sometimes one makes use of accent for differentiating the sense of words which are spelt alike but pronounced differently :

aşà (*adv.*)	[ah-ˈshah]	so
plecà (*v.*)	[ple-ˈkah]	he was going
àflă (*v.*)	[ˈah-flă]	he finds
află (*v.*)	[ah-ˈflă]	he found
còpii (*n.*)	[ˈko-peei̯]	copies
copìi (*n.*)	[ko-ˈpeei̯]	children
dèşi (*adj. m. pl.*)	[deshi̯]	thick
deşì (*conj.*)	[de-ˈshee]	although

1. 6. Conditional Sound Changes

It will be of much help for the understanding of the morphology (declension, conjugation, derivation of words) if we learn some sound changes which arise regularly under the same conditions.

a) When medial **a** loses the accent, in a derived word, it is replaced by **ă** :

barbă (*n.*) [ˈbahr-bă], beard	**bărbat** (*n.*) [băr-ˈbaht], man
(eu) las (*v.*) [i̯eu̯ lahs], I let	**lăsat** (*p. part.*) [lă-ˈsaht], let

mare (*adj.*) [ˈmah-re], great, big — **a mări** (*inf.*) [ah mă-ˈree], to make bigger, to increase

Note.—In some verbal forms stressed ă>a if an ă appears in the following syllable: **spăl** (*v.*), I wash, **spală** (*imp.*); **vărs** (*v.*), I am shedding, **varsă** (*imp.*)

b) If this **a** (see under 1. 6 **a**) is preceded by a palatal or palatalized consonant (**j**, **ş**, **ci**, **chi**, **gi**, **ghi**, **ce**, **che**, **ge**, **ghe**) it changes into **e**:

jale (*n.*) [ˈzhah-le] mourning — **(eu) jelesc** (*v.*) [i̯eu̯ zhe-ˈlesk], I mourn

şarpe (*n.*) [ˈshahr-pe], serpent — **a şerpui** (*inf.*) [ah sher-poo-ˈiee], to wind

chiag (*n.*) [ki̯ahg], rennet — **a închiega** (*inf.*) [ah în-ki̯e-ˈgah], to curdle

ghiaţă (*n.*) [ˈgi̯ah-tsă], ice — **înghieţat** (*p. part.*) [în-gi̯e-ˈtsaht], frozen

c) A stressed medial **o** changes into **u** when it loses the accent:

(eu) port (1*st sing.*) [i̯eu̯ port], I wear — **(noi) purtăm** (1*st pl.*) [noi poor-ˈtăm], we wear

(eu) rog (1*st sing.*) [i̯eu̯ rog], I ask — **(noi) rugăm** (1*st pl.*) [noi roo-ˈgăm], we ask

rugăciune (*n.*) [roo-gă-ˈtchi̯u-ne], prayer

soră (*n.*) [ˈso-ră], sister — **surori** (*n.pl.*) [soo-ˈrori̯], sisters

Note.—This rule, however, does not govern words which have entered the language later:

boltă (*n.*) [ˈbol-tă], vault, dome — **boltit** (*adj.*) [bol-ˈteet], vaulted, arched, curved (like a dome)

colţ (*n.*) [kolts], corner — **colţuros** (*adj.*) [kol-tsoo-ˈros], angular

d) A stressed **a** preceded by a labial (**m**, **f**, **v**, **p**) changes often into **e**, if **e** or **i** appear in the following syllable:

masă (*n.*) [ˈmah-să], table	**mese** (*n. pl.*) [ˈme-se], tables
fată (*n.*) [ˈfah-tă], girl	**fete** (*n. pl.*) [ˈfe-te], girls
vară (*n.*) [ˈvah-ră], summer; girl-cousin	**veri** [veri̯], summers; **vere** (*n. pl.*) [ˈve-re], girl-cousins
o pană (*n.*) [o ˈpah-nă], a feather	**două pene** (ˈdo-u̯ă ˈpe-ne], two feathers
o pană (*n.*) [o ˈpah-nă], a defect (in motor), a puncture (in tyre)	**două pane** [ˈdo-u̯ă ˈpah-ne]
o pară (*n.*) [o ˈpah-ră], a pear	**două pere** (*n. pl.*) [ˈdo-u̯ă ˈpere], two pears

but:

o palmă (*n.*) [o ˈpahl-mă], palm, hand (as a measure)	**două palme** (*n. pl.*) [do-u̯ă ˈpahl-me] and **pălmi** [pălmi̯]
o babă (*n.*) [o ˈbah-bă], an old woman	**două babe** (*n. pl.*) [ˈdo-u̯ă ˈbah-be], two old women

e) A stressed medial **a** changes into **ă** when **i** (instead of **a**, **e** of the nominative singular) appears in the following syllable:

stradă (*n.*) [ˈstrah-dă], street	**străzi** (*n. pl.*) [ˈstrăzi̯], streets
ţară (*n.*) [ˈtsah-ră], country	**ţări** (*n. pl.*) [tsări̯], countries
carte (*n.*) [ˈkahr-te], book	**cărţi** (*n. pl.*) [kărtsi̯], books
mare (*n.*) [ˈmah-re], sea	**mări** (*n. pl*). [mări̯], seas

Note.—Exceptions to this tendency are:

I. The nouns:

vacă [ˈvah-kă], cow	**vaci** (*n.*) [vatchi̯], cows
o fragă (*n.*) [o ˈfrah-gă], a wild strawberry	**două frage** (*n.*) [ˈdo-u̯ă ˈfrah-dzhe], two wild strawberries

II. The adjectives:

mare (*sing.*), **mari** (*pl.*), great
tare (*sing.*), **tari** (*pl.*), strong

f) A medial ă changes into **e** if **e** or **i** appear in the following syllable :

măr (*n.*) [măr], apple	**mere** (*n. pl.*) [ˈme-re], apples **meri** (*n. pl.*), apple-trees
băţ (*n.*) [băts], stick	**beţe** (*n. pl.*) [ˈbe-tse], sticks
tânăr (*n.*) [ˈtî-năr], young	**tineri** (*n. pl.*) [ˈtee-neri̯], youths
(**eu**) **cumpăr** (1*st sing.*) [ˈkoom-păr], I buy	(**tu**) **cumperi** (2*nd sing.*) [ˈtoo ˈkoom-peri̯], you buy

Note.—After a guttural, however, ă, in this position, remains unchanged :

strigăt (*n.*) [ˈstree-găt], scream	**strigăte** (*n. pl.*) [ˈstree-gă-te], screams
flacără (*n.*) [ˈflah-kă-ră], flame	**flăcări** (*n. pl.*) [ˈflă-kări], flames

g) **î** changes sometimes into **i** if **e** or **i** appears in the following syllable :

sfânt (*adj.*) [sfînt], saint	**sfinţi** (*n.*, *adj. pl.*) [sfeentsi̯], saints
cuvânt (*n.*) [koo-ˈvînt], word	**cuvinte** (*n. pl.*) [koo-ˈveen-te], words
mormânt (*n.*) [mor-ˈmînt], tomb	**morminte** (*n. pl.*) [mor-ˈmeen-te], tombs

Note.—This rule is not without exceptions :

mânz (*n.*) [mînz], foal	**mânji** (*n. pl.*) [mînzhi], foals
stâncă (*n.*) [ˈstîn-kă], rock	**stânci** (*n. pl.*) [stîntchi̯], rocks
blând (*adj. m.*) [blînd], tame	**blânzi** (*adj. m. pl.*) [blînzi̯], tame
săptămână (*n.*) [săp-tă-ˈmî-nă], week	**săptămâni** (*n. pl.*) [săp-tă-ˈmîni̯], weeks
mână (*n.*) [mînă], hand	**mâini** (*n. pl.*) [mîini̯], hands
(**eu**) **plâng** (1*st sing.*) [i̯eu̯ plîŋg], I weep	(**tu**) **plângi** (2*nd sing.*) [too plîndzhi̯], thou weepest

h) A stressed **e** changes into a diphthong **ea** when **a** or **ă** appears in the following syllable :

(eu) **alerg** (1*st sing.*) [i̯eu̯ ah-ˈlerg], I run
(el) **aleargă** (3*rd sing.*) [i̯el ah-ˈle̯ar-gă], he runs

întreg (*adj. m.*) [în-ˈtreg], whole
întreagă (*adj. f.*) [în-ˈtre̯a-gă], whole

întregi (*m. pl.*) [în-ˈtredzhi̯]
întrege (*f. pl.*) [în-ˈtre-dzhe]

negru (*adj. m.*) [ˈne-groo], black
neagră (*adj. f.*) [ˈne̯ah-gră], black

i) A stressed **ea** (**ia**) changes into **e** when **-e** or **-i** appears in the following syllable :

împărăteasă (*n.*) [îm-pă-ră-ˈte̯ah-să], empress
împărătese (*n. pl.*) [ˈîm-pă-ră-ˈte-se], empresses

viaţă (*n.*) [ˈvi̯ah-tsă], life
vieţi (*n. pl.*) [ˈvi̯etsi̯], lives

băiat (*n.*) [bă-ˈiaht], boy
băieţi (*n. pl.*) [ba-ˈi̯etsi̯], boys

j) A stressed **o** changes into **oa** if an **ă**, **a** or **e** appears in the following syllable :

frumos (*adj. m.*) [froo-ˈmos], beautiful
frumoasă (*adj. f.*) [froo-ˈmo̯ah-să]

port (1*st sing.*) [i̯eu̯ port], I carry
(el) **poartă** (3*rd sing.*) [i̯el ˈpo̯ahr-tă], he carries

domnul (*n.*) [ˈdom-nool], the master
doamna (*n.*) [ˈdo̯ahm-nah], the mistress

servitor (*n.*) [ser-vee-ˈtor], servant man
servitoare (*n.*) [ser-vee-to̯a-re], maid

Note.—Recently borrowed words, however, are not affected by this rule : **modă** (*n.*) [ˈmo-dă], **mode** (*pl.*) [ˈmo-de], fashion ; **poftă** (*n.*) [ˈpof-tă], **pofte** (*pl.*) [ˈpof-te], desire ; **uniform** (*adj. m.*) [oo-nee-ˈform], uniform ; **uniformă** (*adj. f.*) [oo-nee-ˈfor-mă], uniform.

k) A stressed **oa** changes into **o** when it loses the accent or when an **i** appears in the following syllable :

floare (*n.*) [ˈflo̯ah-re], flower — **înfloresc** (1*st sing.*) [în-floˈresk], I flourish

o moară (*n.*) [o ˈmo̯ah-ră], a mill — **două mori** (*n. pl.*) [ˈdo-u̯ă mori̯], two mills

ploaie (*n.*) [ˈplo̯ah-i̯e], rain — **ploi** (*n. pl.*) [ploi̯], rains

l) **e**, **i** and the semivowel **i̯** change the foregoing **c** and **g**, transforming them in palatals :

(eu) merg (1*st sing.*) [i̯eu̯ merg], I go — **(el) merge** (3*rd sing.*) [i̯el ˈmer-dzhe], he goes

fiică (*n.*) [ˈfee-kă] [ˈfi̯i-kă], daughter — **fiice** (*n. pl.*) [ˈfee-tche] [ˈfi̯i-tche], daughters

un amic (*n.*) [oon ah-ˈmeek], a friend — **doi amici** (*n. pl.*) [doi̯ ah-ˈmeetchi̯], two friends

m) **sc**, **şc** followed by **i** or by **e** is transformed into **şti** or **şte** :

(eu) cunosc (1*st sing.*) [i̯eu̯ koo-ˈnosk], I know — **(tu) cunoşti** (2*nd sing.*) [too koo-ˈnoshti̯], you know

o broască (*n.*) [o ˈbroas-kă], a frog — **două broaşte** (*n. pl.*) [ˈdo-u̯ă ˈbro̯ahsh-te], two frogs

o puşcă (*n.*) [o ˈpoosh-kă], a gun — **două puşti** (*n. pl.*) [ˈdo-u̯ă pooshti̯], two guns

n) In unstressed syllables of derived forms :

t	followed by	**i**	(semivowel)	changes	into	**ţ** ;
d	,,	**i**	,,	,,	,,	**z** ;
s	,,	**i**	,,	,,	,,	**ş** ;
st	,,	**i**	,,	,,	,,	**şt** ;
z	,,	**i**	,,	,,	,,	**j** ;
l	,,	**i**	,,	,,	,,	**i** ;
n	,,	**i**	,,	,,	,,	**i** ;
r	,,	**i**	,,	,,	,,	**i** ;
şc	,,	**i**	,,	,,	,,	**şt.**

înalt (*adj. m.*) [î-ˈnahlt], high	**înalţi** (*adj. m. pl.*) [î-ˈnahltsi̯], high
brad (*n.*) [brahd], a fir-tree	**brazi** (*n. pl.*) [brahzi̯], fir-trees
urs (*n.*) [oors], bear	**urşi** (*n. pl.*) [oorshi̯], bears
o veste (*n.*) [o ˈves-te], news	**două veşti** (*n. pl.*) [ˈdo-u̯ă veshti̯], two news
prost (*adj. m.*) [prost], stupid	**proşti** (*adj. m. pl.*) [proshti̯], stupid
treaz (*adj. m.*) [tre̯az], awake	**treji** (*adj. m. pl.*) [trezhi̯], awake
copil (*n.*) [ko-ˈpeel], one child	**copii** (*n. pl.*) [ko-ˈpii̯], children
(eu) sar (1*st sing.*) [i̯eu̯ sahr], I jump	**(tu) sari** (2*nd sing.*) [too sahri̯], **(tu) sai** (2*nd sing.*) [too sahi̯], you jump
spun (1*st sing.*) [spoon], I say	**tu spui** (2*nd sing.*) [too spui̯], you say
împroşc (1*st sing.*) [îm-ˈproshk], I sprinkle	**împroşti** (2*nd sing.*) [îm-ˈproshti̯], you sprinkle

Note 1.—If **t** is followed by **i** and another vowel, it changes to **ci**:

înţelept (*adj.*) [în-tse-ˈlept], wise	**înţelepciune** (*n.*) [ˈîn-tse-lep-ˈtchoo-ne], wisdom
răutate (*n.*) [ră-oo-ˈtah-te], wickedness	**răutăcios** (*adj.*) [ˈră-oo-tă-ˈtchos], wicked

If **d** is followed by **i** and another vowel, it changes to **gi**:

grămadă (*n.*) [gra-ˈmah-dă], heap	**grămăgioară** (*n.*) [gră-mă-ˈdzhi̯o̯ah-ră], small heap
oglindă (*n.*) [o-ˈgleen-dă], mirror	**oglingioară** (*n.*) [o-gleen-ˈdzhi̯o̯ah-ră], small mirror

Note 2.—Apparent exceptions to this rule are explained by the history of the language, e.g. from **verde** (*adj.*) [ˈver-de], green, the derived verb is: **a înverzi** (*inf.*) [ah în-ver-ˈzee], to become green; but from **gând** (*n.*) [gînd], thought, the verb is **a gîndi** (*inf.*) [ah gîn-ˈdee], to think; from **lipsă** (*n.*) [ˈleep-să], lack, the verb is **a lipsi** (*inf.*) [ah leep-ˈsee], to be absent. Words where this sound-change did not take place are of later non-Latin origin. For the same reason **l** is not changed into **i** in:

hamal (*n.*) [hah-ˈmahl], porter	**hamali** (*n.*) [hah-ˈmahli̯], porters
şacal (*n.*) [shah-ˈkahl], jackal	**şacali** (*n.*) [shah-ˈkahli̯], jackals

1. 7. Division of Words into Syllables

a) There is a tendency in Rumanian to have open syllables, i.e. syllables ending in vowels. Therefore a consonant between two vowels belongs to the following syllable:

ca-să (*n.*)	[ˈkah-să]	house
gră-di-nă (*n.*)	[gră-ˈdee-nă]	garden
e-xa-men (*n.*)	[e-ˈksah-men]	test, examination

b) A group of consonants is divided between the foregoing and the following syllable:

îm-pă-rat (*n.*)	[îm-pă-ˈraht]	emperor
mier-lă (*n.*)	[ˈmi̯er-lă]	blackbird
dom-ni-tor (*n.*)	[dom-nee-ˈtor]	ruler

c) If the last consonant of the group is **l** or **r**, it belongs, with the preceding consonant, to the following syllable:

su-fla-re (*n.*)	[soo-ˈflah-re]	breath
so-cru (*n.*)	[ˈso-kroo]	father-in-law
as-pru (*adj.*)	[ˈahs-proo]	severe
in-tra-re (*n.*)	[in-ˈtrah-re]	entrance

d) Diphthongs belong to the same syllable:

zi-ua (*n.*)	[ˈzee-u̯ah]	the day
noas-tră (*pos. pron.*)	[no̯ahs-tră]	our
moa-le (*adj.*)	[mo̯ah-le]	soft

e) If two neighbouring vowels do not form diphthongs (vowels in hiatus) they are divided between two syllables:

aur (*n.*)	[ˈah-oor]	gold
coaliţie (*n.*)	[ko-ah-ˈlee-tsee-i̯e]	coalition
maestru (*n.*)	[mah-ˈi̯es-troo]	maestro

1. 8. Use of Capital Letters

Proper names are written with capitals, but adjectives derived from them with small letters:

Englez [en-ˈglez], Englishman — **limba engleză** [ˈleem-bah en-ˈgle-ză], the English language
Român [ro-ˈmîn], Rumanian — **limba română** [ˈleem-bah ro-ˈmî-nă], the Rumanian language

When the adjective is part of a proper name it is written with a capital:

Ţara Românească [ˈtsah-rah ro-mî-ˈne̯as-kă], Walachia
Mihai Viteazul [mee-ˈhai̯ vee-ˈte̯a-zool], Michael the Brave

Capital letters are used: at the beginning of a sentence or of a verse, after colon in direct speech, for the name of God, of Christ, of the Saints, and for the names of feast days, as well as for pronouns referring to God and to Christ:

Şi a zis Dumnezeu: " Să fie lumină ! " (Gen. i. 3.)
[Shee ah ˈzees doom-ne-ˈzeu̯: să ˈfee-i̯e loo-ˈmee-nă.]
And God said, Let there be light.

Sf. Niculaie [ˈsfîn-tool nee-koo-ˈlah-i̯e], St Nicholas
Paştele (*pl.*) [ˈpahsh-te-le], Easter
Crăciunul [kră-ˈtchoo-nool], Christmas

Capitals are also used for pronouns of deference and for titles:

Dvoastră, Domnia voastră [dom-ˈnee-i̯a ˈvo̯ahs-tră], You
Universitatea din Bucureşti [oo-nee-ver-see-ˈtah-te̯a deen boo-koo-ˈreshti̯], University of Bucharest

Banca Naţională [ˈbahŋ-ka nah-tsee-o-ˈnah-lă], National Bank

Finally, they are used for the names of the months :

Ianuarie	[i̯ah-noo-ˈah-ree-i̯e]	January
Februarie	[fe-broo-ˈah-ree-i̯e]	February
Martie	[ˈmahr-tee-i̯e]	March
Aprilie	[ah-ˈpree-lee-i̯e]	April
Mai	[mai̯]	May
Iunie	[ˈi̯u-nee-i̯e]	June
Iulie	[ˈi̯u-lee-i̯e]	July
August	[ˈau̯-goost]	August
Septemvrie	[sep-ˈtem-vree-i̯e]	September
Octomvrie	[ok-ˈtom-vree-i̯e]	October
Noemvrie	[no-ˈi̯em-vree-i̯e]	November
Decemvrie	[de-ˈtchem-vree-i̯e]	December

The official spelling of the Rumanian Academy demands that the names of the weekdays be written with small letters, but many use capital letters :

luni	[looni̯]	Monday
marţi	[mahrtsi̯]	Tuesday
miercuri	[ˈmi̯er-koori̯]	Wednesday
joi	[zhoi̯]	Thursday
vineri	[ˈvee-neri̯]	Friday
sâmbătă	[ˈsîm-bă-tă]	Saturday
duminică	[doo-ˈmee-nee-kă]	Sunday

The names of the points of the compass are written with capital letters. This rule, however, is not always respected, and they are often written with small letters :

Est [est] or **Răsărit** [ră-să-ˈreet]	East
Vest [vest] or **Apus** [ah-ˈpoos]	West
Nord [nord] or **Miază-noapte** [ˈmi̯a-ză ˈno̯ahp-te]	North
Sud [sood] or **Miază zi** [ˈmi̯a-ză ˈzee]	South
Nord-Vest [nord-ˈvest]	North-West
Sud-Est [sud-ˈest]	South-East

1. 9. Rumanian Punctuation

corresponds generally to English :

. = **punct** [pooŋkt], *full-stop*, is used at the end of a sentence and after abbreviations.

, = **virgulă** [ˈveer-goo-lă], *comma*, is used to separate—
(*a*) coordinate parts of a compound sentence,
(*b*) subordinate from principal clauses,
(*c*) the noun in apposition,
(*d*) a series of words or parts of the sentence having the same construction,
(*e*) the vocative case.

; = **punct şi virgulă** [pooŋkt shee ˈveer-goo-lă], *semicolon*, is used between sentences grammatically independent but closely connected in sense.

: = **două puncte** [ˈdo-ŭă ˈpooŋ-kte], *colon*, is used before a series of enumerated nouns and before quotations.

— = **liniuţă** [lee-nee-ˈoo-tsă], *dash*, is used to separate parentheses introduced in the sentence. It serves also to mark the beginning of " direct speech."

- = **trăsura de unire** [tră-ˈsoo-rah de oo-ˈnee-re], *hyphen*, serves to unite two or more words which are closely related in sense.

? = **semnul întrebării** [ˈsem-nool în-tre-ˈbă-reeĭ], *question mark*, is used after direct questions.

! = **semn de exclamaţie** [semn de eks-klah-ˈmah-tsee-ĭe], *exclamation mark*, is used after interjections and exclamations.

„ " = **semnele citării** [ˈsem-ne-le tchee-ˈtă-reeĭ] or **ghilemetele (ghilemelele)** [ghee-le-ˈme-te-le], *inverted commas*, are used to introduce and to end a quotation or direct speech.

... = **punctele de suspensiune (întrerupere)** [ˈpooŋk-te-le de soos-pen-ˈsi̯oo-ne, în-tre-ˈroo-pe-re], marks an interruption of speech made with a stylistic purpose.

( ) = **paranteze rotunde** [pah-rahn-ˈte-ze ro-ˈtoon-de], *brackets.*

{ } = **paranteze duble** [pah-rahn-ˈte-ze ˈdoob-le].

[ ] = **paranteze unghiulare** [pah-rahn-ˈte-ze oon-ˈghi̯u-lah-re].

' = **apostroful** [ah-pos-ˈtro-fool], the *apostrophe* is the sign that a letter has been omitted.

Reading Exercise No. 4

Cine tace merge'n pace.
[ˈtchee-ne ˈtah-tche ˈmer-dzhen ˈpah-tche.]
(He) who is silent goes (lives) in peace.

Vorba îşi are vremea ei.
[ˈvor-bah îshi̯ ˈah-re ˈvre-me̯a i̯ei̯.]
(Every) word has its time.

Tăcerea-i dulce ca mierea.
[tă-ˈtche-reai̯ ˈdool-tche kah ˈmi̯e-re̯a.]
Silence is sweet as honey.

Calea flămândului e cea mai lungă.
[ˈkah-lea flă-ˈmîn-doo-looi̯ i̯e ˈtche̯a mai̯ ˈloo-ŋă.]
The way of the hungry is the longest.

Ziua bună se cunoaşte de dimineaţă.
[ˈzee-uah ˈboo-nă se koo-ˈno̯ash-te de dee-mee-ˈne̯ah-tsă.]
Fine day is recognized in the morning.

Fă bine şi nu te teme de nime.
[fă ˈbee-ne shee noo te ˈte-me de ˈnee-me.]
Do (what is) good and don't fear anybody.

Neturburarea sufletului, sănătatea minţii.
[ne-toor-boo-ˈrah-re̯ah ˈsoof-le-too-looi̯, să-nă-ˈtah-tea ˈmeen-tseei̯.]
The calm of the soul is the health of the mind.

Munca dreaptă nu se pierde.
[ˈmooŋ-kah ˈdre̯ahp-tă noo se ˈpi̯er-de].
Honest work is never lost.

Lupul păru-şi schimbă dar năravul ba.
[ˈloo-pool ˈpă-rooshi̯ ˈskim-bă dahr nă-ˈrah-vool bah].
The wolf changes his hair but does not change his habit.

Datoria nu moare niciodată.
[dah-to-ˈree-i̯ah noo ˈmoah-re neetchi̯-o-ˈdah-tă].
Debt never dies.

PART II

GRAMMATICAL FORMS

2. THE NOUN

THE noun can belong to either of two grammatical genders: masculine or feminine. A great many nouns are masculine in the singular and feminine in the plural. These nouns form a class of mixed nouns, called in Rumanian: **ambigene** (*adj. n. pl.*), **eterogene** (*adj. n. pl.*) or **neutre** (*adj. n. pl*). The gender of a noun is recognized by the definite article. The definite article is suffixed to the noun; the indefinite article precedes the noun.

2. 1. The Indefinite Article

Singular:

Masc.	*un* **om**,	a man
	un **epure**,	a hare
Fem.	*o* **fată**,	a girl
	o **femeie**,	a woman

Plural:

The plural has no special form for the indefinite article. One can express the indefinite form of a noun in the plural without an article or by the indefinite pronoun **nişte**=some, **unii**=some:

Masc.	**(nişte) oameni**,	(some) men
	(nişte) epuri,	(some) hares
Fem.	**(nişte) fete**,	(some) girls
	(nişte) femei,	(some) women

Note.—The indefinite pronoun **nişte** before a noun in the plural has the sense of *some*, which can be translated also by **câţiva**; **unii**. Popular forms for **nişte** are **niscai, niscaiva. Nişte cărţi**=some (kind of) books; **unii oameni**=some people; **câţiva copii**=a few children.

Nişte before a noun in the singular or before collective nouns in the plural denotes an indefinite quantity: **nişte făină**=some flour; **nişte cireşe**=some cherries. **Nişte** cannot be used without a noun.

2. 2. The Plural without the Article of Feminine Nouns is formed by suffixes added to the stem of the nouns. The vowels of these suffixes produce phonetic alterations in the stem of the nouns, according to the principles set forth above under *Conditional Sound Changes* (1. 6). If we take into consideration these tendencies of vowel changes, all plural formations are clear.

a) With the suffix **-e**:

Singular	*Plural*
faţă, face	**feţe**, faces
piatră, stone	**pietre**, stones
muscă, fly	**muşte**, flies

b) With the suffix **-i** (semivowel):

Singular	*Plural*
carte, book	**cărţi**, books
floare, flower	**flori**, flowers
grădină, garden	**grădini**, gardens
vale, valley	**văi**, valleys
puşcă, gun	**puşti**, guns

Note.—Some feminine nouns have both plurals, in **-e** and in **-i**; sometimes each form has a slightly different sense:

o şcoală, a school	**două şcoli**, two schools
	două şcoale, ,,
o roată, a wheel	**două roţi**, two wheels
	două roate, ,,
o stradă, a street	**două străzi**, two streets
	două strade, ,,

This tendency of forming feminine plurals in **-i** is based on a phonetical peculiarity of Rumanian. Unstressed **e** has the tendency to change into **i**. At the end of plural feminine nouns **e** being unstressed has the tendency to change into **i** and to cause changes in the preceding syllable according to the conditional sound-changes. (Cp. 1. 6 **e**, **k**.)

c) The nouns, whose form without the article ends in a stressed **-a**, form the plural in **-le** :

Singular	*Plural*
stea, star	**stele**, stars
măsea, molar tooth	**măsele**, molar teeth
basma, kerchief	**basmale**, kerchiefs
zi, day	**zile**, days

Diminutives in **-ică** form the plural in **-le** :

Singular	*Plural*
floricică, little flower	**floricele**, little flowers
viorică, violet	**viorele**, violets
părticică, small part	**părticele**, small parts
ulcică, a mug (earthenware)	**ulcele**, mugs

However, nouns which are not felt to be diminutives form the plural regularly :

Singular	*Plural*
bunică, grandmother	**bunici**, grandmothers
furnică, ant	**furnici**, ants

d) A few feminine nouns have an irregular plural :

Singular	*Plural*
soră, sister	**surori**, sisters
noră, daughter-in-law	**nurori**, daughters-in-law
iarbă, grass	**ierburi**, many plants
lână, wool	**lâneţe**, wools (washed)
	lânuri, pieces of wool
pânză, linen	**pânzeturi**, kinds of linen
brânză, cheese	**brânzeturi**, kinds of cheese
aramă, copper, brass	**arămuri**, copper objects
marfă, goods, merchandise	**mărfuri**, goods

2. 3. The Plural without the Article of Masculine Nouns is formed with the termination **-i**. If the noun ends in a consonant, the **-i** is added to this consonant; if the noun ends in **-u** or **-e**, the **-i** is added to the preceding sound after **-u** or **-e** have been dropped:

Singular	*Plural*
ban, coin	**bani**, coins, money
împărat, emperor	**împăraţi**, emperors
băiat, boy	**băieţi**, boys
copil, child	**copii**, children
cal, horse	**cai**, horses
brad, fir-tree	**brazi**, fir-trees
viteaz, brave man	**viteji**, brave men
fiu, son	**fii**, sons
peşte, fish	**peşti**, fishes, fish
rege, king	**regi**, kings

Note.—If the noun ends in **-ru**, the plural ends in a full vowel **i**:

socru, father-in-law	**socri**, fathers-in-law
codru, forest	**codri**, forests

2. 4. The Feminine Singular with Definite Article

In the singular the article for feminine nouns is **-a** and it is suffixed to the noun in the following ways:

a) The nouns whose indefinite form ends in **-ă** replace this **-ă** by the article **-a**:

apă, water	**apa**, the water
casă, house	**casa**, the house
bancă, seat, bench; bank	**banca**, the seat, the bench; the bank
mână, hand	**mâna**, the hand

b) The feminine nouns whose indefinite forms end in **-a** or in **-i** (only **zi**, *day*) add to this indefinite form the definite article **-a** with the intermediary of an **-u-**:

cafea, coffee	**cafeaua**, the coffee
vâlcea, valley	**vâlceaua**, the valley
zi, day	**ziua**, the day

c) To the indefinite feminine nouns which end in **-e** the article **-a** is added after **-e**:

pâine, bread	**pâinea**, the bread
libertate, liberty	**libertatea**, the liberty
floare, flower	**floarea**, the flower

Note.—If the **-e** is preceded by **-i**, **-j**, **-ş**, the article is added directly to these sounds:

femeie, woman	**femeia**, the woman
grijă, **grije**, task, worry	**grija**, the task
cenuşe, ashes	**cenuşa**, the ashes

d) The nouns treated under **a**), **b**) and **c**) form the class of the feminine or **-a** declension.

Nouns of this **-a** class, however, which express a masculine being, are masculine:

tată, father	**tata**, the father; **tatăl**, the Heavenly Father, or solemnly: father
popă, priest	**popa**, the priest
vlădică, bishop	**vlădica**, the bishop
călăuză, guide	**călăuza**, the guide
sentinelă, sentry	**sentinela**, the sentry
slugă, servant	**sluga**, the servant
Papă, Pope	**Papa**, the Pope
bade, a term of friendly respect, used when addressing an elder man, an elder brother, or even by a girl addressing her sweetheart	**badea**
bădiţă (*dim.*)	**bădiţa**

2. 5. a). The Feminine Plural with Definite Article is obtained by adding to the indefinite form of the plural the article **-le**:

Singular	*Plural*	*Plural*
masă, table	**mese**, tables	**meşele**, the tables
carte, book	**cărţi**, books	**cărţile**, the books
stea, star	**stele**, stars	**stelele**, the stars
soră, sister	**surori**, sisters	**surorile**, the sisters

b) Some masculine nouns in **-a** form the plural like the feminine in **-a**, some like the masculine in **-l**:

călăuză	**călăuze**	**călăuzele**, the guides
sentinelă	**sentinele**	**sentinelele**, the sentries
slugă	**slugi**	**slugile**, the servants
popă	**popi**	**popii**, the priests
tată	**taţi**	**taţii**, the fathers

Exercise No. 5

Pe masă este pâine şi apă. Paserile cântă ziua şi noaptea. Un pitic e un om mic. Nu văd nimic. Piatra e pe pământ. În vas nu-i apă. Tu ai un prieten bun. Cânt un cântec de jale. În râu este apă. Pe câmp este fân. El e stăpân pe pământ. Paserile au cuib pe câmp. Floarea de crin este albă. În pământ este aur şi cărbune. Mama e în casă cu sora.

Pe câmp sunt trei cai şi patru boi. Mama are un măr şi o pară. Cartea e aici. Vezi, cine vine? Nu văd nimic pe cer. Vecina are o fiică şi trei fii. Surorile sunt în grădină. Om cu inimă de copil. Primăvara e cald. În perete este un cui. În moară e grâu. Fântâna din grădină are apă rece.

Noaptea sunt multe stele pe cer. Doina e un cântec de jale. În pădure sunt multe păsări. Viorelele sunt flori de grădină. Nora şi soacra-s la biserică.

2. 6. The Masculine Singular with Definite Article

The definite masculine article in the singular is **-l** or **-le**.

a) The masculine article **-l** is added directly to the nouns ending in **-u** :

Dumnezeu, God	**Dumnezeul**, the God
ou, egg	**oul**, the egg
lucru, work, thing	**lucrul**, the work

b) The article **-l** is added with the intermediary of **-u-** to nouns ending in **-i** (semivowel) or in a consonant :

pui, chicken ; young animal	**puiul**, the chicken
animal, animal	**animalul**, the animal
oraş, town	**oraşul**, the town

c) The masculine article **-le** is added to the masculine nouns in **-e** :

peşte, fish	**peştele**, the fish
cărbune, coal	**cărbunele**, the coal
nume, name	**numele**, the name

Note 1.—There are two categories of nouns, without the article, ending in **-e** :

I. *Fem* :	**carte**, book	**cartea**, the book
	moarte, death	**moartea**, the death
II. *Masc.* :	**frate**, brother	**fratele**, the brother
	dinte, tooth	**dintele**, the tooth

Note 2.—The nouns **foarfece**, *scissors*, **cleşte**, *pliers*, **spate**, *back*, are used either as masculine singular or as feminine plural forms.

2. 7. The Masculine Plural with Definite Article is obtained by adding to the form without article of plural the article **-i** (see 2. 3) :

Singular	*Plural*	*Plural*
lup, wolf	**lupi**, wolves	**lupii**, the wolves
bou, ox	**boi**, oxen	**boii**, the oxen
copil, child	**copii**, children	**copiii**, the children
socru, father-in-law	**socri**, fathers-in-law	**socrii**, the fathers-in-law

2. 8. a). The Mixed Nouns have a masculine form in the singular and a feminine one in the plural :

Singular	*Plural*	*Plural*
scaun, chair	**scaune**, chairs	**scaunele**, the chairs
studiu, study	**studii**, studies	**studiile**, the studies
picior, foot	**picioare**, feet	**picioarele**, the feet
umăr, shoulder	**umere**, shoulders	**umerele**, the shoulders

b) Many nouns of this class form the feminine plural in **-uri** :

Singular	*Plural*	*Plural*
câmp, field	**câmpuri**, fields	**câmpurile**, the fields
lucru, thing	**lucruri**, things	**lucrurile**, the things
râu, river	**râuri**, rivers	**râurile**, the rivers
vin, wine	**vinuri**, wines	**vinurile**, the wines

Note.—Some feminine nouns form the plural in **-uri** :

Singular	*Plural*
aramă, copper	**arămuri**, copper objects
leafă, salary	**lefuri**, salaries
treabă, business	**treburi**, businesses
	trebi, businesses
vreme, time ; weather	**vremuri**, times
	vremi, times

Singular	*Plural*
iarbă, grass	**ierburi**, plants
făină, flour	**făinuri**, kinds of flour
mătasă, silk	**mătăsuri**, silks
blană, fur coat	**blănuri**, fur coats
	blăni, planks
brânză, cheese	**brânzeturi**, kinds of cheese
lână, wool	**lânuri**, pieces of wool (from a sheep)
	lâneţe, wool (prepared)

2. 9. Irregular Plural Forms

a) A few nouns have irregular plural forms :

Singular	*Plural*	*Plural*
om (*m.*), human being, man	**oameni** (*m.*), men	**oamenii**, the men, the people
cap (*m.*), head	**capete** (*f.*), heads	**capetele** (*f.*), the heads
	capi (*m.*), leaders	**capii** (*m.*), the leaders
	capuri (*f.*), promontories	**capurile** (*f.*), the promontories
oaspe, guest	**oaspeţi**, guests	**oaspeţii**, the guests
părâu, pârău (*m.*), brook	**păraie, pâraie** (*f.*), brooks	**păraiele** (*f.*), the brooks, the streams
brâu (*m.*), belt	**brâie, brâne** (*f.*), belts	**brâiele** (*f.*), the belts
grâu (*m.*), wheat	**grâie** (*f.*), wheat-fields	**grâne** (*f.*), cereals
ou (*m.*), egg	**ouă** (*f.*), eggs	

b) Some nouns have only plural forms :

în zori (*f.*), in the dawn	**zorile** (*f.*), the dawn
şale (*f.*), small of the back	**şalele** (*f.*), the back
merinde (*f.*), provisions (of food)	**merindele** (*f.*), the provisions

pantaloni (*m.*), trousers	**pantalonii,** the trousers
Paşti (*f.*), **Paşte** (*m. sing.*), Easter	**Paştile,** the Eastern
Bucureşti (*m.*),	**Bucureştii,** Bucharest

c) Some nouns have in the plural a different meaning from that of the singular, or have two plural forms with different meanings:

Singular	*Plural*
frig, cold (frost)	**friguri** (*pl. f.*), fever
fum, smoke	**fumuri** (*pl. f.*), snobbery
raport, report	**rapoarte** (*pl. f.*), reports
	raporturi (*pl. f.*), relations

Exercise No. 6

Lângă carte este un creion. N'ai carte, n'ai parte. Pe masă este o floare. Fratele e în grădină, sora e în oraş. Vecinul este în stradă. Băiatul are o piatră în mână. Lângă fântână e un copac. În grădină e un băiat şi o fată. În casă nu-i foc. Pâinea este pe masă.

Lângă râu este o câmpie. În stradă e un om. Pe câmp este o vacă. Boul este flămând. Animalul din curte se numeşte câine. Am un creion în mână. Fratele are un cal. Nu se vede nimic pe câmp. Vecinul are o fată şi un băiat. Lângă masă e un scaun şi o bancă. Lupul, ursul, calul şi boul sunt animale; şi câinele este animal. Sângele apă nu se face.

Pe cer sunt numai două stele. În pădure sunt multe flori. Am avut multe parale, acum n'am nimic. În oraş sunt multe grădini, dar în grădini nu-s frage. Numai în păduri sunt frage; în grădini sunt căpşune. Am numai cinci lei. N'am fost niciodată în Paris.

2. 10. Declension of the Noun

Every noun has two different forms for the singular and two for the plural. One form is used for *Nominative* and

Accusative and the second for *Genitive* and *Dative.* When it is necessary to make a distinction between the *Nominative* and *Accusative* or between the *Genitive* and *Dative* (see 14. 5) Rumanian uses special particles: the possessive article **a** (**al, ai, ale**) for the *Genitive* (cp. 5. 1. **b**; 14. 2) and the preposition **pe** for the *Accusative* (cp. 8. 3, Note 3, **c**; 14. 2; and 15. 4.) For the *Vocative* case, cp. 16. 1-5.

a) *Feminine Singular*

	With Indefinite Article	*With Definite Article*
1. *N. A.*	**o casă**, a house	**casa**, the house
G. D.	**unei case**, of a house to a house	**casei**, of the house to the house
	Voc. **casă!**	
2. *N. A.*	**o masă**, a table	**masa**, the table
G. D.	**unei mese**, of a table to a table	**mesei**, of the table to the table
	Voc. **masă!**	
3. *N. A.*	**o gâscă**, a goose	**gâsca**, the goose
G. D.	**unei gâşte (gâşti)**, of a goose, to a goose	**gâştei (gâştii)**, of the goose to the goose
	Voc. **gâscă! (gâsco!)**	
4. *N. A.*	**o ţară**, a country	**ţara**, the country
G. D.	**unei ţări**, of a country to a country	**ţării**, of the country to the country
	Voc. **ţara!**	
5. *N. A.*	**o barcă**, a boat	**barca**, the boat
G. D.	**unei bărci**, of a boat to a boat	**bărcii**, of the boat to the boat
	Voc. **barcă!**	
6. *N. A.*	**o uşă (uşe)**, a door	**uşa**, the door
G. D.	**unei uşi**, of a door to a door	**uşii**, of the door to the door
	Voc. **uşe!**	
7. *N. A.*	**o cruce**, a cross	**crucea**, the cross
G. D.	**unei cruci**, of a cross to a cross	**crucii**, of the cross to the cross
	Voc. **cruce!**	

		With Indefinite Article	*With Definite Article*
8.	*N. A.*	**o floare**, a flower	**floarea**, the flower
	G. D.	**unei flori**, of a flower	**florii**, of the flower
		to a flower	to the flower
		Voc. **floare !**	
9.	*N. A.*	**o pălărie**, a hat	**pălăria**, the hat
	G. D.	**unei pălării**, of a hat	**pălăriei**, of the hat
		to a hat	to the hat
		Voc. **pălărie !**	
10.	*N. A.*	**o cheie**, a key	**cheia**, the key
	G. D.	**unei chei**, of a key	**cheii**, of the key
		to a key	to the key
		Voc. **cheie !**	
11.	*N. A.*	**o vale**, a valley	**valea**, the valley
	G. D.	**unei văi**, of a valley	**văii**, of the valley
		to a valley	to the valley
		Voc. **vale !**	
12.	*N. A.*	**o zi**, a day	**ziua**, the day
	G. D.	**unei zile**, of a day	**zilei**, of the day
		to a day	to the day
		Voc. **zi !**	
13.	*N. A.*	**o soră**, a sister	**sora**, the sister
	G. D.	**unei surori**, of a sister	**surorii**, of the sister
		to a sister	to the sister
		Voc. **soră !**	**(soro !)**
14.	*N. A.*	**o stea**, a star	**steaua**, the star
	G. D.	**unei stele**, of a star	**stelei**, of the star
		to a star	to the star
		Voc. **stea !**	
15.	*N. A.*	**o basma**, a kerchief	**basmaua**, the kerchief
	G. D.	**unei basmale**, of a kerchief	**basmalei**, of the kerchief
		to a kerchief	to the kerchief
		Voc. **basma !**	
16.	*N. A.*	**o sentinelă**, a sentry	**sentinela**, the sentry
	G. D.	**unei sentinele**, of a sentry	**sentinelei**, of the sentry
		to a sentry	to the sentry
		Voc. **sentinelă !**	

	With Indefinite Article	*With Definite Article*
17. *N. A.*	**un tată**, a father	**tata, tatăl**, the father
G. D.	**unui tată**, of a father to a father	**tatei, tatălui**, of the father to the father

Voc. **tată !**

Note 1.—The Genitive and Dative of **vlădica**, *the bishop*, is **vlădicii**, but also **vlădicăi.**

Note 2.—The masculine nouns in **-a** have the Vocative in **-ă** (**-e**) or in **-o** :

Voc. **popă ! popo ! vladică ! vlădico ! bade ! badeo !**

b) *Feminine Plural*

	Without Article	*With Definite Article*
1. *N. A.*	**case**, houses	**casele**, the houses
G. D.	**case**, of houses to houses	**caselor**, of the houses to the houses

Voc. **caselor ! (case !)**

2. *N. A.*	**mese**, tables	**mesele**, the tables
G. D.	**mese**, of tables to tables	**meselor**, of the tables to the tables

Voc. **meselor ! (mese !)**

3. *N. A.*	**gâşte**, geese	**gâştele**, the geese
G. D.	**gâşte**, of geese to geese	**gâştelor**, of the geese to the geese

Voc. **gâştelor ! (gâşte !)**

4. *N. A.*	**ţări**, countries	**ţările**, the countries
G. D.	**ţări**, of countries to countries	**ţărilor**, of the countries to the countries

Voc. **ţărilor ! (ţări !)**

5. *N. A.*	**bărci**, boats	**bărcile**, the boats
G. D.	**bărci**, of boats to boats	**bărcilor**, of the boats to the boats

Voc. **bărcilor ! (bărci !)**

		Without Article	*With Definite Article*
6.	*N. A.*	**uşi**, doors	**uşile**, the doors
	G. D.	**uşi**, of doors to doors	**uşilor**, of the doors to the doors
		Voc. **uşilor !** (**uşi !**)	
7.	*N. A.*	**cruci**, crosses	**crucile**, the crosses
	G. D.	**cruci**, of crosses to crosses	**crucilor**, of the crosses to the crosses
		Voc. **crucilor !** (**cruci !**)	
8.	*N. A.*	**flori**, flowers	**florile**, the flowers
	G. D.	**flori**, of flowers to flowers	**florilor**, of the flowers to the flowers
		Voc. **florilor !** (**flori !**)	
9.	*N. A.*	**pălării**, hats	**pălăriile**, the hats
	G. D.	**pălării**, of hats to hats	**pălăriilor**, of the hats to the hats
		Voc. **pălăriilor !** (**pălării !**)	
10.	*N. A.*	**chei**, keys	**cheile**, the keys
	G. D.	**chei**, of keys to keys	**cheilor**, of the keys to the keys
		Voc. **cheilor !** (**chei !**)	
11.	*N. A.*	**văi**, valleys	**văile**, the valleys
	G. D.	**văi**, of valleys to valleys	**văilor**, of the valleys to the valleys
		Voc. **văilor !** (**văi !**)	
12.	*N. A.*	**zile**, days	**zilele**, the days
	G. D.	**zile**, of days to days	**zilelor**, of the days to the days
		Voc. **zilelor !** (**zile !**)	
13.	*N. A.*	**surori**, sisters	**surorile**, the sisters
	G. D.	**surori**, of sisters to sisters	**surorilor**, of the sisters to the sisters
		Voc. **surorilor !** (**surori !**)	
14.	*N. A.*	**stele**, stars	**stelele**, the stars
	G. D.	**stele**, of stars to stars	**stelelor**, of the stars to the stars
		Voc. **stelelor !** (**stele !**)	

	Without Article	*With Definite Article*
15. *N. A.*	**basmale**, kerchiefs	**basmalele**, the kerchiefs
G. D.	**basmale**, of kerchiefs to kerchiefs	**basmalelor**, of the kerchiefs to the kerchiefs

Voc. **basmalelor !** (**basmale !**)

16. *N. A.*	**sentinele**, sentries	**sentinelele**, the sentries
G. D.	**sentinele**, of sentries to sentries	**sentinelelor**, of the sentries to the sentries

Voc. **sentinelelor !** (**sentinele !**)

17. *N. A.*	**taţi**, fathers	**taţii**, the fathers
G. D.	**taţi**, of fathers to fathers	**taţilor**, of the fathers to the fathers

Voc. **taţilor !** (**taţi !**)

c) The following diagram shows all the endings of the feminine noun :

Singular

	Without the Article	*With the Definite Article*
N. A.	**-ă, -e, (-a)**	**-a, -ea, (-ua)**
G. D.	**-e, -i, (-le)**	**-ei, -ii, (-lei)**

Voc. **-ă, (-o), -e, (-a)**

Plural

	Without the Article	*With the Definite Article*
N. A.	**-e, -i, (-le)**	**-le**
G. D.	**-e, -i, (-le)**	**-lor**

Voc. **-lor, (-e, -i, -le)**

Note 1.—The final **-i** in the feminine ending is always a semivowel.

Note 2.—The plural form without article of the feminine nouns is identical with the Genitive-Dative form of the singular.

Note 3.—For the syntax of the Vocative see chapter 16.

Exercise No. 7

Codru-i frate cu Românul. Carpaţii au multe râuri şi văi. În România sunt codri de stejar şi de fag. Munţii Carpaţi se întind dela Dunăre, prin România, prin Polonia, prin Cehoslovacia şi prin Austria, până la Viena. Dunărea este un fluviu adânc. În codri sunt păsări şi animale, în râuri sunt peşti.

Dacii au fost un popor viteaz. Ei au avut regi. România este aşezată unde a fost altă dată Dacia. Mulţi oameni n'au bani. Noi avem bani, dar nu avem pâine. Primăvara râurile au apă multă. Ţara are munţi şi codri.

A fost odată un împărat. Împăratul avea o împărăţie mare cu păduri, cu munţi, cu câmpii şi cu râuri. Împărăteasa nu avea copii. Un om sărac avea trei feciori şi o fată.

Fiarele sălbatece trăiesc în păduri. În munţi sunt : urşi şi râşi, lupi şi vulpi, cerbi şi căprioare, mistreţi şi pisici sălbatece. Mistreţi şi lupi sunt şi pe câmpii şi în Delta Dunării. În câmpia Munteniei sunt multe dropii. În Delta Dunării trăiesc multe păsări. Acolo sunt pelicani şi lebede, bâtlani şi cocostârci de toată frumuseţa, raţe şi gâşte sălbatece şi multe alte paseri. Chiar raţele polare trăiesc în bălţile Deltei. Flamingi trandafirii cu gât lung, cu picioare roşii vin aici din regiunea Africei. În Deltă şi în Carpaţi trăiesc vulturi cu aripi mari.

2. 11. Declension of Masculine Nouns

a) *Masculine Singular*

	With Indefinite Article	*With Definite Article*
1. *N. A.*	**un domn**, a gentleman	**domnul**, the gentleman
G. D.	**unui domn**, of a gentleman to a gentleman	**domnului**, of the gentleman to the gentleman

Voc. **domnule !** (**Doamne !** (for God)

2. *N. A.*	**un copil**, a child	**copilul**, the child
G. D.	**unui copil**, of a child to a child	**copilului**, of the child to the child

Voc. **copile !** (**copilule !**)

		With Indefinite Article	*With Definite Article*
3.	*N. A.*	**un fiu**, a son	**fiul**, the son
	G. D.	**unui fiu**, of, to a son	**fiului**, of, to the son
		Voc. **fiule !** (**fiu !**)	
4.	*N. A.*	**un pui**, a chicken	**puiul**, the chicken
	G. D.	**unui pui**, of, to a chicken	**puiului**, of, to the chicken
		Voc. **puiule !** (**pui !**)	
5.	*N. A.*	**un fluviu**, a river	**fluviul**, the river
	G. D.	**unui fluviu**, of, to a river	**fluviului**, of, to the river
		Voc. **fluviule !** (**fluviu !**)	
6.	*N. A.*	**un socru**, a father-in-law	**socrul**, the father-in-law
	G. D.	**unui socru**, of, to a father-in-law	**socrului**, of, to the father-in-law
		Voc. **socrule !** (**soacre !**)	
7.	*N. A.*	**un frate**, a brother	**fratele**, the brother
	G. D.	**unui frate**, of, to a brother	**fratelui**, of, to the brother
		Voc. **frate !**	

b) *Masculine Plural*

		Without Article	*With Definite Article*
1.	*N. A.*	**domni**, gentlemen	**domnii**, the gentlemen
	G. D.	**domni**, of, to gentlemen	**domnilor**, of, to the gentlemen
		Voc. **domnilor !** (**domni !**)	
2.	*N. A.*	**copii**, children	**copiii**, the children
	G. D.	**copii**, of, to children	**copiilor**, of, to the children
		Voc. **copiilor !** (**copii !**)	
3.	*N. A.*	**fii**, sons	**fiii**, the sons
	G. D.	**fii**, of, to some sons	**fiilor**, of, to the sons
		Voc. **fiilor !** (**fii !**)	
4.	*N. A.*	**pui**, chickens	**puii**, the chickens
	G. D.	**pui**, of, to chickens	**puilor**, of, to the chickens
		Voc. **puilor !** (**pui !**)	

	Without Article	With Definite Article
5. *N. A.*	**fluvii** (*f.*), rivers	**fluviile**, the rivers
G. D.	**fluvii**, of, to rivers	**fluviilor**, of, to the rivers
	Voc. **fluviilor !**	(**fluvii !**)
6. *N. A.*	**socri**, fathers-in-law	**socrii**, the fathers-in-law
G. D.	**socri**, of, to fathers-in-law	**socrilor**, of, to the fathers-in-law
	Voc. **socrilor !**	
7. *N. A.*	**fraţi**, brothers	**fraţii**, the brothers
G. D.	**fraţi**, of, to brothers	**fraţilor**, of, to the brothers
	Voc. **fraţilor !**	(**fraţi !**)

c) *Diagram Showing the Endings of the Masculine Noun*

Singular

	Without the Article	With the Definite Article
N. A.	cons., **-u**, (**-i**), **-e**	**-l**, (**-ul**), **-le**
G. D.	cons., **-u**, (**-i**), **-e**	**-lui**, (**-ului**)
	Voc. **-e**, (**-ule**), cons.	

Plural

	Without the Article	With the Definite Article
N. A.	**-i**	**-i**
G. D.	**-i**	**-lor**
	Voc. **-lor**, (**-i**)	

Note 1.—For the way the article is added to the noun, *vide* 2. 4; 2. 5; 2. 6; 2. 7.

Note 2.—The final **-i** is a semivowel, except after cons.+**r** (e.g. **codri**).

2. 12. Declension of Proper Names

(1) Masculine proper names form the Genitive and Dative by placing the article **lui** before them (see 14. 4). The feminine, however, are declined like the noun, except those

that end in sounds which cannot take the endings of the Genitive (new names):

Masculine

Nom.	**Petru**	**Ionescu**	**Horia**
Gen.	**lui Petru**	**lui Ionescu**	**lui Horia**
Dat.	**lui Petru**	**lui Ionescu**	**lui Horia**
Acc.	**pe Petru**	**pe Ionescu**	**pe Horia**
Voc.	**Petru! (Petre!)**	**Ionescu (le)!**	**Horia!**

Feminine

Nom.	**Maria**	**Mabel**
Gen.	**Mariei**	**lui Mabel**
Dat.	**Mariei**	**lui Mabel**
Acc.	**pe Maria**	**pe Mabel**
Voc.	**Mario! Marie!**	**Mabel!**

(2) Geographical names are declined according to their gender:

Târgul Brăilei (*Gen.*),	the market of Brăila
străzile Londrei (*Gen.*),	the streets of London
Luna Bucureştilor (*Gen.*),	the Month (market) of Bucharest
apele Prutului (*Gen.*),	the waters of the river Pruth
pustiurile Africei (*Gen.*),	the deserts of Africa
grădinile Iaşilor (*Gen.*),	the gardens of Jassy

(3) A special category of geographical names are the compound ones. These are considered as determined nouns:

Nom.	**Turnul-Severinului** (town)
Gen.	(al) **Turnul-Severinului** (al) **Turnului-Severin**
Dat.	**Turnului-Severin**

Note.—Geographical names after prepositions, see 13. 3.

Exercise No. 8

În curtea vecinului meu sunt multe paseri. El are găini, gâşte, raţe, curci şi curcani. În pădure sunt alte feluri de paseri ; acolo trăiesc : vulturi, corbi, mierle, privighitori şi sturzi. Pe câmpie trăiesc : prepeliţe şi ciocârlii, iar în lunci trăiesc fasanii.

O pasere are două picioare şi două aripi. Corpul paserilor este acoperit cu pene. Penele sunt albe sau negre sau sure. Vulturii trăiesc pe stânci. Ciocul vulturilor este ascuţit.

Lângă casă trăiesc animale domestice. În codri şi în păduri sunt multe animale sălbatece. Corpul animalelor este acoperit cu păr. Culoarea părului este albă, neagră, roşie sau castanie. Lângă casa omului trăiesc : câinele, pisica, vaca, calul, oaia, porcul şi altele.

Am fost astă vară în Poiana-Sibiului. Regii României sunt îngropaţi în Curtea-de-Argeş. Catedrala Curţii-de-Argeş este o clădire veche. Gara din Târgu-Frumos este departe de oraş. Râmnicu-Vâlcea este un oraş de munte. Dela Turnu-Severin până la Bucureşti e drum lung. Târgu-Jiu (lui) este capitală de judeţ. Vatra-Dornei e o staţiune balneară în Bucovina, pe Valea Bistriţei.

3. 1. THE ADJECTIVE

Adjectives have the same declension forms as nouns.

a) Adjectives having a form for masculine and a form for feminine :

		Singular	*Plural*	
Masc.		*Fem.*	*Masc.*	*Fem.*
bun,	good	bună	buni	bune
frumos,	beautiful	frumoasă	frumoşi	frumoase
acru,	sour	acră	acri	acre
albastru,	blue	albastră	albaştri	albastre
nou,	new	nouă	noi (noui)	noue (noi)
greu,	heavy, difficult	grea	grei	grele
rău,	bad	rea	răi	rele
roşu, roş,	red	roşe, roşie	roşi (-i)	roşi (-i)
greoi,	awkward	greoaie	greoi	greoaie
cenuşiu,	ashen	cenuşie	cenuşii	cenuşii

		Singular	*Plural*	
Masc.		*Fem.*	*Masc.*	*Fem.*
vechi, (vechiu)	old	veche	vechi	vechi
silitor,	diligent	silitoare	silitori	silitoare
domnesc,	of the gentleman	domnească	domneşti	domneşti
românesc,	Rumanian	românească	româneşti	româneşti
român,	Rumanian	română	români	române
englez,	English	engleză	englezi (engleji)	engleze

Note 1.—Some adjectives ending in a guttural have the plural in **-i** both for masculine and for feminine :

Singular		*Plural*
Masc.	*Fem.*	*Masc.-Fem.*
adânc, deep	adâncă	adânci
drag, dear, beloved	dragă	dragi
larg, broad	largă	largi
lung, long	lungă	lungi
mic, small	mică	mici
românesc, Rumanian	românească	româneşti

Those, however, ending in **-nic**, **-tec** (**-tic**), and other adjectives ending in guttural which can be used as nouns, have in plural different forms for masculine and feminine :

Singular		*Plural*	
Masc.	*Fem.*	*Masc.*	*Fem.*
amarnic, bitter	amarnică	amarnici	amarnice
unic, only, alone, unparalleled	unică	unici	unice
voinic, strong (physically)	voinică	voinici	voinice
nebunatec (-tic), foolish	nebunatecă	nebunateci	nebunatece

Singular		*Plural*	
Masc.	*Fem.*	*Masc.*	*Fem.*
sălbatec (**-tic**), wild	**sălbatică**	**sălbatici**	**sălbatice**
singuratec (**-tic**), lonely, solitary	**singuratecă**	**singurateci**	**singuratece**
sărac, poor	**săracă**	**săraci**	**sărace**
pribeag, homeless hiker, refugee	**pribeagă**	**pribegi**	**pribege**
năuc, stupid	**năucă**	**năuci**	**năuce**

Note 2.—Some masculine nouns are transformed into feminine by receiving a feminine termination :

prieten,	friend	**prietenă**,	lady friend
naş,	sponsor (at wedding and christening)	**naşe**, (**naşă**)	lady sponsor
cumătru,	godfather at christening (in relation to the child's parents)	**cumătră**,	godmother

b) Adjectives having the same form for masculine and for feminine :

Singular		*Plural*
călare,	on horseback	**călări**
verde,	green	**verzi**
dulce,	sweet	**dulci**
mare,	big, great	**mari**
fierbinte,	hot	**fierbinţi**
moale,	soft	**moi**
repede,	fast	**repezi**

c) A third category is that of the diminutive adjectives, masculine ending in **-el**, feminine in **-ică** :

Singular			*Plural*	
Masc.		*Fem.*	*Masc.*	*Fem.*
frumuşel,	pretty	**frumuşică**	**frumuşei**,	**frumuşele**
mititel,	little, tiny	**mititică**	**mititei**	**mititele**
măricel,	fairly big	**măricică**	**măricei**	**măricele**
uşurel,	fairly light	**uşurică**	**uşurei**	**uşurele**

3. 2. The Position and the Declension of the Adjective

a) The adjective is placed after the noun and agrees with it in gender and in number (cp. 17. 1). The adjective in this position is without a definite article :

Feminine

	Singular	*Plural*
N. A.	**mama bună**, the good mother	**mamele bune**
G. D.	**mamei bune**, of the, to the good mother	**mamelor bune**
V.	**mamă bună !**	**mame bune ! (mamelor bune !)**
N. A.	**marea limpede**, the clear sea	**mările limpezi**
G. D.	**mării limpezi**	**mărilor limpezi**
V.	**mare limpede !**	**mări limpezi ! (mărilor limpezi !)**

Masculine

N. A.	**omul bun,** the good man	**oamenii buni**
G. D.	**omului bun**	**oamenilor buni**
V.	**om bun !**	**oameni buni ! (oamenilor buni !)**
N. A.	**arborele verde**, the green tree	**arborii verzi**
G. D.	**arborelui verde**	**arborilor verzi**
V.	**arbore verde !**	**arbori verzi ! (arborilor verzi !)**

b) The adjective may be placed before the noun (cp. 17. 1). This position gives to the adjective a special emphasis. In this position the adjective takes the definite article, but the noun is without an article :

Feminine

	Singular	*Plural*
N. A.	**buna mamă**, the good mother	**bunele mame**
G. D.	**bunei mame**	**bunelor mame !**
V.	**bună mamă !**	**bunelor mame ! (bune mame !)**

Masculine

	Singular	*Plural*
N. A.	**limpedele râu**, the clear stream	**limpezile râuri**
G. D.	**limpedelui râu**	**limpezilor râuri**
V.	**limpede râu !**	**limpezilor (limpezi) râuri !**

c) The adjective may be used in both positions with the indefinite article :

Feminine

	Singular	*Plural*
N. A.	**o mamă bună**, a good mother **o bună mamă**	**nişte mame bune**, some good mothers **nişte bune mame**
G. D.	**unei mame bune** **unei bune mame**	**nişte mame bune** **nişte bune mame**
V.	**mamă bună !** **bună mamă !**	**mame bune !** **bune mame !**

Masculine

	Singular	*Plural*
N. A.	**un râu limpede**, a clear stream **un limpede râu**	**nişte râuri limpezi**, some clear streams **nişte limpezi râuri**
G. D.	**unui râu limpede** **unui limpede râu**	**nişte râuri limpezi** **nişte limpezi râuri**
V.	**râu limpede !** **limpede râu !**	**râuri limpezi !** **limpezi râuri !**

Note.—These instances show that the adjective, like the noun, has a declension with the definite article and a declension with the indefinite article.

d) Another way to connect the adjective with the noun is by using the demonstrative pronoun : e.g. **Cugetul cel bun, cea mai moale pernă**, The good thought (is) the softest pillow.

Masculine

	Singular	*Plural*
N. A.	**cel**, that	**cei**
G. D.	**celui**	**celor**

Feminine

N. A.	**cea**, that	**cele**
G. D.	**celei**	**celor**

Masculine

	Singular	*Plural*
N. A.	**primăvara cea frumoasă**, the beautiful spring	**primăverile cele frumoase**
G. D.	**primăverii celei frumoase**	**primăverilor celor frumoase**

Feminine

N. A.	**copilul cel bun**, the good child	**copiii cei buni**
G. D.	**copilului celui bun**	**copiilor celor buni**

3. 3. Comparison of Adjectives

a) The *positive* degree :

înalt (*m.*),	**înaltă** (*f.*),	high
jos (*m.*),	**joasă** (*f.*),	low
mare (*m.* and *f.*),		big, great

b) The *comparative* degree is formed with the adverb **mai**, more, placed before the positive form :

mai înalt (*m.*),	**mai înaltă** (*f.*),	higher
mai jos (*m.*),	**mai joasă** (*f.*),	lower
mai mare (*m.* and *f.*),		bigger, greater

The comparison is expressed by the adverb **decât**, *than* :

Pomul e mai înalt decât casa.
The fruit-tree is higher than the house.

Scaunul e mai jos decât masa.
The chair is lower than the table.

Comparison of equality is expressed by :

tot atât . . . ca şi,	as . . . as
tot aşa . . . ca şi,	as . . . as
la fel (de) . . . ca şi,	the same . . . as (like)

Teiul e tot atât de înalt ca şi nucul.
The lime-tree is as high as the walnut-tree.

Perele sunt tot aşa de bune ca şi merele.
Pears are as good as apples.

Câinele e la fel de inteligent ca şi calul.
The dog is as intelligent as the horse.

Comparison of inferiority is expressed by **mai puţin . . . decât**, less than :

Pisica e mai puţin inteligentă decât câinele.
The cat is less intelligent than the dog.

c) The *superlative* is expressed by the comparative form preceded by the demonstrative pronoun : *fem. sing.* **cea**, *that* ; *fem. pl.* **cele** ; *masc. sing.* **cel** ; *masc. pl.* **cei**. The demonstrative article is declined like the noun :

	Singular	*Plural*
N. A.	**apa cea mai adâncă**	**apele cele mai adânci**
G. D.	**apei celei mai adânci**	**apelor celor mai adânci**
N. A.	**cea mai limpede mare** the clearest sea	**cele mai limpezi mări**
G. D.	**celei mai limpezi mări**	**celor mai limpezi mări**
N. A.	**copacul cel mai înalt** the highest tree	**copacii cei mai înalţi**
G. D.	**copacului celui mai înalt**	**copacilor celor mai înalţi**
N. A.	**cel mai frumos arbore**	**cei mai frumoşi arbori**
G. D.	**celui mai frumos arbore**	**celor mai frumoşi arbori**

The *absolute superlative* is formed with the adverb **foarte,** *very*, or with other adverbs :

foarte frumos,	very (most) beautiful
tare bine,	very well
grozav de mult,	terribly much
prea înalt,	too high, very high

3. 4. Adverbial Forms of Adjectives

(See also Chapter 7)

a) The adverbial form of the adjective is, as a rule, identical with the masculine form of the adjective :

Privighitoarea nu e frumoasă, dar ea cântă frumos.
The nightingale is not beautiful, but it sings beautifully.

Cartea este scumpă. The book is expensive.

Am plătit scump (pentru) această carte.
I paid much for this book.

Un om fericit. A happy man.

Un om trăia fericit în casa sa.
A man lived happily in his house.

b) Adjectives ending in masculine **-esc**, feminine **-ească,** have the adverb in **-eşte** :

masc. **bărbătesc,** *fem.* **bărbătească,** *adv.* **bărbăteşte,** manly
masc. **românesc,** *fem.* **românească,** *adv.* **româneşte,** Rumanian
masc. **englezesc,** *fem.* **englezească,** *adv.* **englezeşte,** English
masc. **omenesc,** *fem.* **omenească,** *adv.* **omeneşte** humanly

port bărbatesc, man's dress	**s'a purtat bărbăteşte,** he behaved like a man
Ţara Românească, Walachia	**vorbesc româneşte,** I speak Rumanian

literatura engleză, English literature
firea omenească, human nature

vorbesc englezeşte, I speak English
se poartă omeneşte, he behaves like a human being

The adverbial form of **bun, -ă-**, good, is **bine**, well.

c) The comparative and superlative from adverbs are formed with **mai** and **cel mai**, like the degrees of adjectives:

E mai bine să dai decât să iai.
It is better to give than to take.

Cel mai frumos s'a purtat fratele tău.
Your brother behaved himself best.

EXERCISE No. 9

Animalele domestice sunt mai folositoare decât cele sălbatece. Caii sunt mai repezi decât boii, dar boii sunt tot atât de tari ca şi caii.

Mai bine un măgar sănătos decât un leu bolnav. În ţara orbilor cel cu un ochi este împărat.

Decât toată vara cioară
Mai bine şoim o zi de vară.
Mai bine o împăcare strâmbă decât o judecată dreaptă.

În parcurile Londrei cresc cei mai frumoşi ulmi. Cel mai înalt vârf al Carpaţilor, în România, este Negoiul (2540 m.), în Munţii Făgăraşului. Concurentul Negoiului este muntele Moldovanu, care e numai cu două zeci de metri mai jos. Cel mai înalt munte din Carpaţii de răsărit este Ceahlăul (1904 m.) numit Olimpul Moldovei, din cauza multelor legende în legătură cu acest majestos munte.

Frasinul şi paltinul sunt copaci înalţi. Teiul din grădina de lângă parc este mai înalt decât plopul din parc. În pădurile Carpaţilor sunt stejeri foarte înalţi. Bistriţa este un râu de munte foarte repede, Dunărea este lină dar foarte adâncă.

Înalt cât casa
Verde ca mătasa
Dulce ca mierea
Amar ca fierea.

(Nucul şi nuca.)

Apa liniştită e adâncă. Râul lin sapă adânc. Lemnul de stejar e mai vârtos decât lemnul de fag. Adună bani albi pentru zile negre !

4. NUMERALS

4. 1. Cardinal Numerals

1 **unu(l)** (*substantival m.*)
un (*adjectival m.*)
una (*subst. f.*)
o (*adj. f.*)
2 **doi** (*m.*), **două** (*f.*)
3 **trei**
4 **patru**
5 **cinci**
6 **şase**
7 **şapte**
8 **opt**
9 **nouă**
10 **zece**

From 11 to 20 the cardinal numeral is formed with the help of the preposition **-spre-** inserted between the unit and ten :

11 **unsprezece (unsprece)** (*m.* and *f.*)
12 **doisprezece (doisprece)** (*m.*), **douăsprezece (douăsprece)** (*f.*)
13 **treisprezece (treisprece)**
14 **patrusprezece (patrusprece, paisprezece, paisprece)**
15 **cincisprezece (cinsprece)**
16 **şasesprezece (şaisprece)**
17 **şaptesprezece (şapsprece)**
18 **optsprezece (opsprece)**
19 **nouăsprezece (nouăsprece)**
20 **douăzeci**

21	douăzeci şi unu (*m.*), douăzeci şi una (*f.*)				
22	douăzeci şi doi (*m.*), douăzeci şi două (*f.*)				
23	douăzeci şi trei				
30	treizeci	31	treizeci şi unu, etc.		
40	patruzeci	50	cincizeci (cinzeci)		
60	şasezeci (şaizeci)	70	şaptezeci		
80	optzeci	90	nouăzeci		
100	o sută	200	două sute	300	trei sute
1000	o mie	2000	două mii	3000	trei mii
1100	o mie (şi) o sută				
7354	şapte mii trei sute cincizeci şi patru				
1,000,000	un milion	2,000,000	două milioane		
1,000,000,000	un miliard ; două miliarde.				

a) *Declension of Numerals.*

	Masc.	*Fem.*
Nom.	unu(l), un	una, o
Gen.	a unui(a)	a unei(a)
Dat.	unui(a)	unei(a)
Acc.	pe unu(l)	pe una, pe o

	Masc.	*Fem.*
Nom.	doi	două
Gen.	a doi, a duor(a)	a două, a duor(a)
Dat.	la doi, duor	la două, duor
Acc.	pe doi	pe două

b) All the numerals form the Genitive with the help of the possessive article **a** or with the preposition **dela** ; and the Dative with the help of the preposition **la** :

Munca a zece bărbaţi şi a cinci femei.	The work of ten men and five women.
Hrana a cincizeci de soldaţi.	The food of 50 soldiers.
Miei dela zece oi.	Lambs of ten sheep.
Hainele a zece copii.	The clothes of ten children.

Laptele dela două vaci.	The milk of two cows.
Dau mâncare la şase copii.	I gave food to six children.

c) **O sută** (100) and **o mie** (1000) are declined like feminine nouns.

d) The noun after a numeral above 19 is jointed to the numeral with the help of the preposition **de**:

	unsprezece oameni,	11 men
	nouăsprezece cărţi	19 books
but:	**douăzeci de pomi,**	20 trees
	trei sute de cai,	300 horses
	o mie de oameni,	1000 men

patru sute cinci zeci şi doi soldaţi (or **de soldaţi**), 452 soldiers

e) **amândoi** (*m.*), **amândouă** (*f.*)—*both* are used like **doi, două**, and are followed by the noun with a definite article:

Amândoi băieţii vecinului se joacă în grădină.
Both boys of the neighbour are playing in the garden.

Amândouă mâinile i-au fost legate.
Both his hands have been bound.

Gen.	**a amânduror băieţilor**	**a amânduror mâinilor**
Dat.	**amânduror băieţilor**	**amânduror mâinilor**
Acc.	**pe amândoi băieţii**	**pe amândouă mâinile**

f) Synonymous with **amândoi** is **ambii** (*m.*), **ambele** (*f.*). After this numeral the noun is used without an article:

Nom.	**ambii prieteni** both friends	**ambele surori** both sisters
Gen.	**a ambilor prieteni**	**a ambelor surori**
Dat.	**ambilor prieteni**	**ambelor surori**
Acc.	**pe ambii prieteni**	**pe ambele surori**

g) **Tustrei** (*m.*), **tustrele** (*f.*) (from **toţi trei**), all three :

Gen. **a tustreilor, a tustrelelor**

Tuspatru, **câteşi patru**, all four :

Gen. **a tuspatru**
Dat. **la tuspatru**

Tuscinci, câteşi cinci, all five ; **tusşase, câteşi şase**, all six.

h) The Cardinal Numerals use, like the adjective, the demonstrative pronoun **cel**, etc., to express the idea of objects already known :

Cei 12 oameni, pe cari i-ai văzut zugrăviţi pe peretele bisericii, sunt cei 12 apostoli.
The 12 men you have seen painted on the wall of the church are the 12 apostles.

Am primit cele cinci sute de lei ce-mi datorai.
I received the 500 lei you owed me.

Cei doi condamnaţi au fost executaţi în zorii zilei.
The two people condemned to death have been executed at dawn.

4. 2. Ordinal Numerals

The Ordinal Numerals, except the first, are formed by the suffix **-le(a)** (*m.*), **-a** (*f.*) attached to the cardinal number and by placing before them the possessive article **al** (*m.*), **a** (*f.*) :

1st	**întâiul, întâia ; primul, prima ; cel dintâi, cea dintâi**
2nd	**al doile(a), a doua ; cel de al doilea, cea de a doua**
3rd	**al treile(a), a treia**
4th	**al patrule(a), a patra**
5th	**al cincile(a), a cincia**
6th	**al şasele(a), a şasa**
7th	**al şaptele(a), a şaptea**

8th	**al optule(a) (al optăle), a opta**
9th	**al noule(a) (al noăle), a noua**
10th	**al zecele(a), a zecea**
11th	**al unsprezecele(a), a unsprezecea**
12th	**al doisprezecele(a), a douăsprezecea**
21st	**al douăzeci şi unule(a), a douăzeci şi una**
32nd	**al treizeci şi doile(a), a treizeci şi doua**
100th	**al sutăle(a), a suta**
101st	**al o sută şi unulea**
138th	**al o sută trezeci şi optule(a)**
591st	**al cinci sute nouăzeci şi unule(a), a cinci sute nouăzeci şi una**
1000th	**al o miile(a), a o miia**

Note.—**întâiul** and **primul** are adjectives. Other ordinal numerals have no declension. When the forms with **cel** are used the latter has the declension of a pronoun.

Examples:

Intâiul care a sosit; or, **primul care a sosit**; or, **cel dintâi care a sosit.** The first who arrived.

Intâia zi de iarnă; or, **cea dintâi zi de iarnă**; or, **prima zi de iarnă.** The first winter day.

Primii oameni pe pământ au fost Adam şi Eva.
The first people on earth were Adam and Eve.

Primele flori de primăvară sânt ghioceii.
The first spring flowers are the snowdrops.

Elevului al doilea i-am dat un premiu.
To the second schoolboy I gave a reward.

Celui de al treilea elev din banca a cincia.
To the third schoolboy in the fifth bench.

4. 3. Adjectival Numerals

These numbers are formed from the cardinal numbers with the help of the prefix **în-** and the past participle from a verb of the fourth conjugation derived from the respective cardinal number:

îndoit, -ă (dublu (*m.*), **dublă** (*f.*)), twofold, double
întreit, -ă (triplu (*m.*), **triplă** (*f.*)), threefold, treble, triple
împătrit, -ă (cuadruplu (*m.*), **cuadruplă** (*f.*)), fourfold
încincit, -ă, fivefold
înşesit, -a, six times one
înşeptit, -ă
înoptit, -ă
înzecit, -ă
însutit, -ă
înmiit, -ă

These numbers are treated as adjectives. Their adverbial form is therefore identical with the masculine form:

Am plătit un preţ însutit (*adj.*). I paid a hundredfold price.

Am plătit însutit cât face (*adv.*).
I paid a hundred times more its value.

4. 4. Distributive Numerals

These numerals are formed with the help of the adverb **câte**:

câte unu(l) (*m.*), **câte una** (*f.*)	one by one, singly
câte doi (*m.*), **câte două** (*f.*)	by twos
câte trei, câte patru, câte cinci, etc.	by threes, fours, fives, etc.
unul câte unu(l),	one by one

doi câte doi, trei câte trei, patru câte patru, etc.

4. 5. Fractional Numerals

These are nouns of feminine declension. They are formed from cardinals with the help of the suffix **-ime**:

$\frac{1}{2}$ **o jumătate**
$\frac{1}{3}$ **o treime (una a treia).** *Sing.* **treimea,** *Pl.* **treimile**
$\frac{1}{4}$ **o pătrime (una a patra).** *Sing.* **pătrimea,** *Pl.* **pătrimile**
$\frac{1}{5}$ **o cincime (una a cincia)**

$\frac{2}{6}$ două şesimi (două a şasea)
$\frac{1}{10}$ o zecime (una a zecea) (a zecea parte)
$\frac{1}{100}$ o sutime (una a suta, a suta parte)
$\frac{1}{1000}$ o miime (una a mia, a mia parte)

Note 1.—In the same way one derives:

unime from **unu**, unit (units, tens, hundreds, etc.), oneness
doime ,, **doi**, duality
treime ,, **trei**, trinity

Note 2.—*Fractional Substantives*:

$\frac{1}{2}$ **o jumătate, jumătatea,** *gen.* **jumătăţii,** *pl.* **jumătăţile,** half
$\frac{1}{4}$ **un sfert, sfertul,** *gen.* **sfertului,** *pl.* **sferturile,** quarter
un pătrar, pătrarul, *gen.* **pătrarului,** *pl.* **pătrarele,** quarter

Şase luni sânt jumătate de an.	Six months make half a year.
Am aşteptat un sfert de oră.	I waited for half an hour.
Primul pătrar al lunei.	The first quarter of the moon.
O jumătale plus o treime fac cinci şesimi.	A half plus one-third are five-sixths.

4. 6. Multiplicative Numerals

odată	once
de două ori	twice
de zece ori	ten times
de o sută de ori	a hundred times
de o mie de ori	a thousand times
întâia oară, întâia(şi) dată	the first time
a doua oară	the second time
a suta oară	the hundredth time

A venit a doua oară să mă vadă.
He came the second time to see me.

Inamicul a atacat de zece ori într'o zi.
The enemy attacked ten times in one day.

Note.—Indefinite numerals, see 5. 9.

Exercise No. 10

Calcule şi măsuri

a) Cele patru operaţiuni aritmetice sunt:
adunarea, scăderea, înmulţirea şi împărţirea.
Opt plus (şi cu) opt fac şasesprezece.
Cincisprezece minus (fără) doi fac treisprezece.
De cinci ori patru fac douăzeci.
Zece înmulţit cu cinci fac cincinzeci.
Şaptezeci (împărţit) prin zece fac şapte.
A cincia parte dintr'o sută e douăzeci.
Doi dela opt fac şase.

b) Un sfert de chilogram sunt două sute cincizeci de grame.
Patruzeci şi cinci de minute fac trei sferturi de oră.
Am plătit şaptezeci şi cinci de lei pentru un chilogram (un litru) de vin de Cotnari.
Două jumătăţi fac un întreg.

c) o milă are un chilometru şi şase sute şi nouă (de) metri.
un *yard* are trei picioare sau 0,914 m. (zero întregi nouă, unu, patru).
un *inch* are 25,4 milimetri.
un *gallon* are 4,546 litri.
un *pint* este 0,568 litri.
un *pound* (lb.) are 0,454 kg.
o tonă (*ton*) are 1,016 kg.
un metru are 39,370 *inches* sau 3,28 picioare sau 1,093 *yards* (iarzi).
un chilometru are 0,62137 *mile*.
apa fierbe la o temperatură de 212 grade Fahrenheit sau la 100 grade Celsius, sau la 80 grade Reaumur.
apa înghiaţă la 32 grade Fahrenheit sau la 0 grade Celsius şi Reaumur.
temperatura normală a corpului e 98,4 grade Fahrenheit sau 36,7 grade Celsius sau 29,3 grade Reaumur.
o liră sterlină (un *pound*, £) are 20 de şilingi, un şiling are 12 penşi.
15% (procente, la sută) la o liră sunt 3 şilingi.
5 şilingi sunt 25% dintr'o liră.

Timpul

a) **Ora : Cât e ceasul? (Câte ceasuri?—Ce oră e?)**
What is the time?

E ora unu.
E ora trei.
E cinci şi un sfert.
E patru fără cinci.
E ora opt şi douăzeci.
La ora nouă trebuie să plec.
Te rog să vii la ora şase.
Merge bine ceasul dumitale?
Ceasul meu s'a oprit.
Am uitat să-l întorc aseară.
Al meu e în urmă cu zece minute.
Cât timp durează concertul?
O oră şi zece minute, dela trei treizeci până la cinci fără zece.

b) **Ziua: În câte sântem (avem) astăzi?**

Azi e în 15 Ianuarie 1944.
Mâine e zi întâi.
La 16 Februarie se împlineşte anul de când ai plecat.
Primăvara durează dela 21 Martie până la 23 Iunie.

c) **Anul: În care an?**

Când sânteţi născut?
Sânt născut în ziua de 17 August 1914.
Ştefan cel Mare a domnit dela 1457 până la 1504.
Lupta dela Hastings a avut loc în anul 1066.
Primul răsboi mondial a isbucnit în anul 1914.
Băiatul e de cinci ani, fetiţa are trei ani şi jumătate.
La vârsta de şapte ani băiatul a mers la şcoală.
Când aveam douăzeci şi unul de ani am fost recrutat.
Lupta a durat cinci zile.
În ziua a şasa armatele s'au retras.

5. PRONOUNS

5. 1. a) **Personal Pronouns** (cp. 18. 1-18. 4)

First Person

	Singular	*Plural*
Nom.	**eu**, I	**noi**, we
Dat.	**mie, îmi, mi**	**nouă, ne, ni**
Acc.	**pe mine, mă**	**pe noi, ne**

Second Person

Nom.	**tu**, thou	**voi**, you
Dat.	**ţie, îţi, ţi**	**vouă, vă, vi**
Acc.	**pe tine, te**	**pe voi, vă**

Third Person

	Masc.	*Fem.*	*Masc.*	*Fem.*
Nom.	**el**, he	**ea**, she	**ei**, they	**ele**, they
Dat.	**lui, îi, i**	**ei, îi, i**	**lor, le, li**	**lor, le, li**
Acc.	**pe el, îl, l**	**pe ea, o**	**pe ei, îi, i**	**pe ele, le**

b) *The Genitive* has no special form (see 14. 2). The corresponding form of the possessive pronoun with the possessive article is used instead :

al (a, ai, ale) meu (mea, mei, mele)
al (a, ai, ale) tău (ta, tăi, tale)
al (a, ai, ale) său (sa, săi, sale)

Only the third person has a proper form for the Genitive :

al (a, ai, ale) lui	**al (a, ai, ale) lor**
al (a, ai, ale) ei	**al (a, ai, ale) lor**

c) Another pronoun for the third person is **dânsul** (*m.*), **dânsa** (*f.*) :

Singular

	Masc.	*Fem.*
Nom.	**dânsul**, he	**dânsa**, she
Gen.	**al (a, ai, ale) dânsului**	**al (a, ai, ale) dânsei**
Dat.	**dânsului**	**dânsei**
Acc.	**pe dânsul**	**pe dânsa**

Plural

	Masc.	*Fem.*
Nom.	**dânşii**, they	**dânsele**, they
Gen.	**al (a, ai, ale) dânşilor**	**al (a, ai, ale) dânselor**
Dat.	**dânşilor**	**dânselor**
Acc.	**pe dânşii**	**pe dânsele**

Dânsul mi-a spus că nu va veni.
He told me that he wouldn't come.

Pe dânşii nu i-am văzut în grădină.
I did not see them in the garden.

Aceasta-i haina dânsei. That is her coat.

d) The Dative and Accusative forms noted in the first place in the paradigm (5. 1 a) (**mie, ţie, lui, ei**; **pe mine, pe tine, pe el, pe ea**; **nouă, vouă, lor**; **pe noi, pe voi, pe ei, pe ele**) are stressed (disjunct) pronominal forms. They are used:

(i) Without a verb:

Cui am dat cartea?—Mie (mi-ai dat-o).
To whom did I give the book?—To me (you gave it).

Pe cine ai văzut în oraş?—Pe ei (i-am văzut).
Whom have you seen in the town?—(I saw) them.

(ii) In support of one of the conjunct (unstressed) forms noted in the second and third place of the same paradigm:

Pe tine nu te-am văzut azi. I did not see you to-day.
Vouă nu vă trebuie haine. You do not need clothes.

The conjunct pronominal forms can be used alone, the stressed (disjunct) forms must be supported by a conjunct when used with a verb :

Ţi se cuvine laudă ; ţie ţi se cuvine laudă (*but not* : **ţie cuvine laudă**). You deserve praise.

e) The Dative and Accusative forms noted in the second and in the third place of the paradigm (**îmi, mi, mă, ne, ni ; îţi, ţi, te, vă, vi ; îi, i, îl, l, o, le, li**) are always *unstressed pronominal forms*. Those of them which begin with an **î-**, are used, always proclitically, immediately before the verb. The others are proclitic or enclitic and hyphenated with the stressed word in the sentence :

Îmi aduc aminte de acea zi de vară.
I remember that summer day.

Nu-mi place să te văd trist.
I do not like to see you sad.

Pâinea noastră cea de toate zilele dă-ne nouă astăzi.
Give us this day our daily bread.

Şi ne iartă nouă păcatele noastre.
(Şi iartă-ne nouă păcatele noastre.)
And forgive us our trespasses.

Dece ţi-i frică de aceea nu scapi.
You won't escape that which you are afraid of.

Vecina nu-i acasă, am văzut-o în oraş.
The neighbour (*f.*) is not at home, I saw her in the town.

De te latră un câine astupă-i gura cu pâine.
If a dog barks at you, fill his mouth with bread.

Nu ţi-a fost frică să umbli singur prin codru ?
Were you not afraid to wander through the forest alone ?

The conjunct forms are used enclitically in the affirmative imperative, and in the gerund form :

Adă-mi apă.	Bring me some water.
Daţi-le mâncare.	Give them something to eat.
Faceţi-vă cruce.	Cross yourselves.
Nu-i spune nimic.	Do not tell him anything.
Nu vă speriaţi.	Do not be frightened.
Spunându-i acestea plecă.	Telling him this he left.

In the Subjunctive the conjunct forms are placed between **să** and the verb :

Să te păzeşti de el.	Beware of him.
Să vă fie milă de cei ce suferă.	Have pity with those who suffer.
Să nu-i spui nimic.	Do not tell him anything.

f) The use of the forms of the Dative and Accusative plural :

First person.	**ne**	or	**ni,**
Second ,,	**vă**	,,	**vi,**
Third ,,	**le**	,,	**li,**

can be learned by observing the following rules :

(i) **ne, vă, le** are used when they immediately precede their verb :

Ne pare bine.	We are glad.
Vă spunem adevărul.	We are telling you the truth.
Le-am dat să mănânce.	We gave them something to eat.

(ii) **ni, vi, li** are used when they are separated from the verb by another pronoun :

Ni se pare că l-am văzut în oraş.
We think we have seen him in the town.

Vi le dau aceste cărţi ca să le cetiţi.
I give you these books to read.

Li s'a dat de ştire să vie mâine dimineaţă.
It has been announced to them that they may be coming to-morrow morning.

5. 2. Emphatic Pronoun

The personal pronoun used to emphasize the identity of the person is called the Emphatic Pronoun :

Singular

	Masc.	*Fem.*
Nom.	(eu) **însumi**, myself	(eu) **însămi**, myself
	(tu) **însuţi**, thyself	(tu) **însăţi**, thyself
	(el) **însuşi**, himself	(ea) **însăşi**, herself
Dat.	**mie însumi**, to myself	**mie însămi**, to myself
	ţie însuţi, to thyself	**ţie însăţi**, to thyself
	lui însuşi, to himself	**ei însăşi**, to herself
Acc.	**pe mine însumi**, myself	**pe mine însămi**, myself
	pe tine însuţi, thyself	**pe tine însăţi**, thyself
	pe sine (el) **însuşi**, himself	**pe sine** (ea) **însăşi**, herself

Plural

Nom.	(noi) **înşine**, ourselves	(noi) **însene**, ourselves
	(voi) **înşivă**, yourselves	(voi) **însevă**, yourselves
	(ei) **înşişi**, themselves	(ele) **înseşi**, themselves
Dat.	**nouă înşine**, to ourselves	**nouă însene**, to ourselves
	vouă înşivă, to yourselves	**vouă însevă**, to yourselves
	lor înşişi, to themselves	**lor înseşi**, to themselves
Acc.	**pe noi înşine**, ourselves	**pe noi însene**, ourselves
	pe voi înşivă, yourselves	**pe voi însevă**, yourselves
	pe ei înşişi, themselves	**pe ele înseşi**, themselves

Note.—This pronoun is also used as an adjective :

Fratele însuşi mi-a spus că n'are să vie.
The brother himself told me he wouldn't come.

Voi înşivă aţi mărturisit. You yourselves have confessed.

Dumnezeu însuşi nu poate ajuta pe cine nu vrea să se ajute.
God Himself cannot help a man who does not want to help himself.

Judecaţi-vă voi înşivă. Be yourselves your own judges.

N.B.—There is no Genitive form from this pronoun (cf. 5. 1 **b**).

5. 3. Reflexive Pronoun

Only the third person has a reflexive pronoun :

	Masc. Fem. Sing.	*Masc. Fem. Plural*
Dat.	**îşi, sie, -şi, sieşi**	**îşi, sie, şi, sieşi**
Acc.	**se, pe sine**	**se, pe sine**

Fiecare se laudă pe sine. Everyone praises himself.

Îşi dă sie (şi) de pomană. He gives alms for himself.

Lauda de sine nu miroase bine.
To praise oneself is bad taste.

Vecinii buni se ajută întreolaltă.
Good neighbours help one another.

5. 4. Pronouns of Deference

The second person singular is used when speaking to friends, to children, and in prayers.

The pronoun used in polite address is **domnia ta**, which in colloquial speech became **dumneata (dumeata)**, followed by the verb in the second person singular.

The usual form of deference addressing everybody, except clergymen, is **domnia voastră**, which in colloquial speech became **dumneavoastră (dumeavoastră)**, followed by the verb in the second person plural. When one speaks with respect about a third person one uses :

dumnealui (*masc. sing.*)
dumneaei (*fem. sing.*)
dumnealor (*masc. fem. pl.*)

or : **domnia sa** (*masc. fem. sing.*)
domniile lor (*masc. fem. pl.*)

Declension of the pronoun of politeness and the abbreviated forms :

Sing.	*N.*	**dumneata, domnia ta, d-ta ; dumneavoastră, domnia voastră, d-voastră, dv**
	G. D.	**dumnitale, dumitale, domniei tale, d-tale ; dumneavoastre, domniei voastre, d-voastre**
	A.	**pe dumneata, pe domnia ta, pe d-ta ; pe dumneavoastră, pe domnia voastră, pe d-voastră**
Plur.	*N.*	**domniile voastre, d-voastre**
	G. D.	**domniilor voastre, d-voastre**
	A.	**pe domniile voastre, d-voastre**

		Masculine	*Feminine*
Sing.	*N.*	**dumnealui, domnia lui, d-lui**	**dumneaei, d-ei**
	G. D.	**dumnealui, domniei lui, d-lui**	**dumneaei, d-ei**
	A.	**pe dumnealui, domnia lui, d-lui**	**pe dumneaei, pe d-ei**

		Masc. (*Fem.*)
Sing.	*N.*	**domnia sa, d-sa**
	G. D.	**domniei sale, d-sale**
	A.	**pe domnia sa, pe d-sa**
Plur.	*N. A.*	**dumnealor, domniile lor, d-lor**
	G. D.	**dumnealor, domniilor lor, d-lor**

The pronoun of deference may be written with capital letters in both parts, or only in the first : **D-Ta, d-ta,** etc. The verb after this pronoun comes in the second person when a person is addressed, in the third person when only mentioned :

D-ta mi-ai spus că vei veni la noi.
You told me that you would come to us.

D-voastră (*sing.*) **nu sunteţi de acord cu mine.**
You do not agree with me.

D-voastre (*pl.*) **nu aşteptaţi ajutorul nostru.**
You do not expect our help.

Purtarea d-sale a fost ireproşabilă.
His behaviour was blameless.

Pe d-lui nu l-am întâlnit nici odată. I never met him.

Cine e d-sa? Who is he (the gentleman)?

D-lor de unde sunt? Where are the gentlemen from?

Spune-i d-sale să mă aştepte.
Tell him (the gentleman) to wait for me.

Pe d-ta cum te chiamă? What are you called?

D-voastră cum vă numiţi?
How are you called? (What is your name?)

Cine e fratele d-voastre (*gen.*) **?** Who is your brother?

The pronouns of deference are used like nouns:

Casele acestea sunt ale d-tale (ale vecinului).
These houses are yours.

Cartea este a d-lui (a elevului). The book is his.

Al d-voastre (al elevului) este acest creion?
Is this pencil yours?

Casele d-tale (vecinului) sunt vechi.
Your houses are old.

Părerea d-lor este greşită.
Their (of these gentlemen) opinion is mistaken.

Ale d-voastre păreri le-am auzit.
I (we) have heard your opinions.

The address on a letter or in a written demand to a civilian is: **D-Sale D-Lui** (*m.*) **(Domniei Sale Domnului)**; **D-Sale D-nei** (*f.*) **(Domniei Sale Doamnei).**

5. 5. Possessive Pronouns and Adjectives

The possessive pronoun and adjective agree with the possessed object to which it refers in gender and number, and with the possessor in person :

	Thing possessed sing.		*Thing possessed plur.*	
Possessor—	*Masc.*	*Fem.*	*Masc.*	*Fem.*
1*st per. sing.*	**al meu (mieu)** mine, my	**a mea**	**ai mei**	**ale mele**
1*st per. pl.*	**al nostru** ours, our	**a noastră**	**ai noştri**	**ale noastre**
2*nd per. sing.*	**al tău** thine, thy	**a ta**	**ai tăi**	**ale tale**
2*nd per. pl.*	**al vostru** yours, your	**a voastră**	**ai voştri**	**ale voastre**
3*rd per. sing.*	**al său**, his	**a sa**	**ai săi**	**ale sale**
3*rd per. pl.*	**al lor**, theirs, their	**a lor**	**ai lor**	**ale lor**
3*rd sing.* (colloq.)	**al lui**, his **al ei**, hers, her	**a lui** **a ei**	**ai lor**	**ale lor**

a) Without the possessive article (**al, a, ai, ale**) these pronouns are adjectives and are declined like adjectives :

N. A. **casa mea**, my house — **casa noastră**, our house
G. D. **casei mele** — **casei noastre**

N. A. **casele mele** — **casele noastre**
G. D. **caselor mele** — **caselor noastre**

N. A. **fratele meu**, my brother — **fratele nostru**, our brother
G. D. **fratelui meu** — **fratelui nostru**

N. A. **fraţii mei** — **fraţii noştri**
G. D. **fraţilor mei** — **fraţilor noştri**

N. A. **grădina ta**, thy garden — **grădina voastră**, your garden
G. D. **grădinei tale** — **grădinei voastre**

N. A. **grădinele tale**, thy gardens — **grădinele voastre**, your gardens
G. D. **grădinelor tale** — **grădinelor voastre**

N. A.	**vecinul tău**, thy neighbour	**vecinul vostru**, your neighbour
G. D.	**vecinului tău**	**vecinului vostru**
N. A.	**vecinii tăi**, thy neighbours	**vecinii voştri**, your neighbours
G. D.	**vecinilor tăi**	**vecinilor voştri**
N. A.	**cartea sa (lui, ei)**, his, her book	**cartea lor**, their book
G. D.	**cărţii sale (lui, ei)**	**cărţii lor**
N. A.	**cărţile sale (lui, ei)**, his, her books	**cărţile lor**, their books
G. D.	**cărţilor sale (lui, ei)**	**cărţilor lor**
N. A.	**elevul său (lui, ei)**, his, her pupil	**elevul lor**, their pupil
G. D.	**elevului său (lui, ei)**	**elevului lor**
N. A.	**elevii săi (lui, ei)**, his, her pupils	**elevii lor**, their pupils
G. D.	**elevilor săi (lui, ei)**	**elevilor lor**

b) When the possessor and the subject of the sentence are identical, Rumanian replaces the possessive adjective by the dative forms of the conjunct personal pronoun :

Părinţii îşi iubesc copiii. Parents love their children.

Îmi caut de treburi. I care for my business.

Mi-am pierdut pălăria. I lost my hat.

Cu toţii ne iubim ţara şi familia.
We all love our country and our families.

Vă pierdeţi vremea aşteptând.
You waste your time waiting.

c) The possessor in the third person singular has two pronouns :

1. **al său, a sa, ai săi, ale sale**, his
2. **al lui (al ei), a lui (a ei), ai lui (ai ei), ale lui (ale ei)**, his (her).

The second (**al lui,** etc.) is preferred in the colloquial speech, which uses the possessive pronoun (**al său,** etc.) only in connection with words of relationship :

soră-sa, his sister
soacră-sa, his mother-in-law
socru-su, his father-in-law
bunică-sa, his grandmother
maică-sa, mă-sa, his mother
frate-su, frate-său, his brother
tată-su, tată-său, his father
cumnată-sa, his sister-in-law
cumnată-su, his brother-in-law
tată-meu, my father
soră-mea, my sister
tată-tău, thy father
tată-tu, thy father
mamă-ta, thy mother
maică-ta, thy mother
mă-ta (not used in polite speech)
stăpână-sa, stăpânu-su, his mistress, his master.

Note 1.—Some of these expressions have an irregular declension :

G.-D. (a) **soacri-sa,** (a) **bunică-sa,** (a) **maică-sa,** (a) **surori-sa** (a) **tătâni-su,** (a) **frăţâni-su**

Note 2.—The literary language uses both pronouns :

1. **al său**, etc., correspond to the reflexive pronoun and should be used when the possessor is the subject of the sentence. Even in these cases it is avoided if the subject is not a person.

2. **al lui**, etc., are personal pronouns and are used when they refer to a possessor which is not the subject of the sentence. This rule is often not respected by the literary language, which, under the influence of foreign languages (French, German), uses either pronouns.

Examples :

Privighitoarea fermeca noaptea cu cântecul ei (său) armonios.
The nightingale was charming the night with its harmonious song.

Privighitoarea cânta şi cântecul ei fermeca noaptea.
The nightingale sang and her song enchanted the night.

Omul ne-a invitat în casa sa (lui).
The man invited us into his house.

Am ajuns îndată, căci casa lui nu era departe de biserică.
We arrived soon, for his house was not far from the church.

A spus întâmplarea unui prieten al său (al lui), prietenul a povestit-o soţiei sale, iar soţia a povestit-o unei prietene a ei (sale).
He told the adventure to a friend of his, his friend told it to his wife, and the wife told it to one of her lady friends.

Moş Ion Roată fiind ţăran nu avea ascunzători în sufletul său (lui).
Old Ion Roadă being a peasant had no hidden places in his soul.

Fiecare elev a mers la locul său (lui).
Every schoolboy went to his place.

Şi-a spus durerea (sa); şi-a mărturisit păcatele (sale).
He told his suffering; he confessed his sins.

Vine iarna cu gerurile ei cumplite.
Winter arrives with its terrible colds.

Fiecare cioară îşi laudă puii săi (ei).
Every crow praises its young.

Soldatul şi câinele său. The soldier and his dog.

Vocea stăpânului său. His master's voice.

Copilul plângea. Ochii lui erau plini de lacrimi (Ochii îi erau . . .).
The child was crying. His eyes were filled with tears.

Fetiţa cânta. Glasul ei de argint răsuna în tăcerea nopţii.
The girl sang. Her silver voice sounded in the still night.

Soldatul este obligat să aibă grije de echipamentul său
The soldier must look after his equipment.

Fiecare luptă pentru patria sa.
Everybody is fighting for his country.

5. 6. Demonstrative Pronouns and Adjectives

a) The demonstrative pronoun for indicating the nearer object is:

Masc. **acest (acesta, ăsta)** this (here), that
Fem. **această (aceasta, asta)**

For indicating remoter objects:

Masc. **acel (acela, ăla)** that (there)
Fem. **acea (aceea, aia)**

Singular

	Masc.	*Fem.*
N. A.	**acest (acesta, ăst(a))**	**această (aceasta, asta, astă)**
G. D.	**acestui (acestuia, ăstui(a))**	**acestei (acesteia, astei(a))**

Plural

N. A.	**aceşti (aceştia, ăşti(a))**	**aceste (acestea, aste(a))**
G. D.	**acestor (acestora, ăstor(a))**	**acestor (acestora, ăstor(a))**

Singular

	Masc.	*Fem.*
N. A.	**acel (acela, ăl(a))**	**acea, (aceea, aia)**
G. D.	**acelui (aceluia, ălui(a))**	**acelei (aceleia, ălei(a))**

Plural

N. A.	**acei (aceia, ăi(a))**	**acele (acelea, ale(a))**
G. D.	**acelor (acelora, ălor(a))**	**acelor (acelora, ălor(a))**

The first and second forms are literary forms, the third form is a dialectal one (Walachian) much used in colloquial speech.

The forms ending in **-a** are used :

1. As pronouns bearing the stress of the sentence :

   Acesta este omul de care-ţi vorbiam.
   This is the man I was telling you about.

   Acelora să nu le daţi nimic.
   Don't give anything to those (them).

2. As adjectives following the noun :

   Omul acesta e om de omenie=acest om e om de omenie.
   This man is a decent man.

   Femeile acestea vin dela oraş=aceste femei vin dela oraş. These women (come) coming from the town.

   În ziua aceea am lucrat mult=în acea zi am lucrat mult. I worked much that day.

   Oamenilor acelora nu le-am putut veni în ajutor=acelor oameni nu le-am putut veni în ajutor.
   I could not help those people.

b) A variant of the demonstrative pronoun for indicating objects further off :

Singular

	Masc.	*Fem.*
Nom.	**cel, cela,** that, who, the, which	**cea, ceea,** that, etc.
Gen.	**a celui, a celuia**	**a celei, a celeia**
Dat.	**celui, celuia**	**celei, celeia**
Acc.	**pe cel, pe cela**	**pe cea, pe ceea**

Plural

Nom.	**cei, ceia,** those, etc.	**cele, celea,** those, etc.
Gen.	**a celor, a celora**	**a celor, a celora**
Dat.	**celor, celora**	**celor, celora**
Acc.	**pe cei, pe ceia**	**pe cele, pe celea**

This pronoun is used :

1. Without final **-a**, to connect the adjective with its noun (see 3. 2 **d**) or to form the superlative of the adjective (see 3. 3 **c**).

2. With final **-a** to indicate a noun known to us beforehand :

Omul cela despre care ţi-am vorbit era foarte sărac.
The man I was speaking to you about was very poor.

Revin la chestiunea ceea despre care v'am vorbit.
I come back to the question I was telling you about.

c) Other Demonstrative Pronouns

Singular

	Masc.	*Fem.*
N. A.	**(a)cestlalt**	**(a)ceastălaltă**, the other (here)
G. D.	**(a)cestuilalt**	**(a)cesteilalte**
N. A.	**(a)celalt (celălalt)**	**(a)cealaltă**, the other (there)
G. D.	**(a)celuilalt**	**(a)celeilalte**

Plural

N. A.	**(a)ceştilalţi**	**(a)cestelalte**
G. D.	**(a)cestorlalţi**	**(a)cestorlalte**
N. A.	**(a)ceilalţi**	**(a)celelalte**
G. D.	**(a)celorlalţi**	**(a)celorlalte**

Dialectal forms :

	Singular		*Plural*	
	Masc.	*Fem.*	*Masc.*	*Fem.*
N. A.	**ăstlalt** (**ăstalalt**)	**astălaltă**, the other (here)	**ăştilalţi** (**ăştialalti**)	**astelalte**
G. D.	**ăstuilalt**	**asteilalte**	**ăstorlalţi**	**ăstorlalte**

	Singular		*Plural*	
	Masc.	*Fem.*	*Masc.*	*Fem.*
N. A.	**istlalt**	**istalaltă**, the other (here)	**iştilalţi**	**istelalte**
G. D.	**istuilalt**	**isteilalte**	**istorlalţi**	**istorlalte**
N. A.	**ălalt**	**alaltă**, the other (there)	**ăilalţi**	**alelalte**
G. D.	**ăluilalt**	**aleilalte**	**ălorlalţi**	**ălorlalte**

Note 1.—The forms **aceasta**, **aceea**, when used as nouns, have a predicative adjective in the masculine form :

Aceasta nu-i frumos.	This is not nice.
Aceea nu-i adevărat.	That is not true.

Note 2.—On the possessive article **a** (*f*.), **al** (*m*.), *vide* 14. 2.

d) Demonstrative Pronoun of Identity

Masc. **acelaş(i)**, the same *Fem.* **aceeaş(i)**, the same

	Singular		*Plural*	
	Masc.	*Fem.*	*Masc.*	*Fem.*
N. A.	**acelaş**	**aceeaş (aceiaş)**	**aceeaşi (aceiaşi)**	**aceleaşi**
G. D.	**aceluiaş**	**aceleiaş**	**aceloraşi**	**aceloraşi**

e) Another demonstrative pronoun is **atare**, *such*, which has only two forms, one for singular and another for plural :

	Singular	
	Masc.	*Fem.*
N. A.	**atare om**, such a man	**atare femeie**, such a woman
G. D.	**unui atare om**	**unei atare femei**
	Plural	
N. A.	**atari oameni**	**atari femei**
G. D.	**unor atari oameni**	**unor atari femei**

5. 7. Interrogative Pronouns

a) **Cine?** *who?* is used to ask only of persons.

Ce? *what?* is used to ask only of things.

Care? *which?* is used as an adjective to ask both of persons and of things.

Cine a venit? Who has come?

Cine-i acolo? Who is there?

Ce faceţi? What are you doing?

Ce ştii despre această chestiune?
What do you know about this question?

Care armată a biruit? Which army won the victory?

Care animale mănâncă vegetale şi carne?
Which animals eat plants and meat?

Declension of Interrogative Pronouns

	Singular	*Plural*
Nom.	**cine, care, ce**	**care (cari)**
Gen.	**a cui, a cărui(a)**	**a căror(a)**
	Fem. **a cărei(a)**	
Dat.	**cui, cărui(a)**	**căror(a)**
	Fem. **cărei(a)**	
Acc.	**pe cine, pe care**	**pe care (cari)**

b) Words used as interrogative pronouns:

cât (*m. sing.*), **câţi** (*m. pl.*), **câtă** (*f. sing.*), **câte** (*f. pl.*) **?**
how much? how many?

ce fel de? what kind of?

Cât costă această haină?
How much does this dress cost?

Câte degete ai la o mână?
How many fingers have you on one hand?

Câţi bani ai? How much money have you?

Ce fel de om e acest străin?
What kind of a person is this foreigner?

Ce fel de cărţi cetiţi?
What kind of books are you reading?

Note.—Before adjectives **cât** is followed by the preposition **de**:

Cât de înalt? How high?

5. 8. Relative Pronouns

In form the relative pronouns are identical with the interrogative; they differ only in their grammatical use:

Nu ştiu pe cine să-ţi recomand.
I do not know whom to recommend to you.

El nu înţelege ce spui.
He does not understand what you say.

Omul despre care-mi vorbeşti este prietenul meu.
The man you are telling me about is my friend.

Cine fură azi un ou, fură mâine un bou.
The man who steals an egg to-day will steal an ox to-morrow.

Cine aleargă după doi iepuri nici unul nu prinde.
He who runs after two hares will catch neither.

Care începe multe, fineşte puţine.
He who begins many things will finish few.

There is another relative pronoun:

cel ce (*m.s.*), **cei ce** (*m.pl.*), **ceea ce** (*f.s.*), **cele ce** (*f.pl.*)=**cine**

Cel ce nu lucrează nici să nu mănânce
=**cine nu lucrează . . .**
He who does not work shall not eat.

Cel ce moare sărac moare cinstit=cine moare sărac . . .
He who dies poor dies an honest man.

5. 9. Indefinite Pronouns and Adjectives

These can be simple or compound. The compound pronouns change in declension only in one part.

Simple Indefinite Pronouns:

un, o, a, an
alt, altă, other
anumit, -ă, certain
atât, -a, so much
cutare, so-and-so
nişte, some
nime, nimeni, nimenea, no one, nobody
nimic, nothing
tot, toată, every
totul, everything
unii, unele, some

Note.—**Tot** is also adverb,

e.g. **Îmi tot spunea.** He always was telling me.

Compound Indefinite Pronouns:

cineva, somebody
careva, someone
niscareva (seldom used), someone
altcineva, somebody else
ceva, something
niscaiva (seldom used), something
câtva (*m.*), **câtăva** (*f.*), some
fiecare, fiecine, everyone
fiece, everything
niciunul (niciun) (*m.*), **niciuna (nicio)** (*f.*), no one
oricare, orişicare, oricine, orişicine, whoever
oarecare, someone, a certain
oarece, something
orice, orişice, whatever
oricât (*m.*), **oricâtă** (*f.*), however much
vreun (vre-un), **vreo** (vre-o), some, any
vreunul, vreuna, someone, anyone

nu ştiu cine (care), somebody, lit. I don't know who

cine ştie cine (ce), someone, something, lit. who knows who, what

te miri cine (ce), someone, something, lit. you are wondering who, what

DECLENSION. Either one or the other of the component parts may be declined, but not both.

cineva : *G. D.* **cuiva.**

oricare : *G. D.* **oricărui(a)** (*m.*), **oricărei(a)** (*f.*) ;
Pl. **oricari**, *G. D.* **oricăror.**

orişicine, orişicare : *G. D.* **orişicărui(a)** (*m.*), **orişicărei(a)** (*f.*), **orişicui** ;
Pl. **orişicari, orişicăror.**

fiecare : *G. D.* **fiecărui(a)** (*m.*), **fiecărei(a)** (*f.*) ;
Pl. G. D. **fiecăror.**

oarecare : *G. D.* **oarecărui(a)** (*m.*), **oarecărei(a)** (*f.*) ;
Pl. **oarecari, oarecăror.**

vreunul, vreuna : *G. D.* **vreunui(a)** (*m.*), **vreunei(a)** (*f.*) ;
Pl. **vreunii** (*m.*), **vreunele** (*f.*), *G. D.* **vreunor(a).**

niciunul, niciuna : *G. D.* **niciunui(a)** (*m.*), **niciunei(a)** (*f.*) ;
Pl. **niciunii, niciunele**, *G. D.* **niciunor(a).**

nimeni : *G. D.* **nimănui(a) (nimărui(a)).**

Sing. **câtva** (*m.*), **câtăva** (*f.*).

Plur. **câţiva** (*m.*), **căteva** (*f.*).

Gen. pl. **câtorva.**

EXERCISE No. 11

Possessive Pronouns :

Grădina este a mea. Caii sunt ai tăi. Munţii şi văile sunt ale noastre. Aceste case sunt ale lor. Cărţile acestea sunt ale mele. Aceasta-i părerea lui, dar nu e şi a ei. Ale tale dintru ale tale.

Possessive Adjectives :

Casele noastre sunt la ţară. Ieri am întâlnit pe fratele vostru cel mai mic. Ale codrilor izvoare cu apa lor limpede. Părinţii tăi mi-au scris că eşti sănătos. Am auzit de succesele tale.

Other Pronouns :

A fost odată o babă şi un moşneag. Altă ţară, alt obicei. Anumiţi oameni nu învaţă nici odată nimic. Atât a rămas de pe urma lui! Nu mă priveşte ce spune cutare sau cutare. Am cumpărat la anticar nişte cărţi vechi. Nimic nu e mai preţios decât sănătatea. Nimeni n'a fost să mă vadă. Tot omul este muritor. Unii cred că numai părerea lor este bună. Nu e totul pierdut dacă onoarea nu este pierdută.

Cineva a bătut la uşe, mergeţi careva afară şi vedeţi cine e. Dă-i ceva să mănânce.

Se lumina de ziuă când am pornit la drum. Am mers cât am mers până am ajuns într'un luminiş. Aici ne-am odihnit puţin, apoi am plecat mai departe, până am ajuns pe celalt mal al râului.

Nu cerceta aceste legi
Că eşti nebun când le'nţelegi!
Din codru rupi o rămurea
Ce-i pasă codrului de ea
Ce-i pasă unei lumi întregi
De moartea mea!

(G. Coşbuc, *Moartea lui Fulger.*)

6. THE VERB

6. 1. Auxiliary Verbs

Present Infinitive		*Verbal Noun*	
a avea	to have	**avere**	wealth, riches
a fi	to be	**averea**	the wealth
a voi	to be about to	**fire**	nature, character
		firea	the nature

Past Infinitive		*Pluperfect Infinitive*
a fi avut	to have had	**a fi fost avut**
a fi fost	to have been	**a fi fost fost**
a fi voit	to have wished	**a fi fost voit**

(*A*) *Indicative Mood*

(*a*) *Present Tense*

1. **(eu) am**, I have	**(eu) n'am**, I have not,
2. **(tu) ai**, thou hast	**(tu) n'ai** etc.
3. **(el, ea) are**, he, she has	**(el, ea) n'are**
1. **(noi) avem**, we have	**(noi) n'avem**
2. **(voi) aveţi**, you have	**(voi) n'aveţi**
3. **(ei, ele) au**, they have	**(ei, ele) n'au**
1. **(eu) sunt (sânt), îs, -s**, I am	**nu sunt, nu-s**, I am not,
2. **(tu) eşti**, thou art	**nu eşti** etc.
3. **(el, ea) este, e, îi, -i**, he, she is	**nu este, nu-i**
1. **(noi) suntem (sântem)**, we are	**nu suntem**
2. **(voi) sunteţi (sânteţi)**, you are	**nu sunteţi**
3. **(ei, ele) sunt (sânt), îs, -s**, they are	**nu sunt, nu-s**

Note 1.—The personal pronoun accompanies the verbal form only if it is stressed or put in opposition : **eu am, dar tu n'ai**, I have, but you have not.

Note 2.—In the third person singular, and in the first and second person plural, the verb **a avea** has special forms for predicative use (principal verb) (**are, avem, aveţi**) and for forming compound tenses (auxiliary verb) (**a, am, aţi**).

Note 3.—The auxiliary **a fi** has short forms in the first and third person singular and in the third person plural. (See Exercises 5 and 6.)

(*b*) *Imperfect*

1. **(eu) eram**, I was (I was being),	**(eu) aveam**, I had (I was having),
2. **(tu) erai** etc.	**(tu) aveai** etc.
3. **(el, ea) era**	**(el, ea) avea**
1. **(noi) eram**	**(noi) aveam**
2. **(voi) eraţi**	**(voi) aveaţi**
3. **(ei, ele) erau**	**(ei, ele) aveau**

(*c*) *Perfect*

1. (**eu**) **am avut**, I have had,	(**eu**) **n'am avut**, I have not had,
2. (**tu**) **ai avut** etc.	(**tu**) **n'ai avut** etc.
3. (**el, ea**) **a avut**	(**el, ea**) **n'a avut**
1. (**noi**) **am avut**	(**noi**) **n'am avut**
2. (**voi**) **aţi avut**	(**voi**) **n'aţi avut**
3. (**ei, ele**) **au avut**	(**ei, ele**) **n'au avut**
1. (**eu**) **am fost**, I have been,	(**eu**) **n'am fost**, I have not been,
2. (**tu**) **ai fost** etc.	(**tu**) **n'ai fost** etc.
3. (**el, ea**) **a fost**	(**el, ea**) **n'a fost**
1. (**noi**) **am fost**	(**noi**) **n'am fost**
2. (**voi**) **aţi fost**	(**voi**) **n'aţi fost**
3. (**ei, ele**) **au fost**	(**ei, ele**) **n'au fost**

(*d*) *Preterite*

1. (**eu**) **avui**, I had,	(**eu**) **fui**	or	(**eu**) **fusei**, I was,
2. (**tu**) **avuşi** etc.	(**tu**) **fuşi**		(**tu**) **fuseşi** etc.
3. (**el, ea**) **avu**	(**el, ea**) **fu**		(**el, ea**) **fuse**
1. (**noi**) **avurăm**	(**noi**) **furăm**		(**noi**) **fuserăm**
2. (**voi**) **avurăţi**	(**voi**) **furăţi**		(**voi**) **fuserăţi**
3. (**ei, ele**) **avură**	(**ei, ele**) **fură**		(**ei, ele**) **fuseră**

(*e*) *Pluperfect Compound*

1. (**eu**) **am fost avut**, I had had,	**am fost fost**, I had been,
2. (**tu**) **ai fost avut** etc.	**ai fost fost** etc.
etc.	etc.

Pluperfect Simple

1. (**eu**) **avusem** (**avusesem**) I had had, etc.	**fuse(se)m**, I had been, etc.
2. (**tu**) **avuseşi** (**avuseseşi**)	**fuse(se) şi**
3. (**el, ea**) **avuse** (**avusese**)	**fuse(se)**
1. (**noi**) **avuse(ră)m** (**avuseserăm**)	**fusese(ră)m**
2. (**voi**) **avuse(ră)ţi** (**avuseserăţi**)	**fusese(ră)ţi**
3. (**ei, ele**) **avuse(ră)** (**avuseseră**)	**fusese(ră)**

(*f*) *Future*

1. (eu) **voi fi ; (eu) o să fiu (eu am să fiu)**, I will be, I shall be,
2. (tu) **vei fi ; (tu) o să fii (tu ai să fii)** etc.
3. (el, ea) **va fi ; (el, ea) o să fie (el, ea are să fie)**

1. (noi) **vom fi ; (noi) o să fim (noi avem să fim)**
2. (voi) **veţi fi ; (voi) o să fiţi (voi aveţi să fiţi)**
3. (ei, ele) **vor fi ; (ei, ele) o să fie (ei, ele, au să fie)**

1. (eu) **voi avea ; (eu) o să am (am să am)**, I shall have,
2. (tu) **vei avea ; (tu) o să ai (ai să ai)** etc.
3. (el, ea) **va avea ; (el, ea) o să aibă (are să aibă)**

1. (noi) **vom avea ; (noi) o să avem (avem să avem)**
2. (voi) **veţi avea ; (voi) o să aveţi (aveţi să aveţi)**
3. (ei, ele) **vor avea ; (ei, ele) o să aibă (au să aibă)**

(*g*) *Future Perfect*

1. (eu) **voi fi avut**, I shall have had,	**voi fi fost**, I shall have been,
2. (tu) **vei fi avut** etc.	**vei fi fost** etc.
3. (el, ea) **va fi avut**	**va fi fost**
1. (noi) **vom fi avut**	**vom fi fost**
2. (voi) **veţi fi avut**	**veţi fi fost**
3. (ei, ele) **vor fi avut**	**vor fi fost**

(*B*) *The Subjunctive Mood*

(*a*) *Present*

1. (eu) **să am**, that I may have,	**să fiu**, that I may be,
2. (tu) **să ai** etc.	**să fii** etc.
3. (el, ea) **să aibă**	**să fie**
1. (noi) **să avem**	**să fim**
2. (voi) **să aveţi**	**să fiţi**
3. (ei, ele) **să aibă**	**să fie**

(b) Past

1. (eu) **să fi avut**, that I may have had, had I had, etc.	**să fi fost**, that I may have been, had I been etc.
2. (tu) **să fi avut**	
3. (el, ea) **să fi avut**	
1. (noi) **să fi avut**	
2. (voi) **să fi avut**	
3. (ei, ele) **să fi avut**	

(c) Pluperfect

1. (eu) **să fi fost avut,** etc. — **să fi fost fost,** etc.

(C) *Optative-Conditional Mood*

(a) Present

1. (eu) **aş avea (avere-aş)**, I should (would) have, etc.	**aş fi (fire-aş)**, I should (would) be, etc.
2. (tu) **ai avea (avere-ai)**	**ai fi (fire-ai)**
3. (el, ea) **ar avea (avere-ar)**	**ar fi (fire-ar)**
1. (noi) **am avea (avere-am)**	**am fi (fire-am)**
2. (voi) **aţi avea (avere-aţi)**	**aţi fi (fire-aţi)**
3. (ei, ele) **ar avea (avere-ar)**	**ar fi (fire-ar)**

(b) Past

1. (eu) **aş fi avut**, I would have had,	**aş fi fost**, I would have been,
2. (tu) **ai fi avut** etc.	etc.

(D) *The Imperative Mood*

2. **ai ! (aibi !)**, have ! etc.	**fii !** be ! etc.
3. **(să) aibă !**	**(să) fie !**
2. **aveţi !**	**fiţi !**
3. **(să) aibă !**	**(să) fie !**

(E) *Gerund*

având, having — **fiind**, being

(F) *Past Participle*

avut, had — **fost**, been

6. 2. Principal Verbs

There are four classes of verbs, each having a slightly different conjugation. The infinitive form of each conjugation has a distinctive ending.

Conj.	*Infinitive*	*Verbal Noun*
1*st*	**a cânta**, to sing	**cântare**, singing
,,	**a lucra**, to work	**lucrare**, working
,,	**a se apăra**, to defend oneself	**apărare**, defence
2*nd*	**a vedea**, to see	**vedere**, seeing
3*rd*	**a merge**, to go	**mergere**, going
4*th*	**a auzi**, to hear	**auzire**, hearing
,,	**a zidi**, to build	**zidire**, building
,,	**a omorî**, to kill	**omorîre**, killing
,,	**a urî**, to hate	**urîre**, hating

Note 1.—The particle **a** of infinitive corresponds to the English *to*.

Note 2.—The *past infinitive* is formed with the help of the infinitive of the auxiliary **a fi**, *to be*, and the past participle of the verb: **a fi cântat**, to have sung; **a se fi apărat**, to have defended oneself. The pluperfect infinitive is formed with the help of past infinitive of **a fi**, *to be*, and the past participle of the verb: **a fi fost cântat**, to have had sung.

a) *Present Tense*

(*A*) *The Indicative*

I

1. **(eu) cânt**, I sing, I am singing,	**lucrez**, I work, I am working,	**mă apăr**, I defend myself, I am defending,
2. **(tu) cânţi** etc.	**lucrezi** etc.	**te aperi** etc.
3. **(el, ea) cântă**	**lucrează**	**se apără**
1. **(noi) cântăm**	**lucrăm**	**ne apărăm**
2. **(voi) cântaţi**	**lucraţi**	**vă apăraţi**
3. **(ei, ele) cântă**	**lucrează**	**se apără**

	II	III
1.	**(ea) văd**, I see, I am seeing, etc.	**merg**, I go, I am going, etc.
2.	**(tu) vezi**	**mergi**
3.	**(el, ea) vede**	**merge**
1.	**(noi) vedem**	**mergem**
2.	**(voi) vedeţi**	**mergeţi**
3.	**(ei, ele) văd**	**merg**

IV

1.	**(eu) aud**, I hear, I am hearing, etc.	**zidesc**, I build, I am building, etc.	**omor**, I kill, I am killing, etc.	**urăsc**, I hate, I am hating, etc.
2.	**(tu) auzi**	**zideşti**	**omori**	**urăşti**
3.	**(el, ea) aude**	**zideşte**	**omoară**	**urăşte, ureşte**
1.	**(noi) auzim**	**zidim**	**omorîm**	**urîm**
2.	**(voi) auziţi**	**zidiţi**	**omorîţi**	**urîţi**
3.	**(ei, ele) aud**	**zidesc**	**omoară**	**urăsc**

Note 1.—Some verbs have the first person of the present tense in **-u**. This group includes verbs with the stem ending in consonant + **-l** or **-r** (which do not form the present in **-ez**, like **lucrez**) and a few other verbs :

a afla	to find	**a da**	to give
aflu	I find	**dau**	I give
a umbla	to walk	**a lua**	to take
umblu	I walk	**iau**	I take
a sufla	to breathe	**a bea**	to drink
suflu	I breathe	**beau**	I drink
a umplea	to fill	**a ştie**	to know
umplu	I fill	**ştiu**	I know
a intra	to enter	**a scrie**	to write
intru	I enter	**scriu**	I write
a sta	to stay		
stau	I stay		

Note 2.—A few verbs have in the present a different stem from the infinitive :

a mânca	to eat	**a usca**	to dry
mănânc	I am eating	**usuc**	I am drying

Note 3.—The verbs of the second, third and fourth conjugations ending in the first person in **-d**, **-t**, **-n** may have, in this person as well as in the third person of the subjunctive, **-z**, **-ţ**, **-i** instead of **-d**, **-t**, **-n** :

văz, să văz, să vază	I see, etc.
crez, să crez, să crează	I believe, etc.
auz, să auz, să auză	I hear, etc.
simţ, să simţ, să simţă	I feel, etc.
viu, să viu, să vie	I come, etc.
ţiu, să ţiu, să ţie	I hold, etc.

These forms, although considered regional, are much used in colloquial speech and also in writing.

The dentals are regularly palatalized in participial forms : **văzând, auzind, şezând, văzător, văzut**, etc.

(*B*) The *Subjunctive* idea is expressed with the help of the particle **să** and with the personal forms :

I

1. **(eu) să cânt**, that I may, that I should sing, etc.	**să lucrez**, that I may, that I should work, etc.	**să mă apăr**, that I may, that I should defend myself, etc.
2. **(tu) să cânţi**	**să lucrezi**	**să te aperi**
3. **(el) să cânte**	**să lucreze**	**să se apere**
1. **(noi) să cântăm**	**să lucrăm**	**să ne apărăm**
2. **(voi) să cântaţi**	**să lucraţi**	**să vă apăraţi**
3. **(ei, ele) să cânte**	**să lucreze**	**să se apere**

II	III
1. **(eu) să văd**, that I may see, that I should see, etc.	**să merg**, that I may go, that I should go, etc.
2. **(tu) să vezi**	**să mergi**
3. **(el, ea) să vadă**	**să meargă**
1. **(noi) să vedem**	**să mergem**
2. **(voi) să vedeţi**	**să mergeţi**
3. **(ei, ele) să vadă**	**să meargă**

IV

1	(eu) **să aud**, that I may, that I should hear, etc.	**să zidesc**, that I may, that I should build, etc.	**să omor**, that I may, that I should kill, etc.	**să urăsc**, that I may, that I should hate, etc.
2.	(tu) **să auzi**	**să zideşti**	**să omori**	**să urăşti**
3.	(el, ea) **să audă**	**să zidească**	**să omoare**	**să urască**
1.	(noi) **să auzim**	**să zidim**	**să omorîm**	**să urîm**
2.	(voi) **să auziţi**	**să zidiţi**	**să omorîţi**	**să urîţi**
3.	(ei, ele) **să audă**	**să zidească**	**să omoare**	**să urască**

Note.—Only the third person singular and plural have special forms for subjunctive. The third person singular (and plural) has in subjunctive **-ă** when the indicative has **-e** and it has **-e** when the indicative has **-ă**. In the other persons the subjunctive is identical with the indicative.

(*C*) The *Optative-Conditional* idea is expressed with the help of a conditional auxiliary and the infinitive form of the verb:

I

1.	(eu) **aş cânta**, I should, I would sing, etc.	**aş lucra**, I should, I would work, etc.	**m'aş apăra**, I should, I would defend myself, etc.
2.	(tu) **ai cânta**	**ai lucra**	**te-ai apăra**
3.	(el, ea) **ar cânta**	**ar lucra**	**s'ar apăra**
1.	(noi) **am cânta**	**am lucra**	**ne-am apăra**
2.	(voi) **aţi cânta**	**aţi lucra**	**v'aţi apăra**
3.	(ei, ele) **ar cânta**	**ar lucra**	**s'ar apăra**

	II	III
1.	(eu) **aş vedea**, I should, I would see, etc.	**aş merge**, I should, I would go, etc.
2.	(tu) **ai vedea**,	**ai merge**
3.	(ei, ea) **ar vedea**	**ar merge**
1.	(noi) **am vedea**	**am merge**
2.	(voi) **aţi vedea**	**aţi merge**
3.	(ei, ele) **ar vedea**	**ar megre**

IV

1. **(eu) aş auzi**, I should, I would hear, etc.	**aş zidi**, I should, I would build, etc.	**aş omorî**, I should, I would kill, etc.	**aş urî**, I should, I would hate, etc.
2. **(tu) ai auzi**	**ai zidi**	**ai omorî**	**ai urî**
3. **(el, ea) ar auzi**	**ar zidi**	**ar omorî**	**ar urî**
1. **(noi) am auzi**	**am zidi**	**am omorî**	**am urî**
2. **(voi) aţi auzi**	**aţi zidi**	**aţi omorî**	**aţi urî**
3. **(ei, ele) ar auzi**	**ar zidi**	**ar omorî**	**ar urî**

(*D*) *The Imperative*

I

2nd sing. **cântă !** sing !
2nd pl. **cântaţi !**

2nd sing. **lucrează !** work !
2nd pl. **lucraţi !**

2nd sing. **apără-te !** defend yourself !
2nd pl. **apăraţi-vă !**

II

2nd sing. **vezi !** see !
2nd pl. **vedeţi !**

III

2nd. sing. **spune !** say !
2nd. pl. **spuneţi !**

IV

2nd. sing. **auzi !** hear! **zideşte !** build!
2nd. pl. **auziţi !** **zidiţi !**
2nd. sing. **omoară !** kill! **urăşte !** hate!
2nd. pl. **omorîţi !** **urîţi !**

Note 1.—The regular imperative of the third conjugation is in **-e** : **a bate**, to beat : **bate !** ; **a cere**, to ask : **cere !** ; **a se teme**, to be afraid of : **teme-te !** ; **a crede**, to believe : **crede !** ; **a trage**, to pull : **trage !** ; **înţelege**, to understand : **înţelege !** A few verbs have imperative in **-i** : **mergi !** go ! ; **treci !** cross, pass.

Note 2.—The following verbs have irregular imperative forms :

Sing.	**a zice—zi !** say !	**a face—fă !** do !	**a lua—ia !** take !
Pl.	**ziceţi !**	**faceţi !**	**luaţi !**
Sing.	**a duce—du !** carry !	**a aduce—adu !** bring !	**a avea—ai ! (aibi !)** have !
Pl.	**duceţi !**	**aduceţi !**	**aveţi !**

Note 3.—The negative imperative for the second person singular is the infinitive form of the verb preceded by the negation; for the plural it is the same as the affirmative form, with the negation:

	I	II	III	IV
2nd sing.	**nu cânta!** do not sing!	**nu vedea!**	**nu merge!**	**nu auzi!**
2nd pl.	**nu cântaţi!**	**nu vedeţi!**	**nu mergeţi!**	**nu auziţi!**
2nd sing.	**nu lucra!**			**nu zidi!**
2nd pl.	**nu lucraţi!**			**nu zidiţi!**
2nd sing.	**nu te apăra!**			**nu omorî!**
2nd pl.	**nu vă apăraţi!**			**nu omorîţi!**
2nd sing.				**nu urî!**
2nd pl.				**nu urîţi!**

N.B.—Some of the irregular imperatives have the same form in the negative:

nu zi! (also: **nu zice!**) don't say!
nu fă! (also: **nu face!**) don't do!
nu du! (**nu duce!**) don't carry!
nu adu! (**nu aduce!**) don't bring!
nu avea! (**n'ai!**) don't have!

(*E*) *The Gerund* is formed with the termination **-ând** for the first, second and third conjugations, and with **-ind**, **-înd** for the fourth conjugation:

I	II	III	IV
cântând, (while) singing	**văzând**	**mergând**	**auzind**
lucrând			**zidind**
apărându-se			**omorînd**
			urînd

The verbs ending in **-de**, **-dea** in the gerund change **d** into **z**:

a vedea	**văzănd**, seeing
a întinde	**întinzând**, stretching

	a prinde	**prinzând**, catching
	a pretinde	**pretinzând**, pretending
but :	**a ucide**	**ucigând**, killing

(*F*) *The Present Participle* (verbal adjective) is an adjective in **-tor** (*m.*), **-toare** (*f.*):

a cânta	**cântător** (*m.*), **cântătoare** (*f.*), singing, singer
a vedea	**văzător** (*m.*), **văzătoare** (*f.*), seeing
a merge	**mergător** (*m.*), **mergătoare** (*f.*), going, goer
a auzi	**auzitor** (*m.*), **auzitoatre** (*f.*), hearing, hearer
a omorî	**omorîtor** (*m.*), **omorîtoare** (*f.*), killing, killer

b) *Imperfect Tense*

This expresses the duration or the repetition of any action in the past. It has only an indicative mood.

I

1. **(eu) cântam**, I was singing, I used to sing, etc.	**lucram**, I was working, I used to work, etc.	**mă apăram**, I was defending myself, I used to defend myself, etc.
2. **(tu, cântai**	**lucrai**	**te apărai**
3. **(el, ea) cânta**	**lucra**	**se apăra**
1. **(noi) cântam**	**lucram**	**ne apăram**
2. **(voi) cântaţi**	**lucraţi**	**vă apăraţi**
3. **(ei) cântau**	**lucrau**	**se apărau**

II	III
1. **(eu) vedeam**, I was seeing, I used to see, etc.	**mergeam**, I was going, I used to go, etc.
2. **(tu) vedeai**	**mergeai**
3. **(el, ea) vedea**	**mergea**
1. **(noi) vedeam**	**mergeam**
2. **(voi) vedeaţi**	**mergeaţi**
3. **(ei, ele) vedeau**	**mergeau**

IV

1. (eu) **auziam**, I was hearing, I used to hear, etc.	**zidiam**, I was building, I used to build, etc.	**omoram**, I was killing, I used to kill, etc.	**uram**, I was hating, I used to hate, etc.
2. (tu) **auziai**	**zidiai**	**omorai**	**urai**
3. (el, ea) **auzia**	**zidia**	**omora**	**ura**
1. (noi) **auziam**	**zidiam**	**omoram**	**uram**
2. (voi) **auziaţi**	**zidiaţi**	**omoraţi**	**uraţi**
3. (ei, ele) **auziau**	**zidiau**	**omorau**	**urau**

c) *Perfect* (*Compound Past Tense*)

This expresses a completed action, viewed either in relation to the present, or as absolute past. It is formed with the present forms of the auxiliary **am**, *I have*, and the past participle :

(*A*) *Indicative*

I

1. (eu) **am cântat**, I have sung, I sang, etc.	**am lucrat**, I have worked, I worked, etc.	**m'am apărat**, I have defended myself, I defended myself, etc.
2. (tu) **ai cântat**		**te -ai apărat**
3. (el, ea) **a cântat**		**s'a apărat**
1. (noi) **am cântat**		**ne-am apărat**
2. (voi) **aţi cântat**		**v'aţi apărat**
3. (ei, ele) **au cântat**		**s'au apărat**

II	III
1. (eu) **am văzut**, I have seen, I saw, etc.	**am mers**, I have gone, I went, etc.

IV

1. (eu) **am auzit**, I have heard, I heard, etc.	**am zidit**, I have built, I built, etc.	**am omorît**, I have killed, I killed, etc.	**am urît**, I have hated, I hated, etc.

(*B*) *Subjunctive*

I

1. (eu) **să fi cântat**, I should have sung, (that) I may have sung, etc.	**să fi lucrat**, I should have worked, (that) I may have worked, etc.	**să mă fi apărat**, I should have defended myself, (that) I may have defended myself, etc.
2. (tu) **să fi cântat**		**să te fi apărat**
3. (el, ea) **să fi cântat**		**să se fi apărat**
1. (noi) **să fi cântat**		**să ne fi apărat**
2. (voi) **să fi cântat**		**să vă fi apărat**
3. (ei, ele) **să fi cântat**		**să se fi apărat**

II	III
1. (eu) **să fi văzut**, I should have seen, (that) I may have seen, etc.	**să fi mers**, I should have gone, (that) I may have gone, etc.

IV

1. (eu) **să fi auzit**, I should have heard, (that) I may have heard, etc.	**să fi zidit**, I should have built, (that) I may have built, etc.	**să fi omorît**, I should have killed, (that) I may have killed, etc.	**să fi urît**, I should have hated, (that) I may have hated, etc.

(*C*) *Optative-Conditional*

I

1. (eu) **aş fi cântat**, I would (should) have sung, etc.	**aş fi lucrat**, I would have worked, etc.	**m'aş fi apărat**, I would have defended myself, etc.
2. (tu) **ai fi cântat**		**te-ai fi apărat**
3. (el, ea) **ar fi cântat**		**s'ar fi apărat**
1. (noi) **am fi cântat**		**ne-am fi apărat**
2. (voi) **aţi fi cântat**		**v'aţi fi apărat**
3. (ei, ele) **ar fi cântat**		**s'ar fi apărat**

	II	III
1.	(eu) **aş fi văzut**, I would have seen, etc.	**aş fi mers**, I would have gone, etc.

IV

1.	(eu) **aş fi auzit**, I would have heard, etc.	**aş fi zidit**, I would have built, etc.	**aş fi omorît**, I would have killed, etc.	**aş fi urît**, I would have hated, etc.

(*D*) *Participle*

I. **-at:**	**cântat**, sung	**lucrat**, worked	**apărat**, defended	
II. **-ut:**	**văzut**, seen			
III. **-s (-ut):**	**mers**, gone	**trecut**, past		
IV. **-it, -ît:**	**auzit**, heard	**zidit**, built	**omorît**, killed	**urît**, hated

d) *Preterite* (*Simple Past*)

Between the perfect (compound past) and the preterite (simple past) there is no essential difference. The difference is rather subjective, i.e. an action which is absolutely past, not related to the present, and indifferent to the speaker is expressed in the preterite. A past action of which the effect still survives in the speaker's mind is expressed in the perfect.

The perfect is more frequently used in colloquial Rumanian except in some regions of the Rumanian-speaking world (i.e. Oltenia), where the preterite is preferred or exclusively used.

I

1.	(eu) **cântai**, I sang, etc.	**lucrai**, I worked, etc.	**mă apărai**, I defended myself, etc.
2.	(tu) **cântaşi**	**lucraşi**	**te apăraşi**
3.	(el, ea) **cântă**	**lucră**	**se apără**
1.	(noi) **cântarăm**	**lucrarăm**	**ne apărarăm**
2.	(voi) **cântarăţi**	**lucrarăţi**	**vă apărarăţi**
3.	(ei, ele) **cântară**	**lucrară**	**se apărară**

	II	III
1.	(eu) **văzui**, I saw,	**mersei**, I went,
2.	(tu) **văzuşi** etc.	**merseşi** etc.
3.	(el, ea) **văzu**	**merse**
1.	(noi) **văzurăm**	**merserăm**
2.	(voi) **văzurăţi**	**merserăţi**
3.	(ei, ele) **văzură**	**merseră**

IV

1.	(eu) **auzii**, I heard,	**zidii**, I built,	**omorîi**, I killed,	**urîi**, I hated,
2.	(tu) **auzişi** etc.	**zidişi** etc.	**omorîşi** etc.	**urîşi** etc.
3.	(el, ea) **auzi**	**zidi**	**omorî**	**urî**
1.	(noi) **auzirăm**	**zidirăm**	**omorîrăm**	**urîrăm**
2.	(voi) **auzirăţi**	**zidirăţi**	**omorîrăţi**	**urîrăţi**
3.	(ei, ele) **auziră**	**zidiră**	**omorîră**	**urîră**

e) The *Pluperfect Tense* expresses a past action completed before another past action.

(A) Indicative

Compound Pluperfect

I

1.	(eu) **am fost cântat**, I had sung, etc.	**am fost lucrat**, I had worked, etc.	**m'am fost apărat**, I had defended myself, etc.
			te-ai fost apărat
			s'a fost apărat
			ne-am fost apărat
			v'aţi fost apărat
			s'au fost apărat

	II	III
1.	(eu) **am fost văzut**, I had seen, etc.	**am fost mers**, I had gone, etc.

IV

1.	(eu) **am fost auzit**, I had heard, etc.	**am fost zidit**, I had built, etc.	**am fost omorît**, I had killed, etc.	**am fost urît**, I had hated, etc.

Simple Pluperfect

I

1. (eu) **cântasem**, I had sung, etc.	**lucrasem**, I had worked, etc.	**mă apărasem**, I had defended myself, etc.
2. (tu) **cântaseşi**		
3. (el, ea) **cântase**		
1. (noi) **cântase(ră)m**		
2. (voi) **cântase(ră)ţi**		
3. (ei, ele) **cântase(ră)**		

II	III
1. (eu) **văzusem**, I had seen, etc.	**merse(se)m**, I had gone, etc.
2. (tu) **văzuseşi**	**merseseşi**
3. (el, ea) **văzuse**	**mersese**
1. (noi) **văzuse(ră)m**	**mersese(ră)m**
2. (voi) **văzuse(ră)ţi**	**mersese(ră)ţi**
3. (ei, ele) **văzuse(ră)**	**mersese(ră)**

IV

1. (eu) **auzisem**, I had heard, etc.	**zidisem**, I had built, etc.	**omorîsem**, I had killed, etc.	**urîsem**, I had hated, etc.
2. (tu) **auziseşi**			
3. (el, ea) **auzise**			
1. (noi) **auzise(ră)m**			
2. (voi) **auzise(ră)ţi**			
3. (ei, ele) **auzise(ră)**			

(*B*) *Pluperfect Subjunctive* (is seldom used)

I

1. (eu) **să fi fost cântat**, I should have sung, (that) I might have sung, etc.	**să fi fost lucrat**, I should have worked, (that) I might have worked, etc.	**să mă fi apărat**, I should have defended myself, (that) I might have defended myself, etc.

II	III
1. (eu) **să fi fost văzut**, I should have seen, (that) I might have seen, etc.	**să fi fost mers**, I should have gone, (that) I might have gone, etc.

IV

1. (eu) **să fi fost auzit**, I should have heard, (that) I might have heard, etc.	**să fi fost zidit**, I should have built, (that) I might have built, etc.	**să fi fost omorît**, I should have killed, (that) I might have killed, etc.	**să fi fost urît**, I should have hated, (that) I might have hated, etc.

(*C*) *Pluperfect Optative-Conditional* (is seldom used)

I

1. (eu) **aş fi fost cântat**, I would have sung, etc.	**aş fi fost lucrat**, I would have worked, etc.	**m'aş fi fost apărat**, I would have defended myself, etc.

II	III
1. (eu) **aş fi fost văzut**, I would have seen, etc.	**aş fi fost mers**, I would have gone, etc.

IV

1. (eu) **aş fi fost auzit**, I would have heard, etc.	**aş fi fost zidit, omorît, urît,** I would have built, killed, hated, etc.

f) *Future Tense*

The future with the auxiliary **a voi** expresses a determination, the future with the auxiliary **a avea** and the subjunctive of the principal verb expresses mere futurity. The auxiliary **a avea** may have an invariable form **o** for all persons.

I

1. (eu) voi (voiu) cânta, I will sing,	am (o) să cânt, I shall sing,
2. (tu) vei cânta etc.	ai (o) să cânţi etc.
3. (el, ea) va cânta	are (o) să cânte
1. (noi) vom cânta	avem (o) să cântăm
2. (voi) veţi cânta	aveţi (o) să cântaţi
3. (ei, ele) vor cânta	au să (o) cânte
1. (eu) voi lucra, I will work,	am să lucrez, I shall work,
2. (tu) vei lucra etc.	ai să lucrezi etc.
3. (el, ea) va lucra	are să lucreze
1. (noi) vom lucra	avem să lucrăm
2. (voi) veţi lucra	aveţi să lucraţi
3. (ei, ele) vor lucra	au să lucreze
1. (eu) mă voi apăra, I will defend myself	am să mă apăr, I shall defend myself
2. (tu) te vei apăra etc.	ai să te aperi etc.

II		III	
1. (eu) voi vedea, I will see, etc.	am să văd, I shall see, etc.	voi merge, I will go, etc.	am să merg, I shall go, etc.
2. (tu) vei vedea	ai să vezi	vei merge	ai să mergi
3. (el, ea) va vedea	are să vadă	va merge	are să meargă
1. (noi) vom vedea	avem să vedem	vom merge	avem să mergem
2. (voi) veţi vedea	aveţi să vedeţi	veţi merge	aveţi să mergeţi
3. (ei, ele) vor vedea	au să vadă	vor merge	au să meargă

IV

1. (eu) voi auzi, I will hear	am să aud, I shall hear	voi zidi, I will build	am să zidesc, I shall build
2. (tu) vei auzi	ai să auzi	vei zidi	ai să zideşti
3. (el, ea) va auzi	are să audă	etc.	etc.
1. (noi) vom auzi	avem să auzim		
2. (voi) veţi auzi	aveţi să auziţi		
3. (ei, ele) vor auzi	au să audă		

1. **(eu) voi omorî,** I will kill	**am să omor,** I shall kill	**voi urî,** I will hate	**am să urăsc,** I shall hate
2. **(tu) vei omorî** etc.	**ai să omori** etc.	**vei urî** etc.	**ai să urăşti** etc.

g) *Future Perfect*

I

1. **(eu) voi fi cântat,** I will (shall) have sung, etc.	**voi fi lucrat,** I will (shall) have worked, etc.	**mă voi fi apărat,** I will (shall) have defended myself, etc.
2. **(tu) voi fi cântat**		
3. **(el, ea) va fi cântat**		
1. **(noi) vom fi cântat**		
2. **(voi) veţi fi cântat**		
3. **(ei, ele) vor fi cântat**		

II	III
1. **(eu) voi fi văzut,** I will (shall) have seen etc.	**voi fi mers,** I will (shall) have gone etc.

IV

1. **(eu) voi fi auzit,** I will (shall) have heard etc.	**voi fi zidit,** I will (shall) have built etc.	**voi fi omorît,** I will (shall) have killed etc.	**voi fi urît,** I will (shall) have hated etc.

6. 3. Some Irregular Verbal Forms

a) Some verbs of the second conjugation have infinitive variants of the third conjugation :

a apăreá (II), to appear	**a apáre** (III)
a rămâneá (II), to remain	**a rămấne** (III)
a ţineá (II), to hold	**a ţíne** (III)
a tăceá (II), to be silent	**a táce** (III)

b) The imperfect tense from **a da**, *to give*, and from **a sta**, *to stay*, may be formed by reduplication :

Regular

	Present		*Imperfect*	
1.	(**eu**) **dau**, I give,	**stau**, I stay,	**dam**, I was giving,	**stam**, I was staying,
2.	(**tu**) **dai** etc.	**stai** etc.	**dai** etc.	**stai** etc.
3.	(**el, ea**) **dă**	**stă**	**da**	**sta**
1.	(**noi**) **dăm**	**stăm**	**dam**	**stam**
2.	(**voi**) **daţi**	**staţi**	**daţi**	**staţi**
3.	(**ei, ele**) **dau**	**stau**	**dau**	**stau**

By Reduplication

	Imperfect	*Imperfect*
1.	(**eu**) **dădeám**, I was giving,	**stăteám** (**steteám**), I was staying,
2.	(**tu**) **dădeái** etc.	**stăteái** (**steteái**) etc.
3.	(**el, la**) **dădeá**	**stăteá** (**steteá**)
1.	(**noi**) **dădeám**	**stăteám** (**steteám**)
2.	(**voi**) **dădeáţi**	**stăteáţi** (**steteáţi**)
3.	(**ei, ele**) **dădeáu**	**stăteáu** (**steteáu**)

The *preterite* (*simple past*) is :

1.	(**eu**) **dădúi**	or	**détei** (**dédei**)	**stătúi**	or	**stétei**
2.	(**tu**) **dădúşi**	,,	**déteşi** (**dédeşi**)	**stătúşi**	,,	**stéteşi**
3.	(**el, ea**) **dădú**	,,	**déte**	**stătú**	,,	**stéte**
1.	(**noi**) **dădúrăm**	,,	**déterăm** (**déderăm**)	**stătúrăm**	,,	**stéterăm**
2.	(**voi**) **dădúrăţi**	,,	**déterăţi** (**déderăţi**)	**stătúrăţi**	,,	**stéterăţi**
3.	(**ei, ele**) **dădúră**	,,	**déteră** (**déderă**)	**stătúră**	,,	**stéteră**

The *pluperfect* is derived from preterite :

1.	(**eu**) **dădúsem**, I had given, etc.	(**dasem**)	**stătúsem**, I had stood, etc.	(**stasem**)
2.	(**tu**) **dădúseşi**	(**daseşi**)	**stătúseşi**	(**staseşi**)
3.	(**el, ea**) **dădúse**	(**dase**)	**stătúse**	(**stase**)
1.	(**noi**) **dădúserăm**	(**daserăm**)	**stătúserăm**	(**staserăm**)
2.	(**voi**) **dădúserăţi**	(**daserăţi**)	**stătúserăţi**	(**staserăţi**)
3.	(**ei, ele**) **dădúseră**	(**daseră**)	**stătúseră**	(**staseră**)

N.B.—The accent is not marked in the orthography.

The third person *subjunctive* present (singular and plural) is :

să dea or **să deie**, that he may give
să stea ,, **să steie**, that he may stay

The *imperative* form :

dă ! give !	**nu da !** don't give !
stai ! (**stăi !**) stay !	**nu sta !** don't stay !

Gerund. **dând**, giving ; **stând**, staying.

Present Participle. **dătător, -toare**, giver (who gives) ; **stătător, -toare**, who stays.

c) The verbs **a lua**, *to take*, **a bea**, *to drink*, have some irregular forms :

Indicative.

	Present		*Imperfect*	
1. **(eu) iau**, I take, etc.	**beau (beu)**, I drink, etc.	**luam**, I was taking, etc.	**beam**, I was drinking, etc.
2. **(tu) iai (iei)**	**beai (bei)**	**luai**	**beai**
3. **(el, ea) ia**	**bea (be)**	**lua**	**bea**
1. **(noi) luăm**	**bem**	**luam**	**beam**
2. **(voi) luaţi**	**beţi**	**luaţi**	**beaţi**
3. **(ei, ele) iau**	**beau (beu)**	**luau**	**beau**

	Preterite	*Pluperfect*	
1. **(eu) luái**, I took, etc.	**băúi**, I drank, etc.	**luásem**, I had taken, etc.	**băúsem**, I had drunk, etc.
2. **(tu) luáşi**	**băúşi**	**luáseşi**	**băúseşi**
3. **(el, ea) luă**	**băú**	**luáse**	**băúse**
1. **(noi) luárăm**	**băúrăm**	**luáserăm**	**băúserăm**
2. **(voi) luárăţi**	**băúrăţi**	**luáserăţi**	**băúserăţi**
3. **(ei, ele) luáră**	**băúră**	**luáseră**	**băúseră**

Subjunctive.

Pres. Tense. (el, ea) **să ia** or **să ieie**, that he may take ; **să bea** or **să beie**, that he may drink.

Imperative. **ia** ! take (thou) ! **nu lua** ! do not take ! **luaţi** ! take (you) ! **bea** ! drink (thou) ! **nu bea** ! do not drink ! **beţi** ! drink (you) !

Gerund. **luând**, taking ; **bând**, drinking.

Present Part. **luător, -toare**, who takes ; **băutor, -toare**, who drinks.

Past Part. **luat, -ă**, taken ; **băut, -ă**, drunk.

d) The verb **a voi**, *to will, to wish*, which serves as auxiliary to form the future tense, has two present forms :

1. *Auxiliary Verb*	2. *Principal Verb*
voi (voiu)	**voiesc**, I will, I wish,
vei	**voieşti** etc.
va	**voieşte**
vom	**voim**
veţi	**voiţi**
vor	**voiesc**

Another verb which means *to will, to wish*, is **a vrea** :

Pres. Tense. **vreau, vreai, vrea, vrem, vreţi, vreau**, I wish.

Imperfect. **voiam**, etc., **vream**, etc., I was wishing.

Future. **vói voì**, etc., **voi vrea**, etc., I will wish.

Preterite. **voíi**, etc., **vrúi**, etc., I wished.

Pluperfect. **voisem**, etc., **vrusem**, etc., I had wished.

Gerund. **voind, vrând**, wishing.

Pres. Part. **voitor** (*m.*), **voitoare** (*f.*), who wishes.

Past Part. **voit, vrut**, wished.

e) The auxiliaries in the future tense, in the perfect and in the optative-conditional may be affixed to the principal verb:

Future. **cânta-voi, cânta-vei, cânta-va**, etc., I will sing.

Past Tense. **cântat-am, cântat-ai, cântat-a**, etc., I have sung.

Conditional. **cântare-aş, cântare-ai, cântare-ar, cântare-am, cântare-aţi, cântare-ar**, I would sing.

N.B.—The form **cântare-** in conditional is a long infinitive which is current in Old Rumanian.

f) Other irregular verbs:

a la (1*st conjug.*), to wash the head.

Pres. Tense. **lau, lai, lă, lăm, laţi, lau**, I wash.

Imperfect. **lam, lai, la, lam, laţi, lau**, I was washing.

Preterite. **lăúi, lăúşi, lăú, lăúrăm, lăúrăţi, lăúră**, I washed.

Perfect. **am lăut, ai lăut, a lăut, am lăut, aţi lăut, au lăut**, I have washed.

Gerund. **lând**, washing.

Pres. Part. **lăutor** (*m.*), **-toare** (*f.*), who washes.

Pluperfect. **lăúsem, lăúseşi, lăúse, lăúserăm, lăúserăţi, lăúseră**, I had washed.

Subjunctive. **să lau, să lai, să leie (lea), să lăm, să laţi, să leie**, (that) I may wash.

Imperative. **lă! laţi!** wash!

a mânca (1*st conjug.*), to eat.

Pres. Tense. **mănânc, mănânci, mănâncă, mâncăm, mâncaţi, mănâncă**, I eat.

Imperfect. **mâncam, mâncai, mânca, mâncam, mâncaţi, mâncau**, I was eating.

Preterite. **mâncai, mâncaşi, mâncă, mâncarăm, mâncarăţi, mâncară**, I ate.

Perfect. am mâncat, etc., I have eaten.

Gerund. mâncând, eating.

Pres. Part. mâncător (*m.*), mâncătoare (*f.*), who eats.

Pluperfect. mâncasem, mâncaseşi, mâncase, mâncase(ră)m, mâncase(ră)ţi, mâncase(ră), I had eaten.

Subj. Pres. să mănânc, să mănânci, să mănânce, să mâncăm, să mâncaţi, să mănânce, (that) I may eat.

Imperative. mănâncă ! mâncaţi ! eat ! ; nu mânca ! nu mâncaţi ! don't eat !

a usca (1*st conjug.*), to dry.

Pres. Tense. usuc (usc), usuci (uşti), usucă (uscă), uscăm, uscaţi, usucă (uscă), I dry (*tr.*).

Imperfect. uscam, uscai, usca, uscam, uscaţi, uscau, I was drying.

Preterite. uscai, uscaşi, uscă, uscarăm, uscarăţi, uscară, I dried.

Perfect. am uscat, etc, I have dried.

Gerund. uscând, drying.

Pres. Part. uscător (*m.*), -toare (*f.*), drier (who dries).

Pluperfect. uscasem, uscaseşi, uscase, uscaserăm, uscaserăţi, uscaseră, I had dried.

Subj. Pres. să usuc, să usuci, să usuce, să uscăm, să uscaţi, să usuce, (that) I may dry.

Imperative. usucă ! uscaţi ! dry !

a scrie (3*rd conjug.*), to write.

Pres. Tense. scriu, scrii, scrie, scriem (scrim), scrieţi (scriţi), scriu, I write, I am writing.

a ştie (4*th conjug.*), to know.

Pres. Tense. ştiu, ştii, ştie, ştim, ştiţi, ştiu, I know, I am knowing.

a veni (*4th conjug.*), to come.

Pres. Tense. **vin (viu), vii, vine, venim, veniţi, vin,** I come, I am coming.

Gerund. **venind (viind),** coming.

Pres. Part. **viitor** (*m.*), **viitoare** (*f.*), future.

Imperative. **vino ! (vină !), veniţi !** come !

a tăia (1*st conj.*), to cut.

Pres. Tense. **tai, tai, taie, tăiem, tăiaţi, taie.**

Gerund. **tăind.**

Pres. Part. **tăitor.**

Imperative. **taie ! tăiaţi !**

g) The first person present has also palatalized forms used in the South, in Walachia. These forms present **z** instead of **d**, **u** instead of **n** :

văd>văz,	I see
aud>auz,	I hear
vin>viu,	I come
ţin>ţiu,	I hold

6. 4. Reflexive Forms

Nearly every transitive verb can be also a reflexive. The only difference between transitive and reflexive conjugation is a pronoun added before the transitive verb.

Only the third person of the reflexive pronoun is used in these forms. The first and second persons, singular and plural, use the accusative or the dative of the personal pronoun.

There are two categories of reflexive verbs, according to the accusative or the dative form of pronoun they use.

a) *Accusative reflexive* verbs have the reflexive object in the accusative case :

a se lăuda, to praise oneself.

Pres. Tense. **mă laud, te lauzi, se laudă, ne lăudăm, vă lăudaţi, se laudă**, I praise myself.

Perfect. **m'am lăudat, te-ai lăudat, s'a lăudat, ne-am lăudat, v'aţi lăudat, s'au lăudat**, I have praised myself.

Preterite. **mă lăudai, te lăudaşi, se lăudă, ne lăudarăm, vă lăudarăţi, se lăudară**, I praised myself.

Future. **mă voi lăuda, te vei lăuda, se va lăuda, ne vom lăuda, vă veţi lauda, se vor lăuda**, I will praise myself.

Opt.-Cond. Pres. **m'aş lăuda, te-ai lăuda, s'ar lăuda, ne-am lăuda, v'aţi lăuda, s'ar lăuda**, I would praise myself.

Opt.-Cond. Past. **m'aş fi lăudat, te-ai fi lăudet**, etc., that I might have praised myself.

Subj. Pres. **să mă laud, să te lauzi, să se laude, să ne lăudăm, să vă lăudaţi, să se laude**, (that) I may praise myself.

Subj. Past. **să mă fi lăudat, să te fi lăudat, să se fi lăudat, să ne fi lăudat, să vă fi lăudat, să se fi lăudat**, (that) I may have praised myself.

Imperative. **laudă-te ! lăudaţi-vă !** praise yourself !

Negative Imper. **nu te lăuda ! nu vă lăudaţi !** do not praise yourself !

Gerund. **lăudându-se**, praising oneself.

Some reflexive verbs do not admit, in addition, a regular transitive form. Most of them, however, are used :

(1) in the normal transitive sense ;

(2) intransitively, with the addition of the reflexive pronoun.

Reflexive only :

a se sfii, mă sfiesc, m'am sfiit, to be timid
a se lenevi, mă lenevesc, m'am lenevit, to be lazy, to be idle
a se teme, mă tem, m'am temut de ceva, to be afraid of something

Transitive and Intransitive-Reflexive :

a bate, bat, bătut, to beat
a se bate cu cineva, to fight with somebody

a afla, aflu, aflat, to find
a se afla undeva, to be (in a place), (to feel oneself)

a duce, duc, dus, to carry
a se duce undeva, to go, to depart somewhere

a juca, joc, jucat, to dance
a se juca cu cineva, to play with somebody

a ruga, rog, rugat, to pray, to beg, to invite
a se ruga la (de) cineva, to say prayers to somebody

a uita, uit, uitat, to forget
a se uita la cineva, to look at somebody

a ascunde, ascund, ascuns, to conceal
a se ascunde undeva, to hide (oneself) somewhere

a îmbrăca, îmbrac, îmbrăcat, to dress
a se îmbrăca cu ceva, to dress (oneself) in something

Note.—The reflexive pronoun **se** does not always give to the verb a reflexive sense. Most verbs with **se** are intransitive :

opresc pe cineva, I stop somebody
mă opresc, I stop

b) *Dative reflexive* verbs have the reflexive object in the dative case :

a-şi aduce aminte de ceva, to remember something
a-şi bate joc de cineva, to make fun of somebody
a-şi închipui ceva, to imagine something
a-şi bate capul cu ceva, to worry about, to think about something

Pres. Tense. **îmi aduc aminte, îţi aduci aminte, îşi aduce aminte, ne aducem aminte, vă aduceţi aminte, îşi aduc aminte,** I remember.

Imperfect. **îmi aduceam aminte,** etc., I was remembering.

Perfect. **mi-am adus aminte, ţi-ai adus aminte, şi-a adus aminte, ne-am adus aminte, v'aţi adus aminte, şi-au adus aminte,** I have remembered.

Preterite. **îmi adusei aminte,** etc., I remembered.

Future. **îmi voi aduce aminte,** etc., I will remember.

Opt.-Cond. Pres. **mi-aş aduce aminte,** etc., I would remember.

Opt.-Cond. Past. **mi-aş fi adus aminte,** etc., I would have remembered.

Imperative. **adu-ţi aminte! aduceţi-vă aminte!** remember!

Gerund. **aducându-şi aminte,** remembering.

Pres. Subj. **să-mi aduc aminte,** etc., (that) I may remember.

Past Subj. **să-mi fi adus aminte,** etc., (that) I may have remembered.

c) The dative reflexive construction should not be confused with the construction of verbs which demand a dative pronominal object:

a plăcea, to like.

Pres. Tense.

Îmi place cartea aceasta. I like this book.
Îţi place să citeşti. Thou likest (you like) reading.
Îi place muzică. He likes music.
Ne place să mergem la plimbare. We like to go for a walk.
Vă plac florile. You like flowers.
Le plac jocurile. They like games.

Imperfect.

Îmi plăcea să călătoresc. I used to like travelling.
Îţi plăceau cărţile. Thou usedst to like books.
etc. (You used to like books.)

Future.

Îmi va place cartea. I shall like the book.
Îţi vor place ţigările. Thou wilt like cigarettes.
Îi va place să citească. He will like to read.
etc.

Perfect. **mi-a (mi-au) plăcut, ţi-a plăcut, i-a plăcut, ne-a plăcut, v'a plăcut, le-a plăcut,** I liked, I have liked.

Preterite. **îmi plăcu (plăcură), îţi plăcu, îi plăcu, ne plăcu, vă plăcu, le plăcu,** I liked.

Opt.-Cond. Present.

mi-ar place cartea, I would like the book.
mi-ar place cărţile, I would like the books.

Opt.-Cond. Past. **mi-ar fi plăcut,** etc., I would have liked.

Subj. Pres. **să-mi placă, să-ţi placă,** etc., (that) I may like.

Subj. Past. **să-mi fi plăcut,** etc., (that) I may have liked.

Gerund. **plăcându-mi,** liking, because I like.

a trebui to need.

îmi trebuie, etc., I need.

a părea rău, to regret.

îmi pare rău, etc., I regret.

a părea bine, to be glad.

îmi pare bine, etc., I am glad.

a se părea, to seem.

Present. **mi se pare, ţi se pare, i se pare, ni se pare, vi se pare, li se pare,** it seems to me.

Imperfect. **mi se părea,** etc.

Future. **mi se va părea,** etc.

Perfect. **mi s'a părut,** etc.

Preterite. **mi se păru**, etc.
Subj. Pres. **să mi se pară**, etc.
Subj. Past. **să mi se părut**, etc.
Opt.-Cond. Pres. **mi s'ar părea**, etc., it would seem to me.
Opt.-Cond. Past. **mi s'ar fi părut**, etc., it would have seemed to me.
Gerund. **părându-mi-se**, seeming to me.

a se cădea, to become, to be suitable.
mi se cade, etc., I am, ought.

a se cuveni, to become.
mi se cuvine, etc., I am, ought.

a se şedea, to suit.
mi se şede, etc., it suits me.

Some nouns form, with the pronominal object in dative and the auxiliary **a fi**, verbal expressions which have the same conjugation as the verbs with a dative pronominal object:

Îmi e foame (mi-i foame). I am hungry.
Îmi e sete (mi-i sete). I am thirsty.
Îmi e cald (mi-i cald). I am warm.
Îmi e frig (mi-i frig). I am cold.
Îmi e frică de ceva (mi-i frică). I am afraid of something.
Îmi e dor de cineva (mi-i dor). I am longing for somebody.
Mi-i a mânca. I am hungry.

Note.—The possessive idea is expressed in these constructions with the help of the auxiliary *to be.*

d) Other verbs demand a pronominal object in accusative:

a durea, to be painful.
Mă doare capul. I have headache.
Te dor dinţii. Thou hast toothache.

Îl va durea piciorul. His foot will be sore.
O durea mâna. Her hand was sore.
Ne-au durut ochii. Our eyes were painful.
Vă dureau măselele. Your molar teeth were painful.
Îi dor picioarele. Their (*m.*) feet are sore.
Le doare pieptul. They (*f.*) suffer from pains in the chest.

a junghia, to stab.

Mă junghie în piept. I have a sharp pain in the chest.

e) Some verbs have only an *impersonal reflexive* in the third person:

a se înopta, to become night.
se înoptează, **s'a înoptat**, **se va înopta**, etc.

a se întuneca, to become dark.
se întunecă, **s'a întunecat**, **se va întuneca**, etc.

a se însera, to become evening.
se înserează, etc.

a se face ziua, to dawn.
se face ziua, etc., it dawns.

6. 5. Passive Construction

The passive voice is formed with the help of the auxiliary **a fi**, *to be*, and the past participle, which is treated as an adjective and agrees in gender and in number with the subject. The Rumanian language avoids, where possible, the passive construction and prefers the active or reflexive instead.

The Passive forms:

Pres. Tense. **sânt văzut (văzută), sântem văzuţi (văzute),** etc., I am seen.

Subj. Pres. **să fiu văzut (văzută), să fim văzuţi (văzute),**etc., (that) I may be seen.

Subj. Past. **să fi fost văzut (văzută), să fi fost văzuţi (văzute),** etc., (that) I may have been seen.

Preterite. **fui văzut (văzută), furăm văzuţi (văzute),** etc., I was seen.

Perfect. **am fost văzut (văzută), am fost văzuţi (văzute),** etc., I have been seen.

Pluperfect. **fusesem văzut (văzută), fuseserăm văzuţi (văzute),** etc., I had been seen.

Future. **voi fi văzut (văzută), vom fi văzuţi (văzute),** etc., I will be seen.

Opt.-Cond. Pres. **aş fi văzut (văzută), am fi văzuţi (văzute),** etc., I would be seen.

Opt.-Cond. Past. **aş fi fost văzut (văzută), am fi fost văzuţi (văzute),** etc., I would have been seen.

Imperfect. **eram văzut (văzută), eram văzuţi (văzute),** etc., I was being seen, I used to be seen.

Gerund. **fiind văzut (văzută), fiind văzuţi (văzute),** being seen.

Elevii sunt lăudaţi de învăţătorul lor.
The schoolboys are praised by their teacher.

Elevele sunt lăudate de învăţătoarea lor.
The schoolgirls are praised by their teacher.

În lumea cealaltă toţi vor fi răsplătiţi după faptele lor.
In the other world everyone will be recompensed according to their deeds.

Mai bine să fii iubit decât temut.
It is better to be loved than feared.

Nu judecaţi, ca să nu fiţi judecaţi.
Do not judge, that you may not be judged.

6. 6. Impersonal Forms

The impersonal idea is expressed:

a) With the help of the third person reflexive:

se spune	they say (one says)
se aude	people hear (one hears)

S'a vorbit în oraş. They told in the town.
Nu se poate. It is not possible.

Se zice că adevărul iese totdeuna la iveală.
They say that truth comes always to light.

Note.—The construction with the reflexive pronoun se can be:

1. *Reflexive:*

Buruienile *se înmulţesc* **mai repede decât florile.**
Weeds multiply quicker than flowers.

2. *Passive:*

Pâinea *se vinde* **mai ieften decât carnea.**
Bread is sold cheaper than meat.

3. *Impersonal:*

Se spune **că cine samănă vânt culege furtună.**
They say that who sows wind reaps storm.

b) A general impersonal sense can have also the first and second person plural and the second singular:

Dacă vreţi pace, lucraţi pentru pace.
If you want peace, work for peace.

Dacă alergi după doi iepuri nu prinzi nici unul.
If you run after two hares you don't catch any.

Încetul cu încetul departe ajungi.
Slow by slow you come far.

Mâncăm ca să trăim, nu trăim ca să mâncăm.
We eat in order to live, we do not live in order to eat.

c) Impersonal expressions:

Present	*Future*	*Perfect*
ajunge, is enough	**va ajunge**	**a ajuns**
trebuie, (I, thou, he, she we, you, they) must	**va trebui**	**a trebuit**
plouă, it rains	**va ploua**	**a plouat**
ninge, snow is falling	**va ninge**	**a nins**
fulgeră, it's lightning	**va fulgera**	**a fulgerat**
tună, is thundering	**va tuna**	**a tunat**
e frig, it is cold	**va fi frig**	**a fost frig**
e cald, it is warm	**va fi cald**	**a fost cald**
e vânt, it is windy	**va fi vânt**	**a fost vânt**
e ger, it is frost	**va fi ger**	**a fost ger**
e soare, it is sunny	**va fi soare**	**a fost soare**

6. 7. Transitive, intransitive and reflexive verbs can have a prepositional object (instead of a dative or accusative).

a se feri de ceva, to avoid something
a-şi aduce aminte de ceva, to remember something
a asculta de cineva, to obey somebody
a-şi bate joc de cineva, to make fun of somebody
a râde de ceva, to laugh at something
a se teme de ceva, to be afraid of something

6. 8. List of Verbs

a) Common Verbs of the first conjugation; the three forms—infinitive, first singular present and past participle—are basic for the whole verbal system:

a aduna, adun, adunat, to add, to collect, to gather
a întreba, întreb, întrebat, to ask, to question
a învăţa, învăţ, învăţat, to learn, to teach
a ajuta, ajut, ajutat, to help
a alerga, alerg, alergat, to run
a arunca, arunc, aruncat, to throw
a aştepta, aştept, aşteptat, to wait

a **căra**, **car**, **cărat**, to carry, to transport
a **căsca**, **casc**, **căscat**, to yawn
a **căuta**, **caut**, **căutat**, to seek
a **cerceta**, **cercetez**, **cercetat**, to investigate, to examine
a **chema**, **chem**, **chemat**, to call
a **continua**, **continuu**, **continuat**, to continue
a **cugeta**, **cuget**, **cugetat**, to think
a **cumpăra**, **cumpăr**, **cumpărat**, to buy
a **curăţa**, **curăţ**, **curăţat**, to clean
a **ierta**, **iert**, **iertat**, to forgive
a **înceta**, **încetez**, **încetat**, to cease, to finish
a **înşela**, **înşel**, **inşelat**, to cheat, to fool
a **însemna**, **însemn**, **însemnat**, to mark, to signify
a **înştiinţa**, **înştiinţez**, **înştiinţat**, to announce
a **lăsa**, **las**, **lăsat**, to leave, to let
a **lega**, **leg**, **legat**, to tie
a **lupta**, **lupt**, **luptat**, to fight
a **se mira**, **mă mir**, **mirat**, to wonder
a **mişca**, **mişc**, **mişcat**, to move
a **muia**, **moi**, **muiat**, to moisten
a **muşca**, **muşc**, **muşcat**, to bite
a **păstra**, **păstrez**, **păstrat**, to conserve
a **pleca**, **plec**, **plecat**, to depart
a **ploua**, **plouă**, **plouat**, to rain
a **purta**, **port**, **purtat**, to carry, wear
a **ridica**, **ridic**, **ridicat**, to raise
a **schimba**, **schimb**, **schimbat**, to change
a **spăla**, **spăl**, **spălat**, to wash
a **spera**, **sper**, **sperat**, to hope
a **strica**, **stric**, **stricat**, to spoil
a **striga**, **strig**, **strigat**, to shout
a **studia**, **studiez**, **studiat**, to study
a **ţipa**, **ţip**, **ţipat**, to shriek
a **uita**, **uit**, **uitat**, to forget
a **umbla**, **umblu**, **umblat**, to walk
a **urca**, **urc**, **urcat**, to raise
a **urma**, **urmez**, **urmat**, to follow
a **vărsa**, **vărs**, **vărsat**, to spill
a **visa**, **visez**, **visat**, to dream
a **vizita**, **vizitez**, **vizitat**, to call upon

b) *Verbs of the second conjugation:*

a **avea**, **am**, **avut**, to have
a **bea**, **beau**, **băut**, to drink
a **cădea**, **cad**, **căzut**, to fall
a **dispărea**, **dispar**, **dispărut**, to disappear
a **încăpea**, **încap**, **încăput**, to hold, to contain
a **părea**, **par**, **părut**, to seem
a **plăcea**, **plac**, **plăcut**, to please, to like
a **putea**, **pot**, **putut**, to be able
a **scădea**, **scad**, **scăzut**, to decrease, to diminish
a **şedea**, **şed**, **şezut**, to sit, to dwell
a **tăcea**, **tac**, **tăcut**, to be silent
a **ţinea** (a **ţine**), **ţin**, **ţinut**, to hold
a **umplea**, **umplu**, **umplut**, to fill
a **vedea**, **văd**, **văzut**, to see
a **vrea**, **vreau**, **vrut**, to wish, want
a **zăcea**, **zac**, **zăcut**, to lie

c) *Verbs of the third conjugation:*

a **aduce**, **aduc**, **adus**, to bring
a **ajunge**, **ajung**, **ajuns**, to suffice, to reach
a **alege**, **aleg**, **ales**, to select, to choose
a **aprinde**, **aprind**, **aprins**, to light
a **arde**, **ard**, **ars**, to burn
a **ascunde**, **ascund**, **ascuns**, to hide
a **bate**, **bat**, **bătut**, to beat
a **cere**, **cer**, **cerut**, to ask, to beg
a **coace**, **coc**, **copt**, to bake
a **coase**, **cos**, **cusut**, to sew
a **cosî**, **cosesc**, **cosît**, to cut the grass, to mow
a **crede**, **cred**, **crezut**, to believe
a **cuprinde**, **cuprind**, **cuprins**, to contain, to include
a **creşte**, **cresc**, **crescut**, to grow
a **culege**, **culeg**, **cules**, to gather, to collect
a **cunoaşte**, **cunosc**, **cunoscut**, to know, to be acquainted with
a **deschide**, **deschid**, **deschis**, to open
a **dispare**, **dispar**, **dispărut**, to disappear
a **duce**, **duc**, **dus**, to carry
a **face**, **fac**, **făcut**, to do, to make
a **fierbe**, **fierb**, **fiert**, to boil
a **frânge**, **frâng**, **frânt**, to break
a **împinge**, **împing**, **împins**, to push
a **începe**, **încep**, **început**, to begin
a **închide**, **închid**, **închis**, to close
a **întinde**, **întind**, **întins**, to stretch
a **întoarce**, **întorc**, **întors**, to turn
a **paşte**, **pasc**, **păscut**, to pasture, to graze
a **recunoaşte**, **recunosc**, **recunoscut**, to recognize
a **rămâne** (a **rămânea**), **rămân**, **rămas**, to remain
a **rupe**, **rup**, **rupt**, to break
a **scoate**, **scot**, **scos**, to take out
a **scrie**, **scriu**, **scris**, to write
a **sparge**, **sparg**, **spart**, to break
a **spune**, **spun**, **spus**, to tell
a **şterge**, **şterg**, **şters**, to wipe
a **stinge** (**a stânge**), **sting**, **stins**, to extinguish
a **strânge**, **strâng**, **strâns**, to press, to gather, to collect
a **se teme**, **mă tem**, **temut**, to fear
a **trage**, **trag**, **tras**, to pull, to draw
a **trece**, **trec**, **trecut**, to pass
a **trimite**, **trimit**, **trimis**, to send
a **ucide**, **ucid**, **ucis**, to kill
a **vinde**, **vând**, **vândut**, to sell
a **zice**, **zic**, **zis**, to say

d) *Verbs of the fourth conjugation:*

a **acoperi**, **acopăr**, **acoperit**, to cover
a **adormi**, **adorm**, **adormit**, to fall asleep
a **ascuţi**, **ascut**, **ascuţit**, to sharpen
a **auzi**, **aud**, **auzit**, to hear
a **azvârli**, **azvârl**, **azvârlit**, to throw

a **cheltui, cheltuiesc, cheltuit**, to spend
a **citi (ceti), citesc, cetit**, to read
a **coborî, cobor, coborît**, to descend
a **curăţi, curăţ, curăţit (a curăţa, curăţ, curăţat)**, to clean
a **descoperi, descopăr, descoperit.** to discover
a **despărţi, despart (despărţesc), despărţit**, to separate
a **deveni, devin, devenit**, to become
a **dovedi, dovedesc, dovedit**, to prove
a **fugi, fug, fugit**, to run, to flee
a **gândi, gândesc, gândit**, to think
a **glumi, glumesc, glumit**, to jest, to joke
a **hotărî, hotărăsc, hotărît**, to decide
a **hrăni, hrănesc, hrănit**, to feed
a **ieşi, ies, ieşit**, to go out
a **împărţi, împărţesc (împart), împărţit**, to divide
a **împlini, împlinesc, împlinit**, to fulfil
a **încălzi, incălzesc, încălzit**, to warm
a **îngriji, îngrijesc, îngrijit**, to take care of
a **însoţi, însoţesc, însoţit**, to accompany
a **isprăvi, isprăvesc, isprăvit**, to finish
a **iubi, iubesc, iubit**, to love
a **izbi, izbesc, izbit**, to strike, to hit
a **locui, locuesc, locuit**, to dwell
a **lovi, lovesc, lovit**, to hit
a **mirosi, miros, mirosit**, to smell
a **mulţumi (mulţămi), mulţumesc, mulţumit**, to thank
a **munci, muncesc, muncit**, to work
a **porni, pornesc, pornit**, to start
a **porunci, poruncesc, poruncit**, to order
a **potrivi, potrivesc, potrivit**, to adjust
a **primi, primesc, primit**, to receive
a **repeţi, repet (repeţesc), repeţiţ, (a repeta, repet, repetat)**, to repeat
a **sări, sar, sărit**, to jump
a **servi, servesc, servit**, to serve
a **sfătui, sfătuesc, sfătuit**, to advise
a **sili, silesc, silit**, to force, to compel
a **simţi, simt (simţesc), simţit**, to feel
a **sluji, slujesc, slujit**, to serve
a **sosi, sosesc, sosit**, to arrive
a **şti(e), ştiu, ştiut**, to know
a **suferi, sufăr, suferit**, to suffer
a **sui, sui, suit**, to ascend
a **târî, târăsc, târît**, to drag
a **trăi, trăiesc, trăit**, to live
a **trânti, trântesc, trântit**, to throw with force
a **trebui, trebuiesc, trebuit**, must, to be obliged
a **vârî, vâr, vârît**, to thrust, to put into
a **veni, vin, venit**, to come
a **vesti, vestesc, vestit**, to announce
a **vorbi, vorbesc, vorbit**, to talk
a **zări, zăresc, zărit**, to behold, to see

Exercise No. 12

Proverbe

Soarele încălzeşte şi pe buni şi pe răi.
Numai cu vorba nu se face ciorba.
Să cumperi vecinii întâi şi apoi casa.
Timpul trece dar vecinul rămâne.
Spune-mi cu cine te întâlneşti ca să-ţi spun cine eşti.
Pe unde iese vorba iese şi sufletul.
Legea-i după cum o fac domnii.
De atunci se înmulţesc lotrii, de când se înmulţesc legile.
Cine stă în două luntri cade în apă.
Cine sapă groapa altuia cade singur într'ânsa.
Omul înţelept îşi face iarna car, iar vara sanie.
Cum îţi vei aşterne aşa vei dormi.
Păzeşte-mă, Doamne, de prieteni, că de duşmani mă voi păzi singur.
Banul deschide uşile fără chei.
Bate fierul până e cald şi fă tot lucrul la vremea lui.
Cine intră în horă trebuie să joace.
Cel ce se face oaie lupul îl mănâncă.
Nu tot ce sboară se mănâncă.
Buturuga mică răstoarnă carul mare.

7. 1. ADVERBS

For the adverbial form of the adjective *vide* 3. 4.

Adverbs are formed by derivative suffixes or by composition.

a) Adverbs are derived from nouns, adjectives or verbs with the help of the suffixes **-iş** (or **-îş**), **-eşte** :

cruce (*n.*), cross	**cruciş** (*adv.*), crosswise
faţă (*n.*), face	**făţiş** (*adv.*), openly
chior (*adj.*), blind	**chiorîş** (*adv.*), asquint
om (*n.*), man	**omeneşte** (*adv.*), humanly
orb (*adj.*), blind	**orbeşte** (*adv.*), blindly
a fura (*v.*), to steal	**pe furiş** (*adv.*), furtively
a se târî (*v.*), to crawl	**târîş** (*adv.*), crawling

b) Some nouns with the article have the function of the temporal adverbs (see 13. 8):

Lunia, **Marţia**, **Miercurea**, **Joia**, **Vineria**, **Sâmbăta**, **Dumineca**, every Monday, on Mondays, etc.

Luni, **Marţi**, **Mercuri**, **Joi**, **Vineri**, **Sâmbătă**, **Duminică**, Monday, on Monday, etc.

seara, in the evening
anul acesta, this year
anul trecut, last year

c) Nouns without the article may function as adverbs:

a bate măr (*n.*), to beat to death (lit. to beat into a soft apple).
întunerec beznă (*n.*), pitch dark.
mânios foc (*n.*), blazing with anger (lit. angry as fire).
s'a dus glonţ (*n.*), he went quickly and straight (lit. he went like a bullet).

d) *Adverbial expressions* formed with the help of prepositions and nouns or adjectives:

afară din cale (**din cale afară**), excessively, exceptionally
cât pe ce (**cât p'aci**), nearly, on the point of, about to, not short of
cu greu, hardly, scarcely
cu totul, altogether, completely, entirely, absolutely
de-a-dreptul, straightaway, outright, directly
de-andoasele, back to front, contrariwise
de-a ascunselea, hiding; **a se juca de-a ascunselea**, to play hide-and-seek
de bună seamă, surely, for certain
de cu vreme, in good time
de fel, **de loc**, not at all
dintr'odată, suddenly, all at once
din ce în ce, more and more
într'adins, purposely, deliberately
într'adevăr, indeed, truly, really
într'o doară, taking a risk, on the offchance, at a venture
fără doar şi poate, without doubt, without fail
nici de cum, not at all
pe neaşteptate, unexpectedly
pe înserate, towards evening
pe nesimţite, insensibly

pe semne, as it seems, apparently

în zori de zi, at dawn, at daybreak

tot una, all the same, indifferently

la anul, next year
la vară, next summer

7. 2. Adverbs of Place

acolo, colo, acolea, colea, there
aici, aci (aicea, acilea), ici, here
aiurea, elsewhere
alături, alăturea, alongside, next door
altundeva, elsewhere
aproape, near
deasupra, on top, on the surface, overhead
dedesub(t), below, beneath, underneath
dinainte, înainte, before, in front, at the head, ahead
dinapoi, înapoi, behind, in the rear
dincoace, on this side
dincolo, on the other side, beyond
împrejur, around
încoace, hither
încolo, thither
jur-împrejur, all around, right around
nicăiri, nicăirea, nowhere
oriunde, everywhere
pretutindeni, everywhere
undeva, somewhere

7. 3. Adverbs of Time

acum(a), acu, acuş, now, immediately
adese(a), adeseori, often, frequently
adineaori, adineoară, just a minute ago
apoi, afterwards, next
atunci, then, at that time
când, when
cândva, some time
câteodată, sometimes
curând, soon
deunăzi (dăunăzi), the other day, a day or so ago
mereu, always
niciodată, never
odată, once
pururea, always, eternally
totdeuna, always
uneori, sometimes
vreodată, sometimes, ever, at any time

7. 4. Adverbs of Manner

abia, hardly, just
adecă, that is, namely
altfel, otherwise
astfel, so, thus
aşa, so, thus
cum, **precum**, as, likely
întocmai, **tocmai**, exactly
oarecum, somehow

7. 5. Adverbs of Quantity

atât, so much
cam, approximately
cât, how much
câtva, a little, somewhat
ceva, somewhat
întrucâtva, somewhat, in some respects
numai, only
prea, too

7. 6. Affirmation and Negation

da, yes
nu, no, not
ba, no, not at all
poate, perhaps

Note 1.—Another negation is **ne**, which has a restricted use (see also 10. 11 **d**):

bun (*adj.*), good	**nebun** (*adj.*), mad
serios (*adj.*), serious	**neserios** (*adj.*), not serious
om (*n.*), human being	**neom** (*n.*), inhuman creature
a nu putea (*v.*), not to be able	**ne putând** (*v.*), being unable

Note 2.—Some adverbs have a comparative and superlative degree like adjectives (see 3. 4 **c**):

1. **încolo**	2. **mai încolo**	3. **cel mai încolo**
1. **aproape**	2. **mai aproape**	3. **cel mai aproape**
1. **curând**	2. **mai curând**	3. **cel mai curând**

Exercise No. 13

Ziua bună se cunoaşte de dimineaţă.

Pentruce o zi este mai slăvită decât alta, o dată ce toată lumina vine dela soare? (Ecclesiasticul, xxxiii. 7.)

Nu trebuie să zici: ,,Lucrul acesta este mai rău decât celălalt,“ căci fiecare lucru se va dovedi bun, latimpul său. (Ecclesiasticul, xxxix. 34.)

Mai târziu sau mai de vreme adevărul iese la iveală.

Nici lupul flămând, nici capra cu doi iezi.

Cum e bună ziua, aşa-i şi mulţămita.

Nebunul, când râde, râde cu hohote, pe când omul cu simţire deabia zâmbeşte. (Ecclesiasticul, xxi. 23.)

Noaptea toate vacile sunt negre.

A fost odată ca'n poveşti
A fost ca niciodată,
Din rude mari împărăteşti
O prea frumoasă fată.

Eminescu, *Luceafărul.*

E mai bine să fii fruntea cozii decât coada frunţii.

Nu fii sgârcit, căci banii strângătorului intră în mâna cheltuitorului, şi scumpul mai mult păgubeşte, leneşul mai mult aleargă; dar nu fii nici scump la tărâţe şi ieften la făină.

Multe lucruri frumoase sunt în lumea aceasta, numai să ai ochi să le vezi.

8. PREPOSITIONS AND CONJUNCTIONS

On the use of the preposition **pe**, *on*, in the accusative, see 15. 1.

8. 1. After the preposition the pronoun takes the accusative form; the noun takes the form without a definite article (cp. 13. 2). The preposition **cu**, *with*, takes the noun with a definite article, unless there is a suggestion of a partitive genitive in the noun (cp. 13. 2, Notes 2 and 3):

Plec cu trenul. I go by train.
Vine cu gândul să-mi spuie totul.
He comes with the intention to tell me everything.

but : **Plecă cu supărare.** He went away with anger.
Îmi spuse cu durere. He told me painfully.
Vine cu gânduri bune. He comes with good intentions.

8. 2. Simple and compound prepositions :

afară de, with exception of
către, towards, to
de, of, from, about
dela, from
despre, about
din (cp. 8. 3, Note 1), from, out of
dinspre, from
dintre, from, between
dincolo de, beyond, over
din jos de, down
după, after
fără, without
în (cp. 8. 3, Note 1), in
între, between
înspre, towards, to
la, to
lângă, near, by the side of
până (la), till, until
pe, on, upon ; near, about, over
pe lângă, beside, apart from
pentru, for, on account of ; towards, to
peste, over
prin (cp. 8. 3, Note 1), through
printre, among
spre, to, towards
sub (subt, supt), under, beneath, below

Note.—The particle **a** is used as preposition in expressions like :

Miroase a bătaie. It looks (smells) like trouble.
Calcă a popă. He steps like a would-be priest.

8. 3. Nominal Prepositions

Prepositions with substantival termination and nouns preceded by prepositions are used as prepositions. After them the noun is in the Genitive-Dative form :

asupra vrăjmaşului, against the enemy
deasupra oraşului, over the town

dedesubtul pământului, beneath the earth
de-a-lungul râului, along the river
dinaintea casei, before the house
în susul apei, upstream
împrejurul casei, round the house
de-a-curmezişul şoselei, across the highway
în ruptul capului, not at all (lit. if you break your neck)
în ciuda ploii, in spite of
împotriva voinţii sale, against his will
în preajma vântului, against the wind

The pronoun used after these prepositions is a possessive, which shows that they are adverbial expressions felt by the speaker as nouns :

asupra mea, ta, noastră, voastră, lui, sa, lor against me, etc.
dinaintea mea, ta, noastră, voastră, lui, sa, lor in face of me, etc.
în jurul, tău, nostru, vostru, lui, său, lor round me, etc.
în spatele meu, tău, nostru, vostru, lui, său, lor behind me, etc.

Note 1.—The prepositions **în**, **din**, **prin** have also longer forms: **întru**, **dintru**, **printru**, which should not be confused with **între**, between ; **dintre**, from ; **printre**, among. The longer forms, **întru**, **dintru**, **printru**, are used when the word following begins with a vowel :

într'un an	(în un an)	in a year
dintr'un codru	(din un codru)	from a forest
printr'o minune	(prin o minune)	by a miracle
dintr' odată	(din odată)	suddenly

Note 2.—The preposition **de** is much used, and has varied meanings (see 14. 3) :

a) It expresses the material of which something is made, or the value of an object :

o masă de lemn, a wooden table
pădure de stejari, oak forest
obiect de valoare, object of value

un păhar de apă, a glass of water
haină de lână, wool coat
o pâine de cinci lei, a 5 lei loaf

b) It is used after numbers from twenty upwards:

douăzeci de ani, twenty years
treizeci şi doi de oameni, thirty-two men

c) It expresses duration:

de doi ani, for (since) two years
de-o săptămână, for a week

d) It is found with the object of some verbs:

a se teme de Dzeu, to fear God
a fugi de răspundere, to avoid responsibility

e) It is used with other prepositions or adverbs to modify their meaning:

de pe masă, from the table
un om de la ţară, a villager, a peasant
de pe la munte, from the mountain region
n'am mâncat de ieri, I have not eaten since yesterday

f) **de** has sometimes the sense of the conditional particle **dacă**, *if*:

de o fi să mor, if I should die

g) **de** with the infinitive:

arta de a vorbi, the art of speaking
dreptul de a lupta, the right to fight

h) **de** after some adverbs:

Cât de scump e? How dear is it?
Oricât de bine ar fi. However well it may be.

i) **de** before adverbs expresses the idea *from*:

Vine de departe. He comes from far.
De unde vine? Where does he come from?

Note 3.—I.) The preposition **pe** (pre) can mean *on, through*:

Pune cartea pe masă! Put the book on the table!
Aleşi pe sprânceană. Especially (lit. by eyebrow) selected.
A intrat pe uşe. He entered the door.

II.) It enlarges the sense of another preposition, giving it a more general sense:

la noi, at us — **pe la noi**, in our region
lângă boi, near the oxen — **pe lângă boi**, round the oxen
la prânz, at noon — **pe la prânz**, about noon
la oraş, in the town — **pe la oraş**, in town

III.) It helps to form the accusative (cp. 15. 1):

Pe cine nu-l laşi să moară, nu te lasă să trăieşti.
(The man) whom you don't let die, won't let you live.

IV.) It gives another sense to a preposition:

Pe lângă mâncare a cerut şi băutură.
Apart from eating he asked for drink as well.

8. 4. Conjunctions are joining together words, phrases or co-ordinate clauses. They are simple or compound words.

a) *Copulative* conjunctions:

şi, and — **nici**, neither, nor
nici chiar, not even

b) *Alternative* conjunctions:

sau (au), or — **ori**, or

c) *Adversative* conjunctions:

dar, but — **ci**, but
însă, but — **iar, iară**, but, and, whereas
totuş(i), nevertheless, however

d) *Conductive* conjunctions introducing a noun clause :

că, that | **cum că**, that

e) *Conclusive* conjunctions :

deci, then | **de aceea**, therefore

f) *Causative* conjunctions :

căci, because, for | **de vreme ce**, since, because

g) *Interrogative* conjunctions :

oare ? (**au ?**), isn't ? indeed ? is it true ? don't you think?

h) *Explicative* conjunctions :

oricum, anyhow, however, in any case
precum, as
întrucât, as far as
cu atât mai mult, so much the more

i) *Correlative* conjunctions :

şi . . . şi, both . . . and
ori . . . ori, either . . . or
atât . . . cât, as . . . as, both . . . and
când . . . când, sometimes . . . at other times
cu atât . . . cu cât, the more . . . the more
deşi . . . totuş(i), though . . . yet
nici . . . nici, neither . . . nor
sau . . . sau, either . . . or
fie . . . fie, either . . . or
nu numai . . . ci şi, not only . . . but also
dacă . . . sau, whether . . . or
cum . . . aşa, as . . . so
de ce . . . de ce, more . . . more

Note.—Conjunctions joining subordinate clauses, see 20.

Exercise No. 14

Proverbe

Graba strică treaba.
Gura lumii, numai pământul o astupă.
Boul se leagă de coarne şi omul de limbă.
Năravul din fire n'are lecuire.
Fuge de ploaie şi dă în noroaie
Unde e înţelepciune multă, e şi nebunie multă.
Unde nu e cap, vai de picioare.
De multe ori nu aduce anul, ce aduce ceasul.
Vorba lungă e sărăcia omului.
Bogatul mănâncă atunci când îi e foame, săracul când găseşte.
Banul muncit nu se prăpădeşte.
Lăcomia strică omenia.
Cine îmbrăţişează multe puţine adună.
Pune-ţi căciula înainte şi te judecă singur.
Câinele îmbătrâneşte de drum şi nebunul de grija altora.
Cine se face oaie îl mănâncă lupii.
Fă-te tovarăş cu dracu, până treci cu el lacu.
Mai bine cu cel cuminte la pagubă, decât cu cel prost la câştig.
Fă-mă, mamă, cu noroc, şi m'aruncă'n foc.
Cinci degete sânt la o mână şi unul cu altul nu se potriveşte.
După război mulţi viteji se găsesc.
Decât slugă mare, mai bine stăpân mic.
La copacul căzut toţi aleargă să taie crengi.
Mai bine sărac şi curat.
Ce-i în mână nu-i minciună.
Cine împarte, parte-şi face.
Paza bună trece primejdia rea.
Soarele e soare, şi tot nu poate încălzi toată lumea.
Ce se naşte din pisică, şoareci prinde.
Mai bine un dram de noroc decât o oca de minte.
Leagă sacul la gură până e plin.
Cine se frige cu ciorba, suflă şi în iaurt.
Corb la corb nu scoate ochii.

Să nu dea Dumnezeu omului cât poate să rabde.
Omul înţelept nu aprinde moara ca să scape de şoareci.
Cine nu lucrează'n tinereţe, n'are ce mânca la bătrâneţe.

9. INTERJECTIONS

These are :

9. 1. Onomatopeics, which reproduce natural sounds :

buf ! bang ! (imitation of the sound of a falling object)
boc ! rat-tat-tat ! (imitation of the knocking sound)
cioc ! cioc ! (imitation of the sound of a hammer or similar object)
plosc ! (pleosc !) slap ! splash !
bobâlc ! bâldâbâc ! splash !
trosc ! snap ! (sound of breaking twig)
cotcodac ! cluck ! cluck ! (hen)
cucurigu ! cock-a-doodle-doo !
cucu ! cuckoo !
miau ! meeow !
ham ! bow-wow !

9. 2. Those expressing Sentiments and Volitions

a ! ah ! aha !
ah ! aha ! (expressing surprise)
auleu ! au ! aoleo ! of ! uf ! vai ! woe ! oh dear !
aleu ! valeu ! ow ! (cry of pain)
alei ! alelei ! alas !
aferim ! wonderful !
zău ! by Jove !
de ! apoi de ! well ! (grudging assent)
aida de ! aş ! ei aş ! go on ! (expressing incredulity)
ehei ! ehehei ! ah me ! (expressing sentimental regret)
ia ! ian ! now ! (lit. *imper.* from a lua=to take)
ei ! well !
hait ! got it !
bre ! hey, you ! (familiar)
mă(i) ! (*m.*), hallo ! (familiar) (to a man)
fă ! **fa** ! (*f.*), hallo ! (familiar) (to a woman)
hai ! haide ! come (on) ! let us go !
haidem ! let us go ! (1*st pers. pl.*)
haideţi ! let us go ! (2*nd pers. pl.*)
pentru Dumnezeu ! for God's sake !
Doamne fereşte ! God forbid
vai de mine ! oh dear !
nani ! nani ! hushaby !

9. 3. Those calling or inciting animals

aho ! **ho** ! stop ! (oxen)
prr ! whoa ! (horses)
hăi ! go ! (oxen)
hi ! **de** ! gee up ! (horses)
hăis ! **hăisa** ! (turning oxen to the left)
cea ! **ceala** ! (turning oxen to the right)
nea ! come here !
cuţu ! **cuţu** ! here, doggie !
pui ! **pui** ! chick ! chick !
ţîba ! get down ! (dogs)

9. 4. Greetings

Bună dimineaţa ! Good morning !
Bună ziua ! Good day !
Bună seara ! Good evening !
Noapte bună ! Good night ! (when leaving).
Seara bună ! Good evening ! (when leaving).
Salutare ! Good-bye !
La revedere ! Good-bye ! Au revoir !
Cu bine ! Good luck !
Sănătate bună ! Good-bye ! (Good health !) (on leaving).
S'auzim de bine ! Good-bye ! (on leaving).
Doamne ajută ! God aid you ! (greeting somebody at work).
Noroc ! Good luck !
Felicitările mele ! My congratulations !
La mulţi ani ! Many happy returns !
Hristos a înviat ! **Adevărat c'a înviat** ! (at Easter). Christ has risen ! Truly, He has risen !
Mulţumesc ! **Mulţumim** ! Thank you !
Să trăieşti ! May you live long !
La mai mare ! May you advance in your career ! (congratulation on promotion).
Sărbători fericite ! Merry Christmas ! Happy New Year !

Exercise No. 15

Ghicitori

Ghici ghicitoarea mea :

(1) Cine s'a născut şi încă n'a murit ?

(2) Cine nu s'a născut şi a murit ?

(3) Am un copil — dacă-l iau în braţe plânge — dacă-l pun jos tace ?

(4) Cu coarne ca boul, cu şea ca un cal, se urcă pe copac ca un şarpe ?

(5) Două merg, două stau — două judecată n'au ?

(6) Am un car cu fân, şi merge pe patru resteie ?

(7) Patru fraţi într'un cojoc ?

(8) Spuneţi-mi acum anume — ce pom e acel în lume — care ramurile sale — toate le are la vale — şi vinele rădăcina — îi stau în sus cu tulpina ?

(9) Sânt albă sulemenită — şi urîtă şi iubită — vara nu vor să mă vadă — şi iarna mă'nbrăţişează ?

(10) Ce e dulce şi mai dulce — şi nu poate să se'nbuce ; — dar din el gustă tot omul — şi argatul ca şi domnul ?

(11) Am o găină, c'o aripă albă şi cu una neagră ; cu cea albă împrăştie, şi cu cea neagră adună ?

(12) Am un măr de aur, joacă pe-o piele de taur ?

(13) Am un copaci cu 12 craci şi în tot cracul câte patru cuiburi, şi'n tot cuibul câte şapte ouă ?

(14) La cap pieptene, la trup pepene, la coadă secere, — cucoşul, boule, pricepe-te ?

(15) Am patru surori — tot fug una după alta şi nu se mai ajung ?

(16) Am o casă văruită — nicăiri nu-i găurită ?

(17) Minte are — suflet n'are — umblă făr'astâmpărare — ce nu ştii te învaţă — de-i ghici'ţi voi frige-o raţă ?

(18) Ce vieţuitoare umblă dimineaţa în patru picioare, la prânz în două şi seara în trei ?

(19) Câmpul alb — oile negre — cine le paşte le cunoaşte ?

(20) Unul trecând pe drum şi văzând o femeie şi un bărbat că lucrau împreună le zise : — ,,bună ziua, om cu soţie ! —" Iar femeia a răspuns : —,,nu e om cu soţie, cu ochii nu ne-ai pătruns, cu mintea nu ne-ai înţeles. Uită-te şi ia seana : mama acestui om este soacra mamei mele. Cine sânt eu ? "

(1) eu, *I* ; (2) *Adam* ; (3) lanţul, *the chain* ; (4) melcul, *the snail* ; (5) soarelo şi luna, cerul şi pământul, focul şi apa ; (6) oaia ; (7) nuca, *the nut* ; (8) omul ; (9) soba, *the stove*; (10) somnul, *the sleep*; (11) ziua şi noaptea ; (12) soarele ; (13) anul, lunile, săptămânile şi zilele ; (16) oul, *the egg* ; (17) ceasul, *the watch* ; (18) omul, când e mic umblă d'a buşile, când e mare umblă în două, iar la bătrâneţe ia un băţ ; (19) cartea şi literele ; (20) fiica omului cu care lucrează.

PART III

WORD FORMATION

10. COMPOSITION

COMPOUND words are not usual in the Rumanian language. There exist, however, on a reduced scale, the following compounds :

10. 1. Verb with noun.
10. 2. Noun with verb.
10. 3. Noun with noun.
10. 4. Noun with adjective.
10. 5. Pronoun with verb.
10. 6. Adverb with verb.
10. 7. Preposition with noun.
10. 8. Preposition with preposition.
10. 9. Preposition with conjunction.
10. 10. Preposition with noun and pronoun, etc.

Examples :

10. 1. Verb with noun :

Sfarmă-Piatră, a mythological personage, strong enough to crush a stone in the hand

Strâmbă-Lemne, a mythological personage, strong enough to bend a tree

sgârâie-brânză, Scrooge (lit. scratch-cheese)

pierde-vară, a lazy fellow (lit. who loses the summer without working)

papă-lapte, a good-for-nothing, a very soft fellow (lit. milk-eater)

linge-blide, a fellow licking the plates, a man sitting in the kitchen, a parasite

încurcă-lume, a man who only produces confusion, who muddles things

ucigă-l crucea, devil (lit. Let him be killed by the Cross)

10. 2. Noun with verb:

gură-cască, stupidly gaping

10. 3. Noun with noun:

Barbă-Cot, a mythological personage, dwarf with a beard one ell long
Statu-Palmă, a mythological personage whose stature is only one hand high
tren-fulger, a very fast train
ceas-brăţară, wrist-watch
Moş Crăciun, Father Christmas

10. 4. Noun with adjective; adjective with noun:

Făt-Frumos, Prince Charming
burtă-verde, a suburban, narrow-minded
Duminica Mare, Whit-Sunday
miază-noapte, midnight

10. 5. Pronoun with verb; verb with pronoun:

cineva, someone
altceva, something else
fiecare, everyone
vreunul (*m.*), **vreuna** (*f.*), someone

10. 6. Adverb with verb; verb with adverb:

cândva, sometime
cumva, somehow
oriunde, anywhere

10. 7. Preposition with noun:

cuminte, clever
diseară, this evening
fără de lege, crime
confrate, fellow, colleague

10. 8. Preposition with preposition:

dintre, from
printre, among

10. 9. Preposition with conjunction:

pentru că, because

10. 10. Preposition with noun and with pronoun:

de vreme ce, because
în vreme ce, while

Note.—Phrases equivalent to compound words are formed in Rumanian with the help of the preposition **de**:

om de omenie, a man of honour
om de cuvânt, a man of his word
pui de lup, wolf-cub
societate de binefacere, benevolent society
flori de câmp, wild flowers
frunză de stejar, oak leaf
om de nădejde, a reliable man
haină de sărbătoare, Sunday clothes
câine de vânătoare, hunting dog

10. 11. Compound words formed with the help of prefixes, which modify entirely or partially the sense of the stem words:

a) **a-**:

mestec, I mix	**amestec**, I mix
pun, I put	**apun**, I set (the sun)
lunec, I slip	**alunec**, I slip
dorm, I am sleeping	**adorm**, I fall asleep
mân, I drive	**amân**, I postpone

b) **des-**:

fac, I do	**desfac**, I undo
leg, I bind	**desleg**, I unbind
învăţ, I teach, learn	**desvăţ**, I make forget
mă încalţ, I put on my shoes	**mă descalţ**, I take my shoes off
înfund, I stop up	**desfund**, I uncork
închid, I close	**deschid**, I open

c) **în-, îm-**:

mormântul, the grave	**a înmormânta**, to bury
verde, green	**a înverzi**, to grow green
floare, flower	**a înflori**, to bloom
rău, bad	**a înrăutăţi**, to make worse

d) ne-

bun, good	**nebun**, mad
firesc, natural	**nefiresc**, unnatural
voie, permission	**nevoie**, need
drept, right ; straight	**nedrept**, unjust

e) pre- :

fac, I do	**prefac**, I change, I remodel
a lua, to take	**a prelua**, to take over
a pune, to put	**a prepune**, to suspect

f) răs- :

bun, good	**răsbun**, I avenge
putere, power	**răsputere**, all power
mă scol, I rise	**mă răscol**, I revolt
a bate, to beat	**a răsbate**, to penetrate

g) stră- :

a împunge, to stick in	**a străpunge**, to pierce
a bate, to beat	**a străbate**, to pierce
moş, old man, grandfather	**strămoş**, ancestor
nepot, nephew, grandson	**strănepot**, great grandson
bunic, grandfather	**străbunic**, great grandfather
vechi, old	**străvechi**, very old

11. DERIVATION

There is more variety of word formations with the help of suffixes. Each suffix serves to change the meaning of the stem-word. Here are the principal suffixes :

11. 1. Diminutive.

-andru :

băiat, boy	**băieţandru**, young boy
căţel, puppy	**căţelandru**, puppy

-el :

băiat, boy	**băieţel**, little boy
scaun, chair	**scăunel**, a small chair
mare, big, large, great	**măricel**, biggish.

-ică :

viorea, violet	**viorică**, violet
Ion, John	**Ionică**, Johnny
pasăre, bird	**păsărică**, little bird
frumos, beautiful	**frumuşel** (*m.*), **frumuşică** (*f.*), nice, pretty
mic, small	**mititel** (*m.*), **mititică** (*f.*), tiny

-iţă :

gură, mouth	**guriţă**, little mouth
poartă, gate	**portiţă**, small gate
mioară, young sheep	**mioriţă**, young sheep

-işor :

pod, bridge	**podişor**, a small bridge
băţ, stick	**beţişor**, a small stick
bine, well	**binişor**, pretty well

-ioară, -ior :

grămadă, heap	**grămăgioară**, a small heap
soră, sister	**sorioară**, little sister
uliţă, street	**ulicioară**, narrow, short street
casă, house	**căscioară**, a small house
frate, brother	**frăţior**, little brother

-uică :

fereastră, window	**ferestruică**, small window
pasăre, bird	**păsăruică**, small bird

-uleţ :

râu, river	**râuleţ**, small river
brâu, belt	**brâuleţ**, small belt
sac, bag	**săculeţ**, small bag

-uliţă :

furcă, fork	**furculiţă**, fork (for eating)
puică, chicken, sweetheart	**puiculiţă**, chicken, sweetheart

-uţ, -uţă :

cal, horse	**căluţ**, little horse
bou, ox	**bouţ**, calf
masă, table	**măsuţă**, a small table
casă, house	**căsuţă**, small house

11. 2. Augmentative.

-an :

băiat, boy	**băietan**, lad
curcă, she-turkey	**curcan**, he-turkey
lung, long	**lungan**, a long man

-ilă :

buză, lip	**buzilă**, with large lips
ger, frost	**Gerilă** (myth. personage)
flămând, hungry	**Flămânzilă** (myth. personage)

-oaie :

casă, house	**căsoaie**, large house

-oi :

piatră, stone	**pietroi**, a big stone
furcă, fork	**furcoi**, large fork
vulpe, she-fox	**vulpoi**, he-fox

-os :

nas, nose	**năsos** (*m.*), **năsoasă** (*f.*), with big nose
spate, back	**spătos, spătoasă**, with wide shoulders
păr, hair	**păros, paroasă**, hairy

11. 3. *Nomina Agentis* (persons who perform the action expressed in the stem of the word).

-ar :

plug, plough	**plugar**, ploughman
zid, wall	**zidar**, builder, bricklayer
bucate, meals	**bucătar**, cook

-aş :

arc, bow	**arcaş**, archer
frunte, forehead	**fruntaş**, leader
plai, mountain path	**plăieş**, mountaineer
ucid, I kill	**ucigaş**, murderer
luntre, boat	**luntraş**, boatman

-giu :

han, inn	**hangiu**, innkeeper
cafea, coffee	**cafegiu**, coffee-maker

-tor, -toare :

a învăţa, to teach, to learn	**învăţător** (*m.*), **învăţătoare** (*f.*) teacher
a lucra, to work	**lucrător** (*m.*), **lucrătoare** (*f.*), worker

11. 4. Abstract Nouns derived from verbs.

-anie, -enie :

a pierde, to lose	**pierzanie**, destruction, loss
a păţi, to happen, to come to pass	**păţanie**, happening, adventure
surd, deaf	**surzenie**, deafness

-are, -ere, -ire, -îre :

a se purta, to behave	**purtare**, behaviour
a curge, to flow	**curgere**, flowing
a ceti, to read	**cetire**, reading
a ocărî, to scold	**ocărîre**, scolding

-ciune :

a se ruga, to pray	**rugăciune**, the prayer
a ierta, to forgive	**iertăciune**, forgiveness
a urî, to hate	**urîciune**, hated thing, ugliness

-eală :

a se îndoi, to bend oneself, to doubt	**îndoială**, doubt
a cheltui, to spend	**cheltuială**, expense
a greşi, to make a mistake	**greşală**, mistake

-et, -ăt :

a urla, to howl	**urlet**, howling
a striga, to shout	**strigăt**, shout
a umbla, to walk	**umblet**, walking

-inţă :

a crede, to believe	**credinţă**, belief, faith
a ştie, to know	**ştiinţă**, science
a putea, to be able	**putinţă**, possibility

-oare :

a ninge, to snow	**ninsoare**, fallen snow (at one time)
a scrie, to write	**scrisoare**, letter
a unge, to smear	**unsoare**, ointment
a mulge, to milk	**mulsoare**, milked milk (at one milking time)

-tură :

a sări, to jump	**săritură**, jump
a umfla, to swell	**umflătură**, swelling
a rupe, to break	**ruptură**, breaking

11. 5. Abstract Nouns derived from adjectives and from nouns.

-eaţă, -eţă :

alb, white	**albeaţă**, whiteness
frumos, beautiful	**frumuseţă**, beauty
bătrân, old (aged)	**bătrâneţe** (*pl.*), old age
tânăr, young	**tinereţe** (*pl.*), youth

-ie :

vesel, gay	**veselie**, gaiety
sărac, poor	**sărăcie**, poverty
bărbat, man	**bărbăţie**, manhood

-ime :

mult, much	**mulţime**, crowd
înalt, high	**înălţime**, height
lat, wide, broad	**lăţime**, breadth, width
tânăr, young	**tinerime**, young people

-ate, -tate :

bun, good	**bunătate**, kindness
rău, bad	**răutate**, badness
drept, right	**dreptate**, right, justice

11. 6. Collective Nouns.

-et :

tânăr, young	**tineret**, youth
brad, fir-tree	**brădet**, fir-thicket
pom, fruit-tree	**pomăt**, orchard

Note.—The same suffix derives nouns from verbs (cp. 11. 4):

a ţipa, to shriek	**ţipăt**, the shrieking
a râde, to laugh	**râset**, the laughing
a umbla, to walk	**umblet**, the walking

-iş :

frunză, leaf	**frunziş**, leaves
piatră, stone	**pietriş**, gravel
acopăr, I cover	**acoperiş**, roof

11. 7. Nouns from other Nouns.

a) To indicate origin.

-an, -ean (*m.*), **-ancă, -eancă** (*f.*) :

ţară, country	**ţăran**, peasant	**ţărancă**, peasant woman
sat, village	**sătean**, villager	**săteancă**, village woman
cetate, fortress	**cetăţean**, citizen	**cetăţeancă**, citizeness
munte, mountain	**muntean**, mountaineer	**munteancă**, mountain woman
Focşani (name of a town)	**Focşănean**, citizen of F.	**Focşăneancă**, woman of F.
Brăila (name of a town)	**Brăilean**, citizen of B.	**Brăileancă**, woman of B.

b) Feminine Nouns from Masculine.

-easă :

mire, bridegroom	**mireasă**, bride
împărat, emperor	**împărăteasă**, empress
bucătar, cook	**bucătăreasă**, cook (woman)

-că :

pui, chicken	**puică**, chicken (*f.*); sweetheart
fiu, son	**fiică**, daughter
Român, Rumanian	**Româncă**, Rumanian (woman)

-oaică :

lup, wolf	**lupoaică**, she-wolf
urs, bear	**ursoaică**, she-bear
Bulgar, Bulgarian	**Bulgăroaică**, Bulgarian woman

c) To indicate the place where the noun expressed by the stem is to be found.

-ar :

grâne (*pl.*), cereal	**grânar**, barn, granary

-ărie :

lapte, milk	**lăptărie**, dairy
cârnaţ, sausage	**cârnăţărie**, butcher

-işte :

cânepă, hemp	**cânepişte**, place where hemp grows
porumb, maize	**porumbişte**, place where maize grows

11. 8. Adjectival Suffixes.

-at :

buză, lip	**buzat**, with big lips
ureche, ear	**urechiat**, with big ears
patru, four	**pătrat**, square

-atec :

lună, moon	**lunatec**, moonstruck
nebun, fool, mad	**nebunatec**, foolish
toamnă, autumn	**tomnatec**, autumnal
moale, soft	**molatec**, soft
singur, alone	**singuratec**, lonely

-esc :

bărbat, man	bărbătesc, manly
om, man	omenesc, human
Român, Rumanian	Românesc, Rumanian

-eş :

chip, figure, looks	chipeş, good-looking
gură, mouth	gureş, talkative
ochi, eye	oacheş, dark-eyed

-eţ, -reţ, -ăreţ :

glumă, joke	glumeţ, joker
drum, road	drumeţ, hiker
vorbă, word	vorbăreţ, talkative
lung, long	lungăreţ, oblong
a sălta, to jump, dance	săltăreţ, jumping

-iu, -liu, -niu :

aur, gold	auriu, golden
haz, joke	hazliu, joker
cafea, coffee	cafeniu, coffee-coloured

-nic :

jos, down	josnic, mean, base
amar, bitter	amarnic, bitterly
dar, gift, present	darnic, generous

-oi :

greu, heavy, difficult	greoi, clumsy
viu, alive	vioi, lively

-os :

păcat, sin	păcătos, sinful
bucurie, joy	bucuros, glad, joyful
credinţă, faith	credincios, faithful
sirguinţă, diligence	sirguincios, diligent

-ui :

alb, white	**albui**, whitish
verde, green	**verzui**, greenish

11. 9. Verbal Suffixes.

-ez :

a lucra, to work	**lucrez**, I am working
a fuma, to smoke	**fumez**, I am smoking

-esc, -iesc :

a înflori, to blossom	**înfloresc**, I am blossoming
a preţui, to prize	**preţuiesc**, I am prizing
a păcătui, to sin	**păcătuiesc**, I am sinning

11. 10. Every adjective and most of the past participles may be used as a noun, and take the definite article (cp. 17. 2):

verde, green	**verdele**, the green
frumos, beautiful	**frumosul**, the beautiful
bine, well	**binele**, the good action, deed
a vâna, to hunt	**vânatul**, the hunting, the hunted animal

Exercise No. 16

Idiomatic Expressions

A aduce vorba despre ceva, to raise a question (in a discussion).
A o apuca la sănătoasa, to turn tail, to take to one's heels.
A apucat-o la sănătoasa. } He ran away.
A luat-o la sănătoasa. }
A avea mână lungă, to steal (lit. to have a long hand).
A bate apa'n piuă, to talk nonsense (lit. to beat water in a fulling mill).
A bate capul cuiva, to insist, to keep on.

A-şi bate capul cu ceva, to think about something ; to rack one's brains.
A bate câmpii, not to keep to the point, to talk extravagantly.
A bate şeaua să'nţeleagă iapa, to make somebody understand something indirectly.
Cât ai bate'n palme, (as quickly as you clap), in the twinkling of an eye.
A căuta nod în papură, to seek a non-existent defect (a knot in a rush plant).
Cât ai clipi din ochi, in the twinkling of an eye.
A se da pe (la) brazdă, to improve oneself ; to get accustomed.
A se da de gol, to betray oneself.
A da de gol pe cineva, to expose ; to compromise somebody.
A-şi da în petec, to expose oneself, to betray oneself.
A da de belea, } to get into trouble.
A-şi găsi beleana, }
A da drumul, to deliver, to let go.
A da (a veni) de hac cuiva, to get the better of.
A-şi face de cap, to be unruly.
A face din ţânţar armăsar, to exaggerate.
A se face luntre şi punte, to leave no stone unturned.
A făgădui marea cu sarea, to promise the impossible.
A-şi ieşi din fire, to lose one's temper, to get angry.
A învăţa pe de rost, to learn by heart.
A se lăsa pe tânjală, to become lazy, idle.
A-şi lua inima'n dinţi, to take all your courage.
A mânca bătaie, to get a thrashing.
A ploua cu găleata, to rain cats and dogs.
A pune la inimă, to take to heart.
A pune beţe'n roate, to make difficulties to somebody.
A pune mână dela mână, to make a collection.
A-şi pierde firea, to lose one's senses ; to get frightened.
A spune verde, to tell straight, sincerely, frankly.
A îndruga verzi şi uscate, to talk nonsense.
A taia frunze la câini, to do nothing, to waste one's labour.
A tăcea peşte, to be dead silent.
A ţinea minte, to remember, to retain in the memory.
A vorbi cai verzi pe pereţi, to talk nonsense ; to fancy.

Asta-i floare la ureche, that does not trouble me at all; that is easy to do.
A fi bun de mână, to have a lucky hand.
Bun de gură, talkative; garrulous.
Din fir în păr, in detail; very thoroughly.
La Sfântul Aşteaptă, till Doomsday.
La Paştile cailor, on the Greek calends.
A se face în patru, to do all, everything possible.
Nici una nici două, quickly; without ceremony.
A trage nădejde, to hope.
Nici în ruptul capului, not at any price; over my dead body.
A umfla pe sus, to lift and carry away.
A fi cu cale, to be right.
A găsi cu cale, to think it right.
A pune la cale, to arrange.

PART IV

SYNTAX

12. 1. The order of words in the sentence is determined by one rule: first things come first! There are, however, grammatical laws observed generally for the sake of clearness, euphony and good style.

The order of words in an *affirmative sentence* is: subject, verb, direct object, indirect object:

Petru a dat o carte lui Ioan.	Peter gave a book to John.
Soarele încălzeşte pe buni şi pe răi.	The sun warms the good and the bad.
Am văzut casa din parcul oraşului.	I saw the house in the town park.
Am pus cheile pe masă.	I put the keys on the table.
Părintele iubeşte pre (pe) Fiul şi a dat toate în mâna lui. (Ioan, iii. 35.)	The Father loveth the Son and hath given all things into his hands.

The order of words is not so fixed as in English; as a rule, what you think of first, or what you wish to emphasize, comes first:

Petru a dat *lui Ion* **o carte.**	Peter gave John a book.

The *rule of proximity* is another hint for the order of words in a sentence: what you think of together you express together:

Amicul meu este bolnav în spital.	My friend is ill in hospital.
Am plecat la Londra cu fratele meu.	I left for London with my brother.
Soru-mea vorbeşte bine englezeşte.	My sister speaks English well.

In general, it is *the sense* which fixes the place of the words in a sentence. The predominant idea is expressed first:

Spusu-mi-a frunza de vie că dragostea nu-i moşie.	The leaf of the vine told me that love is not an estate, i.e. money.
A început atunci pentru băiatul sărac frecuşul vieţii. (I. L. Caragiale, „Norocul culegătorului".)	Then there began for the poor boy the chafing of the yoke of life.
S'a dus moş Ion şi n'a putut face treaba singur; dar când v'aţi mai dus câţiva într'ajutor, treaba s'a făcut cu mare uşurinţă, greutatea n'a mai fost aceeaş. (I. Creangă, „Moş Ion Roată şi Unirea".)	Old John went and he could not do the thing alone; but when several of you went to help him, it was done with great ease, the weight was no longer the same.

12. 2. The order of words in an *interrogative sentence* is the same as in an affirmative. The intonation of voice, pointing out the psychological subject, marks the interrogation:

Affirmative. **Îţi pláce cartea.**	You like the book.
Interrogative. **Îţi plãce cartea?**	Do you like the book?
Aff. **Ai văzút pe fráte-său.**	You have seen his brother.
Int. **Ai văzũt pe frãte-său?**	Have you seen his brother?
Aff. **Vorbíţi englezéşte.**	You speak English.
Int. **Vorbĩţi englezeşte?**	Do you speak English?
Aff. **Plecáţi.**	You leave.
Int. **Plecãţi?**	Are you leaving?
Aff. **Éste.**	He is, there is.
Int. **Ẽste?**	Is there?
Aff. **Únde ai fóst.**	Where you were.
Int. **Ũnde ai fost?**	Where were you?

Aff.	**Sóru-mea va cântá diseară.**	My sister will sing to-night.
Int.	**Soru-mea va cântă diseară?**	Shall my sister sing to-night?

12. 3. When the sentence is introduced by an adverb or by an interrogative pronoun the verb follows immediately after the adverb:

Aff.	**Trenul pleacă la ora opt.**	The train leaves at eight.
Int.	***Când pleacă* trenul?**	When does the train leave?
Aff.	**Traian a trecut Dunărea la Turnu-Severin.**	Trajan crossed the Danube at Turnu-Severin.
Int.	**Pe *unde a trecut* Mihai Viteazul Carpaţii?**	Where did Michael the Brave cross the Carpathians?
Aff.	**Ştefan cel Mare a domnit dela 1457 până la 1504.**	Stephen the Great reigned from 1457 to 1504.
Int.	***Când a domnit* Ştefan cel Mare?**	When did Stephen the Great reign?
Int.	***Cine este* prietenul d-tale?**	Who is your friend?
Int.	**Cu *cine a mers* băiatul la plimbare?**	With whom did the boy go for a walk?
Aff.	***Când au ajuns* drumeţii lângă pădure.**	When the travellers reached the wood.
Aff.	***Unde nu-i* cap, vai de picioare!**	Where there is no head, i.e. intelligence, woe to the legs!
Aff.	***După ce sau sosit* oaspeţii, am intrat în casă.**	After the guests arrived, we entered the house.

Note.—Interrogative sentences may be introduced by interrogative particles: **au** (*archaic*), **oare, doar(ă)**:

— ***Au doar* nu sunt şi Eu Unsul lui Dumnezeu? *Au doar* nu mi-aţi jurat şi mie credinţă, când eram numai Stolnicul Petre? Nu m'aţi ales voi? Cum a fost oblăduirea mea?**

Ce sânge am vărsat? Care s'a întors dela uşa mea fără să câştige dreptate şi mângâiere? Şi încă acum nu mă vreţi, nu mă iubiţi? (C. Negruzzi, „Alexandru Lăpuşneanu".)

— But am not I also the Anointed of God? Have you not sworn to be faithful to me also, when I was only Peter the Chamberlain? Have you not chosen me? How was my reign? What blood have I shed? Who was turned away from my door without receiving justice and consolation? And yet you do not want me now, you do not love me?

> **Şi când se va întoarce pământul în pământ**
> **Au cine o să ştie de unde-s, cine sânt?**
> **M. Eminescu.**

> And when earth returns into earth
> Who will know wherefrom I come and who I am?

12. 4. The order of words in *negative sentences* is the same as in affirmative. The negation **nu**, *not*, *no*, is placed before the verb. Double and treble negations in the same sentence are possible, without changing the negative sense of the sentence, and they are compulsory after a negative indefinite pronoun:

Aff.	**Suntem mulţumiţi.**	We are pleased.
Neg.	***Nu suntem* mulţumiţi.**	We are not pleased.
Aff.	**A venit.**	He has come.
Neg.	***N'a venit* încă.**	He has not come yet.
Aff.	**L-am văzut ieri în oraş.**	I saw him yesterday in the town.
Neg.	***Nu l-am văzut* niciodată nicăiri.**	I have never seen him anywhere.
	***N'a pierdut* nimic niciodată.**	He has never lost anything.
	***N'avem* decât o viaţă.**	We have only one life.
	***N'a plouat* de loc pe-aici.**	It has not rained at all here.
	Nimeni *nu ştie* când i se va sfârşi viaţa.	Nobody knows when his life will end.

Neg. *N'a venit* **nimeni.**	Nobody came.
N'am văzut **nici pe frate-meu, nici pe soru-mea.**	I have seen neither my brother, nor my sister.
N'am **amici.**	I have no friends.
N'am **nici un amic.**	I have not a single friend.
N'am **bani.**	I have no money.
N'am **nici un ban.**	I haven't a penny.
N'am **de spus nimic.**	I have nothing to say.
Nimeni *n'a fost* **de faţă.**	Nobody was present.
Nu-i **de făcut nimic.**	There is nothing to be done.
Negăsind **pe nimeni acasă am lăsat o scrisoare.**	Because I didn't find anybody at home I left a letter.

12. 5. The imperative concept is expressed by the imperative or by the subjunctive form of the verb ; the latter has a future sense. The negative imperative of the second singular is identical with the infinitive form without the particle **a**. The reflexive pronoun and the unstressed pronominal object are suffixed to the affirmative imperative form :

Mergi ! Go ! (*sing.*)	**Mergeţi !** Go ! (*pl.*)
Nu merge ! Don't go ! (*sing.*)	**Nu mergeţi !** Don't go ! (*pl.*)
Aleargă ! Run ! (*sing.*)	**Alergaţi !** Run ! (*pl.*)
Nu alerga ! Don't run ! (*sing.*)	**Nu alergaţi!** Don't run! (*pl.*)
Ascunde-te imediat ! (*sing.*)	Hide yourself immediately.
Ascundeţi-vă ! (*pl.*)	Hide yourselves !
Nu te ascunde ! (*sing.*)	Don't hide yourself !
Nu vă ascundeţi ! (*pl.*)	Don't hide yourselves !
Pleacă la ţară ! (*sing.*)	Go to the country !
Plecaţi de aici ! (*pl.*)	Go from here !
Nu pleca din oraş ! (*sing.*)	Don't leave the town !
Nu plecaţi încă ! (*pl.*)	Don't go yet !
Să faci repede focul ! (*sing.*)	Put the fire on quickly !
Să nu faceţi nedreptate ! (*pl.*)	Don't do injustice !
Să nu faci nici un rău ! (*sing.*)	Don't do a wrong thing !
Să spui adevărul ! (*sing.*)	Thou shalt tell the truth.
Să spuneţi adevărul ! (*pl.*)	You shall tell the truth !

Vino la noi ! (*sing.*)	Come to us !
Veniţi la mine ! (*pl.*)	Come to me !
Nu veni ! (*sing.*)	Don't come !
Chiamă-mă ! (*sing.*)	Call me !
Chiemaţi-mă ! (*pl.*)	Call me !
Nu mă chiema ! (*sing.*)	Don't call me !
Nu mă chiemaţi ! (*pl.*)	Don't call me !
Să nu ucizi ! (Ex. xx. 13.)	Thou shalt not kill !
Cinsteşte pe tatăl tău şi pe muma ta ! (Ex. xx. 12.)	Honour thy father and thy mother !
Pâinea noastră cea spre fiinţă dă-ne-o nouă astăzi. Şi ne iartă nouă greşalele noastre, precum şi noi iertăm greşiţilor noştri. (Mat. vi. 11-12.)	Give us this day our daily bread. And forgive us our debts, as we also have forgiven our debtors.
Nu judecaţi şi nu veţi fi judecaţi ; nu osândiţi şi nu veţi fi osândiţi ; iertaţi şi veţi fi iertaţi. (L. vi. 37.)	Judge not, and ye shall not be judged ; condemn not, and ye shall not be condemned ; forgive, and ye shall be forgiven.

Note.—In exclamatory sentences the verb is placed before the subject :

Trăiască regele !	Long live the King !
Vie ploaie şi furtună !	Come wind, come rain !

12. 6. The place of the conjunct pronoun is before the verb :

Ţi-am spus să vii.	I told you to come.
Nu *ne-a dat* de ştire.	He did not let us know.

In subjunctive forms the conjunct pronouns are placed after **să** ; the negation comes between **să** and the pronoun ; in imperative forms the conjunct pronouns are affixed to the imperative :

Am *să-ţi* dau ceva.	I will give you something.
Dă-mi voie *să-ţi* spun pentru ce am venit.	Allow me to tell you why I have come.

Să-ţi dau un exemplu.	To give you an example.
Aş vrea *să-l* văd la lucru.	I would like to see him at work.
Să nu vă duceţi fără mine.	Don't go without me.
Să nu-i spui nimic.	Don't tell him anything.
Să se facă dreptate !	Let justice be done !
Să nu se schimbe nimic !	Let nothing be changed !

13. 1. Syntax of the article ; Nominative case

The definite article is needed by any noun used in a general sense :

Iubesc *florile*.	I like flowers.
Plumbul e greu.	Lead is heavy.
Viaţa este scurtă.	Life is short.
Sintaxa articolului.	Syntax of the article.
Dreptatea este lumina vieţii.	Justice is the light of life.
Copilăria e primăvara vieţii noastre.	Childhood is the spring of our life.

13. 2. The definite article is not used in unqualified nouns following prepositions (cp. 8. 1) :

pe lângă *boi*, near the oxen	:	pe lângă *boii noştri*, near our oxen
după *casă*, behind the house	:	în *casa noastră*, in our house
sub *pat*, under the bed	:	sub *patul din dormitor*, under the bed in the bedroom
din *grădină*, from the garden	:	din *grădina vecinului*, from the neighbour's garden

Note 1.—If the noun is a well-known person, it may take the definite article after the preposition :

Vine *dela regele*.	He comes from the King.
A fost *la împăratul*.	He was at the emperor's.
Se duce *la popa*.	He goes to the priest.

Note 2.—The preposition **cu**, *with*, is followed by a noun with article, when this noun is used in a general sense:

Boul se apără *cu coarnele.*	The ox defends himself with his horns.
Numai *cu vorba* **nu se face ciorba.**	With words only you can not make broth.
Încetul *cu încetul* **departe ajungi.**	Little by little you may go far.

Note 3.—When, however, the noun expresses a part of the whole (forming with **cu** an adverbial phrase), it does not take the article:

A vorbit *cu demnitate.*	He spoke with dignity.
A înaintat *cu pași* **repezi.**	He advanced with quick steps.
A plecat *cu supărare.*	He went angrily away.
Cafea *cu lapte.*	White coffee (i.e. with milk).
Dulceaţă *cu apă.*	Preserves with water.
Mâncare *cu legume.*	Vegetable meal.

13. 3. Geographical names as subjects or after prepositions take the definite article:

Anglia, Scoţia, Ţara Galilor **şi** *Irlanda* **formează Regatul Unit al Marei Britanii.**	England, Scotland, Wales and Ireland form the United Kingdom of Great Britain.
Parisul **e capitala Franţei.**	Paris is the capital of France.
Dunărea **e cel mai mare fluviu din Europa.**	The Danube is the largest river in Europe.
Vin din *America.*	I come from America.
Prietenul meu trăieşte în *Spania.*	My friend is living in Spain.

Masculine geographical names and feminine ones in **-e** take no article after prepositions (if they are without determinative):

Plec la *Paris.*	I am going to Paris.
Am fost în *Focşani.*	I have been in Focşani.
Venind *dela Cluj* **mă voi opri** *în Braşov.*	Coming from Cluj I shall stop in Braşov.
Ne-am oprit o oră *în Târgo-vişte.*	We stopped for an hour in Targovişte.
Din Egipt **a sburat** *spre Irac.*	From Egypt he flew to Iraq.

Feminine geographical nouns in **-a** retain the article after prepositions:

Mă duc *la Brăila.*	I am going to Braila.
Am fost *la Londra.*	I was in London.
Am fost *în Londra.*	I was in London, I have visited London.
Trăiesc *în Roma.*	I am living in Rome.
Vin *dela* (*din*) *Copenhaga.*	I am coming from Copenhagen.
Am călătorit cu el *dela Suceava* **până la Cernăuţi.**	I travelled with him from Suceava as far as Cernăuţi.

N.B.—To express direction, geographical names of localities demand the preposition **la**; to express "being in" they demand the preposition **în**.

The rule concerning the article applies also to the names of countries and continents; these names use, however, the preposition **în**, *in*, to express "in which direction" as well as "where":

Plec mâine *în Franţa.*	I leave to-morrow for France.
Am trăit cinci ani *în America.*	I lived five years in America.
Venind *din Anglia* **m'am oprit, trei zile,** *în Grecia.*	On the way from England I stopped for three days in Greece.

Masculine plural geographical names in **-eşti, -i** do not

take the article after prepositions ; in colloquial speech these names are often used in the singular :

Am fost *la Bucureşti.*	I was in Bucharest.
Dela Galaţi până la **Iaşi este mai aproape decât** *dela Focşani până la Craiova.*	From Galatz to Jassy is nearer than from Focşani to Craiova.

But :

Bucureştii sunt capitala ţării.	Bucharest is the capital of the country.
Cernăuţii **sunt în nordul ţării.**	Cernautsi is in the North of the country.
Bucureştiul **e un oraş frumos.**	Bucharest is a lovely town.
Cernăuţul **e aşezat pe malul Prutului.**	Cernautsi is situated on the bank of the river Pruth.

13. 4. The definite article is used with nouns in apposition and with titles preceding proper names :

Ştefan cel Mare, *Voevodul Moldovei.*	Stephen the Great, Prince of Moldavia.
Ludovic al 14-lea, *regele Franţei.*	Louis XIV, King of France.
Regina Victoria **a Angliei.**	Queen Victoria of England.
Împăratul **Traian.**	Emperor Trajan.
Domnul **profesor Ionescu.**	Professor Ionescu.
Doamna **Popovici.**	Mrs. Popovici.

Note.—The noun in apposition does not vary its case with the defined noun (see 14. 2, Note 4).

13. 5. In proverbial sentences and in general statements the subject takes the article :

Fuga-i **ruşinoasă, dar e sănătoasă.**	Flight is shameful, but is safe.
Calul **de dar nu se caută de dinţi.**	Don't look a gift horse in the mouth.

Pe lângă *lemnul* uscat arde şi cel verde.	Beside dry wood, the green also burns.
***Copiii* au nevoie de îngrijire.**	Children need care.
***Îmi* plac *cireșele*.**	I like cherries.

In general comparisons the noun takes the definite article :

Trăiau ca *frații*.	They lived like brothers.
Verde ca *iarba*.	Green as grass.
Dulce ca *mierea*.	Sweet as honey.

13. 6. When the noun is preceded by an adjective, the adjective takes the article :

***Înțeleptul* împărat.**	The wise emperor.
***Săracul* om !**	Poor man !
***Biata* femeie!**	Poor woman !
***Bunul* meu părinte.**	My good father.

13. 7. After **tot** (*m.*), **toată** (*f.*), *every*, and **amândoi** (*m.*), **amândouă** (*f.*), *both*, the noun always takes the definite article :

Tot *omul* e muritor.	(Every) man is mortal.
Toate *felurile* de mărfuri.	All kinds of goods.
Toţi *oamenii* trebuie să moară.	All men must die.
Amândoi *frații* au plecat la şcoală.	Both brothers have gone to school.
Amândouă *femeile* erau triste.	Both women were sad.

But :

***Ambii* fraţi.**	Both brothers.

13. 8. The names of seasons, the names of weekdays and the nouns **ziua**, *the day*, and **noaptea**, *the night*, take the article, when they are used as temporal adverbs :

***Vara* e cald.**	In summer it is warm.
***Toamna* plouă.**	In autumn it rains.

Iarna ninge.	In winter it snows.
Primăvara e frumos.	In spring it is fine.
Oamenii lucrează *ziua*.	The people work by day.
Lucrătorii dorm *noaptea*.	The workers sleep by night.
Duminica mergem la biserică.	On Sundays we go to church.

13. 9. The definite article is replaced by the demonstrative pronoun **cel, cea** with numbers and sometimes also with adjectives :

Cei doi nu prea voiau să primească, dar după multă stăruinţă din partea *celui al treilea* au primit. (I. Creangă, „Cinci pâni".)	The two (men) were not too willing to accept, but after much insistence on the part of the third they accepted.
Cei buni şi *cei răi*.	The good ones and the bad ones.

Genitive and Dative Cases

14. 1. The Genitive and the Dative have identical forms. The Genitive is the possessive case, the Dative is the case of the indirect object :

Soarta *oamenilor* (*Gen.*) e în mâinile *zeilor*.	The fate of men is in the hands of the gods.
A spus *oamenilor* (*Dat.*) să intre în casă.	He told the men to enter the house.
Femeia *unui om* (*Gen.*) s'a înecat într'un râu.	The wife of a certain man was drowned in a river.
Unui om (*Dat.*) i s'a înecat femeia în mare.	The wife of a certain man was drowned in the sea (lit. to a man the wife was drowned in the sea).

14. 2. To express the Genitive it is necessary to use the demonstrative pronoun (called possessive article) **al** (*m. sing.*),

ai (*m. pl.*), **a** (*f. sing.*), **ale** (*f. pl.*) in the following circumstances:

a) When the Genitive is an attribute of a noun with indefinite article:

o casă *a vecinului*, a house of the neighbour	: **casa vecinului**, the neighbour's house
nişte case *ale vecinului*, some houses of the neighbour	: **casele vecinului**, the neighbour's houses
un băiat *al vecinului*, a boy of the neighbour	: **băiatul vecinului**, the boy of the neighbour
doi băieţi (de) *ai vecinilor*, two boys of the neighbours	: **băieţii** *vecinilor*, the boys of the neighbours

b) When the Genitive forms the predicate with the auxiliary **a fi**, *to be*:

Casa este *a surorii.*	The house belongs to (is of the) sister.
Casele sunt *ale noastre.*	The houses belong to us.
Calul este *al fratelui* **meu.**	The horse belongs to my brother.
Caii sunt *ai voştri.*	The horses are yours.

c) When the noun is followed by two or more Genitives (or by possessive pronouns) the second and following Genitives (or pronouns) are preceded by the demonstrative pronoun:

Hainele băiatului, *ale fetiţei* **şi** *ale servitorului.*	The clothes of the boy, of the girl and of the servant.
Prietenul nostru, *al vostru* **şi** *al lor.*	Our friend, your friend and their.

d) When the noun is separated from the Genitive by one or more words:

Casa cea frumoasă *a vecinului.*	The neighbour's beautiful house.

Drepturile eterne *ale poporului.*	The eternal rights of the people.
Prietenul cel mai bun *al nostru.*	Our best friend.

Note 1.—The demonstrative pronoun **al**, etc., may be preceded by the preposition **de**:

Un om *de-al împăratului.*	One of the emperor's men.
But:	
Un om *al împăratului.*	A man of the emperor.
Câţi-va cunoscuţi *de-ai noştri.*	Some of our acquaintances.

Note 2.—Followed by **de**, or preceded and followed by **de**, the demonstrative pronoun **al** is placed before proper names, sometimes also before common nouns, to express the kind or quality of a noun describing a group:

Al de **Popescu.**	A Popescu, a man like Popescu.
De al de **Ionescu.**	Persons like Ionescu.
De al de **el.**	Persons like him.

Note 3.—On the use of **al** with ordinal numbers, see 4. 2.

Note 4.—A noun in apposition does not change its case (see 13. 4).

Casa lui Ion, *pădurarul* **din deal, este acoperită, cu paie.**	The house of John, the wood-keeper on the hill, is thatched.
Moartea lui Ştefan cel Mare, *Voevodul* **Moldovei, s'a întâmplat în anul 1504.**	The death of Stephen the Great, Prince of Moldavia, happened in the year 1504.

But also:

La moartea părintelui ei, *bunului* **Petru Rareş, . . .**	At the death of her father, the good Petru Rareş, . . .

(C. Negruzzi, „Al. Lăpuşneanu".)

14\. 3. Another way of expressing the Genitive concept is the preposition **de** with the Nom.-Acc. form :

O pădure *de brazi.*	A wood of fir-trees.
Douăzeci *de oameni.*	Twenty people.
O masă *de lemn.*	A wooden table.
O mulţime *de copii.*	A crowd of children.

To express a part of a category the preposition **dintre,** *from, among*, is used :

Cei mai buni *dintre elevi.*	The best pupils.
Care *dintre voi* **îmi poate spune.**	Which of you can tell me ?

14\. 4. The Genitive and Dative cases are formed by aid of the demonstrative pronoun **(a) lui** (*Gen.*), **lui** (*Dat.*) placed before the noun :

a) Names of persons (see 2. 12) :

Operele *lui Eminescu.*	The works of Eminescu.
Băiatul *lui Ştefan* **al** *lui Petrea.*	The boy of Stephen Peter's son.
Casa aceasta este *a lui Constantin.*	This house belongs to Constantine.
Lui Gheorghe **nu-i plac glumele.**	George does not like jokes.
Spune *lui Ion* **să vie la noi.**	Tell John to come to us.

b) Names of months :

În luna *lui Septemvrie.*	In the month of September.
Primăvara începe în luna *lui Martie.*	Spring begins in the month of March.

c) Nouns which are indeclinable :

În ţara *lui Verde Împărat.*	In the country of Emperor Green.
Judecata *lui Vodă* **a fost dreaptă.**	The Prince's judgment was right.

A dat bună ziua *lui Făt Frumos.*	He said good day to Prince Charming.

d) Nouns which design a relationship:

Această carte este *a lui frate-său.*	This books belongs to his brother.
Acest creion este *al frăține-său.*	This pencil belongs to his brother.
Băiatul a scris *lui tată-său.*	The boy has written to his father.

Or:

Băiatul a scris tătâne-său.	The boy has written to his father.

14. 5. The Dative concept can be expressed also with the help of a preposition, **la**, **către**, *to*, with the Nom.-Acc. form:

A dat de mâncare *la vite.*	He gave food to the cattle.
Corb *la corb* **nu scoate ochii.**	One raven doesn't scratch out another's eyes.
Sătul la flămând nu crede.	One who has eaten enough does not understand the hungry.
N'a spus *la nimeni* **că pleacă.**	He did not tell anybody he was going.
A vorbit *către boieri.*	He spoke to the boyars.

Binele nu se face	Good is not done
Numai *la cine-***ţi place,**	Only to whom you like,
Ci binele este bine	But it is well
Să-l faci *la fiecine.*	To do good to everyone.

Note.—The Pronominal Dative of the first and second person is used as an *Ethical Dative*:

Mi-l **apucară de barbă şi** *mi ți-l* **bătură măr.**	They took him by the beard and beat him to pulp.
El prea *mi* **se laudă.**	He praises himself too much.

Accusative Case

15. 1. The Accusative is the case of the direct object. It may be expressed with the preposition **pe**, *on*; more frequently, however, it is without a preposition. The order of the words in the sentence and the sense help to recognize the Accusative.

It is impossible to give precise rules with regard to the use of **pe** (archaic **pre**) in Accusative. A few hints and examples grouped in categories may guide the beginner.

a) The use of **pe** in Accusative is compulsory:

(i) with common and proper names indicating persons;
(ii) with pronouns (not with the pronoun **ce**, *what*) when they replace persons;
(iii) with ordinal numbers and with cardinal numbers when the latter are defined with **cei, cele**;
(iv) after **decât, ca** in comparisons which enlarge the object;
(v) with **amândoi, ambii**, *both*, and with **nimenea**, *nobody*, **toţi**, *all*, etc., when used as nouns:

A chemat la masă pe împăratul.	He invited the Emperor to dinner.
Lăudăm pe Dumnezeu.	We praise God.
Nu-l cunosc pe Al. Ionescu.	I do not know Al. Ionescu.
Sărută pe băiat şi-i zise.	He kissed the boy and said to him.
Pe tine nu te-a întrebat.	He did not ask you.
Apa pe care o beau.	The water which I drink.
N'am văzut pe cine căutam.	I did not see the person I was looking for.
Pe oricine vei întreba îţi va spune aceasta.	Ask whom you will, he will tell you that.
A întrebat pe al doilea copil.	He asked the second child.
Isus chemă la sine pe cei doisprezece apostoli.	Jesus called the twelve apostles to him.

Îl iubia mai mult, decât pe frate-său.	He used to love him more than his brother.
Nu mă lăsa ici străină ca pe-o floare în grădină.	Do not leave me here alone like a flower in the garden.
A întrebat pe toţi câţi erau de faţă.	He asked all who were present.
I-a luat pe amândoi cu sine.	He took both with him (her).

b) The use of **pe** in Accusative is possible, but not compulsory :

(i) with a well-known object which has an attribute ;
(ii) with the pronouns and with **toţi**, *all*, used as adjectives ;
(iii) with nouns indicating persons and having the indefinite article ;
(iv) with cardinal numbers used as nouns :

Voi întâlni (pe) omul cel cu capra.	I shall meet the man with the goat.
Chemară (pe) primarul din comuna vecină.	They called the Mayor of the neighbouring commune.
Adună (pe) toţi oamenii din sat.	He summoned all the men in the village.
A omorît (pe) o sută pe alţi zece i-a rănit.	He slew a hundred, another ten he wounded.
Îşi alese mire (pe) un fiu de împărat.	She chose as her bridegroom an Emperor's son.

c) The use of **pe** in Accusative is *not* possible :

(i) with the conjunct pronouns ;
(ii) when the object is conceived as partitive ;
(iii) when the object is in connection with a dative pronominal object ;
(iv) with a well-known object which has no attribute or in a general statement :

Văzându-mă în primejdie a sărit să-mi dea ajutor.	Seeing me in danger he leapt to my rescue.

Pe mine nu mă poate convinge.	I cannot be convinced.
Trimise soldaţi să ocupe podul.	He despatched soldiers to occupy the bridge.
N'a avut copii viciodată.	She has never had children.
Mi-a bătut băiatul.	He beat my boy.
Unui om i-au omorît femeia.	They have killed the wife of a man.
Îşi cunoştea fratele prea bine.	He used to know his brother very well.
Iubesc copiii.	I like children.
Sărută băiatul şi-l urcă în trăsură.	He killed the boy and put him into the carriage.

Note.—These rules can only give a rough outline of the use of **pe** in Accusative. In general it is required by persons, or other nouns used as persons, and arises from the necessity to distinguish between Nominative and Accusative, e.g. :

Dacă (pe) iarba câmpului care astăzi este şi mâine se aruncă în cuptor Dumnezeu aşa o îmbracă, oare nu cu mult mai vârtos pe voi . . . (Mat. vi. 30.)	If God so clothe the grass of the field, which to-day is, and to-morrow is cast into the oven, shall he not much more clothe you . . .
Aseară am văzut pe toată lumea în teatru : pe Ionescu, pe Georgescu, etc.	Last night I saw everyone in the theatre : Mr. Ionescu, Mr. Georgescu, etc.
Acest om a călătorit mult, a văzut toată lumea.	That man travelled much, he saw the whole world.

Vocative Case

16. 1. The Vocative of masculine nouns ending in consonants is in **-e**. This termination is added as a rule to the form with the definite article. In a few cases **-e** is added to the form without the article :

Fiule ! Son !
Copilule ! Child ! **Copile !** Child !

Dumnezeule ! God !	
Domnule ! Sir !	**Doamne !** (in prayers) Lord !
Dracule ! Devil !	**Drace !** Devil !

16. 2. If the Vocative has an attribute, the Vocative form is identical with the Nominative :

Fiul meu !	My son !
Iubiţi copii !	Beloved children !
Oameni buni !	Good people !

16. 3. Sometimes, when the adjective precedes the noun, both adjective and noun take the Vocative termination :

Scumpe prietene ! (scumpe prieten !)	Dear friend !
Iubite frate !	Beloved brother !
Dragă amice !	Dear friend !
Stimate domnule ! (stimate domn !)	Dear Sir ! (Esteemed Sir !)
Înalte Stăpâne !	My Lord ! (ecclesiastical).

16. 4. In the Vocative case, feminine nouns in **-a** have the termination **-ă** or **-o**. The latter has a restricted use, and is applied also to feminine adjectives used as nouns, as well as to some masculine nouns in **-a**, **-ea** :

Mamă !	Mother !
Soro !	Sister !
Babă ! Babo !	Old woman !
Bunică ! Bunico !	Grandmother !
Ileană ! Ileano !	Helen !
Scumpo ! (*f.*)	Dear !
Iubito ! (*f.*)	Beloved !
Popo !	Priest ! (used contemptuously).
Badeo !	Brother !

16. 5. The Vocative is often used in colloquial speech with the particles **măi** (for *masc.*), **bre** (for *masc.*), *fa* (for *fem.*), **hăi** (*masc.*, *fem.*). This construction is considered familiar, but not polite. The interjection **măi** can be used also with feminines :

Măi frate !	Hello, brother !
Bre omule !	Man !
Fa muiere !	Woman !
Măi muiere !	Woman !

Strigătură satirică :

Nu te uita, lele hăi,
Că mi-s cioarecii cam răi,
C'am acasă două oi
Şi mi-oi face alţii noi !

Satiric verse :

Don't look at me, young woman,
That my woollen trousers are worn out,
Because I have at home two sheep
And I will make myself some other new ones.

The Adjective

17. 1. The Modifying Adjective is normally placed after the noun and agrees with the noun in gender, number and case :

Un bătrân *înţelept.*	A wise old man.
O casă *bătrânească, moştenită* **din moşi strămoşi, şi slugi** *îmbătrânite* **în curte,** *iubitoare* **şi** *credincioase.* **(I. Al. Brătescu-Voineşti, „Moartea lui Castor".)**	An old house, handed down from father to son, and servants grown old in the service of the household, loving and faithful.
Calea *dreaptă* **e cea mai scurtă.**	The right way is the shortest.
Bărbat *bun* **şi usturoi** *dulce* **nu se poate.**	A good man (husband) and sweet garlic do not exist.

The attribute may be placed before the noun, when the quality expressed is especially stressed; in this case the adjective takes the article:

Sărmanul **bătrân.**	The poor old man.
Răpăusatul **meu tată.**	My late father.
Nu judecaţi după înfăţişare, ci judecaţi după *dreaptă* **judecată.** (Ioan, vii. 24.)	Judge not according to appearance, but judge righteous judgement. (John vii. 24.)

If an adjective refers to several nouns of different gender it takes the masculine form:

În satul acela trăiau un om şi o femeie, *bătrâni* **şi** *săraci.*	In that village were living a man and a woman, old and poor.

The Rumanian language avoids such constructions however, or even makes the agreement with the nearer noun:

Bărbaţii şi femeile *prezente* **au ascultat conferinţa.**	The men and women present listened to the lecture.
Codrii şi văile *pline* **de căprioare.**	Woods and valleys full of roes.

An adjective, used as an adverb, followed by another adjective or by a supine (**de**—past participle) does not agree with the noun:

O poziţie *puternic* **fortificată.**	A strongly fortified position.
Dealuri *greu* **de arat** (also: **grele**).	Hills difficult to plough.
Probleme *uşor* **de rezolvat.**	Problems easily to be solved.

17. 2. The same rules of agreement (cp. 17. 1) apply to the **Predicative Adjective:**

Tatăl şi mama mea vor fi *prezenţi* **la serbare.**	My father and mother will be present at the festival.
Soru-sa şi frate-său îmi sunt *prieteni.*	His sister and brother are friends of mine.

Studenţii şi studentele sunt *obligaţi* să fie *prezenţi* la cursuri.	Men and women students are compelled to attend the lectures.
Camera era *largă* de trei metri şi *lungă* de doi metri.	The room was three metres wide and two metres long.

Every adjective with the help of an article can be used as a noun (cp. 11. 10):

Adj.	Un bărbat *voinic.*	A strong man.
	O femeie *voinică.*	A strong woman.
Noun.	*Voinicul* acesta nu se teme de nimic.	This brave man is not afraid of anything.
Adj.	Câmpul este *verde.*	The field is green.
	Florile sunt *galbene.*	The flowers are yellow.
Noun.	Îmi place mai bine *verdele* decât *galbenul.*	I prefer green to yellow.
	Bogatul greşeşte şi *săracul* îţi cere iertare.	The rich man makes mistakes and the poor asks for pardon.

17. 3. The **Adverb** normally follows the verb which it qualifies:

Am ajuns *târziu* la gară.	I arrived late at the station.
Soarele răsare *dimineața* şi apune *seara.*	The sun rises in the morning and sets in the evening.
Să fii în gară *cel mai târziu* la ora opt.	Be at the station by eight o'clock, at the latest.
L-am rugat să vie *la mine.*	I begged him to come to me.
I-am spus *sincer* pentru ce am venit.	I told him sincerely why I had come.
A intrat *pe furiș* în grădină, a sărit *repede* peste gard şi a ajuns în faţa casei.	Stealthily he entered the garden, leapt quickly over the fence, and arrived at the front of the house.
Eu nu vorbesc *grecește.*	I do not speak Greek.
Cine n'are cal să urce *pe jos la deal.*	He who has no horse may walk up the hill on foot.

Note.—It is, however, the meaning which the speaker wants to convey which fixes the position of the adverb :

Un autor *bine* cunoscut.	A well-known author.
Cine se scoală de dimineaţă *departe* ajunge.	He who rises early goes far.
***La început* era cuvântul.**	In the beginning was the word.
Munţii, *în depărtare*, păreau că ard în flăcări.	The mountains, far away, seemed to be burning into flames.

The Pronoun

18. 1. The Personal Pronouns (see 5. 1) are used with the verb only when they need to be emphasized :

***Noi* vrem pământ**	We want land.
***Eu* însă nu puteam uita înfruntul ce-mi făcuse. (C. Negruzzi, „Cum am învăţat româneşte".)**	But I could not forget the outrage he had done me.

As a rule, however, the verb is used without a pronoun :

***Am fost* aseară la teatru.**	I was at the theatre last night.
Nu mi-*ai scris* demult.	You haven't written to me for a long time.
Nu ştiu când *ne vom mai întâlni*.	I don't know when we will meet again.
Seara *am citit* tatălui meu tot cântul întâi din moartea lui Avel. (C. Negruzzi, *ibid.*)	In the evening I read to my father the whole of the first Canto of "The Death of Abel."

18. 2. The personal pronouns of the first and second person singular (**eu, tu**) cannot be used in comparison or after a preposition; the accusative forms (**mine, tine**) are used instead:

Fratele meu era mai mare *decât mine* **cu doi ani.**	My brother was two years older than I.
Dela tine **a venit direct** *la mine.*	From you he came direct to me.

18. 3. The conjunct pronoun as object immediately precedes the verb. The stressed pronoun as object precedes the conjunct or follows after the verb; it is, however, suffixed to imperative forms:

L-am **văzut în oraş.**	I saw him in the town.
Îi **întâlnesc, în fiecare zi, la aceeaş oră.**	I meet them every day at the same hour.
I-am **găsit în grădină.**	I found them in the garden.
Le-am **dat bună ziua.**	I bade them good day.
Vă voi **spune când vom pleca de-acasă.**	I shall tell you when we leave home.
Pe tine te lăudăm.	Thee we praise.
Dă-ne nouă astăzi.	Give us this day.

18. 4. The conjunct pronoun as object is used to repeat the direct or indirect object of the sentence:

Pe aceşti oameni *i-am* **mai văzut undeva.**	I have seen these people somewhere else.
Or:	
Am mai văzut undeva pe aceşti oameni.	I have seen these people somewhere else.
Copiilor nu *le* **lipseşte nimic.**	The children do not lack anything.
Or:	
Nu lipseşte nimic copiilor.	The children do not lack anything.
Pe frate-său nu *l-am* **văzut, dar am înţâlnit-***o* **pe soră-sa şi** *i-am* **dat cartea.**	I did not see his brother, but I met his sister and I gave her the book.

— **Pentru aceea obştia** *ne-a* **trimis pe noi să-ţi spunem că norodul nu te vrea, nici te iubeşte şi măria Ta să te întorci înapoi. . . .**	" For that reason the community has sent us to tell you that the people do not want you, do not love you, and that Your Majesty must return. . . ."
— **Dacă voi nu mă vreţi, eu vă vreau, dacă voi nu mă iubiţi, eu** *vă* **iubesc pe voi. . . . (C. Negruzzi, „Alexandru Lăpuşneanu".)**	" If (though) you do not want me, I want you, if (though) you do not love me, I love you. . . ."

The feminine pronoun as object in the third person singular is added as a suffix to the past participle of the compound verbal form :

Pe Maria o văd plimbându-se în grădină, pe Ileana am *văzut-o* **în piaţă.**	I see Mary walking in the garden, I saw Helen in the market.

Note.—For the syntax of other pronouns see 5. 2—5. 8.

Syntax of the Verb

19. 1. Auxiliary Verbs. The verbs **a avea**, *to have*, **a fi**, *to be*, **a voi**, *to wish*, *will*, are used both as principal verbs and as auxiliaries for the formation of compound tenses. In the latter function, **a avea** has different forms from those of the principal verb for the third person singular and the first and second person plural :

Auxiliary	*Principal Verb*
am fost, I have been, I was,	**am**, I have,
ai fost etc.	**ai** etc.
a fost	**are**
am fost	**avem**
aţi fost	**aveţi**
au fost	**au**

As an auxiliary, **a voi** has different forms from the principal verb **a voi, a vrea**, *to wish, will*:

Auxiliary	*Principal Verb*
voi (voiu) merge, I will go, I shall go, I should go,	**voiesc** or **vreau**, I will, I wish, etc.
vei merge etc.	**voieşti** ,, **vreai**
va merge	**voieşte** ,, **vrea**
vom merge	**voim** ,, **vrem**
veţi merge	**voiţi** ,, **vreţi**
vor merge	**voiesc (vor)** ,, **vreau**

19. 2. The Indicative Mood is the mood expressing an action or a situation conceived as a fact:

A sosit.	He has arrived.
A plecat?	Has he gone?
Îmi *pare* **bine că** *ești* **sănătos.**	I am glad you are in good health.
Cine *sapă* **groapa altuia** *cade* **singur într'ânsa.**	Whoever digs a grave for another falls in himself.

19. 3. a) The Subjunctive Mood expresses an action conceived as possible. It is preceded by the particle **să**:

Să mergem **ori să nu mergem?**	Should we go or not?
Să fie **oare posibil?**	Is it possible?
Să fi fost **pela trei după miezul nopţii.**	It might have been about three o'clock in the morning.
Să fi **tot mers cinci chilometri.**	He might have gone 5 km. altogether.

b) The subjunctive is used in main clauses to express a wish (optative-subjunctive) or even an order (imperative-subjunctive):

Să tot trăieşti, să nu mai mori! (I. Creangă.)	(You would like) ever to live, never to die.
Să trăieşti!	May you live (long)!
Să-ţi fie **de bine!**	Good luck to you!
Dumnezeu *să te păzească*!	God protect you!
Dumnezeu *să-l ierte*!	God forgive him!
Să pleci **de-aici!**	Get out of this!
. . . Începură a striga :	. . . They started to shout :
— *Să micşoreze* **dăjdiile!**	" Let him lower the taxes! "
— *Să* **nu ne** *zăpciască*!	" Don't let him oppress us! "
— *Să* **nu ne mai** *împlinească*!	" Don't let him punish us! "
— *Să* **nu ne mai** *jefuiască*!	" Don't allow him to rob us any longer! "
. . . — Moţoc *să moară*!	. . . " Let Moţoc die! "
— Capul lui Moţoc vrem!	" We want Moţoc's head! "

(C. Negruzzi, „Alexandru Lăpuşneanu".)

c) The subjunctive can have future meaning in exclamative clauses :

Să vezi **ce am să fac!**	You will see what I will do!
Să fi văzut **cum fugiau Turcii!**	You should have seen how the Turks fled!
Să-i fi plătit **şi nu-ţi făcea acest serviciu!**	(Even) if you had paid him, he would not have done you this service.

d) The subjunctive with the auxiliary **a avea** forms the future :

Am să plec **la ţară.**	I shall leave for the country.
O să vedeţi **ce** *are să se întâmple* **mâine.**	You will see what will happen to-morrow.

e) In the third person, the subjunctive can be used without the particle să in the imperative sense :

Meargă **unde vrea!**	Let him go where he pleases!
Ducă-se **pe pustii!**	Let him go to the wilds! (i.e. the devil).

f) The subjunctive also expresses a concession:

(*Să*) *fie pâinea* cât de rea, tot mai bine'n ţara mea.	However bad the bread may be, it tastes better in one's own land (than in exile).
Nu voi spune măcar *să mă omori* (=*să mă omori* şi nu-ţi spun).	I will not tell it, even though you should kill me.

g) The subjunctive also expresses a possibility, whose realization was very near:

Era *să cad*.	I almost fell.
Eram (era) *să vă spun*.	I was going to tell you.

h) A feature of Rumanian syntax is the use of the subjunctive mood, when English and other western languages use the infinitive, or other grammatical forms:

Am hotărît *să părăsim* ţara.	We decided to leave the country.
Vreau *să mai văd* şi altă lume.	I wish to see other people too.
Trebuie *să plecaţi*, căci e târziu.	You must go, for it is late.
Plecă fără *să-şi ia* ziua bună.	He went without saying good-bye.

i) **The Infinitive**, in constructions like the above, is exceptional, although it is sometimes used by the best authors for a stylistic effect and also in official correspondence:

Lesne a ierta, dar anevoie a uita.	It is easy to forgive, but difficult to forget.
A binevoit *a-i da* de ştire. **A binevoit *să-i dea* de ştire.**	He was so good as to inform him.
Ştiu lucra.	I know how to work.
Nu ştie (*a*) *vorbi*. **Nu ştie *să vorbească*.**	He does not know how to talk.
Începu a cânta.	He started to sing.
A început *a-mi spune*. **A început *să-mi spuie*.**	He began to tell me.

Până *a nu-l fi* întâlnit nu-l cunoşteam.	I did not know him, until I met him.
Îmi vine a plânge.	I am on the point of crying.
Cine nu ştie *a asculta*, nu va ştie *să poruncească.*	He who does not know to obey, will not know how to command.
Şi cu adevărat, era groază *a privi* această scenă sângeroasă. (C. Negruzzi, „Alexandru Lăpuşneanu".)	And truly it was terrifying to look at this bloody scene.
Se arătă a fi mulţumit.	He showed himself to be satisfied.
Ei puseră şarpele într'un putinei şi aşa nu lipsiau *a-l culca* între dânşii. (P. Ispirescu, „Împăratul şerpilor".)	They put the serpent in a barrel and so they always put him to bed between them.

j) The infinitive without **a** is used preferably after the verbs **a putea**, *to be able*; **a avea**, *to have*; **a şti**, *to know*; after **a începe**, *to begin*; **a învăţa**, *to learn*; **a crede**, *to believe*, and after other verbs, the infinitive is used with **a**:

Nu pot *merge.*	I cannot go.
Îţi pot *spune.*	I can tell you.

Or:

Pot să-ţi spun.	I can tell you
În deşert se învârtia în patul durerii, căci nu putea *afla* răgaz. (C. Negruzzi, „Alexandru Lăpuşneanu".)	In vain he tossed on his bed of suffering, and he could not find peace.

But:

. . . Înfrăţirea dorită de strămoşii noştri, pe care ei n'au putut *s'o facă.* (I. Creangă, „Moş Ion Roată şi Unirea".)	. . . The brotherhood desired by our forefathers, which they were not able to realize.

N'am cu cine *sta* **de vorbă.**	I have no one to talk to.
N'am pe cine *întreba.*	I have nobody to ask.
Văd că ai ce *lucra.*	I see you have work (to do).
N'am când *scrie* **o scrisoare.**	I have not time to write a a letter.
Când aveam şase ani am învăţat *a ceti.*	At the age of six years I learned to read.
A început *a vorbi.*	He began to talk.
S'a apucat să înveţe *a cânta.*	He began to learn singing.

19. 4. a) The Optative-Conditional is the mood expressing a wish or a hypothetical condition:

Aş mânca ceva.	I should (like to) eat something.
Am vrea **să trăim la ţară.**	We should like to live in the country.
Ar fi vrut **să sboare ca să ajungă mai repede acasă.**	They would have liked to fly to get home more quickly.
Dare-ar **Dumnezeu să ajungă cu bine!**	May God allow (help) him to arrive safely!
Arză-te-ar **focul om drag;**	May the fire burn you, beloved man;
De mână mă duci la iad! (Cântec popular.)	You are leading me by the hand to hell! (Folk-song.)

b) In a conditional sentence the Optative-Conditional is used in the main clause, as well as in the conditional clause itself:

Aş merge **dacă** *aş putea.*	I would go, if I could.
Dacă *ai vrea* **să mă ajuţi,** *ţi-aş fi* **recunoscător.**	If you would like to help me, I should be grateful to you.
Nu *ţi-aş spune* **adevărul, dacă** *aş şti* **că te superi.**	I should not tell you the truth, if I knew that it would anger you.
Dacă *aş fi* **avut timp,** *aş fi* **venit mai adesea.**	If I had had time, I should have come more often.

Constructions like the following are also possible, where the condition is expressed in the indicative:

Dacă *vrei*, ai putea să mă ajuţi.	If you like, you could help me.
Aş vrea să te ajut, dacă *pot*.	I would like to help you, if I can (could).

c) The perfect Optative-Conditional in conditional sentences can be replaced by the imperfect:

De (dacă) *veniai* mai de vreme, mă *găsiai* acasă= dacă *ai fi venit* mai de vreme, *m'ai fi găsit* acasă.	If you had come earlier, you would have found me at home.
Dacă-ţi *spuneam*, nu mă *credeai*.	If I had told you, you would not have believed me.

The perfect Optative-Conditional may be replaced by the imperfect in the conditional clause, although it is used in the main clause:

Dacă-mi *spuneai* că nu vii, nu te-aş fi aşteptat.	If you had told me that you weren't coming, I would not have waited for you.
Dacă *veniai* mai de vreme, l-ai fi întâlnit.	If you had come earlier, you would have met him.

d) The Optative-Conditional is used also to express an action whose fulfilment is not certain:

Se spune că *ar avea* mulţi bani.	It is said that he has a lot of money.
S'a zvonit că *ar fi intrat* Turcii în ţară.	It was rumoured that the Turks had entered the country.

e) The Optative-Conditional is used to express a comparison in clauses introduced by: **parcă, caşicând, caşicum,** *as if*:

Cel înţelept trăieşte caşicând *ar avea* să moară în clipă următoare.	The wise man lives as if he were to die in the next moment.
Mi-aduc aminte de el, parcă *l-aş vedea* înaintea ochilor.	I remember him, as if I saw him before my eyes.

19. 5. The Infinitive is compound of the particle **a**, *to*, and the stem of the old infinitive in **-re**. The infinitive forms in **-re** are used as feminine verbal nouns :

Infinitive	*Verbal Noun*
a mânca, to eat	**mâncare**, food
a putea, to be able	**putere**, power
a creşte, to grow	**creştere**, growth
a vorbi, to speak	**vorbire**, speech
a coborî, to descend	**coborîre**, descent

N'are poftă de mâncare.	He has no appetite for food.
A ieşit la plimbare.	He went for a walk.

The use of the infinitive is restricted in Rumanian because it has been replaced by the subjunctive construction (see 19. 3 h, i, j).

The infinitive is used after the prepositions : **de**, *of* ; **spre**, *in order that* ; **pentru**, *for* ; **până**, *until* ; **înainte de**, *before* ; **fără**, *without* :

Arta *de a vorbi.*	The art of speaking.
Plăcerea *de a asculta.*	The pleasure of listening.
Gândeşte înainte *de a vorbi.*	Think before you speak.
Departe *de a mă lămuri.*	Far from enlightening me.
Până *a nu-mi spune*, **nu ştiam nimic.**	Until you told me, I knew nothing.
Citeşte acest studiu, pentru *a te deprinde* **cu stilul concis.**	Read this study, to accustom yourself to concise style.

19. 6. The Present Participle in **-tor** (*m.*), **-toare** (*f.*), can be used as an adjective and also as a noun (*nomen agentis*) :

a **lucra**, to work ; **lucrător** (*m.*), **lucrătoare** (*f.*), worker, working.

Lucrătorii **şi** *lucrătoarele* **din fabrici.**	The men and women factory workers.
Zi *lucrătoare.*	Working day.

a tăia, to cut ; **tăietor** (*m.*), **tăietoare** (*f.*), cutter, cutting.

Tăietorii **de lemne.**	The wood-cutters.

a strânge, to gather, to hoard ; **strângător** (*m.*), **strângătoare** (*f.*), gathering, he, she who gathers.

Un om *strângător.*	A man careful (with money).

a iubi, to love ; **iubitor** (*m.*), **iubitoare** (*f.*), he, she who loves.

Iubitorii **de dreptate.**	Those who love justice.
Copiii *iubitori* **de adevăr.**	The truth-loving children.

19. 7. a) The Gerund in **-nd** expresses a continuous action in the present or in the past. It has always an active sense and can be used with every person without changing its form for number or gender. It has also the function of a present participle :

Pofta vine *mâncând.*	Appetite comes with eating.
L-am auzit *urcând* **scările.**	I heard him going upstairs.
Spunându-ţi **aceasta, te las cu bine.**	Saying this to you, I bid you good-bye.
Am văzut lumea *alergând* **din toate părţile.**	I saw people running from all directions.
Mă întrebam şi nu-mi puteam răspunde, ce ne despărţise aşa şi pentruce nu veniam să trăim cu toţii împreună, cu mama, *îngrijind-o, ajutând-o.* **(Al. Brătescu-Voineşti, ,,Moartea lui Castor".)**	I was asking myself and I was unable to find an answer, what had separated us in such a way that we did not all come to live together with our mother, taking care of her and helping her.
După aceasta *salutând* **pe Doamna Ruxandra de regentă în vremea minorităţii fiului ei, proclamară pe Bogdan de Domn. (C. Negruzzi, ,,Alexandru Lăpuşneanu".)**	Afterwards, greeting the Princess Ruxandra as Regent, during the minority of her son, they proclaimed Bogdan as Prince.

Care cu poveri de muncă	Carts loaded with labour's burden
Vin încet şi *scârţiind* ;	Come, slowly and creaking ;
Turmele s'aud *mugind*	The flocks can be heard lowing
Şi flăcăii vin pe luncă	And the lads come singing
Hăulind.	through the meadow.
(G. Coşbuc, „Noapte de vară".)	

Note.—The negation of the gerund form is the prefix **ne** :

Ne băgând de seamă a călcat pe un şarpe.	He trod on a snake because he was inattentive.
Ne mai fiind bolnav părăsi patul.	Being no longer ill he got up.
Vrând-nevrând.	Willy-nilly.

b) The Gerund is used instead of the present adjectival participle in **-tor, -toare**, when this latter has acquired another sense. This use, however, has a poetical touch and is restricted to the literary language :

Apele mereu *crescânde.*	The steadily rising waters.
Crescător.	Breeder (e.g. of livestock).
Crescând.	Growing, rising.
Lebeda *murindă* (*muribundă*).	The dying swan.
Muritor.	Mortal.
Ruxandra ieşi *tremurândă* **şi galbenă, şi rezemându-se de perete (zise) . . . (C. Negruzzi, „Alex. Lăp.".)**	Ruxandra came out, trembling and pale and leaning on the wall (said) . . .

c) The Gerund of a reflexive verb has the pronoun suffixed to it :

Văzându-se **atacaţi din toate părţile.**	Seeing themselves attacked from all sides.
Urcându-ne **pe o scară, am ajuns în pod.**	By climbing up a ladder, we reached the attic.

d) The future of **a fi**, *to be*, with the Gerund expresses an incertitude, sometimes being equivalent to the future perfect in English :

Vei fi *dorind* **dta să pleci, dar nu se poate.**	You will want to leave, but it is impossible.
Va fi *făcând* **el multe cereri, până va fi ascultat.**	He will have made many demands, before he is heard (until he will be heard).
Unde o fi *fiind* **el acum ?**	Where is he now ?
Ce va fi *gândind* **?**	What will he be thinking ?

e) The Gerund is used with the subjunctive, the conditional and the infinitive. These constructions, however, are seldom heard and seem awkward :

Să fi *crezând* **el una ca aceasta ?**	Could he believe such a thing ?
Mi s'a spus că ar fi *plângând* **toată ziua.**	It was told me he would weep all day.
Crede a fi *ştiind* **toate.**	He thinks he knows everything.
. . . un leneş, care nu credem *să mai* **fi** *având* **păreche în lume . . . (I. Creangă, „Povestea unui om leneş".)**	. . . a lazy man who, we believe, has no equal in the world . . .

f) The sentence use of the Rumanian Gerund does not always conform with the use of the English Gerund ; e.g. it cannot function as a noun :

Understanding is loving.	**A înţelege înseamnă a iubi.**
After seeing the play, we went home.	**Dupăce am văzut piesa, am mers acasă.**
A reading-room.	**O sală de lectură.**
The art of writing letters.	**Arta de a scrie scrisori.**
I did not know of his leaving the town.	**N'am ştiut că el părăseşte oraşul.**

The habit of speaking.	**Obiceiul de a vorbi.**
Worn out by long watching, the soldier fell asleep.	**Istovit de veghe lungă, soldatul adormi.**

19. 8. a) The Past Participle always forms the perfect tense with the help of the auxiliary **a avea**, *to have.* The past participle is used also as an adjective which agrees in number and gender with its noun :

Aţi *văzut* **piesa** *jucată* **aseară la Teatrul Naţional ?**	Did you see the play at the National Theatre (acted) last night ?
Copiii nu sunt *întrebaţi* **ce părere au.**	Children are not asked their opinion.

b) Reflexive verbs have no reflexive pronoun in past participle forms used attributively :

	Întors **acasă.**	Back home.
But :	**S'a întors acasă.**	He returned home.
	Deşteptat **din somn.**	Awakened from sleep.
But :	**S'a deşteptat din somn.**	He woke up.

c) After some verbs the past participle has the meaning of the past infinitive passive :

Ea se lăsă *sărutată.*	She allowed herself to be kissed.
Ea se lăsă a fi (să fie) *sărutată.*	
Chestiunea trebuie *înţeleasă.*	The question must be understood.

d) Some adverbial expressions are formed with the help of the past participle feminine plural preceded by a preposition :

Pe *nerăsuflate.*	Breathlessly.
Din *auzite.*	From hearsay.

19. 9. The invariable masculine past participle preceded by the prepositions **de**, *of*, **la**, *to*, **pe**, *on*, **din**, *from*, etc., has the force of a noun and is called a *Supine* :

Bun *de mâncat.*	Good to be eaten.
A sfârşit *de vorbit.*	He finished speaking.
Fată *de măritat* **şi flăcău** *de însurat.*	A marriageable girl and a marriageable lad.
De urat **am mai ura, dar ni-i că vom însera.**	As far as wishing goes we would wish more, but we are afraid that night will fall. (*From a New Year carol.*)
De văzut **am văzut, dar nimic n'am priceput.**	As far as seeing is concerned, I did see but I understood nothing.
Frumos *la văzut* **şi plăcut** *la auzit.*	Pretty to see and pleasing to hear.
A mers *la arat.*	He went to plough.
S'a pus *pe cetit.*	He has settled down to reading.
Trăieşte *din cerşit.*	He lives by begging.
Umblă *după miluit.*	He is looking for pity (alms).
A fost plătit *pentru tăiat* **lemne.**	He was paid for cutting wood.
Am cam întârziat . . . trebuia să plec mai de vreme, dar în sfârşit . . . *de aşteptat*, **mă aşteaptă. . . . (I. L. Caragiale, „La Hanul lui Mânjoală".)**	I am a little late . . . I ought to have left sooner, but I am sure they will be waiting for me. . . .

Note.—The English infinitive construction is often translated by a Rumanian supine :

I have nothing to read.	**N'am nimic** *de cetit.*
What have you to do to-day ?	**Ce ai** *de făcut* **azi ?**

19. 10. a) The Present Tense, apart from its regular use in expressing a present action, is also used as a historic tense in dramatically narrative prose :

Călătorul străin, flămând cum era, nemai aşteptând multă poftire, *se aşează* jos lângă cei doi şi *încep* a mânca cu toţii la pâne goală şi a bea apă rece din fântână, căci altă udătură nu aveau. Şi *mănâncă* ei launloc tustrei, şi *mănâncă*, până ce *gătesc* de mâncat toate cele cinci pâni, de par'că n'au fost. (I. Creangă, „Cinci pâni".)	The foreign traveller, hungry as he was, without waiting for any further invitation seats himself beside the other two and all three begin to eat dry bread and to drink cold water from the well, because they had had no other drink. They eat and eat all three together until they finish eating the five loaves as if there had never been any.
Calul *se scoală* scuturându-şi capul ca de buimăceală ; *se ridică* în două picioare, *se smuceşte* într'o parte şi mă *trânteşte* în partea ailalta ; pe urmă o *ia* la goană pe câmp ca de streche şi *piere'n* întunerec. (I. L. Caragiale, „La Hanul lui Mânjoală".)	The horse rises shaking his head as if he were giddy. He raises himself on two feet, he springs to one side and flings me down on the other ; then he makes off across the field, as if bitten by the horse-fly, and disappears in the darkness.

b) As in English, the present tense may be used with a future sense :

***Plec* mâine la Bucureşti.**	I am leaving to-morrow for Bucharest.
Să vii îndată ce-ţi *scriu*.	Come as soon as I write you.

c) The present tense expresses *the English simple* and *continuous present* tenses, as well as *the English present perfect* :

***Văd* că nu *vii*.**	*I see* you *are* not *coming*.
***Merg* în oraş.**	I *am going* into the town.

Trăiesc aici de trei ani.	I *have lived* here for three years.

19. 11. The Imperfect Tense expresses an unfinished or repeated action in the past; it is translated by the continuous past, but sometimes by the simple past:

Se însera când am ajuns acasă.	It was growing dark when I arrived home.
Când *eram* copil, *mergeam* la biserică în fiecare Duminică.	When I was a child, I used to go to church every Sunday.
Cocoana Marghioala *era* frumoasă, voinică, şi oacheşe, *ştiam* . . . *Eram* tânăr, curăţel şi obraznic. (I. L. Caragiale, „La Hanul lui Mânjoală".)	Mrs. Marghioala was beautiful, buxom and dark, I knew . . . I was young, smart and impudent.
La 1857, pe când *se fierbea* Unirea în Iaşi, boierii moldoveni liberali, ca de-alde Costache Hurmuzache, Mihai Kogălniceanu şi alţii, au găsit cu cale să cheme la Adunare şi câţiva ţărani fruntaşi. (I. Creangă, „Moş Ion Roată şi Unirea".)	In 1857, when the Union was brewing in Jassy, the liberal Moldavian boyars, like C. H., M. K. and others, thought fit to call to the Assembly some of the leading peasants as well.
Nenorocitul Domn *se svârcolia* în spasmele agoniei; spume *făcea* la gură, dinţii îi *scrâşniau* şi ochii săi sângeraţi se holbaseră; o sudoare îngheţată, tristă a morţii prevestitoare, *ieşia* ca nişte nasturi pe obrazul lui. (C. Negruzzi, „Alexandru Lăpuşneanu".)	The unhappy Prince writhed in spasms of agony; he was foaming at the mouth, his teeth grinding, his bloodshot eyes were staring; a cold perspiration, the sad forerunner of death, was rising in beads on his brow.

19. 12. The Perfect Tense (compound past) expresses a past action from the point of view of the present time;

the **Preterite** (aorist, simple past) expresses a past action which has no relation with the present. The preterite is used as the historic tense. In some regions the preterite is used exclusively.

The use of the preterite or of the perfect is determined by regional and by stylistic factors. In the north of the country (in Moldavia) (see Borta Vântului, p. 224) the preterite is less used than in the south (in Walachia) (see Împăratul şerpilor, p. 226), where in some parts (in Oltenia or Little Walachia) the perfect is not used at all:

Când *sosi* Alexandru Vodă, sfânta slujbă începuse şi boierii erau toţi adunaţi. . . .	When the Prince Alexander arrived the Sacred Liturgy had begun, and the boyars were all assembled. . . .
Apropiindu-se de Alexandru Vodă, boierii *se închinară* până la pământ, fără a-i săruta poala după obicei.	Drawing near to Prince Alexander they bowed down to the ground, without kissing the hem of his garment according to custom.
— Bine *aţi venit*, boieri, *zise* acesta silindu-se a zâmbi.	" Welcome, boyars," he said, forcing himself to smile.
— Să fii Măria Ta sănătos, *răspunseră* boierii.	" Good health to Your Highness," replied the boyars.
— *Am auzit*, urmă Alexandru, de bântuirile ţării şi *am venit* s'o mântuim ; ştim că ţara m'aşteaptă cu bucurie. (C. Negruzzi, „Alexandru Lăpuşneanu".)	" I have heard," continued Alexander, " of the misfortunes of the country and I came to save it ; I know that the country awaits me with joy."

Din Moldova	*From Moldavia*
Era un om sărac, sărac şi avea o mulţime de copii. Acu era în vremea foametei şi el *a muncit* o săptămână pe un căuş de grăunţe. Apoi *s'a dus* la râşniţă cu	(Once) there was a poor, poor man, and he had a crowd of children. Now it was in time of famine and he worked for a week on a scoop full of grain. Then

ele. Dupăce *le-a râşnit, a ieşit* afară cu căuşul cu făină şi *s'a pornit* o furtună mare şi *i-a luat* toată făina din căuş. Da el straşnic *s'a mâniat*. (M. Eminescu, „Borta Vântului".)	he went with it to the hand-mill. After he had ground it, he went outside with the scoop full of flour, and there arose a great storm of wind and took all his flour from the scoop. And he was furiously angry.
Din Muntenia	*From Walachia*
Deci într'o dimineaţă, *porniră* amândoi pentru acest sfârşit : atât de mare era dorul lor să aibă un copil. *Găsiră* un pui micuţ de şarpe, îl *luară*, îl *aduseră* acasă, îl *puseră* într'o ţeavă de trestie şi îl *culcară* între dânşii. . . . Şarpele *crescu* până ce într'o zi *crepă* ţeava. Îl *puseră* într'un mosor. (P. Ispirescu, „Împăratul şerpilor".)	So one morning they both set out with this object in view: so great was their desire to have a child. They found a wee baby snake, took it, brought it home, placed it in a hollow reed and put it to bed between them. . . . The serpent grew until one day the reed burst. They put it into a hollow elder-branch (used as a bobbin).

Note 1.—The perfect is always formed with the help of the auxiliary **a avea**, *to have*. The past participle of a verb with the auxiliary **a fi**, *to be*, expresses the result of an action :

Mama *e dusă* **de acasă.**	Mother is away from home.
Copiii *sunt plecaţi* **la şcoală.**	The children have gone to (are at) the school.

Note 2.—The English past tense, when it expresses the duration in the present of an action which began in the past, is translated in Rumanian with a present (cp. 19. 10 **c**) :

How long *have you been* in London ?	**De când** *sunteţi* **în Londra ?**
I have been ill now for three days.	*Sunt* **bolnav de trei zile.**

19. 13. a) The Future Tense formed with the auxiliary **a voi**, *to will*, expresses determination; the future formed with the auxiliary **a avea**, *to have*, and the subjunctive expresses futurity:

voi face, I will do **am să merg**, I shall go

b) The Future Perfect corresponds to the English Future Perfect; it expresses an action which takes place before a future action:

Eu voi fi ajuns, **când tu** *vei porni* **de-acasă.**	I shall have arrived, when you leave home.

c) The Future Perfect with the auxiliary **voi** (**o**), *I will*, sometimes expresses a doubt or a possibility:

O fi venit **oare?**	Will he have arrived?
Va fi primit **scrisoarea mea?**	Will he have received my letter?
I-o fi spus, **ceea ce l-am rugat să-i spuie?**	Will he have said what I told him to say?
Eu voi fi rămas **să capăt vreo laviţă lângă cuptor. (I. L. Caragiale, „La Hanul lui Mânjoală".)**	I shall be left to get (to sleep on) a wooden bench near the fireplace.

19. 14. The Pluperfect expresses an action fulfilled before another past action. In colloquial speech it is often replaced by the perfect:

Se făcuse **ziua când am ajuns în sat.**	Daylight had dawned when we arrived in the village.
I-am fost scris **să vie, dar n'a primit scrisoarea.**	I had written him to come, but he did not get the letter.
Frate-său a dat să vorbească, dar n'a putut — *amuţise*. **(I. L. Caragiale, „La Hanul lui Mânjoală".)**	His brother tried to speak, but could not—he had become dumb.

Numele acesta îi aduse aminte de toate cele ce ***se petrecuseră.*** **(C. Negruzzi, „Alexandru Lăpuşneanu“.)** — This name reminded him of all that had happened.

N'a fost în stare să-mi spuie unde ***l-a văzut.*** — He was unable to tell me where he had seen him.

19. 15. When the verb of the main clause is in the past tense, and the verb of the dependent clause expresses an action which is still going on, the verb of the dependent clause has the present form :

Am auzit că ***se găseşte*** **în oraş şi am mers să-l văd.** — I heard that he was in the town, and I went to see him.

Pânăce nu mi-a spus nu ştiam că mama ***e bolnavă.*** — Until he told me, I did not know that my mother was ill.

Mi-a părut bine ***că-l întâlnesc.*** — I was glad to meet him.

Îl întrebă unde ***pleacă.*** — He asked me where he was going.

Se întoarse să vadă cine ***vorbeşte.*** — He turned round to see who was speaking.

When, however, both actions are accomplished, from the point of view of the speaker, in the past, the perfect is used in the main as well as in the dependent clause :

Am auzit că ***a sosit*** **în oraş şi am mers să-l văd.** — I heard that he had arrived in the town, and I went to see him.

Mi-a părut bine că l-am întâlnit. — I was glad that I had met him.

Se întoarse să vadă cine ***a vorbit*** **(=vorbise).** — He turned to see who had spoken.

20. Adverbial Clauses. The following classification gives a survey of the adverbial clauses in Rumanian :

Type	*Conjunctions*
1. Time.	**când**, when, as; **cât timp**, while, as long as; **de când**, since; **pe când**, as, while; **până când**, until; **înainte de**, before; **îndatăce**, as soon as; **dupăce**, after; **în vreme ce**, while; **până ce**, till, until. Adverbial Clauses of Time are often replaced by constructions with the gerund.
2. Place.	**unde**, where; **de unde**, wherefrom; **oriunde**, wherever; **până unde**, to where; **încotro**, whither.
3. Cause.	**căci, de vreme ce, din cauză că, deoarece, fiindcă, pentrucă**, as, because, for, since.
4. Purpose.	**ca să, să, pentru ca să, pentru a**, that, so that, in order that; **ca să nu**, lest.
5. Result.	**că, de, încât**, so . . . that.
6. Condition.	**dacă, de, când**, if, when; **numai să**, only if; **dacă nu**, unless.
7. Concession.	**cu toate că, deşi, măcar că**, though, although; **chiar dacă**, even if; subjunctive.
8. Comparison and Manner.	**aşa . . . (pre)cum**, so . . . as; **ca şi când**, as if; **cum . . . aşa**, as . . . as; **decât**, than; **ca**, like; **tot atât . . . ca şi**, as . . . as; **întrucât**, inasmuch.

Examples of above:

1. **_Când_ doi se ceartă, al treilea câştigă.**	When two argue, the third gains.
Gândeşte _înainte de_ a vorbi.	Think before speaking.
Bate fierul _până e_ cald.	Strike the iron while it is hot.

Dupăce a trecut războiul, mulţi viteji se găsesc.	When the war is over, many heroes are found.
Că *de când* nu ne-am văzut multă vreme a trecut. (M. Eminescu.)	Because much time has passed since we saw each other.
Iar Iisus *auzind* s'a dus de acolo cu corabia, în loc singuratic, dar *aflând* mulţimile au venit după el, pe jos, din oraşe. (Mat. xiv. 13.)	When Jesus heard of it, he departed thence by ship into a desert place apart: and when the people had heard thereof, they followed him on foot out of the cities. (Matt. xiv. 13.)
2. *Unde* nu-i cap, vai de picioare.	Where there is no head, woe to the feet.
A mers *încotro* a văzut cu ochii.	He went whither he saw with his eyes.
Oriunde vei verge, te voi urma.	Wherever you go, I will follow you.
3. Apoi se roagă să-i dee şi lui ceva de mâncare, *căci* e tare flămând. . . .	Then he begs them to give him also something to eat, because he is very hungry. . . .
Primiţi, vă rog, oameni buni, această mică mulţămită dela mine, *pentrucă* mi-aţi dat de mâncare la nevoie. (I. Creangă, „Cinci pâni".)	Good people, please accept this small recompense from me, because you gave me something to eat in my necessity.
Nu ştiam nimic, *de vreme ce* nu mi-ai scris.	I did not know anything, since you have not written to me.
4. Omul înţelept nu aprinde moara *ca să* scape de soareci.	The wise man does not set fire to the mill in order to get rid of the mice.

A intrat *să*-şi ia rămas bun.	He entered to say good-bye.
Pentru a urmări vânatul, a intrat în pădure.	To hunt the game he entered the wood.
5. A alergat *de* era mort de oboseală.	He ran so hard that he was dead tired.
A crescut atât (aşa) de mare, *că* (*încât*) nu mai încăpea în casă.	He grew so big that he could not enter the house.
6. *Dacă* vei veni de vreme, mă vei găsi acasă.	If you come early, you will find me at home.
De vrei să trăieşti bine şi să aibi tihnă, să te sileşti a fi totdeuna la mijloc de masă şi la colţ de ţară. (C. Negruzzi, ,,Sfaturi bătrâneşti".)	If you wish to live well and to have peace, strive to be always at the middle of the table and in a corner of the country.
Dacă nu-ţi place, nu mânca.	Don't eat, unless you like it.
7. A plecat *deşi* ploua ca din galeată (cu găleata).	He set out although it was raining cats and dogs.
Cu toate că ştia că se apropie sfârşitul, nu înceta să lucreze.	Although he knew that the end was approaching, he did not cease to work.
Chiar dacă ar fi să fim înfrânţi, trebuie să luptăm până la capăt.	Even if we should be defeated, we must fight to the end.
Măcar că a suferit mult, nu şi-a pierdut nădejdea.	Although he suffered much, he did not despair.
Bărbatul să aducă cu sacul, muierea să scoată cu acul, tot se isprăveşte.	The husband may bring (stores) by the sackful, and the wife use them by the thimbleful (lit. needle), but it all goes.

8. S'a luptat *ca* un erou.	He fought like a hero.
Mai bine un dram de noroc. *decât* un car de minte.	Better a grain of luck than a cartload of brains.
Cu cât ai mai mult, *cu atât* doreşti mai multe.	The more you have, the more you want.
Deci, *după cum* se alege neghina şi se arde în foc, *astfel* va fi la sfârşitul veacului. (Mat. xiii. 40.)	As therefore the tares are gathered up and burned with fire; so shall it be in the end of the world. (Matt.xiii. 40.)
Cum îţi vei aşterne, *aşa* vei dormi.	As you make your bed, so you will sleep.
Or:	
Cum îţi aşterni, *aşa* dormi.	
Cum ne aşternem, *aşa* vom dormi.	
Adevăr grăiesc vouă, *întrucât* nu aţi făcut unuia dintre aceşti prea mici, nici mie nu mi-aţi facut. (Mat. xxv. 45.)	Verily I say unto you, inasmuch as ye did it not to one of the least of these, ye did it not to me. (Matt. xxv. 45.)
Ca răbdarea la necaz, nici un leac.	Like patience in trouble, no other remedy (exists). (Patience is the best remedy.)

Predoslovie [1]

Nu sânt vremile sub cârma omului, ci bietul om sub vremi.

. . . .

Puternicul Dumnezeu, cinstite şi iubite cetitorule, să-ţi dăruiască, după aceste cumplite vremi a anilor noştri, cândva şi mai slobode veacuri, întru care, pre lângă alte trebi, să aibi vreme şi cu cetitul cărţilor a face iscusită zăbavă [2]; că nu este alta şi mai frumoasă şi mai de folos în toată viaţa omului zăbavă, decât cetitul cărţilor.

MIRON COSTIN.
(1633-1691.)

[1] Archaic for **precuvântare** or **prefaţă**=preface.
[2] Archaic : retardation, occupation, enjoyment.

READER

CONTENTS

Conversational Phrases

a) În călătorie. On the journey

Bună dimineaţa, domnule Ionescu!	Good morning, Mr. Ionescu!
Bună ziua!	Good day!
Bună seara!	Good evening!
Noapte bună!	Good night!
La revedere!	Good-bye!
Salutare!	Greetings!
Ce mai faceţi? Nu v'am văzut de mult.	How are you? I haven't seen you for a long time.
Mulţumesc, sunt sănătos.	Thank you, I am well.
Când aţi sosit în oraş?	When did you arrive in the town?
Azi dimineaţă la ora zece.	This morning at 10 o'clock.
De unde veniţi?	Where have you come from?
Îmi pare bine că v'am întâlnit.	I am glad to have met you.
Şi mie-mi pare bine.	I am glad too.
Vreţi să stăm puţin de vorbă?	Would you like to have a talk with me?
Când plecaţi la ţară?	When do you leave for the country?
Plec, diseară, dar mă întorc săptămâna viitoare.	I am going to-night, but I return next week.
La ce oră pleacă trenul spre Brăila?	What time does the train leave for Brăila?
Aveţi un accelerat la ora 9 şi treizeci şi un personal la ora 11.	You have a fast train at 9.30 and a slow train at 11.
Când ajungem în Galaţi?	When do we arrive in Galaţi?
Unde schimbăm pentru Constanţa?	Where do we change for Constanţa?
Trebuie să plecaţi neapărat?	Must you really go?

Nu pot amâna căci am scris că sosesc mâine dimineaţă.	I cannot postpone it because I wrote that I am arriving to-morrow morning.
Îmi pare foarte rău.	I am very sorry.
Vă rog să mă iertaţi că trebuie să plec. Am o întâlnire la ora trei şi un sfert.	Excuse me, please, I must go. I have an appointment for 3.15.
Care e drumul cel mai scurt la gară?	Which is the shortest way to the station?
Mergeţi pe linia tramvaiului până la colţ, apoi apucaţi la dreapta şi gara e drept în faţă.	Go along the tram line to the corner, then turn to the right and the station is straight ahead.
Şofer, du-mă la gară.	Driver, take me to the station.
Sunt foarte grăbit căci vreau să prind trenul de 9 pentru Cernăuţi.	I am in a great hurry, for I want to catch the 9 o'clock train for Cernăuţi.
În zece minute sunteţi în Gara de Nord.	In ten minutes you are in the North Station.
Vă rog un bilet clasa a doua (până la) Braşov.	A second-class ticket to Braşov, please.
Cu care tren plecaţi?	What train are you taking?
Cât costă biletul?	What does the ticket cost?
Daţi-mi restul, vă rog.	My change, please.
Unde-i casa de bagaje?	Where is the luggage office?
Daţi-mi voie să vă conduc.	Allow me to show you.
Schimbaţi-mi, vă rog, o mie de lei?	Can you change me 1000 lei, please?
Nu aveţi mărunte?	Haven't you any change?
Are trenul acesta un vagon-restaurant?	Has this train a restaurant-car?
Vă rog ajutaţi-mă să mă înţeleg cu cu conductorul trenului.	Please, help me to make me understood to the conductor.
Ce limbă vorbiţi?	Which language do you speak?

Vorbesc englezeşte şi franţuzeşte, înţeleg puţin româneşte.	I speak English and French, and I understand a little Rumanian.
Vorbiţi vă rog mai clar.	Speak more distinctly, please.
Daţi-mi voie să vă întreb de unde veniţi.	May I ask you where you have come from ?
Vin din Anglia şi plec la Bucureşti.	I have come from England and I am going to Bucharest.
Unde-i vagonul de dormit ?	Where is the sleeping-car ?
Aveţi paturi libere ?	Have you any vacant berths?
Doresc două paturi la clasa întâia.	I want two second-class beds.
E ocupat acest loc ?	Is this place taken ?
Acesta e ocupat, cel de alături e liber.	This one is taken, but that one beside it is disengaged.
Am un loc rezervat în acest compartiment.	I have a reserved seat in this compartment.

b) **În prăvălie.** In the shop. **La hotel.** In the hotel. **În restaurant.** In the restaurant.

Ce doriţi, vă rog ?	What do you want, please ?
Cu ce vă putem servi ?	What can we do for you ?
Doresc să văd pe patronul librăriei.	I want to see the owner of the bookshop.
Cât costă cartea aceasta ?	How much does this book cost ?
Am nevoie de un dicţionar Englez-Român.	I want an English-Rumanian dictionary.
Nu aveţi o ediţie mai nouă ?	Haven't you a more recent edition ?
Aveţi ziare engleze ?	Have you any English newspapers ?
Unde pot schimba bani ?	Where can I exchange money?
Ce valută aveţi ?	What kind of money have you ?
Am lire sterline şi dolari.	I have pounds and dollars.

Care e cursul oficial al dolarului ?	What is the official rate of exchange of the dollar ?
Astăzi e mai scăzut decât săptămâna trecută.	To-day it is lower than last week.
Cât costă aceste haine ?	How much is this suit ?
Preţul e destul de mare pentrucă sunt de lână.	The price is pretty high because they are woollen.
Nu aveţi un rând de haine de sport mai ieftine ?	Haven't you a less expensive sports suit ?
Unde pot cumpăra articole de sport ?	Where can I buy sports kit ?
Am nevoie de o pereche de ghete.	I need a pair of shoes.
În ce stradă e hotelul Victoria ?	In which street is the Hotel Victoria ?
Aveţi o cameră cu baie ? Doresc una mai liniştită spre curte.	Have you a room with a bathroom ? I want a quiet one overlooking the courtyard.
La ce etaj e această cameră ?	On which floor is the room ?
Etajul al 5-lea e prea sus ; n'aveţi una mai jos ?	The fifth floor is too high ; haven't you one on a lower floor ?
Vă rog să mă deşteptaţi la ora 8.	Please wake me at 8 o'clock.
Chelner, dă-mi, te rog, lista de bucate.	Waiter, give me the menu, please.
Doriţi un aperitiv ?	Would you like an aperitive ?
Aduceţi-mi o ţuică cu masline.	Please bring me a ţuica with olives.
Luaţi vin sau bere ?	Will you have wine or beer ?
Ce fripturi aveţi ?	What joints have you ?
Doresc o jumătate de Drăgăşani.	I want half a bottle of wine of Drăgăşani.
Am cerut o friptură de miel.	I asked for roast lamb.
Carnea aceasta nu-i destul de bine friptă.	This meat isn't cooked enough.

Doriţi o costiţă de purcel la grătar ?	Would you like a grilled pork chop ?
Luaţi o cafea turcească ?	Do you take Turkish coffee ?
Dă-mi, te rog, fructe : struguri şi mere.	Please give me some fruit : grapes and apples.
Doriţi brânză ?	Would you like any cheese ?
Nu, mulţumesc.	No, thank you.
Daţi-mi nota de plată. Doresc să fac plata.	Give me the bill, please. I want the bill.
Ce-aţi avut supă sau ciorbă ?	Which did you take, soup or sour broth ?

c) La bancă.	In the bank
Aş dori să vorbesc cu directorul băncii într'o chestiune personală. Vă rog anunţaţi-mă. Mi-a dat întâlnire pentru ora 11.	I should like to speak to the manager on a personal matter. Please tell him I'm here. He made an appointment with me for 11 o'clock.
Poftiţi în birou.	Come into the office, please.
Pot schimba acest cec ?	Can I cash this cheque?
Este barat ?	Is it crossed ?
Doresc să deschid nu cont curent.	I should like to open a current account.
Unde e casieria ?	Where is the cash-desk ?
Aici în dreapta, lângă biroul contabilului.	Here to the right, next to the accountant's office.
Doresc plata în numerar.	I want cash.
Ce procente se plătesc pentru depuneri ?	How much interest are bank deposits giving ?
Cu ce procente se acordă împrumuturi ?	What is the interest on loans ?
Faceţi operaţiuni de schimb ?	Do you exchange money ?
Numai Banca Naţională cumpără şi vinde devize străine.	Only the National Bank buys and sells foreign money.
Poliţa aceasta este scadentă astăzi.	This bill is due to-day.

Cine sunt giranţii?	Who are the guarantors?
Am o scrisoare de credit.	I have a letter of credit.
Puteţi ridica banii astăzi.	You may cash it to-day.
Semnaţi această recipisă.	Sign this receipt, please.
Nu primesc chitanţă pentru banii depuşi?	Don't I get a receipt for the deposit?
Casierul eliberează chitanţe.	The cashier gives the receipts.
Am un cont curent.	I have an account.

d) La poştă. At the post office

Unde e poşta?	Where is the post office?
Poşta Centrală e în Calea Victoriei, dar un oficiu poştal se găseşte aici aproape în Piaţa Mare.	The Central Post Office is in the Calea Victoria, but there is a post office near here in the Great Market Place.
Până la ce oră e deschisă poşta?	Until what time is the post office open?
Orele de serviciu sunt până la şase, dar telegrame se pot trimite oricând.	Business hours are up to six o'clock, but you can send telegrams any time.
Unde pot cumpăra timbre?	Where can I buy some stamps?
La ghişeul din dreapta.	At the counter on the right.
Daţi-mi, vă rog, cinci cărţi poştale pentru străinatate, zece timbre de câte zece lei şi un mandat poştal.	Please give me five postcards to send abroad, ten ten-lei stamps each and a money order.
Cu cât se franchează o scrisoare pentru Anglia?	What is the postage for a letter to England?
Cu zece lei scrisoarea simplă, cu 20 scrisoarea recomandată.	Ten lei for an ordinary letter, twenty for a registered.
Unde e o cutie pentru scrisori?	Where is there a letter-box?
Care e taxa pentru o convorbire telefonică cu Londra?	What is the cost for a (telephone) call to London?
Daţi-mi legătura cu Cernăuţii, numărul şapte opt zero nouă.	Please connect me with C., number seven eight zero nine.

Aveţi vreo scrisoare poste restante pe numele James Brown?	Have you a poste-restante letter for Mr. James Brown?
Cât cântăreşte pachetul acesta?	How much does this parcel weigh?
Îl pot expedia recomandat?	Can I send it registered?
Da, dacă-l sigilaţi cu ceară roşie.	Yes, if you seal it with wax.
Când pleacă poşta pentru Anglia?	When does the mail for England go?
Cu trenul de seară.	By the evening train.
Am nevoie de hârtie şi de cerneală.	I need paper and ink.
Găsiţi pe biroul din sala de aşteptare.	You'll find it on the desk in the waiting-room.
Daţi-mi, vă rog, un blanchet pentru o telegramă.	Please give me a telegram form.
Unde se scrie adresa?	Where do you write the address?
Cum pot trimite bani?	How can I send some money?
Cumpăraţi un mandat poştal.	Buy a postal-order.
Unde e biroul de informaţii?	Where is the inquiry office?
Pe coridor în fund, la dreapta.	On the bottom of the corridor on the right.

e) La doctor.	At the doctor
Îmi puteţi recomanda un internist?	Could you recommend me a specialist for internal diseases?
În ce stradă stă doctorul Ionescu Alexandru?	In which street is Dr. Ionescu Alexander staying?
Doctorul Popescu G. dă consultaţii în strada Stelelor 43.	Dr. Popescu G.'s consulting-rooms are at No. 43 Stelelor Street.
E acasă domnul doctor?	Is doctor at home?
Vă rog luaţi loc în sala de aşteptare.	Please take a seat in the waiting-room.

Aşteaptă mulţi pacienţi ?	Are there many patients waiting ?
Voi veni mâine.	I will call again to-morrow.
Am dureri de cap.	I have a headache.
Sufăr de ficat.	I am suffering with my liver.
Am răcit, tuşesc.	I have a cold, I am coughing.
N'am suferit nici odată de stomac.	I have never had stomach-ache.
Am avut demult o operaţie de apendicită.	I had an operation for appendicitis long ago.
Mă doare braţul stâng.	I have a pain in my left arm.
Nu pot mişca piciorul.	I can't move my foot.
N'am dormit toată noaptea.	I haven't been to sleep all night.
Nu am temperatură.	I haven't a temperature.
Sper că nu e nimic serios.	I hope it is nothing serious.
Pulsul e regulat.	The pulse is regular.
Trebuie să consultaţi un laringolog.	You must consult an ear and throat specialist.
Va trebui să intraţi într'un sanatoriu.	You must go into a nursing-home.
E o operaţie uşoară.	It is a minor operation.
Ce pot mânca.	What may I eat ?
Mergeţi cu această recetă la farmacie.	Go to the chemist's with this prescription.
Luaţi de trei ori pe zi câte o linguriţă din acest medicament.	One teaspoonful of this medicine to be taken three times a day.
Care e onorarul Dvoastre ?	What is your fee ?

Luca viii. 4-10

4. În vremea aceea, adunându-se mult norod şi cei care, de prin toate oraşele, veneau la el, a vorbit în parabolă :

5. Eşit-a sămănătorul să samene sămânţa sa. Şi când sămăna el, o parte a căzut lângă drum şi a fost călcată cu picioarele şi păsările cerului au mâncat-o.

6. Altă parte a căzut în loc pietros şi dacă a răsărit s'a uscat, pentru că nu avea umezeală.

7. Altă parte a căzut în mijlocul spinilor, şi spinii crescând cu ea odată, au înnăbuşit-o.

8. Iar altă parte a căzut în pământul cel bun şi crescând a făcut rod însutit. Şi după ce a spus aceasta a strigat : Cine are urechi de auzit să auză.[1]

9. Ci ucenicii lui l-au întrebat : Ce este pilda aceasta ?

10. El atunci a răspuns : Vouă vă este dat să cunoaşteţi tainele Împărăţiei lui Dumnezeu, dar celorlalţi (le vorbesc) în pilde, ca (nu cumva) văzând să nu vază [1] şi auzind să nu înţeleagă.

Pământul României

Pământul românesc se aseamănă cu o cetate de formă aproape rotundă. Zidul interior al acestei cetăţi îl formează Carpaţii de sud numiţi şi Alpii Transilvăneni spre miazăzi, Carpaţii răsăriteni şi cei păduroşi spre est şi spre nord, şi Munţii Apuseni, numiţi şi Carpaţii de apus, cari închid platoul Transilvaniei spre vest.

Trei văi taie zidurile acestei cetăţi. Valea Mureşului şi Valea Someşului deschid două intrări dinspre apus, Valea Oltului deschide o intrare spre sud. Spre răsărit trecătorile

[1] For these palatalized forms, cp. 6. 2, *A*, Note 3.

Carpaţilor către şesul Moldovei sunt strâmtori foarte înguste, numite chei. Cheile Bicazului sunt cele mai înguste, mai prăpăstioase şi mai majestoase în sălbătacia lor fără asemănare. Un drum îngust, prin fundul Cheilor Bicazului, duce din Transilvania în Moldova, la sud de Ceahlău, în regiunea Neamţului.

Legătura principală între platoul Transivaniei şi şesul Munteniei este Valea Prahovei, cunoscută prin bogaţia ei în petrol. Cu Moldova de nord, numită Bucovina, muzeu de artă veche românească, legătura se face peste Măgura, ajungând în Vatra Dornei, cunoscuta staţiune balneară.

Acest cerc de munţi, avansaţi ca o cetate în spre stepa din nordul Mării Negre, este dublat de un cerc de râuri, care înconjoară cetatea cu şanţuri de apă. Nistrul, Dunărea şi Tisa încercuesc şesurile din jurul cetăţii munţilor.

Această regiune se numia în antichitate Dacia Felix. Împăratul Traian a încorporat-o în Imperiul Roman şi a transformat-o într'o provincie romană, în anul 106 după Christos.

În spaţiul dintre râuri şi munţi se întind şesuri mănoase, cu bogăţii agricole, grădini încărcate cu fructe, podgorii cu viţă de vie de toate varietăţile şi lunci înverzite cu păscători bogate.

Munţii adăpostesc bogăţii minerale. Între acestea petrolul şi aurul ocupă primul loc.

Cele mai variate peisaje împodobesc acest pământ. Peisajul dobrogean, cu ţărmul Mării Negre şi cu Delta Dunării produce grâu şi furnisează peşte pentru întreaga populaţie a ţării. Cetăţi antice sânt îngropate în pământul Dobrogei, care în antichitate se numia Scythia Minor sau Dacia Pontica.

Şesul Munteniei, cu Bărăganul întins ca o stepă, şi regiunea Moldovei dela Siret până la Nistru sunt grânarele ţării.

Podgoriile se întind până în regiunea dealurilor carpatine. Această regiune este bogată în livezi de pomi roditori.

Munţii acoperiţi de codri seculari sunt raiul vânătorilor. Cerbii şi căprioarele populează poienile. Mistreţii caută pădurile de fag. Urşii se retrag în desişurile cele mai ascunse

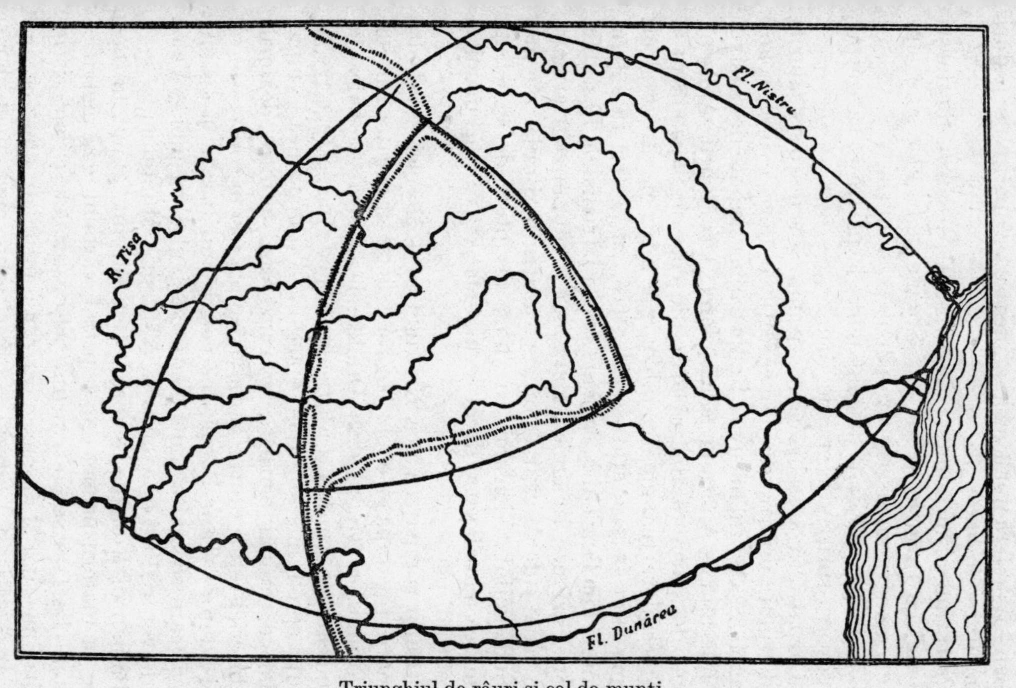

Triunghiul de râuri și cel de munți.

(**A. D. Xenopol**, *Istoria Românilor din Dacia Traiană*, I, 1881.)

şi-şi fac bârlogul în vizuini. Cocoşul de munte şi capra sălbarecă preferă înălţimele stâncoase, acoperite cu păduri de molift şi de brad.

Pretutindeni în munţi, pe unde sunt păscători, întâlneşti ciobanii cu turmele lor de oi. Stânile ciobanilor sunt singurele aşezări omeneşti, care populează munţii.

Râurile cu apă limpede sunt pline de păstrăvi, cari atrag pe pescarii-turişti din oraşele ţării.

„Carpaţii făgărăşeni văzuţi primăvara de pe dealurile Mediaşului, printre caişii încărcaţi cu flori, evocă icoana Pirineilor. Asprul masiv al Rodnei aduce aminte de masivul Brennerului. Apucând calea Jarei, în Munţii Apuseni, stânci de marmoră albă răsărite din covorul pajiştei sau al mestecenilor, reamintesc tablouri elveţiene. În Codrul-Muma sunt peisaje atât de sălbatece, cu peşteri fără fund şi doline una lângă alta, ca şi în Carstul Istrian dela Postumia şi St. Cazian. Imaginea Harz-ului din Câmpia Germană este redată de Munţii Dobrogei văzuţi din Brăila, iar mai la Sud, golful Balcicului, cu dunga argintată de smochini, cu marea mai albastră decât cerul, te face să te crezi în golful Sorentului.

Străinii compară Valea Nistrului cu a Moselei, iar Delta Dunării, tot după ei, e mai bogată în atracţii decât a Nilului.

Pornind cu trenul dela Oradea-Mare, străbaţi valea cu fermecătoare frumuseţi a Crişului-Repede cu perspective de o clipă spre inima Munţilor Apuseni. Tai marginea Câmpiei ardelene, numai ogoare; pătrunzi apoi printre dealurile cu biserici-cetăţi dintre Târnave, spre a ieşi în contrastul cel mai izbitor: Ţara Bârsei, şes neted, numai sate şi ogoare, lângă care se înalţă dintr'odată masivul Bucegilor. Valea Prahovei te duce în câmpia fără sfârşit a Munteniei.

Pământul României cuprinde aur, argint, aluminiu, fier, sare ca materii prime, dar şi petrol, cărbuni, gaz metan ca forţă. La faţă se cultivă din belşug ceralele caracteristice latitudinei, dar şi din acele care au o întindere mare la nord (secara) ori la sud (orezul). Cresc pruni, meri, nuci, dar şi castani, migdali ori smochini. Cu puţină muncă aceştia din urmă ar fi rentabili. Viţa de vie rodeşte din Dunăre până'n

Hotin, dela Cetatea Albă la Arad. Până şi bumbac s'ar putea, cu oarecare trudă, cultiva mai mult. Aproape nimic din ceia ce e strict necesar nu lipseşte. Pânea sau mămăliga se capătă din belşug; lâna, cânepa, inul procură îmbrăcămintea. Cârdurile de vite dau laptele şi carnea necesară; bălţile întinse forfotesc de peşti, aiurea crescuţi cu grea casnă".

după I. SIMIONESCU,
Ţara Noastră, 1937.

Lupul şi mielul

Un lup văzu un miel bând apă dintr'un pârâu, mai la vale de locul unde stătea el la pândă. Căutându-i pricină ca să-l mănânce lupul strigă:

— De ce-mi tulburi apa ca să n'o pot bea?

— Eu nu ţi-o pot tulbura — răspunse mielul — pentrucă apa curge dela tine înspre mine.

Lupul se ruşină de răspunsul mielului, dar nu renunţă la intenţia sa şi strigă cu mai multă furie:

— Dar anul trecut pentru ce ai tulburat apa părinţilor mei?

— Anul trecut eu încă nu mă născusem — răspunse mielul nevinovat.

Atunci lupul strigă cu şi mai multă furie:

— Văd că mai eşti şi obraznic şi ştii să întorci vorba — şi fără să aştepte răspuns se repezi şi sfăşie mielul în bucăţi.

Istoria literaturii române

Introducere

Istoria literaturii române se împarte în patru epoci distincte: *epoca veche*, cea mai lungă, *epoca nouă*, care începe dela naşterea noastră ca popor romanic, *epoca modernă*, al cărei început datează dela întemeierea României unite şi independente, şi *epoca contemporană*, dela Unirea tuturor Românilor încoace.

. . . .

Înainte de întâia carte românească.
Stăpânirea culturii bisericeşti în haină slavonă.

Începuturile literaturii române se pierd în negura deasă care învăluie, pentru cercetătorul de azi, trecutul neamului. Dacă istoria poate totuş reconstrui din datele răsleţe, păstrate prin documente străine, câteva capitole, nu totdeauna limpezi, dar adesea glorioase, din trecutul românesc, datele acestea nu pot spune aproape nimic, nici celei mai ingenioase minţi reconstructive, asupra vieţii culturale a celor mai vechi Români.

Conservarea în limba română a cuvintelor de origine latină *a scrie* şi *carte* sub forma corespunzătoare cu legile fonologiei româneşti, dovedeşte că noţiunile exprimate prin aceste cuvinte au fost în toate timpurile curente la poporul român şi ne îndreptăţeşte să credem că, după stingerea culturii romane în regiunile dunărene, strămoşii Românilor n'au uitat niciodată meşteşugul de a scrie şi de a ceti cărţi. A deduce însă din aceasta că, în veacurile sbuciumate din aproape întreg evul de mijloc, ar fi existat o literatură românească scrisă, este de sigur greşit, şi cu greu se vor împlini vreodată nădejdile acelor optimişti care mai cred că vreo întâmplare norocoasă va scoate la lumină vreun manuscris în limba străveche românească. Chiar dacă, în împrejurările mai mult decât nefavorabile pentru ivirea unei mişcări literare, s'ar fi aflat pe acele timpuri un fiu al neamului nostru care să-şi aştearnă gândurile pe pergament, scrisul său n'ar fi fost românesc, ci în limba modelelor sale, grecească sau slavonă.

Influența slavonă

Influenţa slavonă datează la noi din timpurile vechi. Limba română păstrează urme atât de adânci ale acestei influenţe, încât nu ne mai putem îndoi o clipă că comunitatea noastră cu Slavii a dăinuit veacuri întregi. Au trebuit să se scurgă mulţi ani, până când masele mai compacte de Slavi din sudul Dunării au înghiţit cele mai multe insule de Români din mijlocul lor, şi s'a scurs vreme îndelungată până ce, printr'o desnaţionalisare lentă, Slavii din ţinuturile româneşti de astăzi, din nordul fluviului, au fost absorbiţi de către strămoşii noştri. Procesul acesta de desnaţionalisare a fost accelerat atuncea când organisaţiile primitive de triburi din sud-estul european se schimbaseră în organisaţii mai înaintate, transformându-se mai în urmă în state naţionale. Slavii de sud ajunseră cu mult înaintea Românilor la aceste organisaţii, silind pe Români să se desvolte sub înrâurirea lor. Influenţa aceasta n'a fost numai politică, ci şi culturală, căci, fiind în nemijlocita apropiere a imperiului bizantin, care pe acea vreme ducea facla culturii mondiale, popoarele slave din sud ajunseseră în curând la o înflorire literară pe care n'au mai ajuns-o de atunci veacuri întregi.

. . . .

Într'o vreme când orice mişcare culturală se reflecta prin biserică, ortodoxismul românesc a fost evenimentul cu cele mai grave urmări pentru desvoltarea culturală a Românilor, căci el i-a legat pe Români pentru veacuri întregi cu cultura Orientului, formând un zid despărţitor faţă de catolicismul vecinilor din vest şi din nord.

Arta în epoca veche

. . . .

Prin invasia Turcilor şi prin cucerirea Bizanţului, o cultură veche ameninţa să se stingă. O parte însemnată din cei ce, în imperiul bizantin, alcătuiau clasa savanţilor, a literaţilor şi a artiştilor, se refugie în Italia, ducând cu ea sâmburele Renaşterii. Biserica apuseană, înţelegând glasul vremii, în marile ei aspiraţiuni de cucerire şi mărire, a ştiut să pună în serviciile sale noul avânt, şi în loc de a ridica stavilă în calea lor, ea a promovat talentele originale ce apăreau în mediul atât de prielnic al Italiei, bogată în centre de cultură.

Altă parte a refugiaţilor a ajuns în Ţările române, unde, ca şi la Muntele Athos, câtva timp existară singurele centre importante ce deveniră depozitarele artei bizantine.

. . . .

Ca şi în literatură şi ca şi în toate manifestările sale, trăsăturile caracteristice ale poporului român se vădesc în manifestările artistice ale Evului Mediu, prelungit mult peste limitele sale fireşti. O putere mare de asimilare face pe artistul român să primească cu plăcere cele mai variate influenţe externe şi să le imite cu uşurinţă ; un simţ foarte desvoltat pentru armonie face însă ca aceste înrâuriri din afară să nu predomine în măsură atât de mare, încât să tulbure proporţiile tradiţionale ; un instinct sănătos îl călăuzeşte totdeuna pe artist, făcând ca ceea ce este esenţial să iasă la iveală, iar amănuntul indiscret să fie sacrificat fără durere. Astfel se explică de ce arta bizantină, deşi a suferit la Români atâtea prefaceri, se continuă totuş în ceea ce e mai caracteristic pentru ea şi apare în cea mai frumoasă puritate.

Eruditul istoric al artei I. Strzygowski,[1] fost profesor la Universitatea din Viena, se exprimă astfel vorbind despre vechea artă românească : ,,În văile părăsite ale Bucovinei sunt comori de artă, cum nu se mai întâlnesc nicăiri pe lume. . . . Pe pereţii exteriori ai bisericilor din Suceviţa, Voroneţ, Mănăstirea Humorului, Vatra Moldoviţei, etc., se văd acele icoane ale bisericii ortodoxe, care te răpesc cu totul şi care, cu culorile lor vii, privite de departe, îţi dau impresia unui covor persian. Aşa frumuseţă strălucitoare nu mai întâlneşti aiurea. Şi această bogăţie de culori te stăpâneşte şi mai mult în interiorul bisericilor unde i se adaugă luciul abundent al aurului, pe care câteva raze discrete de soare, pătrunzând prin ferestre, îl ridică la un puternic efect artistic.“

Iată ce scrie P. Henry, un cercetător francez despre această pictură murală : ,,Epoca cuprinsă între domnia lui Petru Rareş (1527-1538, 1541-1546) şi aceea a Movileştilor (1595-1616) este epoca strălucită a picturii moldoveneşti, urmând apogeul arhitecturii sub Ştefan cel Mare (1457-1504). . . . Nu cunosc nimic mai frumos decât nuanţele imensului Arbore care acopere tot peretele de sud dela Voroneţ, cu cele două culori dominante, verdele şi albastrul, care formează — oricât de surprinzătoare ar părea această asemănare — cel mai moale covor pe care-l poţi visa. Nu cunosc nimic mai somptuos şi în acelaş timp mai dulce pentru ochi decât aurul şi azurul Judecăţii din urmă dela Voroneţ.“

[1] rz in this surname is to be pronounced like *s* in *measure*.

Iar un alt specialist francez în istoria artelor, H. Focillon se exprimă în termenii următori: ,,Făcute pentru plin-aer, expuse de-adreptul luminii cereşti, aceste picturi al-fresco au o frăgezime de accent şi o autoritate decorativă care ne încântă. . . . Dar această îmbrăcăminte exterioară nu trebuie să ne ascundă interesul şi farmecul picturii sanctuarului . . . (care) ne păstrează expresiuni din cele mai înalte ale gândirii bizantine . . . (şi) prin costume şi portrete, o serie întreagă de opere în care se afirmă poesia vieţii româneşti, întinerind formulele antice. . . .“

Arhitectura

Arhitectura a făcut la Români progrese remarcabile şi e, din toate artele, aceea căreia i s'au adăugat mai multe elemente inovatoare. Stilul fundamental rămâne cel bizantin, chiar atunci când meşterii zidari erau străini, ca acel Vitus-Veit, Sas din Ardeal, care a lucrat alături de Dobromir, la biserica episcopală din Argeş. Dar cele dintâi locaşuri sfinte din Oltenia, clădite în formă de cruce, cu cupola la mijloc, arătând o înfluenţă sârbească, ascund în zidurile lor elegante arcaturi oarbe, împrumutate stilului roman, sau au, ca faţada bisericii din Dealu, dela începutul secolului al XVI-lea, elemente armeneşti şi georgiene.

SEXTIL PUŞCARIU.

Snoavă

Unui om i s'a înecat muierea într'un râu. El o căuta pe râu în sus. Îl întrebă un alt om : ,,Ce cauţi în apa râului ? “ — El răspunse : ,,Îmi caut soţia, că s'a înecat acolo jos.“

Celalat zise către el: ,,Caut-o acolo în jos că o fi dus-o apa. De ce o cauţi în susul apei ? “

Răspunse cel ce-şi căuta femeia : ,,Nu cred să fi mers pe apă în jos, căci cât a trăit tare îndărătnică a fost şi cred că şi moartă îndărăt pe apă s'a dus.“

după M. GASTER,
Chrestomatie română, ii, 1891.

Borta Vântului

(Poveste)

Era un om sărac, sărac şi avea o mulţimo de copii. Acu era în vremea foametei şi el a muncit o săptămână pe un căuş de grăunţe. Apoi s'a dus la râşniţă cu ele. După ce le-a râşnit, a ieşit afară cu căuşul cu făină şi s'a pornit o furtună mare şi i-a luat toată făina din căuş. Da el straşnic s'a mâniat.

— ,,Nu mă las eu aşa cu una cu două[1],“ — îşi făcu un şumuiog de paie şi porneşte. Îl întrebă un om:

— ,,Unde te duci, cumetre?“

— ,,Mă duc să astup borta vântului, că mi-a luat făina din căuş.“

— ,,Da unde-i nimeri-o?“

— ,,Unde-o fi, acolo mă duc.“

Mergând el loc îndepărtat, a ajuns pe Dumnezeu şi pe Sfântul Petru, cari umblau pe pământ pe atunci.

— ,,Unde te duci, omule?“

— ,,Mă duc să astup borta vântului, că mi-a luat făina din căuş.“

Da Dumnezeu i-a zis aşa:

— ,,Omule, nu te mai duce. Na-ţi o nucă, da până acasă să nu zici: ‚Nucă, deschide-te!‘“

Întorcându-se el înapoi a ajuns la un om şi s'a rugat să-l primească, să doarmă acolo peste noapte.

— ,,De unde vii, bade?“ — îl întrebă omul cela.

— ,,Mă duceam s'astup borta vântului ş'am întâlnit un nebun pe drum şi mi-a dat o nucă. Si-a zis să nu zic: ‚Nucă deschide-te!‘ Ce-o mai fi şi asta?“

Femeia omului, vicleană, ia o nucă în mână şi zice:

— ,,Ia să-ţi văd nuca!“

Îi schimbă nuca omului. Si pe urmă se duce într'un ocol şi zice:

— ,,Nucă, deschide-te!“

[1] I won't renounce so easily.

Când a zis, atâtea vite ce-au ieşit: oi, cai, miei, o bogăţie întreagă, ştii mata,[1] putere dumnezeiască!

— ,,Hai, bată-mi-l[2] Dumnezeu de vânt, şi pe moşneag lua-l-ar ucigă-l crucea![3] Mă duc să astup borta vântului şi să bat pe moşneag, de ce m'a viclenit."

Ajunge iar pe Dumnezeu. Da Dumnezeu, ştii putere dumnezeiască, aici[4] era altfel la faţă.... Nu l-a cunoscut....

— ,,Unde te duci, bade?"

— ,,S'astup borta vântului şi să ucid moşneagul, că ce[5] m'a viclenit?"

— ,,Na-ţi, bade, un măgar. Dar să nu-i zici până acasă: ,Măgar, fă bani!'"

— ,,N'oi[6] zice."

Se întoarce el iar pe la omul cela. Da[7] omul cela îl ospătează şi-i dă vin să bea şi omul s'o chefăluit ş'a adormit pe laiţă. Da erau nişte ţigani în şatră acolo, ş'aveau, un măgar, şi omul s'a dus şi l-a cumpărat, ş'a schimbat măgarul. Omul a doua zi se scoală, ia măgarul şi se duce acasă şi zice: ,,Măgar, fă bani!" Măgarul de unde? El apucă un drug şi începe a dişela măgarul.

— ,,Acu nu-l mai iert eu!" — Se porneşte să'ntâlnească pe moşneag şi să astupe borta vântului. Întâlneşte pe Dumnezeu.

— ,,Na-ţi, bade, o cârjă, dar să nu zici până acasă: ,Cârje, încârjeşte-te!'"

Ia cârja, vine pe la omul cela. Aici omul i-a dat şi mai straşnic ospăţ şi s'a sfătuit că dac'a[8] vedea că-i mai dă şi cârja, pe urmă să-l omoare, ca să nu prepuie că el i-o luat-o. Acu zice omul femeii: ,,Măi femeie, noi hai cu cârja în zâmnic şi să'nchidem uşa şi să zicem: ,Cârje, încârjeşte-te!'" Se vâră în zâmnic şi spun acele cuvinte. Cârja unde'ncepe a bate şi a sdrobi.

— ,,Bade, ţi-om da şi măgar şi nucă, numai, mă rog, scapă-ne. Omul i-o[9] lăsat de i-o bătut bine, o luat măgarul, cârja şi nuca, şi s'o pornit acasă.

[1] Abreviated for: **dumneata<domniata.** [2] Ethical Dative.
[3] The devil. [4] Local instead of temporal: **acum**, *now*.
[5] **=de ce.** [6] **nu voi.** [7] **dar.** [8] **dacă va.** [9] **=i-a;**

Aşa s'a făcut de bogat acu, de-a ajuns vestea pân la împăratul. Atâţia bani avea el, de-a sămănat şi-a crescut grâu de aur, şi-a trimis doi sufragii să-i deie sămânţă, să semene şi împăratul.

— ,,Să spui împăratului că nu vreau să-i dau, să vedem ce mi-o [1] face. . . .''

Împăratul când a auzit aşa, straşnic s'a mâniat, şi a gătit oştirea să se ducă cu război asupra lui. Împăratul era în frunte, ştii mai mare. Ş'a venit pân'la uşa lui şi-a strigat să ias'afară. Dar el era îmbrăcat tot cu straie de ale noastre nu cu straie leşeşti.[2] El pune cârja sub suman şi iese afară. Acu împăratul cu atâtea mii de oameni i-a fost ruşine singur lui să se ducă el acum cu unul să se lupte. A zis:

— ,,Omule, arată-ţi tu întâi puterea.''

— ,,Bine, vino, Împărate! — Cârje, încârjeşte-te, — la tot soldatul câte două şi la împăratul nouă!''

Cârja cea dumnezeiască tot în cap dădea. O'[3]nebunit şi pe soldaţi şi pe împăratul. Şi-o rămas omul în pace şi-o trăit în pace. Să dea Dumnezeu să trăiască şi copiii mei aşa!

Culeasă de MIHAI EMINESCU.
(1850-1889.)

Împăratul şerpilor

(Fragment de poveste.)

A fost odată, ca niciodată; că de n'ar fi nu s'ar povesti; pe când făcea plopul pere şi răchita micşunele; pe când se băteau urşii în coade; pe când se luau de gât lupii cu mieii de se sărutau înfrăţindu-se; pe când se potcovia puricele la un picior cu nouă zeci de ocale de fier şi s'arunca în slava cerului de ne aducea poveşti;

Pe când scria musca pe perete
Mai mincinos cine nu crede.[4]

[1] =ce-mi va. [2] Town dress. [3] =a.
[4] Usual introduction to fairy tales containing fantastic statements so as to justify the miraculous content which follows of the fairy tale.

A fost odată un unchiaş şi o mătuşe. Ei ajunseseră la sărăcie, cheltuind tot ce aveau după sufletul lor, spre a dobândi un fiu, dar în deşert.[1] Acum, la vreme de bătrâneţe, se hotărîră şi ei să iasă pe câmpie, şi orice vor găsi, să-l ia şi să-l crească ca pe fiul lor.[2]

Deci într'o dimineaţă, porniră amândoi pentru acest sfârşit: atât de mare era dorul lor să aibă un copil. Găsiră un pui micuţ de şarpe, îl luară, îl aduseră acasă, îl puseră într'o ţeavă de trestie şi îl culcară între dânşii. Tot ce puteau, biet, agonisi şi dânşii, cheltuiau pentru hrana fiului lor. Şarpele crescu până ce într'o zi crepă ţeava. Îl puseră într'un mosor. Îngrijirea şi hrana cea bună ce-i da[3] făcură pe şarpe să crească repede, şi plesni şi mosorul. Îl puseră într'un putinei şi aşa nu lipsiau a-l culca între dânşii.

Dupăce mai trecu câtva timp, într'o dimineaţă, auziră crăpând şi putineiul. Atunci unde ieşi din el şarpele şi le zise: — „Vă mulţămesc, tată şi mamă, de îngrijirea cea bună ce mi-aţi dat. Fără voi poate aş fi perit. Acum să faceţi bunătate[4] să mă duceţi de unde m'aţi luat."

Bătrânii nu se cam îndurau de el. Se făcuse un şarpe aşa de frumos cum nu mai văzuseră ei. Solzii lui erau ca de aur. Ochii străluciau în capul lui ca nişte pietre de rubin; îl sărutaseră şi pe-o parte, şi pe alta, şi îi spuseră: — „Dar bine, dragul nostru fiu, tocmai când credeam să avem şi noi o mângâiere la bătrâneţele noastre, tocmai atunci ne părăseşti? Noi credeam că numai moartea ne va despărţi de tine." — „De aceea vă zic să mă duceţi de unde m'aţi luat, ca să vă pot fi de folos. Şezând aici cu voi viaţa mea este în joc [5]."

Cuvintele lui erau aşa de mieroase[6] încât nu se putură opri de a nu-l asculta. Îl duseră deci, de unde l-au luat, moşul ţiindu-l de cap şi baba de coadă.

Cum îl puseră jos, şarpele se ridică în coadă, şi întorcându-se către unchiaş şi babă, le zise: „Să nu vă speriaţi de ce

[1] in vain.

[2] Observe the use, with preference, of the aorist (**preterite**) in this text contrary to the foregoing one. This text is from Walachia, the other one (**Borta vântului**) is from Moldavia.

[3] =**dădeau** (*impf.*). [4] =**bine**. [5] in danger. [6] sweet like honey.

veţi vedea. N'apucă să sfârşească bine vorba, şi unde se porniră din toate părţile şerpii ca frunza şi ca iarba, ce veniau la chemarea împăratului lor şi i se închinară. Dacă văzu însă că moşul şi baba se cam pierd cu firea,[1] făcu un semn, şi toţi şerpii porniră pe unde veniră.

PETRE ISPIRESCU.
(1830-1887.)

De când trăiesc la un loc cei urîţi cu cei frumoşi?

S'a sfătuit odată Dumnezeu şi cu sfântul Petrea, să se ducă în lume şi s'aleagă pe oamenii urîţi din cei frumoşi. Mergând ei prin lume, iacă la o cotitură de drum se întâlnesc c'un urît, da'urît nu ceva.

— Bună calea, om bun.

— Mulţămesc „mnorvoaste"[2] moşule — zice omul. Da'cine sunteţi şi unde vă duceţi?

— Apoi cine suntem, suntem noi; da'ne ducem să alegem pe oamenii urîţi din cei frumoşi.

— Ăăra,[3] bine faceţi, că şi mie tare mi-i greu[4] de oamenii cei urîţi.

Auzind Dumnezeu ce vorbă a vorbit urîtul, zice către sfântul Petrea.

— Să-i lăsăm, Petre, să trăiască la un loc, aşa amestecaţi. N'ai auzit ce-a zis uriciunea asta? Te sperii numai când îl vezi, şi te uită că se socoate frumos şi-i[5] dă[6] că şi lui i-i greu de oamenii urîţi. D'apoi cei frumoşi, ce să mai zică?

Şi de-atunci trăiesc la un loc, cei urîţi cu cei frumoşi.

După AL. VASILIU,
Poveşti şi Legende.

[1] are getting afraid.
[2] Distorted for: **dumnilor voastre<domniilor voastre.**
[3] Interjection: well; bravo.
[4] I am annoyed, disgusted.
[5] Ethic Dative.
[6] sustains.

Movila lui Purcel

Ştefan Vodă cel Bun [1] vrând să meargă la biserică, într'o Duminică dimineaţă la liturgie, în târg în Vaslui, şi ieşind în polimari la curţile domneşti ce erau făcute de dânsul, a auzit un glas mare de om, strigând să aducă boii la plug. Şi mirându-se ce om este acela că ară Duminica, îndată a trimis în toate părţile ca să-l găsească pre acel om, să-l aducă la dânsul. Şi l-au aflat pre om în sus, pre apa Vaslului, cale de patru ceasuri, arând la o Movilă ce se chiamă acum Movila lui Purcel; că pea cel om încă îl chiema Purcel. Şi ducându-l pre acel om la Ştefan Vodă, l-au întrebat Ştefan Vodă: el a strigat aşa tare? Şi pentru ce ară Duminica? El a zis, că a strigat el să aducă boii la plug, şi ară Duminica, că este om sărac, şi într'alte zile n'a vrut frate-său să-i deie plugul, şi acum Duminica i-a dat. Deci Ştefan Vodă au luat plugul fratelui celui bogat şi l-au dat [2] fratelui celui sărac să fie al lui.

Ion Neculce (1672-1745(6)),
O samă de cuvinte.

Alexandru Lăpuşneanu [3]
(Fragment)

IV

. . . .

Ruxandra luă un păhar de argint plin de apă pe care-l aducea sluga; şi apoi maşinaliceşte şi silită mai mult de

[1] **Voevod al Moldovei** (1457-1504). [2] Archaic for : **l-a dat.**

[3] Acţiunsa acestei nuvele istorice se petrece la sfârşitul secolului al 16-lea. Fragmentul ce urmează este încheierea părţii a patra şi ultima a nuvelei. Voevodul Alexandru Lăpuşneanu a domnit în două rânduri în Moldova (1552-1561; 1563-1568). Ajuns domn cu ajutorul Turcilor, el n'a putut câştiga încrederea şi sprijinul boierilor ţării. În a doua a sa domnie prigoana împotriva boierilor a culminat într'un masacru organizat la curtea sa. Doi boieri, Spancioc şi Stroici, scapă din acest masacru şi pribegesc prin ţări străine. Întorcându-se în ţară pentru a se răzbuna ei asistă la moartea prin otrăvire a domnului-tiran.

boieri, lăsă să cadă otrava în el. Boierii o împinseră în camera bolnavului.

— Ce face? întrebă Spancioc pe Stroici, care crăpase uşa şi se uita.

— Întreabă de fiul său — zice că vrea să-l vadă — cere de băut — Doamna tremură — îi dă păharul — nu vrea să-l iee.

Spancioc sări şi scoase junghiul din cingătoare.

— Ba, îl ia, bea. . . . Să-ţi fie de bine Măria Ta!

Ruxandra ieşi tremurândă [1] şi galbenă, şi rezemându-se de perete:

— Voi să daţi seama înaintea lui Dumnezeu, zise suspinând, că voi m'aţi făcut să fac acest păcat.

Mitropolitul veni: Să mergem, zise Doamnei.

— Dar cine va căuta de nenorocitul acesta?

— Noi răspunseră boierii.

— Oh! părinte, ce mă făcuşi să fac! zise Doamna, către mitropolitul, şi se duse cu el plângând. Amândoi boierii intrară la bolnav.

Otrava încă nu începuse a-şi face lucrarea. Lăpuşneanu sta întins cu faţa în sus, liniştit, dar foarte slab. Când intrară boierii, el îi privi îndelung şi necunoscându-i îi întrebă cine sunt şi ce voiesc.

— Eu sunt Stroici, răspunse acesta.

— Şi eu Spancioc, adăogă celalt, şi aceea ce voim este să te vedem până a nu muri cum ţi-am făgăduit.

— Oh! vrăjmaşii mei! suspină Alexandru.

— Eu Spancioc, urmă acesta, Spancioc pe care ai vrut să-l tai, când ai ucis 47 de boieri, şi care a scăpat din ghiarele tale! Spancioc a cărui avere ai jefuit-o, lăsându-i femeia şi copiii să cerşească pe la uşile creştinilor.

— Ah! ce foc simt că mă arde, strigă bolnavul, apucându-se cu mâinele de pântece!

— Zi „*Acum slobozeşte*," căci ai să mori. Otrava lucrează.

— Oh! M'aţi otrăvit, nelegiuiţilor! Doamne, fie-ţi milă de sufletul meu! Oh! Ce foc! Unde-i Doamna? Unde-i copilul meu!

[1] For the use of the gerund see 19. 7.

— S'au dus şi te-au lăsat cu noi.

— S'au dus şi m'au lăsat! M'au lăsat cu voi! Oh! Omorîţi-mă să scap de durere! Oh! Înjunghie-mă tu, tu eşti mai tânăr, fie-ţi milă! Scapă-mă de durerile ce mă sfâşie! Înjunghie-mă! — zise întorcându-se spre Stroici.

— Nu-mi voi spurca vitejescul junghiu în sângele cel pângărit al unui tiran ca tine.

Durerile creşteau. Otrăvitul se zbuciuma în convulsii.

— Oh! strigă, îmi arde sufletul! Oh! Daţi-mi apă, daţi-mi ceva să beau!

— Iată, zise Spancioc, luând păharul de argint de pe masă; au rămas drojdiile otrăvii. Bea şi te răcoreşte.

— Ba, ba, nu, nu vreau, zise bolnavul strângând dinţii. Atunci Stroici îl apucă şi-l ţinu neclintit; iar Spancioc scoţând cuţitul din teacă, îi descleştă cu vârful lui dinţii, şi îi turnă pe gât otrava ce mai era în fundul paharului.

Lăpuşneanu, mugind ca un taur ce vede trunchiul şi securea ce au să-l lovească, voi a se înturna cu faţa spre perete.

— Ce vrei să nu ne mai vezi? ziseră boierii. Ba se cade spre osânda ta să ne priveşti; învaţă a muri, tu care ştiai numai a omorî. Şi apucându-l amândoi îl ţineau nemişcat, uitându-se la el cu o bucurie infernală şi mustrându-l.

Nenorocitul Domn se zvârcolia în spasmele agoniei; spume făcea la gură; dinţii îi scrâşniau şi ochii săi sângeraţi se holbaseră; o sudoare îngheţată, tristă a morţii prevestitoare, ieşia ca nişte nasturi pe obrazul lui. După un chin de jumătate ceas, în sfârşit îşi dete duhul în mâinile călăilor săi.

Acest fel fu sfârşitul lui Alexandru Lăpuşneanu, care lăsă o pată de sânge în istoria Moldovei.

La mănăstirea Slatina, zidită de el, unde e îngropat, se vede şi astăzi portretul lui şi al familiei sale.

COSTACHE NEGRUZZI.
(1808-1868.)

Pe câmpia Bărăganului[1]
(Fragment din Pseudo-Kinegetikos, 1874)

Şi eu am crescut pe câmpul Bărăganului. Şi eu am văzut cârdurile de dropii, cutreerând cu pas măsurat şi cu capul aţintit la pază, acele şesuri fără margine, prin care aerul resfirat în unde diafane sub arşiţa soarelui de vară, oglindeşte ierburile şi bălăriile din depărtare şi le preface dinaintea vederii fermecate, în cetăţi cu mii de minarete, în palate cu mii de încântări.[2]

Din copilărie şi eu am trăit cu Tămădăienii, vânători de dropii de blaştină, cari neam de neamul lor[3] au rătăcit prin Bărăgan, pitulaţi în căruţele lor acoperite cu covergi de rogojină şi mânând în pas a lene gloabele lor de căluşei, am dat roată, ore, zile şi luni întregi, împrejurul falnicilor dropioi, cărora ei le zic Mitropoliţi.

Eu n'am uitat nici pe răposatul Caraiman, veselul şi priceputul staroste al vânătorilor Tămădăieni, carele putea să înghiţă în largele sale pântece atâtea vedre cât şi o butie de la Dealul-Mare; nici pe iscusitul moş Vlad, în căruţa căruia ai adormit tu adesea, pe când el, cu ochi de vulpe, zărea creştetul delicat al dropiei mişcând printre fulgii coliliei; nici pe bietul Gheorghe Giantă, cel care cu o rugină de puşcă pe care orice vânător ar fi asvârlit-o în gunoi, nimerea mai bine decât altul cu o carabină ghintuită, şi care pe mine nemernicul, m'a adus de multe ori cu vânat, la conacul de amiază.

Mie unuia, dacă cumva mi-a plăcut vreo vânătoare, apoi a fost tocmai din acelea în care picioarele şi mânile au mai puţin de lucrat.

Şi în adevăr, să şedem strâmb şi să judecăm drept: oare ce desfătare vânătorească mai deplină, mai neţărmurită, mai senină şi mai legănată în dulci şi duioase visări, poate fi pe lume decât aceea care o gustă cineva când, prin pustiile Bărăganului, căruţa în care stă culcat, abia înaintează pe căi fără de urme? Dinaintea-i e spaţiul nemărginit;

[1] The Walachian plain. [2] description of mirage.
[3] for generations.

dar valurile de iarbă, când înviate de o spornică verdeaţă, când ofilite sub pârlitura soarelui, nu-i însuflă îngrijirea nestatornicului ocean. În depărtare, pe linia netedă a orizontului, se profilează, ca moşoroaie de cârtiţe uriaşe, movilele, a căror urzeală e taina trecutului şi podoaba pustietăţii.

De la movila Neacşului, din preajma Borcei, ele stau semănate în prelargul câmpiei, ca sentinele mute şi gârbovite, sub ale lor bătrâneţi! La poalele lor cuibează vulturii cei falnici cu late pene negre, precum şi cei suri al căror cioc ascuţit şi aprig la pradă răsare hidos din ale lor grumazuri jupuite şi golaşe. E groaznic de a le vedea cum aceste jivine se repăd la stârvuri şi se îmbuibă cu mortăciuni, când prin suhaturi pică de bolesne câte o vită din cirezi! Dar căruţa trece în lături de acea privelişte scârboasă; ea înaintează încetinel şi rătăceşte fără ţel, după bunul plac al mârţoagelor arominde [1] sau după prepusul de vânat al Tămădăianului căruţaş.

De cu zorile, atunci când roua stă încă aninată pe firele de iarbă, căruţa s'a pornit dela conacul de noapte, dela coliba unchiaşului *mărunt*, căruia-i duce acum *dorul*, Bărăganul întreg [2] — şi tocmai când soarele e deasupra amiazului, ea soseşte la locul de întâlnire al vânătorilor.

AL. ODOBESCU.
(1834-1895.)

Amintiri din copilărie
(Fragment)

Odată, vara, pe-aproape de Moşi,[3] mă furişez din casă şi mă duc, ziua-miază-mare, la moş Vasile, fratele tatei cel mai mare, să fur nişte cireşe; căci numai la dânsul şi încă la vro două locuri din sat era câte-un cireş văratec care se

[1] For the use of the gerund cp. 19. 7.
[2] **Dor-Mărunt** (Little Longing) is the nickname of an innkeeper, where the hunters had their meeting-place. Round this inn a village was built.
[3] Saturday, the eve of Whit-Sunday, is the day of the commemoration of the dead, called **Moşi**=ancestors.

cocea-pălea de Duminica-Mare. Şi mă chitesc eu în mine,[1] cum s'o dau ca să nu mă prindă. Intru mai întâi în casa omului şi mă fac [2] a cere pe Ion să ne ducem la scăldat.

— Nu-i acasă Ion, zise mătuşa Mărioara; s'a dus cu moşu-tău Vasile, sub cetate la o chiuă din Condreni, s'aducă nişte sumani.

Căci trebuie să vă spun că la Humuleşti torc şi fetele şi băieţii, şi femeile şi bărbaţii; şi se fac multe giguri de sumani, şi lăi şi de noaten, care se vând şi pănură, şi cusute; şi acolo pe loc la negustori armeni, — veniţi înadins din alte târguri: Focşani, Bacău, Roman, Târgu-Frumos — şi de pe aiurea, precum şi pela iarmaroace în toate părţile. Cu asta se hrănesc mai mult Humuleştenii, răzăşi fără pământuri, şi cu negustoria din picioare: vite, cai, porci, oi, brânză, lână, oloi, sare şi făină de popuşoi; sumane: mari, genunchere şi sărdace; iţari, berneveci, cameşoaie, laicere şi scorţuri înflorite; ştergare de burangic alese, şi alte lucruri, ce le duceau Lunia în târg de vânzare, sau Joia pe la mănăstirile de maici cărora le vine cam peste-mână [3] târgul.

— Apoi dar mai rămâi sănătoasă, mătuşă Marioară! vorba de dinioarea. Şi-mi pare rău că nu-i văru Ion acasă că tare-aş fi avut plăcere, să ne scăldăm împreună. . . . Dar în gândul meu: ştii c'am nimerit-o? Bine că nu-s acasă; şi de n'ar veni degrabă, şi mai bine-ar fi.

Şi scurt şi cuprinzător, sărut mâna mătuşei, luându-mi ziua bună, ca un băiet de treabă [4]; ies din casă cu chip că mă duc la scăldat, mă şupuresc pe unde pot şi când colo, mă trezesc în cireşul femeii şi încep a cărăbăni la cireşe în sân, crude, coapte, cum se găsiau. Şi cum eram îngrijit şi mă siliam să fac ce-oi face mai degrabă, iaca mătuşa Mărioara c'o jordie în mână, la tulpina cireşului! . . .

— Dar bine, ghiavole,[5] aici ţi-i scăldatul? — zise ea, cu ochii holbaţi la mine; scoboară-te jos, tâlharule, că te-oi învăţa eu!

Dar cum să te cobori, căci jos era prăpădenie! Dacă

[1] I am planning with myself, I am thinking.
[2] I pretend.
[3] far, inconvenient.
[4] like a good boy.
[5] For diavole (*voc.*), devil.

vede ea şi vede că nu mă dau jos, zvârr! de vreo două trei ori cu bulgări în mine, dar nu mă chiteşte. Apoi începe a se aburca pe cireş în sus, zicând: Stăi, măi porcane, că te căptuşeşte ea, Mărioara acuş! Atunci eu mă dau iute pe-o creangă mai spre poale, şi odată fac: zup! în nişte cânepă care se întindea dela cireş înainte, şi era crudă şi până la brâu de înaltă. Şi nebuna de mătuşa Mărioara după mine, şi eu fuga iepureşte prin cânepă, până la gardul din fundul grădinii, pe care neavând vreme să-l sar, o cotigeam înapoi iar prin cânepă fugând tot iepureşte, şi ea după mine până'n dreptul ocolului, pe unde-mi era iar greu de sărit; pe de lături iar gard, şi hârsita de mătuşa nu mă slăbea din fugă nici în ruptul capului! Cât pe ce să puie mâna pe mine! Şi eu fuga şi ea fuga, şi eu fuga şi ea fuga, până ce dăm cânepa toată palancă la pământ; căci să nu spun minciuni, erau vro zece, douăsprezece prăjini de cânepă frumoasă şi deasă cum îi peria, de care nu s'a ales nimica. Şi după ce facem noi trebuşoara asta, mătuşa nu ştiu cum se încâlceşte prin cânepă, ori se împiedică de ceva şi cade jos. Eu atunci iute mă răsucesc într'un picior, fac vre două sărituri mai potrivite, mă asvârl peste gard de parcă nici nu l-am atins, şi-mi pierd urma, ducându-mă acasă şi fiind foarte cuminte în ziua aceea. . . . Ion Creangă.

(1837-1889.)

Moş Ion Roată şi Unirea

La 1857, pe când se fierbea Unirea în Iaşi, boierii moldoveni liberali, ca de-alde [1] Costache Hurmuzachi, M. Kogălniceanu şi alţii, au găsit cu cale să cheme la Adunare şi câţiva ţărani fruntaşi, câte unul de fiecare judeţ, spre a lua şi ei parte la facerea acestui măreţ, şi nobil act naţional. Cum au ajuns ţăranii în Iaşi, boierii au pus mână dela mână,[2] de i-au ferchezuit frumos şi i-au îmbrăcat la fel, cu cheburi albe şi cuşme nouă, de se mirau ţăranii ce berechet i-a găsit. Apoi, se zice că i-ar fi dat pe sama unuia dintre boieri să

[1] See 14. 2, Note 2. [2] collected money between them.

le ţie cuvânt, ca să-i facă a înţelege scopul chemării lor la Iaşi.

— Oameni buni, ştiţi pentru ce sânteţi chemaţi aici, între noi, zise boieriul cu blândeţă.

— Vom şti, cucoane, dacă ni-ţi spune, răspunse cu sieală un ţăran mai bătrân, scărpinându-se în cap.

— Apoi iaca ce, oameni buni: de sute de ani, două ţări surori, creştine şi megieşe, Moldova noastră şi Valahiea sau Ţara Muntenească, de care poate-ţi fi auzit vorbindu-se, se sfăşie şi se mănâncă între dânsele spre cumplita urgie şi peire a neamului românesc. Ţări surori şi creştine, am zis, oameni buni; căci precum ne închinăm noi Moldovenii, aşa se închină şi fraţii noştri din Valahiea. Statura, vorba, hrana, îmbrăcămintea şi toate obiceiurile câte le avem noi, le au întocmai şi fraţii noştri Munteni. Ţări megieşe, am zis, oameni buni; căci numai părăuaşul Milcov, ce trece pela Focşani, le desparte. ,,Să-l săcăm dar dintr'o sorbire" şi să facem sfânta Unire, adică înfrăţirea dorită de strămoşii noştri, pe care ei n'au putut s'o facă în împrejurările grele de pe atunci. Iaca, oameni buni, ce treabă creştinească şi frumoasă avem de făcut. Numai Dumnezeu să ne-ajute! Inţeles-aţi, vă rog, oameni buni, pentruce v'am chemat? Şi dacă aveţi ceva de zis, nu vă sfiiţi; spuneţi verde,[1] moldoveneşte, ca la nişte fraţi ce vă sântem. Că de aceea ne-am adunat aici, ca să ne luminăm unii pe alţii şi Dumnezeu să ne lumineze pe toţi, cum a şti el mai bine!

— Înţelegem, cucoane, aşa a fi, răspunseră câţiva ţărani mai ruşinoşi; că dă, dacă nu-ţi şti dumnevoastră ce-i pe lume, noi ţărănimea dela coarnele plugului avem să ştim ce-i bine şi ce-i rău?

— Ba eu drept să vă spun, cucoane, n'am înţeles! ci-că[2] zise cu îndrăzneală unul dintre ţărani, anume *Ion Roată*. Ş'apoi chiar dacă ne-am pricepe şi noi la câte ceva, cine se mai uită în gura noastră? Vorba ceea, cucoane: Ţăranul când merge, tropăeşte, şi când vorbeşte, hodorogeşte, să ierte cinstită faţa dumnevoastră. Eu socot că treaba asta se putea face şi fără de noi: că dă, noi ştim a învârti sapa,

[1] sincerely, openly. [2] =se zice că.

coasa şi secerea, dar dumnevoastră învârtiţi condeiul şi când vreţi, ştiţi a face din alb negru şi din negru alb. . . . Dumnezeu v'a dăruit cu minte, ca să ne povăţuiţi şi pe noi prostimea. . . .

— Ba nu, oameni buni, s'a trecut vremea aceea, pe când numai boierii făceau totul în ţara aceasta ş'o storceau după plac. Astăzi toţi, dela Vlădică până la opincă,[1] trebue să luăm parte la nevoile şi la fericirea ţării. Muncă şi câştig, datorii şi drepturi, pentru toţi deopotrivă.

Le spuse boieriul apoi despre originea Românilor, cum şi de cine au fost ei aduşi pe aceste locuri ; despre suferinţele lor şi cum au ajuns a fi desbinaţi şi împrăştieţi prin alte ţări. Le dă el pilde câte şi mai multe : cu smocul de nuiele, cu taurii învrăjbiţi şi, în sfârşit, se sileşte bietul creştin din răsputeri a-i face să înţeleagă care sânt roadele binefăcătoare ale Unirii, aducându-le aminte că tot „pentru unirea tuturor" se roagă şi sfânta biserică în toate zilele, mai bine de 1850 de ani.

— Ei, oameni buni, cred că acum aţi priceput !

— Priceput, cucoane, cât se poate de bine, răspunseră mai toţi. Dumnezeu să vă ajute la cele bune !

— Ba eu tot nu, cucoane, răspunse moş Ion Roată.

— Dumnezeu să mă ierte, moş Ioane, dar dumneta, cum văd, eşti cam greu de cap ; ia haidem în grădină să vă fac a înţelege şi mai bine. — Moş Ioane, vezi colo în ogradă la mine bolovanul cel mare ?

— Îl vedem, cucoane.

— Ia fă bine, şi adă-l ici lângă mine, zise boieriul, care şedea acum pe un jâlţ în mijlocul ţăranilor.

— S'avem iertare, cucoane, n'om putè,[2] că doar acolo-i greutate, nu şagă.

— Ia cearcă şi vezi.

Moş Roată se duce şi vre să rădice bolovanul, dar nu poate.

— Ia du-te şi dumneta moş Vasile, şi dumneta bade Ilie, şi dumneta bade Pandelachi.

În sfârşit se duc ei vro 3-4 ţărani, urnesc bolovanul din loc, îl rădică pe umere şi-l aduc lângă boier.

[1] peasant sandal=peasant. [2] =putea.

— Ei, oameni buni, vedeţi? S'a dus moş Ion şi n'a putut face treaba singur; dar când v'aţi mai dus câţiva într'ajutor, treaba s'a făcut cu mare uşurinţă, greutatea n'a mai fost aceeaşi. Povestea cântecului:

Unde-i unul, nu-i putere
La nevoi şi la durere;
Unde-s mulţi, puterea creşte
Şi duşmanul nu sporeşte.

Aşa şi cu Unirea, oameni buni! Credeţi dumnevoastră, că d-a ajuta Dumnezeu a se uni Moldova cu Valahiea, avem să fim numai atâţia? Fraţii noştri din Transilvania, Bucovina, Basarabia şi cei de peste Dunărea, din Macedonia şi de prin alte părţi ale lumii, numai să ne vadă că trăim bine, şi ei se vor uni cu noi şi vom face împreună o ţară mare, bogată şi puternică de n'or mai îndrăzni duşmanii în vecii vecilor a se lega de Români. D'apoi fraţii noştri de sânge: Franţujii, Italienii, Spaniolii şi Portugezii ce aşteaptă? La orice întâmplare, Doamne fereşte, stau gata să-şi verse sângele pentru noi. . . . Unirea face puterea, oameni buni.
— Ei, acum cred c'aţi înţeles şi răsînţeles?

— Ba eu unul, să iertaţi dumnevoastră, cucoane, încă tot n'am înţeles, răspunde moş Roată.

— Cum se face asta, moş Ioane? Mai bine ce v'am tălmăcit, şi un copil putea să înţeleagă.

— Mai aşa,[1] cucoane, răspunseră ceilalţi.

— Moş Ioane, zise acum boierul cam tulburat de multă obosală, ia spune dumneta în legea dumitale, cum ai înţeles, cum n'ai înţeles, decând se face atâta vorbă; să auzim şi noi!

— Dă, cucoane, să nu vă fie cu supărare; dar dela vorbă şi până la faptă este mare deosebire. . . . Dumnevoastră, *ca fiecare boier*, numai ne-aţi poruncit să aducem bolovanul, dar n'aţi pus umărul împreună cu noi la adus, cum ne spuneaţi dinioarea, că de acum toţi au să iee parte la sarcini: dela Vlădică până la opincă. Bine-ar fi, dac'ar fi aşa, cucoane, căci la război înapoi şi la pomană năvală, parcă nu prea

[1] of course.

vine la socoteală. . . . Iar dela bolovanul dumnevoastră . . . am înţeles aşa: că până acum noi ţăranii am dus fiecare câte-o piatră mai mare sau mai mică pe umere; însă acum sântem chemaţi a purta împreună tot noi, *opinca*, o stâncă pe umerele noastre. . . . Să dea Domnul, cucoane, să fie altfel, că mie unuia nu mi-a părè [1] rău. . . .

La aceste vorbe, ţăranii ceialalţi au început a strânge din umere, a se uita lung unul la altul şi a zice:

— Ia, poate că şi Roată al nostru să aibă dreptate! . . .

Iar boeriul, luându-i înainte cu glume, a înghiţit găluşca şi a tăcut molcum.

Iaşi, 4 *Mai*, 1880. ION CREANGĂ.

Pe Valea Motrului

Mergem o bucată pe marginea Motrului, ale cărui unde verzui, pripite, se sparg de bolovani. Apoi urcăm pe-un podiş trăgănat. Mirezme'mbătătoare se'mprăştie'n aer de pe fâneţele bătute de soare. Lanurile îşi leagănă spicele, ca de farmecul unui cântec. În depărtare se pierd liniile încâlcite ale dealurilor acoperite de păduri. Pe costişe grânele coapte sânt împânzite de secerători. Cârduri de fete'n cămăşi şi vâlnice roşii se pleacă muncii şi-şi mişcă braţele'n tactul unei doine. Dulce răsună valea de glasurile lor. Pe mirişti şi pe codri alunecă'ncet umbrele călătoare ale norilor. În urma noastră Motrul, tolănit ca un balaur în spintecătura dealurilor, îşi tremură solzii în soare. Copaci bătrâni se pleacă pe undele lui să-i asculte poveştile.

El vine de sus, dinspre Culmea Frumoasă, dela poalele muntelui Oslea, pe care sta'n vechime încolăcit năprasnicul şarpe cu nouă ochi, de groaza căruia se cutremura toată valea Dunării, pân'a sosit Iorgovan, un voinic fără pereche şi s'a aşezat într'o groapă cu tolba de săgeţi; şi când şarpele, flămând a ridicat capul să'nghită o turmă de vite, Iorgovan, întinzând arcul, i-a aruncat o săgeată şi i-a scos un ochi; tot aşa până când şarpele, rămâind numai c'un ochi, a rupt-o

[1] =părea.

de fugă pe la Furca Alunului, pe unde se vede şi azi dâra lui, căreia îi mai zic unii şi ,,brazda lui Novac." Iorgovan s'a luat după el, şi unde-l ajungea îi şi tăia câte o bucată din trup ; la apa Cernei însă voinicul a stat, fermecat de cântecul unei zâne, iar capul, şarpelui a trecut Dunărea pe la Cazane, şi s'a ascuns în peştera de unde iese vara musca cea rea.[1]

AL. VLĂHUŢĂ.
(1858-1919.)

Năpasta

Dramă în două acte

(**Dragomir** *a omorît pe Dumitru soțul Ancăi ca să se poată căsători cu ea.* **Anca** *bănuește că* **Dragomir** *e ucigașul și se căsătorește cu el ca să se poată răsbuna. Un nevinovat, Ion, a fost condamnat la ocnă pentru moartea lui Dumitru. Ion înebunit de suferințe evadează din închisoare și ajunge în casa lui* **Dragomir** *și a Ancăi.* **Anca** *destăinuește lui Ion că adevăratul ucigaș este* **Dragomir**. *Ion încearcă să omoare pe* **Dragomir**, *dar* **Anca** *îl salvează pentru a-i aplica pedeapsa cuvenită pentru crima lui. Ion se sinucide.* **Anca** *îndeamnă pe* **Dragomir** *să-i arunce trupul într'o fântână ca să nu fie bănuiți că ei au omorît pe Ion. Ea cheamă apoi oamenii din sat și învinuește pe* **Dragomir** *că a omorît pe Ion, pentru ca să-l facă să sufere pentru o crimă pe care n'a comis'o, precum a suferit Ion, pentru crima făptuită de el.*)

ACTUL II

SCENA VIII

Anca, Dragomir

Anca (*vine cu pasul grav la* **Dragomir**, *care stă pe scaun cu capul în mâini*). Scoală, Dragomire, c'a sosit ceasul!

Dragomir (*se scoală*). Ceasul!

Anca. Ceasul socotelii. Stăi drept . . . ; adună-ţi minţile

[1] musca columbacă=a fly which kills the cattle.

câte le mai ai şi răspunde la ce te-oi întreba. . . . Pentruce l-ai omorît?

Dragomir (*înnecat de ciudă până la lacrimi*). Nu! nu l-am omorît eu! . . . N'ai fost tu aicea? N'ai văzut tu?

Anca. Nu pe Ion . . . ; pe Ion lasă-l. . . . De altcineva îţi vorbesc eu acuma . . .

Dragomir (*pălind încet*). De cine?

Anca. Ştii de cine; nu te mai preface. . . . Tu vrei să pleci, tu caută să pleci (*el face trist din cap că da; ea aspru*). Ei! . . . nu faci un pas de-aicea până nu-i zici pe nume . . . (*privindu-l cu toată puterea*). Zi-i odată pe nume. . . .

Dragomir (*încet de tot*). Du . . . mi . . . tru!

Anca (*răsuflând din adânc*). Ai văzut? . . . Aşa! Du-mitru (*şade jos; el stă în picioare*). Pentru ce l-ai ucis. . . .

Dragomir. Pentru tine . . .

Anca. Pentru mine . . .

Dragomir. Ca să te iau eu . . .

Anca. Cum l-ai ucis? spune (*îşi pune coatele pe masă şi bărbia în palme şi ascultă nemişcată; el stă drept, se încheie cu îngrijire la mintean şi povesteşte simplu*).

Dragomir. Mă tot goneai. . . . Odată, când ai ieşit dela biserică la Vinerea Mare, seara — ţi-aduci aminte — m'am dat pe lângă tine şi ţi-am zis: ,,Anco! de ce n'ai vrut să mă iei pe mine? Eu tot te iubesc. . . . Lasă-l pe Dumitru şi vino.“ . . . Ţi-aduci aminte? . . .

Anca. Da, mi-aduc.

Dragomir. Tu mi-ai răspuns: ,,Am bărbat, lasă-mă'n pace!“

Anca. Şi tu?

Dragomir. Eu am plecat acasă, n'am dormit toată noaptea şi dimineaţa . . . m'am hotărît.

Anca. Cum ai făcut?

Dragomir. Ştiam când se întoarce dela deal p'în pădure . . . şi l-am aşteptat. . . . Venea şuerând. . . . Ne-am întâlnit, ne-am dat în vorbă . . . i-am arătat o plută înnaltă; el a ridicat ochii în sus. . . . Am tras cuţitul, şi până s'aplece iar ochii . . . (*se opreşte stingându-i-se glasul*).

Anca (*îşi acopere faţa, — un moment — apoi şi-o descopere şi-l priveşte aşteptând*). Ei? . . . înnainte.

Dragomir. Ce să-ţi mai spui?

Anca. El ce-a făcut?

Dragomir. A ţipat ş'a căzut în genunchi . . . ; a dat să scoată cuţitul . . . da m'am repezit şi l-am lovit peste mână şi la beregată . . . ; când m'am plecat la el, m'a muşcat de mână.

Anca. Dela el era muşcătura! (*îi face semn să urmeze*).

Dragomir. Pe urmă l-am întors cu faţa în jos, am mers la fântână de m'am spălat şi m'am dus acasă să mă culc, că nu mai puteam, cădeam d'an picioarele de ostenit. . . . Ion l-a găsit acolo. . . . Pe urmă . . . ştii.

I. L. Caragiale.
(1852-1912.)

Petrea Dascalul

. . . .

Se isprăvise răsboiul Crimeiei, trupele austriace se retrăseseră din ţară şi pacea dela Paris ne promitea Unirea Principatelor, mărirea teritoriului cu o parte din Basarabia, neatârnarea politică şi multe altele care ne înflăcărau minţile.

În timpul acela dar, de frumoasă amintire, doi lorzi engleji care luase parte la comanda superioară a oştirilor aliate din Crimea, auzind că Moldova e o ţară încă primitivă, cu obiceiuri patriarcale şi cu munţi plini de urşi, veniră anume din Sevastopol în Galaţi cu hotărîrea de a se desfăta la un vânat de urşi, ceea ce de mult timp locuitorii Angliei nu mai pot face în insulele lor. Ei erau bogaţi căci lirele sterling sunau în buzunarele lor, erau serioşi căci mai nu vorbiau unul cu altul, erau fudui căci se ţineau totdeuna cu gâturile ţapene şi abia de scoborau ochii pe vre-un obraz omenesc. Nalţi şi subţiri, şi totdeuna bine îmbrăcaţi şi pieptănaţi ei priviau lumea cu gravitate prin geamul ochelarilor, vroind parcă înadins să puie oarecare distanţă între ei şi lume.

Ei plecară într'o trăsură cu opt cai de poştă pregătită de pârcălabul de Galaţi, şi apucară drumul spre munte la o moşie către proprietarul căreia aveau anume scrisori de recomendaţie.

. . . .

Vremea era frumoasă, aerul viu şi răcoros, şi spre partea şesului la răsărit, soarele se înălţa vesel pe un cer cuprins de foc.

Tăcuţi urcau Englejii la deal, cu pas regulat şi cu aerul serios a unor oameni ce merg într'o gravă întreprindere. Numai Petrea Dascalul blajin cum era el şi cam slobod la gură, mai schimba din când în când câte o şagă cu tovarăşii săi din sat. Trei ceasuri întregi ei suiră mereu în sudoarea frunţii.

. . . .

Pe la amiazăzi Petrea Dascalul îi opri într'o desime mare unde era o mulţime de bolovani şi cioate răsturnate, care păreau a fi aduse de puhoi. — Aice e ursul! — zise Petrea Dascalul. Atunci figurile lungi şi solemne ale lorzilor se făcură şi mai lungi şi mai solemne, căci dorul lor era acum aproape să fie împlinit: aveau în sfârşit să deie ochii cu sihastrul Carpaţilor şi să aibă ce istorisi despre lupta cu dânsul când se vor întoarce în ţara lor.

. . . .

— Aici e ursul, adaose Petrea Dascalul, arătând gura vizuinei. . . . — Doarme ca boerii după masă, băgă de samă Petrea Dascalul.

În vremea aceasta flegmaticii Englezi începură să deie semne de nerăbdare, crezând că Petrea Dascalul în care dela început nu prea avusese încredere, era cu adevărat un şiret ce-i purta cu vorba.

— E trândav ursul, zise Petrea cam necăjit, nu-l scoţi cu una cu două dela tabietul lui. . . . Dar eu i-s popa!

Apoi el băgă mâna în torbă, scoase o lumănărică de ceară albă, o lipi la buza puştii deasupra ţelului, o aprinse zicând că la prohod trebuie şi lumănare, se dase pe brânci şi cu puşca întinsă şi înarmată intră voiniceşte în visunie. Lordul cel mai înalt şi mai necrezător, care nu se aştepta la una ca aceasta, se uita acum nemişcat şi cu ochii holbaţi cum Petrea Dascalul se târâia încet, încet în visunie, cum îşi introduse mai întâi capul, pe urmă umerii, apoi picioarele, iar, după ce nu mai văzu nimic, strigă: "*How original!*" însă cu un glas schimbat cum nu ise întâmplase din fiua asaltului turnului Malacof. Iar celalt lord, cuviincios ca totdeuna, îşi ştergea cu batista sudoarea de pe frunte provenită negreşit[1] din căldura soarelui, însă nu repetă de astă dată cuvintele tovarăşului său ca de obicei.

După câteva minute de aşteptare groaznică în care numai inimile îşi păstrase mişcarea, se auzi deodată un trăsnet de puşcă urmat de un muget sălbatec, înfricoşat, cu atât mai înfricoşat cu cât venea din întunerecul de sub pământ unde era ştiut că numai moartea putea să hotărască între om şi fiară. Apoi se făcu iarăş linişte adâncă, linişte de mormânt în timp de mai multe minute lungi ca secolele, în care lorzii abia de'şi mai puteau păstra sufletul. *Acu-i acu!* . . . gândia fiecare în sine. Dar lucru înfiorător, liniştea ţinea mereu, nici un semn nu venia de sub pământ. . . . Ce se petrecea oare acolo? . . . Negreşit nu era bine de vreme ce Petrea Dascalul după împuşcătura lui nu mai ieşia la lumină, căci dacă ar fi fost el învingătorul ce ar mai fi stat înlăuntru?

Când iată . . . se auzi la gura visuniei un foşnet curios, mai mare decât l-ar fi putat face un om, şi cioatele şi pietrele începură să se mişte. Momentul era suprem; lorzii înţepeniţi, cu ochii îndreptaţi spre visunie, cu puştile la ochi şi degetele pe trăgători stăteau gata să tragă în dihania ce se vestia, şi tâmplele lor se băteau atât de puternic încât ochelarii le jucau pe nas. Dar spre marea şi nemărginita lor mirare, în loc de dihanie se văzură deodată picioarele lui Petrea Dascalul, apoi umerii, apoi capul şi dupăce Petrea ieşi de tot, ţinând într'o mână puşca şi în cealaltă o frânghie, aruncă repede capătul ei celorlalţi patru puşcaşi strigând: — „Trageţi, băieţi, vârtos! . . ." Atunci câteşi cinci prinseră să tragă din răsputeri şi iată că o cogemite ursoaică moartă,

[1] of course.

lovită drept în frunte şi legată cu frânghia de gât eşi de sub pământ.

Uimirea Englejilor fu atât de mare văzând isbânda lui Petrea Dascalul încât de astă dată uitându-şi demnitatea, şi distanţa socială ce-i despărţia de dânsul, începură să-l strângă de mână cu o căldură neobicinuită cumpătatului temperament englez.

Iar Petrea Dascalul care atunci pentru prima oară avu fericirea să facă cunoştinţă cu lirele sterling ale Marei Britanii se uita nedumirit când la strălucitoarea monedă ce curgea gârlă în palma sa, când la lorzii cei cu figurile de un cot, având aerul a zice : ,,Banii, nu-i vorbă îi primesc eu, dar voi ce dracul de vă miraţi aşa de mine, că doar nu mi-i întâia oară să mă bag în bârlogul ursului ?“

. . . .

Cu o parte din lirele sterling Petrea Dascalul şi-a măritat o fată, cea din urmă ce-i rămăsese în casă, iar cu cealaltă parte şi-a făcut sie-şi o mică zestrişoară pentru zilele bătrâneţelor. Nu târziu după aceea, proprietarul moşiei primi din Londra o scrisoare cu rugămintea să înmâneze lui Petrea Dascalul, ca semn de neuitare din partea lorzilor, portretele fotografice ale lor însoţite de două puşti foarte scumpe ieşite din cea mai renumită fabrică a Engliterei, cum şi un număr al ziarului *The Illustrated London News* în care era desemnată cu mult adevăr fioroasa scenă a intrării lui Petrea Dascalul în visunia ursului.

Dar urmarea cea mai de căpetenie, ce a avut această mică întâmplare, a fost că amândoi lorzii iubitori de vânat, au apărat călduros în Camera de sus a Angliei drepturile ciudatelor ţări dunărene cu surugii nebuni şi vânători ce se bagă în visunia ursului, şi nu puţin contribui puternica lor voce întru a fi recunoscută *Unirea* mult dorită a Principatelor române şi alegerea îndoită a *Colonelului Cuza*. Mici lucruri au câte odată mari urmări, căci nime nu ştie unde pot răspunde capetele firelor care leagă una de alta faptele omeneşti.

N. GANE.
(1838-1916.)

Bunicul

Se scuturau salcâmii ca ploaia de miresme.

Bunicul stă pe prispă. Se gândeşte. La ce se gândeşte? La nimic. Numără florile cari cad; se uită în fundul grădinii; se scarpină'n cap, şi iar numără florile scuturate de o adiere călduroasă şi mirositoare.

Pletele albe şi creţe par'că sunt nişte ciorchini de flori albe, sprâncenile, mustăţile şi barba . . . peste toate au nins ani mulţi şi grei.

Numai ochii bunicului au rămas ca odinioară: blânzi şi mângâietori.

Cine a trântit poarta?

— Credeam că s'a umflat vântul. . . . O bată-vă norocul cocoşeii moşului — zise bătrânul.

Un băeţandru şi o fetiţă roşii şi bucălăi, sărutară mâinile lui „tata-moşu".

— Tată moşule, zise fetiţa, de ce sboară pasările?

— Fiin' că au aripi, răspunse bătrânul, sorbind'o din ochi.

— Păi raţele n'au aripi? . . . De ce nu sboară?

— Sboară, zise băiatul, dar pe jos.

Bătrânul cuprinse într'o mână pe fată şi în cealaltă pe băiat.

— O, voinicii moşului, şopti el, şi zâmbi pe sub mustăţi, şi-i privi cu atâta dragoste, că ochii lui erau numai lumină şi binecuvântare.

— Tată moşule, da cocorii un' se duc, când se duc?

— În ţara cocorilor.

— În ţara cocorilor?

— Da.

— Da rândunelele un' se duc când se duc?

— În ţara rândunelelor.

— În ţara rândunelelor?

— Da.

— Tată moşule, aş vrea să-mi crească şi mie aripi şi să sbor sus, sus de tot, până'n slava cerului, — zise băiatul netezindu-i barba.

— Dacă ţi-o creşte ţie aripi, — zise fata, — mie să-mi prinzi o presură şi un sticlete.

— Da . . . hî . . . hî . . . păi ce fel . . . şi mie ?

Fata se întristă. Bătrânul o mângâiă şi zise băiatului :

— Bine, să prinzi şi pentru tine, să prinzi şi pentru ea.

— Ţie două şi mie două . . . nu aşa, tată moşule ?

— Fireşte, ţie două, lui două şi mie una.

— Vrei şi tu, tată moşule ? întrebă băiatul cu mândrie.

— Cum de nu, mie un scatiu.

Ce fericiţi sunt ! Băiatul a încălecat pe un genunchi şi fata pe altul. Bunicul îi joacă. Copiii bat din palme. Bunicul le cântă ,,măi cazace, căzăcele, ce caţi noaptea prin argele. . . .“

O femeie uscăţivă intră pe poartă cu două doniţi mari de apă. Copiii tăcură din râs şi bunicul din cântec. E mama lor şi fata lui. Cum îi văzu începu :

— I . . . tată, şi dumeata . . . iar îi răzgâi . . . o să ţi se suie în cap !

— Bunicul ridică mâna în sus, aducând degetele ca un preot, care binecuvintează, şi zise prelung :

— Lăsaţi pe copii să vină la mine !

— Biiine, tată, biiine . . . dar ştii . . . o bată-i focul de copii. — Femeia intră în casă.

— Să-i bată norocul şi sănătatea, şopti moşul, ca şi cum ar fi mustrat pe cineva, şi sărută în creştetul capului şi pe unul şi pe altul.

Si iar începu râsul şi jocul şi cântecul. Şi se osteni bunicul şi stătu din joc, iar copiii începura să-l mângâie.

Din vorbă în vorbă copiii se făcură stăpâni pe obrajii bunicului.

— Partea asta este a mea.

— Şi partea asta a mea.

— Mustaţa asta este a mea.

— Şi asta a mea.

La barbă se încurcară. Bunicul îi împăcă zicându-le :

— Pe din două.

Şi copiii o şi despicară, cam repede, că bătrânul strânse din ochi.

— Jumătate mie.

— Şi jumătate mie.

Şi dupăce o împărţiră frăţeşte, începu lauda.

Băiatul : — Mustaţa mea e mai lungă.

Fata : — Ba a mea este mai lungă.

Şi băiatul întinse d'o mustaţă şi fata de alta, ba a lui, ba a ei, să fie mai lungă.

Pe bunic îl trecură lacrimile, dar tăcu şi-i împăcă zicându-le : — Amândouă sunt d'o potrivă.

— Ş'a mea ş'a ei !

— Ş'a mea ş'a lui !

La obraji cearta se aprinde mai tare.

— Partea mea este mai frumoasă.

— Ba a mea că e mai albă !

Bunicul zâmbi.

— Ba a mea, că e mai caldă !

— Ba a mea, că e mai dulce !

— Ba a mea, că nu e ca a ta !

— Ba a mea, că are un ochi mai verde !

Bunicul abia se ţinea de râs.

— Ba a mea !

— Ba a mea !

Şi băiatul înfuriindu-se trase o palmă peste partea fetei. Fata ţipă, sări de pe genunchiul bătrânului, se repezi şi trase o palmă peste partea băiatului. Băiatul cu lacrimile în ochi sărută partea lui şi fata suspinând pe a ei.

Mama lor eşi pe uşe şi întrebă răstit :

— Ce e asta ? Viermi neastâmpăraţi ! Obrajii bunicului erau roşii şi calzi. Şi surâzând fericit, răspunse fie-si :

— Lăsaţi pe copii să vie la mine !

Barbu S. Delavrancea.
(1858-1918.)

Învingătorul lui Napoleon

În vara aceia profesorul Caranfil se dusese să petreacă vacanţa la Mănăstirea Neamţului, şi în ziua când i s'a întâmplat cele ce mi-a povestit, făcuse o excursie cu mai mulţi prieteni şi cunoscuţi prin împrejurimile mănăstirii până dincolo de schitul Procovului. Când a ajuns acasă, la părintele Chiprian, la care avea locuinţa, înnoptase dealbinelea şi Caranfil se gândi cu plăcere la aşternutul lui moale, unde avea să se odihnească de oboselile zilei. Intrând înlăuntru, îşi aruncă ca de obicei privirile la gravurile vechi de pe păreţii camerei sale. Pe un părete, portretele lui Alexandru II şi al Împărătesei Maria Feodorovna, pe care vremea lăsase fel de fel de urme, stăteau alăturea de împuşcarea lui Maximiliam, iar pe păretele din faţă era Sfânta Agură, şi mai încolo chipul lui Napoleon, făcut după o ilustraţie a timpului.

Caranfil se pregăti să se culce gândindu-se la tot felul de lucruri. Petrecuse bine în ziua aceia într'o companie veselă şi plăcută. . . . Aici Caranfil surâse. Peste câteva zile va face o nouă escursie, la Cetatea Neamţului, unde nu fusese niciodată. ,,Săracul Ştefan cel Mare, se gândi el, mare om!" Şi Caranfil într'un acces de patriotism îşi scoase surtucul făcând doi paşi prin odae, şi se opri în faţa lui Napoleon.

,,Teribilă figură," continuă profesorul fixând chipul lui Napoleon. ,,Dar a dat şi el de dracul la Waterloo şi ducele de . . ."

Aici Caranfil se opri, căci nu-i veni repede în minte numele eroului dela Waterloo.

. . . .

Caranfil îşi puse mânile sub cap şi închise ochii, hotărît să doarmă, dar ceva îl împiedeca. ,,Stăi, frate, cum îi zice?" . . . Şi el îşi fixă toată atenţia, pentru a scoate din mulţimea cunoştinţelor şi a numelor proprii înmagazinate în capul său, numele eroului englez.

. . . .

Caranfil se trânti în pat, apoi deodată svârli oghialul de pe el, se dădu jos şi începu să se plimbe dela un capăt la celălalt al odăii.

,,Ia să vedem, zise el tare. . . . S'o luăm încetişor. . . . Aşa." Şi începu ca la şcoală să-şi puie întrebări şi să dee tot el răspunsurile:

— Unde a fost învins, mă rog, Napoleon? — La Waterloo. — Foarte bine. — Cine l-a învins? — Ducele de . . ."

Caranfil se opri la figura lui Napoleon, pe care o fixă cu tenacitate, ca şi cum ar fi voit să citească în trăsăturile eroului francez numele duşmanului său. Dar împăratul stătea mândru şi nu voi să se preteze de loc la astfel de manoperă a profesorului. De aceea începu iarăş cu întrebările, plimbându-se prin odae agitat: „Cine a fost învingătorul lui Napoleon? — Ducele de . . ."

Se vede bine că ducele era hotărît, cu tot dinadinsul, ca în noaptea asta să petreacă în locuinţa lui aeriană pe sama amicului nostru.

Caranfil se opri în mijlocul odăii şi zise cu tonul cel mai convingător: „Să fiu raţional . . . să aştept până mâne . . . nu-i cine ştie cât. . . . Atunci voi afla desigur." Şi profesorul, ca încheere la această judecată, iarăş fixă un punct în spaţiu. „Şi apoi serios . . . ce-mi pasă la urma urmei cine l-a învins! . . . Dracul să-i iee pe amândoi! . . . Haide, Caranfile . . . fii om cuminte. . . . La culcare!"

Într'adevăr, în urma acestei admonestări, aşa de raţionale, se culcă iarăş, închise ochii, şi îşi puse şi o pernă peste cap. Dar nu trecură nici cinci minute şi Caranfil scoase capul şi zise încetişor: „Kutusoff, Blücher, Schwarzenberg . . ." Dar nici în tovărăşia soţilor lui de arme generalul englez nu voi să iasă la iveală.

. . . .

Caranfil se sculă, udă un prosop cu apă rece, se legă cu el la cap, apoi începu să se plimbe prin casă furios, repetând ca un şcolar bucher: „Napoleon a fost învins la Waterloo de . . . stăi . . . stăi . . . stăi! — Cine a învins pe Napoleon la Waterloo? — Ducele de . . ."

Cum se plimba astfel prin casă, deodată o licărire fericită îi lumină faţa şi Caranfil se opri pe loc şi zise tare, cu cea mai desăvârşită convingere, uitându-se fix în podele: „Toţi oamenii sânt muritori . . . ducele de . . . e om . . . deci ducele de . . . e muritor."

. . . .

El își adusese aminte că odată, mai demult, învățase la universitate, într'un manual de logică al unui Englez, acest exemplu de silogism, în care ducele învingător era subiectul din propoziția minoră; și dacă istoria îl trădase în noaptea aceasta blăstămată, sperase un moment că cel puțin filosofia îi va veni în ajutor.

. . . .

Caranfil deschise fereastra și o răcoare plăcută veni în odae, răcorindu-i capul înfierbântat. De pe dealul din față, dinspre Pleș, se auzea fâșiitul brazilor. Luna lumina întinderile, și la lumina ei, chipul lui Napoleon se deslușea lămurit pe păretele opus. Caranfil îl fixă încă odată cu aceeaș intenție de mai adineoara, dar împăratul, cu capul întors în profil, cu mâna dreaptă la deschizătura jiletcii și cu cea stângă la spate, îl înfrunta vădit cu aerul lui rece și desprețuitor.

Această chestiune începu să iee pentru Caranfil proporțiile unei adevărate nenorociri.... Cu neputință să doarmă!... Și se plimba prin casă cu pași mari, vorbind singur și gesticulând....

,,A fost în Portugalia.... Cine a fost în Portugalia?... Ducele de Brag... nu.... Toți oamenii sânt muritori.... Cum de l-am uitat?... Ducele de Rag... lua-l-ar dracu....“

. . . .

Unde să se ducă?... Cum să afle? Da! se va duce la amicul său Vasiliu... el singur îl va putea liniști. Până dimineață era prea mult. Caranfil se îmbrăcă, se încălță și eși din casă. Vasiliu stătea tocmai în Vovidenie... dar n'are a face. Caranfil porni într'acolo.

. . . .

Era o noapte dintre cele mai frumoase. De pe cărarea care duce spre deal, în Vovidenie, se vedea o priveliște admirabilă, dar lui Caranfil de altele îi ardea acuma: ,,A comandat cu Blücher.... Prin urmare, cine a comandat cu Blücher la Waterloo?... Toți oamenii sânt muritori.... Ducele de... este om....“

De prisos toate procedeele! Noroc că nu mai era mult până la Vasiliu.

Când a ajuns în Vovidenie era miezul nopţii. O linişte mare stăpânea toate împrejurimile. Numai toaca mănăstirii se auzea lămurit, când mai încet când mai tare, iar din fundul codrilor care împrejmuesc din trei părţi mănăstirea din deal, o altă toacă, dela un schit misterios, răspundea când mai tare, când mai încet. . . .

Caranfil bătu în geamul prietenului său strigânde-l pe nume. — Cine-i acolo? se auzi din lăuntru. — Eu. — Tu eşti? — Da. Dormeai? — Adormisem, dar ce-i? — Te rog, cum îi zice generalului englez care a învins pe Napoleon la Waterloo? . . . Comandantul luptei. . . .

Urmă o mică pauză, după care Vasiliu întrebă: — Ai înnebunit? — Te rog, lasă gluma la o parte, spuse Caranfil, şi răspunde-mi.

Vasiliu nu răspunse, dar se auzi un mic sgomot în casă şi după puţină vreme, uşa sălii se deschise şi o figură îmbrăcată în alb, cu un surtuc între umere, apăru în cerdac.

— Ce ai, bre? — N'am nimic, răspunse Caranfil, am uitat numele învingătorului lui Napoleon, şi mă chinuesc deaseară să aflu cum îi zice şi nu pot. — Pentru asta ai venit? — Pentru asta. — Nu cumva ai fost azi pe la Casa de nebuni? îl întrebă foarte serios Vasiliu. . . . — Nu vorbi prostii te rog, răspunde-mi. Vasiliu se gândi un moment, apoi zise: „Nu-mi aduc aminte."

Caranfil insistă: „Adu-ţi aminte . . . te rog . . . e duce . . . duce de . . . adu-ţi aminte . . . a fost comandantul suprem la Waterloo. . . . A luptat întăi în Portugalia. E duce. . . ."

Vasiliu păru că se gândeşte adânc. Caranfil adăugă: El îi care a zis în focul luptei la Waterloo: „să murim pentru bătrâna Anglie." Ţi-aduci aminte? — Să murim pentru bătrâna Anglie? (repetă Vasiliu pe gânduri). — Da, da, da! zise bucuros Caranfil.

Vasiliu se gândi în urma acestei lămuriri, pe când Caranfil îşi ţinea răsuflarea. — Nu-mi aduc aminte. — Gândeşte-te . . . te rog, gândeşte-te . . . a fost ministru pe la 1828. — La

1828? — Da, în cabinetul lui Robert Peel. — Metternich? . . . zise cu oarecare sfială Vasiliu.

Caranfil se înfurià. — Bine, măi, Metternich e Englez? Atâta istorie ştii tu? Să-ţi fie ruşine să spui asemenea prostii, ce dracu?! Şi o mare descurajare cuprinse pe Caranfil.

Vasiliu îi răspunse liniştit: — Ia ascultă, bre, ai venit să-mi faci scandal . . . în mijlocul nopţii? Haide pleacă de-aici, căci mi-i frig. . . . — Te rog, zise Caranfil schimbând tonul. Nu te supăra . . . mai gândeşte-te o leacă. Nu-i Metternich. . . .

Vasiliu se gândi, ce-i dreptul, dar răspunse: — Nu . . . nu-mi aduc aminte. — Nu-ţi aduci aminte, sau nu ştii? — Nu-mi aduc aminte. — Te rog adu-ţi. — Lasă-mă în pace, mi-ai stricat somnul . . . nu-mi aduc aminte? Şi Vasiliu intră în lăuntru şi încuià uşa.

Caranfil rămase un moment pe gânduri. Îşi duse mâna la frunte, după care operaţie urmă o vorbă grozavă, plină de năduh, probabil la adresa ducelui de . . . căruia, desigur, nici un Englez şi nici un alt om nu i-o adresase până atunci. După aceia porni încetişor la vale, tot cum venise.

Pe drum se oprea din când în când: ,,Nu se poate . . . nu se poate . . . ducele de . . . ducele de Mag . . . nu . . . ducele de Bag . . . nu . . . stăi. . . .“ Şi el deslănţui imediat un torent de vorbe grozave, care învăluiră deopotrivă pe duce, mănăstirea, pe amicul Vasiliu, în special, şi toate trebile omeneşti în general. Apoi întocmai cum ar striga la telefon: ,,Waterloo! . . . Ducele de . . .“

Caranfil ajunse acasă, fără să poată stabili nici o asociaţie psichologică, etimologică sau cronologică între diferitele lucruri scoase de dânsul la lumină în acea noapte şi numele ducelui victorios. De la uşă, se asvârli desperat pe pat. Stătu un moment aşa, fără să se mişte, apoi se sculă, deschise geamul, se plimbă prin casă uitându-se cu o ură feroce la Napoleon. Împăratul sta rece şi nepăsător!

În urmă se desbrăcă şi se vârî în aşternut trăgându-şi oghealul peste cap.

Dar deodată sări din pat ca muşcat de şerpe şi se aruncă

asupra unei lăzi, care stătea în fundul odăii. „Dobitoc ce sânt!" strigă tare Caranfil dându-şi o tiflă. Apoi, de la ladă alergă la masă, pe care o pipăi pe deasupra căutând chibriturile, gratificându-se întru una cu titul de dobitoc, pe urmă dete fuga le geam, unde iar făcu nişte mişcări ca şi cum ar fi cântat pe un instrument cu clape, apoi îşi înşfăcă hainele şi tremurând de nerăbdare le căută prin buzunar. Negăsind ce căuta nici aici, se aruncă iar asupra lăzii începând să bojbăjească înlăuntru prin întuneric, dete peste o carte mică şi groasă şi stăpânit de un singur gând, se repezi afară ca un turbat, oprindu-se din fugă lângă un felinar care era cam la vr'o două sute de metri de la casa lui. Acolo el deschise dicţionarul şi ceti cuvântul *Napoleon*: „Fu învins la Waterloo în ziua de 18 Iunie, de către armatele coalizate, subt comanda ducelui de Wellington şi . . ."

„A, ha! bun!" strigă Caranfil uşurat. „Ducele de Wellington!" Urmă încă o vorbă românească, adresată exclusiv Englezului, de astădată de satisfacţie însă. . . .

Şi tremurând de frig, temându-se să nu-l vadă cineva desculţ şi în costumul acela, Caranfil fugi iute înnapoi, se culcă liniştit, şi adormi îndată.

D. D. PĂTRĂŞCANU.
(1872-1937.)

Puiul

Sandi, să asculţi de mamica.

Într'o primăvară o prepeliţă aproape moartă de oboseală, — că venea de departe tocmai din Africa, — s'a lăsat din zbor într'un lan verde de grâu, la marginea unui lăstar. Dupăce s'a odihnit vre-o câteva zile, a început să adune beţişoare, foi uscate, pae şi fire de fân şi şi-a făcut un cuib pe un moşoroi de pământ, mai sus, ca să nu i-l înece ploile; e urmă şeapte zile de-a rândul a ouat câte un ou, în tot, şapte ouă mici ca nişte cofeturi, şi a început să le clocească. Ai văzut cum stă găina pe ouă? Aşa sta şi ea, doar că ea în loc să stea în coteţ, sta afară în grâu; şi ploua, ploua, de vărsa şi ea nu se mişca, ca nu cumva să pătrundă o picătură de ploae la ouă. După trei săptămâni i-au ieşit nişte pui drăguţi, nu goi ca puii de vrabie, îmbrăcaţi cu puf galben ca puii de găină, dar mici, parcă erau şeapte gogoşi de mătasă şi au început să umble prin grâu după demâncare. Prepeliţa prindea câte o furnică, ori câte o lăcustă, le-o firimiţa în bucăţele mici şi ei, pic! pic! pic! cu cioculeţele lor, o mâncau numai decât. Şi erau frumoşi, cuminţi şi ascultători; se plimbau prinprejurul mamei lor şi când îi strigă: pitpalac! — repede veneau lângă ea. Odată prin Iunie, când au venit ţăranii să secere grâul, ăl mai mare dintre pui n'a alergat repede la chemarea mă-si, şi cum nu ştia să zboare, haţ! l-a prins un flăcău sub căciulă. Ce frică a păţit, când s'a simţit strâns în palma flăcăului, numai el a ştiut; îi bătea inima ca ciasornicul meu din buzunar; dar a avut noroc de un ţăran bătrân. care s'a rugat pentru el:

— Lasă-l jos, mă Marine, că e păcat de el, moare. Nu-l vezi că deabia e cât luleaua.

Când s'a văzut scăpat, fuga speriat la prepeliţă să-i spue ce-a păţit. Ea l-a luat, l-a mângâiat şi i-a spus:

— Vezi ce va să zică să nu mă asculţi? Când te-oi face mare, o să faci cum oi vrea tu, dar acum că eşti mic, să nu eşi niciodată din vorba mea, că poţi să păţeşti şi mai rău.

Şi aşa trăiau acolo liniştiţi şi fericiţi. Din seceratul grâului şi din râdicarea snopilor se scuturaseră pe mirişte o groază de boabe cu care se hrăniau, şi măcar că nu era vre-o apă prin apropiere, nu sufereau de sete, că beau dimineaţa picături de rouă de pe firele de iarbă. Ziua, când era căldură mare, stau la umbră în lăstar: după amiază, când se potolia vipia, eşiau cu toţii pe mirişte; iar în nopţile răcoroase se adunau grămadă ca sub un cort, sub aripele ocrotitoare ale prepeliţei. Încet, încet puful de pe ei s'a schimbat în fulgi şi în pene şi cu ajutorul mamei lor, au început să zboare. Lecţiile de zbor se făceau dimineaţa spre răsăritul soarelui, când se îngâna ziua cu noaptea, şi seara în amurg, căci ziua era primejdios din cauza hereţilor, care dădeau târcoale pe deasupra miriştei.

Mama lor îi aşeza la rând şi îi întreba : ,,Gata ?" — ,,Da," răspundeau ei. ,,Una, două, trei !" Şi când zicea ,,trei," frrrrr ! zburau cu toţii dela marginea lăstarului tocmai coló lângă cantonul de pe şosea şi tot aşa îndărăt. Şi mama lor le spunea că-i învaţă să zboare pentru o călătorie lungă, pe care trebuia s'o facă în curând, când o trece vara. ,,Şi o să zburăm pe sus de tot, zile şi nopţi, şi o să vedem dedesubtul nostru oraşe mari şi râuri şi marea."

. . . .

Într'o după-amiază pe la sfârşitul lui August, pe când puii se jucau frumos în mirişte împrejurul prepeliţei, aud o căruţă venind şi oprindu-se în drumeagul de pe marginea lăstarului. Au râdicat toţi în sus capetele cu ochişorii ca nişte mărgele negre şi ascultau.

— Nero ! înnapoi ! — s'a auzit un glas strigând. Puii n'au priceput, dar mama lor, care înţelesese că e un vânător, a rămas încremenită. Scăparea lor era lăstarul, dar tocmai dintr'acolo venia vânătorul. După o clipă de socoteală, le-a poruncit să se pituleascǎ jos, lipiţi cu pământul, şi cu nici un preţ să nu se mişte.

— Eu o să zbor ; voi să rămâneţi nemişcaţi ; care zboară e pierdut. Aţi înţeles ?

Puii au clipit din ochi c'au înţeles, şi au rămas aşteptând în tăcere.

Se auzia fâşiitul unui câne care alerga prin mirişte şi din când în când glasul omului : ,,Unde fugi ? Înapoi, Nero !"

Fâşiitul se apropie, — uite cânele : a rămas împietrit, cu o labă în sus, cu ochii, ţintă în spre ei.

,,Nu vă mişcaţi," — le şopteşte prepeliţa şi se strecoară binişor mai departe. Cânele păşeşte încet după ea. Se apropie grăbit şi vânătorul. Uite-l : piciorul lui e acum aşa de aproape de ei, încât văd cum i se urcă o furnică pe carâmbul cizmei. Vai ! cum le bate inima. După câteva clipe prepeliţa zboară ras cu pământul, la doi paşi dela botul cânelui, care o urmăreşte ; vânătorul se depărtează strigând : ,,Înnapoi ! înnapoi !" Nu poate trage de frică să nu-şi împuşte cânele ; dar prepeliţa se preface aşa de bine că e rănită încât cânele vrea cu orice preţ s'o prindă; iar când socoteşte ea că e în afară de bătaia puştii, zboară repede scăpată spre lăstar.

În vremea asta puiul ăl mai mare, în loc să stea nemişcat ca fraţii lui, după cum le poroncise mă-sa, zboară; vânătorul îi aude pârâitul zborului, se întoarce şi trage. Era cam departe. O singură alice l-a ajuns la aripă. N'a picat, a putut zbura până la lăstar; dar acolo de mişcarea aripii, osul, la început numai plesnit s'a crăpat de tot, şi puiul a căzut cu o aripă moartă. Vânătorul cunoscând desimea lăstarului, şi văzând că trăsese într'un puiu, nu s'a luat după dânsul, socotind că nu face truda de a-l căuta prin lăstar.

Ăilalţi pui nu s'au mişcat din locul, unde-i lăsase prepeliţa. Ascultau în tăcere. Din când în când se auzeau pocnete de puşcă şi glasul vânătorului strigând: ,,apporte!" Mai târziu căruţa s'a depărtat înspre vânător de drumeagul lăstarului; încet-încet pocnetele şi strigătele s'au pierdut, s'au stâns, şi în tăcerea sării care se lăsă nu se mai auzia decât cântecul greerilor; iar când s'a înnoptat şi răsărea luna despre Cornăţel, au auzit desluşit glasul mamei lor chemându-i din capul miriştei: ,,Pitpalac! Pitpalac!"

Repede au zburat spre ea, şi au găsit-o. Ea i-a numărat; lipsea unul.

— Unde e nenea?

— Nu ştim, — a zburat.

Atunci prepeliţa desperată a început să-l strige tare, mai tare, ascultând din toate părţile. Din lăstar i-a răspuns un glas stâns: ,, piu! piu! . . ."

Când l-a găsit, când i-a văzut aripa ruptă, a înţeles că era pierdut: dar şi-a ascuns durerea, că să nu-l desnădăjduiască pe el. . . .

D'atunci au început zile triste pentru bietul puiu. Abia se mişca cu aripa târîş după dânsul; — se uita cu ochii plânşi cum fraţii lui se învăţau la zbor dimineaţa şi seara; iar noaptea, când ăilalţi adormeau sub aripa mamei, el o întreba cu spaimă:

— Mamă, nu e aşa că o să mă fac bine? Nu e aşa c'o să merg şi eu să-mi arăţi cetăţi mari şi râuri şi marea?

— Da, mamă, răspundea prepeliţa silindu-se să nu plângă.

Şi a trecut vara. Au venit ţăranii cu plugurile de au arat miriştea, prepeliţa s'a mutat cu puii într'un lan de porumb de alături ; dar peste câtăva vreme au venit oamenii de au cules porumbul, au tăiat cocenii şi au întors locul ; atunci s'au mutat în nişte pârloage din marginea lăstarului. În locul zilelor mari şi frumoase au venit zile mici şi posomorîte, a început să cadă brumă şi să se rărească frunza lăstarului. Pe înserate se vedeau rândunici întârziate zburând în rasul pământului, ori pâlcuri de alte păsări călătoare, iar în tăcerea nopţilor friguroase se auziau strigătele cocorilor, mergând toate în aceiaş parte, către miazăzi.

În inima bietei prepeliţe era o luptă sfâşietoare. Ar fi vrut să se rupă în două, — jumătate să plece cu copiii sănătoşi care suferiau de frigul toamnei înaintate, iar jumătate să rămâie cu puiul schilod care se agăţa de ea cu desperare. Suflarea duşmănoasă a Crivăţului, pornită fără veste într'o zi, a hotărît-o. Decât să-i moară toţi puii, mai bine numai unul, — şi fără să se uite înapoi, ca să nu-i slăbească hotărîrea, a zburat cu puii zdraveni, pe când ăl rănit striga cu desnădejde :

— Nu mă lăsaţi ! Nu mă lăsaţi !

A încercat să se târască după ei, dar n'a putut, şi a rămas în loc urmându-i cu ochii până au pierit în zarea despre miazăzi.

Peste trei zile toată preajma era îmbrăcată în haina albă şi rece a iernii. După o ninsoare cu viscol, urmă un senin ca sticla, aducând cu dânsul un ger aprig.

. . . .

La marginea lăstarului un puiu de prepeliţă cu aripa ruptă stă zgribulit de frig. După durerile grozave de până adineaori, urmează acum o piroteală plăcută. Prin mintea lui fulgeră crâmpee de vedenii . . . mirişte . . . un carâmb de cismă pe care se urcă o furnică . . . aripa caldă a mamei. Se clatină într'o parte şi într'alta, şi pică mort, cu degetele ghiarei împreunate ca pentru închinăciune.

Ioan Al. Brătescu-Voineşti.
(1868.)

Neagra Şarului [1]
(Fragment)

. . . .

A-doua-zi, mătuşa Floarea iar găsi de cuviinţă să râdă de dracul dela izvor. Deşi nu cobora devale, ea părea a şti mai multe decât mine.

— Oile lui Calistru, zicea ea, behăiesc pe Rarău,[2] şi el umblă cu baltagul prin fundul văilor. Dragostea lui a fost de trei seri, poate nici trei, ş'a rămas cu inima friptă. A căzut [3] nu ştiu de unde Iordăchel cu brâul roşu, l-a dat cu coarnele la o parte.[4]

— Ş'acuma Calistru se dă pe ici, s'arată pe dincolo, şi se uită pe sub sprâncene. . . .

— La ce se uită, mătuşă Floare? întrebai eu c'un râs cam jalnic.

— Oi, domnişorule, îmi răspunse ea; rău să nu-ţi pară. . . . De-aici nu poate ieşi lucru curat!

Nu ştiu dacă gazda mea a vrut numai să mă mângâie. Poate ştia multe şi mărunte lucruri,[5] căci tainele văii nu-i erau necunoscute, deşi ea sta cu nasu'n vatră la căsuţa de pe coastă. Le ştia. Curând le-am înţeles şi eu, căci deseori dela cuibarul ieruncii am auzit un glas de hulubiţă sălbatică. Ştia de-bună samă şi Calistru, pentru că de multe ori trupu-i uriaş, strâns în chimir larg ciobănesc, umbla încovăiat în preajma celor trei mesteceni.

Şi'ntr'un rând, îmi aduc aminte că era într'o Miercuri, pe la toacă, — stam pe malul Negrei şi aşteptam să deie drumul din sus haitului. Asta era pentru mine una din cele mai frumoase privelişti ale muntelui. Apa curgea puţintel scăzută, în solzi fumurii, — când auzii dela deal strigătele prelungi ale plutaşilor. Un şuiet uşor ca de vânt

[1] Name of a village and of a river in the mountains in the region of Vatra Dornei, on the Bistriţa river.
[2] Mountain in southern Bucovina.
[3] =came suddenly, appeared.
[4] comparison, i.e. like does a bull with his horns.
[5] multe şi mărunte=many things in detail.

se apropie, crescu, şi deodată, cu vuiet, se arătară nahlapii încordaţi ca nişte grumazuri cu coamele în spulber. Veneau cu iuţeală fugind pe creţii fumurii ai Negrei. Fruntea trecu ca'n goană de cai, şi după ea haitul venea sunând plin. Trecu o plută uşoară ca'n furtună. Trecu a doua. La a treia, sângele îl simţii cum mi se grămădeşte la piept în stânga. Venea pe puntea albă Catrina. Toporul plăieşului era înfipt într'un brad şi ea îşi ţinea cumpăna sprijinindu-se c'o mână de coada toporului. Flăcăul, Iordăchel a Roşului, încordat, cu muşchi ca de criţă, cu ochii pe salturile clocotitoare ale Negrei, purta cârma. Veneau cu repeziciunea năprasnicului pârău de munte, şi femeia râdea, ca o văduvă slobodă şi fericită ce se afla, stăpână pe zilele tinereţelor ei.

Dar omul cel cu'ntuneric sub frunte, care-şi lăsase pe ţancuri oile pentru o târzie şi aspră dragoste, pândea ca şi mine. Din dosul unor butuci îşi arătă trupul mare, şi ca o fiară se zvârli între cei doi, tocmai când pluta, adusă de unde cotite, ştergea malul. Am auzit un ţipăt ascuţit, prelung; pluta dispăru brusc la cotitură; şi peste freamătul nahlapilor căzu, fără să bag de samă, cu sunet mare, o furtună grabnică dinspre Călimani. Prin brazi şerpuiau şuiete şi învolburări, ploaia se învălui în vârtejuri; trecu — şi ropotul ei suna departe pe codri, iar când ajunsei acasă, cu ochii plini de icoana unei clipe grozave, o suliţă lungă de soare străpunse dela asfinţit negura opcinilor.

Mătuşa Floarea venea şi ea din vale, depe Neagra. Parcă scoborîse şi ea să vadă trecerea năhlapilor şi a plutelor. Se opri lângă prispă. Se aşeză, privind spre vale. Voiam să-i cer o lămurire; nu îndrăzneam. Ea-mi vorbi încet, fără s'o întreb:

— Domnişorule, la noi furtunile sunt vârtej şi apele viforoase. . . .

MIHAI SADOVEANU.
(1880.)

Mioriţa [1]

Pe un picior de plai,	On a low hillside,
Pe-o gură de rai,[2]	Where heaven spreads wide,

[1] Diminutive from **mioară**=young sheep.
[2] (beautiful) like the entry into paradise.

Iată vin în cale,	O'er the pathway wending,
Se cobor în vale,	To the plain descending,
Trei turme de miei	Three shepherds keep
Cu trei ciobănei.	Three flocks of sheep.
Unu-i Moldovean,	One Moldavian,
Unu-i Ungurean,[1]	One Hungarian,
Şi unu-i Vrâncean.[2]	And one from Vrancea-land.
Iar cel Ungurean,	Now the Hungarian,
Şi cu cel Vrâncean,	And the Vrancea-man,
Mări se vorbiră	Were scheming the while
Ei se sfătuiră,	And plotting with guile,
Pe l'apus de soare	At the fall of day
Ca să mi-l omoare	Their kinsman to slay,
Pe cel Moldovean	Working great wrong
Că-i mai ortoman,[3]	For that he was strong,
Ş'are oi multe,	His folds were full,
Mândre şi cornute,	His lambs well for wool,
Şi cai învăţaţi,	Steeds swift for running,
Şi câni mai bărbaţi. . . .	Hounds fierce and cunning....
Dar cea mioriţă	Now there was a sheep
Cu lână plăviţă,	With fleece soft and deep,
De trei zile'ncoace	Three days ere this
Gura nu-i mai tace,	Had mourned his miseries,
Iarba nu-i mai place.	Grass all amiss.
— Mioriţă laie,[4]	" Dear little black sheep,
Laie, bucălaie,[5]	Black-nosed, clad deep,
De trei zile'ncoace	Three days ere this
Gura nu-ţi mai tace !	Mourn'st thy miseries
Ori iarba nu-ţi place,	How ! Grows thy grass amiss,
Ori eşti bolnăvioară,	Or wherefore dost pine,
Drăguţă mioară ?	Darling lamb of mine ?"
— Drăguţule bace,[6]	" O shepherd dear,

[1] The people often call the Rumanians of Transylvania **Ungurean**=from Hungaryland, not **Ungur**=Hungarian.

[2] From the region of **Vrancea** in the district of Putna.

[3] wealthy, rich in sheep.

[4] **lău** (*m.*), **laie** (*f.*)=grey.

[5] **bucălău** (*m.*), **bucălaie** (*f.*)=with black mouth.

[6] Vocative from **baci**=first (chief) shepherd.

Dă-ţi oile'ncoace,	Draw thy lambs near,
La negru zăvoi,	Seek the forest deep,
Că-i iarba de noi.	Where is grass for thy sheep
Şi umbră de voi.	And shade for thy sleep.
Stăpâne, stăpâne,	Also, master dear,
Îţi chiamă ş'un câne,	Call thy dog near,
Cel mai bărbătesc	Thy fiercest hound
Şi cel mai frăţesc,	Thou hast faithful found,
Că l'apus de soare	For at fall of day
Vreau să mi te-omoare	Purpose thee to slay
Baciul Ungurean	The Hungarian
Şi cu cel Vrâncean !	And the Vrancea-man ! "
— Oiţă bârsană,[1]	" Little lamb, dear heart,
De eşti năsdrăvană [2]	If thou hast this art,
Şi de-o fi să mor	If life I must yield
În câmp de mohor,	In the millet-field,
Să spui lui Vrâncean	Speak to the Vrancean
Şi lui Ungurean	And the Hungarian
Ca să mă îngroape	To bury me here
Aicia pe-aproape,	Where I may be near,
În strunga de oi	In the fold, to sleep
Să fiu tot cu voi,	Ever with my sheep,
În dosul stânii	By my hut of logs
Să-mi aud cânii.	Still to hear my dogs.
Astea să le spui,	Tell them what I say,
Iar la cap să-mi pui	And close by me lay
Flueraş de fag,	My little pipe of beech,
Mult zice cu drag !	Silver of speech !
Flueraş de os,	My little pipe of bone,
Mult zice duios !	With melting moan !
Flueraş de soc,	My pipe of elder-tree,
Mult zice cu foc ! [3]	Fiery and free !
Vântul când va bate	Then the rising breeze
Prin ele-a răsbate	Shall play on these
Ş-oile s'or strânge	And shall draw my sheep

[1] From the **Bârsa**-land in Transylvania.
[2] with supernatural powers, uncanny.
[3] which plays with much passion (fire).

Pe mine m'or plânge	Their master to weep
Cu lacrămi [1] de sânge!	With heart's blood deep!
Iar tu de omor	But of this murdering
Să nu le spui lor.	Tell my lambs nothing;
Să le spui curat	Only shall thou say
Că m'am însurat	I am gone away
C'o mândră crăiasă,	With a princess-bride,
A lumii mireasă;	Spouse of all earth wide;
Că la nunta mea	Her when I wed
A căzut o stea;	Fell a star dead;
Soarele şi luna	Sun and moon shone down
Mi-au ţinut cununa,	For my bridal crown,
Brazi şi păltinaşi	Firs and maple trees
I-am avut nuntaşi,	Were my witnesses,
Preoţi, munţii mari,	My priests the high hills,
Pasări lăutari,	My music, birds' trills,
Păsărele mii,	Birds all in flight,
Şi stele făclii!	And the stars for light!
Iar dacă-i zări,	But shouldst thou see,
Dacă-i întâlni,	As well may be,
Măicuţă bătrână,	My old mother dear,
Cu brâul de lână,	Girt with white wool, here
Din ochi lăcrămând,[2]	Weeping woefully,
Pe câmp alergând,	Wand'ring o'er the lea,
De toţi întrebând,	With anxious plea,
Şi la toţi zicând:	Demanding of ye:
— Cine-a cunoscut	'Who here has known
Cine mi-a văzut,	Has seen mine own,
Mândru ciobănel,	A shepherd trim,
Tras printr'un inel?	As a willow slim?
Feţişoara lui,	His skin to sight,
Spuma laptelui;	Like milk-foam white;
Mustăcioara lui,	His moustaches, fair
Spicul grâului;	As the wheaten ear;
Perişorul lui,	His curly hair,
Pana corbului;	Like raven rare;
Ochişorii lui	His eyes deep glow

[1] =lacrimi. [2] =lăcrimând.

Mura câmpului. . . .	Like the coal-black sloe. . . .'
Tu, mioara mea,	Thou, sweet lamb, shall take
Să te'nduri de ea.	Pity, for her sake.
Şi-i spune curat	Only shall thou say
Că m'am însurat	I am gone away
Cu-o fată de crai,	With a princess-bride,
Pe-o gură de rai.	Where heaven spreads wide.
Iar la cea măicuţă,	But let her not hear,
Să nu-i spui, drăguţă,	My old mother dear,
Că la nunta mea	That when we wed
A căzut o stea ;	A star fell, dead ;
C'am avut nuntaşi	That my witnesses
Brazi şi păltinaşi ;	Were the maple trees ;
Preoţi munţii mari,	My priests, the high hills,
Pasări, lăutari,	My music, birds' trills,
Păsărele mii ;	Birds all in flight ;
Şi stele făclii.	And the stars light.

V. ALECSANDRI (1821-90),
Poesii populare ale Românilor,
Bucureşti, 1866.

Translated by
N. W. Newcombe.

Cucul

Frunză verde de pelin,
Ce [1]-mi eşti, cucule, hain,
De cânţi vara'n jumătate
Ş'apoi sbori în altă parte ?

Cuculeţ, pasere sură,
Muşca-ţi-aş limba din gură
Cântecul să nu-ţi mai zici
Nici să mai colinzi pe-aici.

Vara vii, vara te duci
Când îs dragostele [2] dulci
Cântă-mi mie înc'odată
Că mi-e mintea tulburată.

[1] =why. [2] Plural for singular.

Cântă'n dreapta [1] mea cu foc
Să am parte de noroc.
Cântă'n faţa mea cu drag
Că ţi-oi da frunze de fag
Să nu mai fii tot pribeag.

V. Alecsandri, *Poesii populare ale Românilor*, Bucureşti, 1866.

Cântec

Frunză verde măr uscat,
Astă noapte m'am visat [2]
Că mândrul m'a sărutat.
M'am trezit ş'am pipăit
Şi nimica n'am găsit :
Numai dorul inimei
Scris pe faţa perinei
Cu mătasa genelor
Şi cu roua ochilor.

O. Densusianu, *Flori alese din cântecele poporului*, Bucureşti, 1920.

Malul Siretului

Aburii uşori ai nopţii ca fantasme se ridică
Şi, plutind de-asupra luncii, printre ramuri se despică ;
Râul luciu se'ncovoaie subt copaci, ca un balaur
Ce, în raza dimineţii, mişcă solzii lui de aur.

Eu mă duc în faptul zilei,[3] mă aşez pe malu-i [4] verde
Şi privesc cum curge apa şi la cotituri se pierde,
Cum se schimbă'n vălurele pe prundişul lunecos,
Cum adoarme la bulboace, săpând malul nisipos ;

[1] The right side is considered the lucky one.
[2] =m'am văzut pe mine în vis.
[3] =at break of day.
[4] =pe malul lui, on his bank.

Când o salcie pletoasă lin pe baltă se coboară,
Când o mreană saltă'n aer dup'o viespe sprinteioară,
Când sălbatecile raţe se abat din sborul lor,
Bătând apa'ntunecată de un nour trecător.

Şi gândirea mea furată se tot duce'ncet la vale
Cu cel râu care'n veci curge făr'a se opri din cale.
Lunca'n juru-mi [1] clocoteşte. O şopârlă de smarald
Cată ţintă [2] lung la mine, părăsind nisipul cald.

VASILE ALECSANDRI (1821-1890).

Trecut-au anii

(Sonet)

Trecut-au anii ca nori lungi pe şesuri
Şi nici odată n'or să vie iară,
Căci nu mă'ncântă azi cum mă mişcară
Poveşti şi doine, ghicitori, eresuri,

Ce fruntea-mi de copil o'nseninară,
Abia'nţelese, pline de'nţelesuri;
Cu-a tale umbre azi în van mă'mpresuri,
O ceas al tainei, asfinţit de sară.

Să smulg un sunet din trecutul vieţii,
Să fac, o suflet, ca din nou să tremuri?
Cu mâna mea în van pe liră lunec:

Pierdut e totu'n zarea tinereţii
Şi mută-i gura dulce-a altor vremuri,
Iar timpul creşte'n urma mea . . . mă'ntunec!

MIHAI EMINESCU (1850-1889).

[1] =în jurul meu, round me.
[2] a căută ţintă la cineva, to stare at somebody.

Somnoroase păsărele

Somnoroase păsărele
Pe la cuiburi se adună.
Se ascund în rămurele —
Noapte bună !

Doar izvoarele suspină
Pe când codrul negru tace ;
Dorm şi florile'n grădină —
Dormi în pace !

Trece lebeda pe ape
Între trestii să se culce —
Fie-ţi îngerii aproape.
Somnul dulce !

Peste-a nopţii feerie
Se ridică mândra lună,
Totu-i vis şi armonie —
Noapte bună !

MIHAI EMINESCU (1850-1889).

Noapte de vară

Zările, de farmec pline,
Strălucesc în luminiş ;
Sboară mierlele'n tufiş
Şi din codri noaptea vine,
Pe furiş.

Care cu poveri de muncă
Vin încet şi scârţiind ;
Turmele s'aud mugind,
Şi flăcăii vin pe luncă
Hăulind.

Cu cofiţa, pe'ndelete,
Vin neveste dela râu;
Şi cu poala prinsă'n brâu
Vin cântând în stoluri fete
Dela râu.

Dela gârlă'n pâlcuri dese
Sgomotoşi copiii vin:
Satul e de vuet plin;
Fumul alb alene ese
Din cămin.

Dar din ce în ce s'alină
Toate sgomotele'n sat,
Muncitorii s'au culcat
Linîştea-i acum deplină
Şi-a'noptat.

Focul e'nvelit pe vatră
Iar opaiţele-au murit,
Şi prin satul adormit
Doar'vr'un câne'n somn mai latră
Răguşit.

Iat'o! Plină, despre munte,
Ese luna din brădet
Şi se'nalţă'ncet-încet,
Gânditoare ca o frunte
De poet.

Ca un glas domol de clopot
Sună codrii mari de brad;
Ritmic valurile cad,
Cum se sbate'n dulce ropot
Apa'n vad.

Dintr'un timp şi vântul tace ;
Satul doarme ca'n mormânt —
Totu-i plin de duhul sfânt :
Linişte'n văzduh şi pace
Pe pământ.

Numai dorul mai colindă,
Dorul tânăr şi pribeag,
Tainic se'ntâlneşte'n prag
Dor cu dor să se cuprindă
Drag cu drag.

GHEORGHE COŞBUC (1875-1918).

Cântec sfânt

Corinei.

Cântecul ce ades ţi-l cânt
Când te-adorm în fapt de seară,
Puiule, e-un cântec sfânt,
Vechi şi simplu dela ţară.

Mama mi-l cânta şi ea
Şi la viersul ei cel dulce
Puiul ei se potolea
Şi-o lăsa frumos să-l culce.

Azi te-adorm cu dânsul eu,
Eri-el m'adormia pe mine,
Şi-adormi pe tatăl meu
Când era copil ca tine. . . .

Mâne, când voiu fi pământ,
Nu-l uita nici tu, — şi zi-le,
Zi-le doina, cântec sfânt,
La copiii tăi, copile !

ST. O. IOSIF (1875-1913).

Romanţa celor trei corăbii

Porniră cele trei corăbii . . .
Spre care ţărm le-o duce vântul ? . . .
Ce porturi tainice,
Ascunse cercetătoarelor priviri,
Le vor vedea sosind mânate de dorul tristei pribegiri ? . . .
Ce valuri nemiloase,
Mâine
Le vor deschide'n drum mormântul ? . . .

Porniră cele trei corăbii, purtând în pântecele lor
Grămezi de aur,
Chihlimbare,
Smaralde verzi
Şi-opale blonde ;
Iar sus pe bord,
Tristeţea-acelor romanţe veşnic vagabonde,
Cântate,
Azi în drum spre Poluri
Iar mâne'n drum spre Equator ! . . .

Porniră cele trei corăbii . . .
Şi-abia se mai zăresc —
Se'ngroapă
În golul zărilor pătate de violetul înserării ;
Iar albul pânzelor întinse,
În cenuşiul depărtării
Zideşte trei mauzoleuri în care dorm cei duşi pe apă.

Porniră cele trei corăbii . . .
Şi'n urma lor rămase portul
Mai trist ca muntele Golgotei însângerat de-un asfinţit ;
Şi'n urma lor pe cheiul umed,
Un singur albatros rănit
Mai stă la pază
Ca Maria
Venită să vegheze mortul ! . . .

Ion Minulescu (1881-1944),
Romanţe pentru mai târziu, 1922.

Lacrimi

(Copilă)

Copilă, copilă
Mi-e a mâhnire [1] şi milă.
Grivei [2] plânge şi el.
Lacrimile noastre sunt la fel.
I s'a urît şi lui cu lacrimile mute.
Un gând i-a spus : aşteaptă. Alt gând îi spune : du-te.

Îi este dor, ca nouă,
De făgăduelile-amândouă.
Îl cotropeşte ceaţa ca pe fiecare.
Seceră, poate, şi'n el semnul de'ntrebare.

Flămânde sunteţi de altă pâine,
Lacrimi de om şi lacrimi de câine.

Ce e Grivei ?
Ce-i, moşule ? Ce vrei ?

Glasul, ca o bătaie de armă,
Ţi s'a 'ncetinat şi ţi se destramă
Şi latră'nnăbuşit la noapte
Sfaturi, şi şoapte.

A stat cu mine'n bătătură o viaţă,
El într'o ceaţă, eu într'altă ceaţă.

Copilă,
Mi-e a mâhnire şi milă.

Tovarăşi, prieteni, vecini,
Dar singurateci, dar streini.

Un òstrov fără luntre, fiecare,
Ostròave 'n bălţi, în depărtare,
Zărite'n ochii tăi, în ochii ei . . .

Îmbătrânim, Grivei.

TUDOR ARGHEZI (1880).

[1] For this construction, see 6. 4 c and 8. 2, note. [2] Name of a dog.

Gorunul

În limpezi depărtări aud din pieptul unui turn [1]
Cum bate, ca o inimă, un clopot —
Şi'n svonuri [2] dulci
Îmi pare
Că stropi de linişte îmi curg prin vine, nu de sânge . . .

Gorunele din margine de codru,
De ce mă'nvinge
Cu aripi moi atâta pace
Când zac în umbra ta
Şi mă desmierzi cu frunza-ţi jucăuşă ? [3] . . .

,,. . . O, cine ştie ? — Poate că
Din trunchiul tău îmi vor ciopli
Nu peste mult sicriul, —
Şi liniştea
Ce voi gusta-o între scândurile lui,

O simt pe semne [4] de acum [5] :
O simt, cum frunza ta mi-o picură în suflet —
Şi mut
Ascult cum creşte'n trupul tău sicriul,
Sicriul meu,
Cu fiecare clipă care trece,
Gorunule din margine de codru. . . .

LUCIAN BLAGA (1895),
Poemele luminii, 1919.

[1] steeple, bell-gable. [2] sounds. [3] playing, moving.
[4] probably. [5] yet, now.

VOCABULARY

Note 1

a) Verbs and adverbs not included in this vocabulary are to be found in chapters 6. 8 ; 7. 1—7. 5 of the book.

b) Interjections and greetings are included in this vocabulary only if they appear in the reading texts. Otherwise they are to be found in chapters 9. 1—9. 4 of the Grammar.

c) The words of Part III (Word Formation) are not comprised in this vocabulary if they do not occur elsewhere in the book.

Note 2

The forms of the verb recorded in this vocabulary are: infinitive, first person sing. present, and past participle. The conjugation of the verb is marked with the Roman figures I, II, III, IV.

The forms of the noun and of the adjective are: the singular and the plural without the article.

All other morphological forms can be found with the help of these forms.

Note 3

a) For the convenience of the student the stressed syllable has been marked with an acute accent. In diminutives (nouns and adjectives) the accent is shifted from the stem to the derivative suffix (see 1. 5. **b**, **c**). In the forms of the declension the accent remains on the same syllable.

b) In the conjugation the accent is shifted on to the last syllable in the following verbal forms (see 1. 5. **b**):

i) 1st and 2nd pl. pres., I, II and IV conj.;
ii) gerund;
iii) adj.-part. in -tor (-toáre);
iv) past participle;
v) imperfect;
vi) preterite sing. I, II and IV conj.; in plur. the accent is on the last but one syllable.

A

a, al, ále, ái, *poss. art.* (see 14. 2); **al de** (see 14. 2, note 2).

abáte (a), abát, abătút, *v. tr.* III, to divert, to turn away from; **a se —**, to turn off, to go round.

absorbí (a), absórb, -ít, *v. tr.* IV, to absorb, to soak in.

abundént, -ă, *adj.*, abundant.

ábur, *n. m.*, **-i,** *pl.*, steam; vapour; damp.

aburcá (a), abúrc, -át, *v. tr.* I, to push upwards, to help climb a tree; **a se —**, to climb; cf. **urcá**.

ac, *n. mix.*, **-e,** *pl.*, needle.

acásă, *adv.*, at home.

acceler-á (a), -éz, -át, *v. tr.* I, to accelerate, to hasten; to urge.

accelerá-t, *adj. m.*, **-tă**, *f.*, **-ţi**, *m. pl.*, **-te**, *f. pl.*, accelerated; *n. mix.*, fast train.
accént, *n. mix.*, **-e**, *pl.*, accent, stress, emphasis.
accept-á (a), **accépt**, **-át**, *v. tr.* I, to accept.
accés, *n. mix.*, **-e**, *pl.*, access; fits.
acéla, **acél**, *m.*, **acéea**, **aceá**, *f.*, *dem. pron.*, that (see 5. 6. **a**); **de acéea**, *conj.*, therefore.
acélaş(i), **acéeaş(i)** (**acéiaş**), *dem. pron.*, the same (see 5. 6. **d**).
acéstalalt, **aceástălaltă**, *dem. pron.*, the other (see 5. 6. **c**).
acést, **aceásta**, *dem. pron.*, this (see 5. 6. **a**).
acólo, *adv.*, there.
acoperí (a), **acópăr**, **acoperít**, *v. tr.* IV, to cover.
acórd, *n. mix.*, **-uri**, *pl.*, accord, agreement.
acordá (a), **acórd** (**-éz**), **-át**, *v. tr.* I, to accord, to allow, to grant; to tune.
ácr-u, **-ă**, *adj.*, **-i**, **-e**, *pl.*, sour.
act, *n. mix.*, **-e**, *pl.*, act, deed, action; document.
acúm (**acú**), *adv.*, now.
acúş, *adv.*, immediately.
acuz-á (a), **acúz**, **-át**, *v. tr.* I, to accuse.
adânc, **-ă**, *adj.*, **-i**, *pl.*, deep.
adăogá (**adăugá**) (**a**), **adáog**, **adăogát**, *v. tr.* I, to add, to adjoin.
adăpost-í (a), **-ésc**, **-ít**, *v. tr.* IV, to shelter, to harbour.
adésea (**adése**), *adv.*, often, frequently.
adéseori, *adv.*, often, frequently.
adevăr, *n. mix.*, **-uri**, *pl.*, truth, verity; **într'adevăr**, *adv.*, indeed, truly, really.
adevărá-t, **-tă**, *adj.*, **-ţi**, **-te**, *pl.*, true, genuine.
adiér-e, *n. f.*, **-i**, *pl.*, breeze.
adineoárea (**adineáori**, **adinioáră**), *adv.*, just before.
adíns (see **într'adíns**).
admirábil, **-ă**, *adj.*, **-i**, **-e**, *pl.*, wonderful, admirable.
admonest-áre, *n. f.*, **-ări**, *pl.*, admonition, exhortation.
adormí (a), **adórm**, **-ít**, *v. intr.* IV, to fall asleep.
adrés-ă, *n. f.*, **-e**, *pl.*, address.
adres-á (a), **-éz**, **-át**, *v. tr.*, *intr.*, to address.
adúce (a), **adú-c**, **-s**, *v. tr.* III, to bring, to fetch; **a-şi aduce aminte de ceva**, to remember something; **a aduce aminte cuiva ceva**, to remind somebody something (see 6. 4. **b**; 6. 7).
aduná (a), *v. tr.* I, **adún**, **-át**, to gather, to collect; **a se —**, to assemble.
adun-áre, *n. f.*, **-ări**, *pl.*, addition; meeting, assembly.
adús, *n. mix.*, **-uri**, *pl.*, bringing, carrying.
áer, *n. m.*, air; **a-şi da áere**, *pl.*, to give himself airs.
aerián, **-ă**, *adj.*, aerial, airy.
aerisí-t, **-tă**, *adj.*, **-ţi**, **-te**, *pl.*, aerated.
afácer-e, *n. f.*, **-i**, *pl.*, business.
afáră, *adv.*, out of doors, outside; **afáră de**, *prep.*, beside, excepting.
afirmá (a), **afírm**, **-át**, *v. tr.* I, to affirm, to assert.
aflá (a), **áflu**, **aflát**, *v. tr.* I, to find, to discover.
África, *n. f.*, Africa.
agăţá (a), **agăţ**, **-át**, *v. tr.* I, to hang up; **a se — de**, to cling to.
agitá (a), **agít**, **-át**, *v. tr.* I, to agitate, to stir; **agitát**, **-ă**, *adj.*, in agitation.
agoní-e, *n. f.*, **-i**, *pl.*, agony.

agonis-í (a), **-ésc**, **-ít**, *v. tr.* IV, to earn, to gain.
agrícol, **-ă**, *adj.*, **-i**, **-e**, *pl.*, agricultural.
ai, see **aveá** (a).
áia, *dem. pron.*, that (see 5. 6. **a**).
aíci (**aícia**), *adv.*, here.
aiúrea, *adv.*, elsewhere, somewhere else.
ajúnge (a), **ajúng**, **ajúns**, *v. tr.*, *intr.* III, to reach, to come at; to suffice, to be sufficient.
ajut-á (a), **ajút**, **-át**, *v. tr.* I, to help.
aju-tór, *n. mix.*, **-toáre**, *pl.*, help, aid, support.
al, see **a**; **al de**, see 14. 2, note 2.
ăl, **ắla**, *dem. pron.*, that (see 5. 6. **a**).
ắlalt, **álaltă**, *dem. pron.*, that other (see 5. 6. **c**).
alắturi, **alắturea**, *adv.*, next, by, beside.
alb, **-ă**, *adj.* **-i**, **-e**, *pl.*, white.
albástr-u, **-ă**, *adj.*, **-i**, **-e**, *pl.*, blue.
albatrós, *n. m.*, **albatróşi**, *pl.*, albatross.
albín-ă, *n. f.*, **-i** (**-e**), *pl.*, bee.
alcătuí (a), **-ésc**, **-ít**, *v. tr.* IV, to form, to compose, to arrange.
aléne, *adv.*, lazily.
alerg-á (a), **alérg**, **-át**, *v. intr.* I, to run.
Alexándru, *prop. n.*, Alexander.
aliá-t, **-tă**, *adj.*, **-ţi**, **-te**, *pl.*, allied; *n.*, ally.
alíce, *n. f.* (**alíci**, *n. m.*), **-le**, *pl.*, small shot, slug.
aliná (a), **alín**, **-át**, *v. tr.* I., to soothe, to calm; **a se** —, to get calm.
Álpi, *prop. n. m. pl.*, Alps.
ált, **-ă**, *indef. pron.*, **al-ţi**, **-te**, *pl.*, another, other, next (see 5. 9).
áltădată, *adv.*, another time.
áltcineva, *indef. pron.*, somebody else (see 5. 9).
ált-ul, **-a**, *indef. pron.*, **álţii**, **áltele**, *pl.*, another (see 5. 9).
aluát, *n. mix.*, **-uri**, *pl.*, dough, paste.
alumíniu, *n. m.*, aluminium.
alún, *n. m.*, **-i**, *pl.*, hazel-tree.
alún-ă, *n. f.*, **-e**, *pl.*, hazel-nut.
alunecá (a), **alúnec**, **-át**, *v. intr.* I, to slip, to glide out, to slide.
amâná (a), **amấn**, **-át**, *v. tr.* I, to postpone, to delay, to adjourn.
amân-dói, *m.*, **-dóuă**, *f. adj.*, *num.*, both.
amănúnt, *n. mix.*, **-e**, *pl.*, detail, particular.
amár, **-ă**, *adj.*, **-i**, **-e**, *pl.*, bitter.
amárnic, **-ă**, *adj.*, **-i**, **-e**, *pl.*, bitter.
ambigén, **-ă**, *adj.*, **-i**, **-e**, *pl.* *Gram. gender*: belonging to masculine in sing. and to feminine in plur.
ámb-ii, *m.*, **-ele**, *f.*, *adj.*, *num.*, both.
amenințá (a), **amenínţ**, **-át**, *v. tr.* I, to menace, to threaten.
América, *prop. n. f.*, America.
amestecá (a), **améstec**, **-át**, *v. tr.* I, to mix, to mingle, to blend; **a se** —, to meddle with, to interfere, to intervene.
amiázăzi, **amiáză**, **amiázi** (**la**), *adv.*, at noon; **amiáz**, *n. mix.*, **-uri**, *pl.*, noon.
amíc, *n. m.*, **-i**, *pl.*, friend.
amínte, see **adúce**.
amintír-e, *n. f.*, **-i**, *pl.*, recollection, memory, reminiscence.
amúrg, *n. mix.*, **-uri**, *pl.*, twilight, dusk.
amuţ-í (a), **-ésc**, **-ít**, *v. intr.* IV, to become dumb.
an, *n. m.*, **-i**, *pl.*, year; **la anul**, *adv.*, next year.
andoásele, see **de-andoásele**.
Ánglia, *prop. n. f.*, England.
animál, *n. mix.*, **-e**. *pl.*, animal.

aniná (a), **anín**, **-át**, *v. tr.* I, to hang on, to hook ; to bind.
antíc, **-ă** (**ántic**), *adj.*, ancient, antique.
anticár, *n. m.*, **-i**, *pl.*, antiquarian bookseller, antique dealer.
antichit-áte, *n. f.*, **-ăţi**, *pl.*, antiquity.
anúme, *adv.*, namely ; purposely.
anumít, **-ă**, *adj.*, **anumi-ţi**, **-te**, *pl.*, *indef. pron.*, certain (see 5. 9).
anunţá (a), **anúnţ**, **-át**, *v. tr.* I, to announce, to inform.
aórt-ă, *n. f.*, **-e**, *pl.*, aorta.
áp-ă, *n. f.*, **-e**, *pl.*, water.
apărá (a), **ápăr**, **-át**, *v. tr.* I, to defend ; **a se** —, *v. refl.*, to defend oneself.
apăreá (a), (**apáre**), **apár**, **apărút**, *v. intr.* II (III), to appear.
apendicít-ă, *n. f.*, **-e**, *pl.*, appendicitis.
aperitív, *n. mix.*, **-e**, *pl.*, aperitive.
aplecá (a), **apléc**, **-át**, *v. tr.* I, to incline, to bend, to bow.
aplicá (a), **aplíc**, **-át**, *v. intr.* I, to apply, to lay on.
apogé-u, *n. mix.*, **-e**, *pl.*, acme, apogee.
apói, *adv.*, then, afterwards.
apóstol, *n. m.*, **-i**, *pl.*, apostle.
apostróf, *n. mix.*, **apostroáfe**, *pl.*, apostrophe.
apporte ! (French imperative used as a hunting term), bring !
áprig, **-ă**, *adj.*, brisk, quick ; sharp ; vehement.
Aprílie, **Apríl**, *n. m.*, April.
aprínde (a), **aprínd**, **apríns**, *v. tr.* III, to set fire to, to kindle ; **a se** —, *intr.*, to catch fire.
aproápe, *adv.*, near, by, close, nearly.
apropi-á (a), **-éz** (**aprópiu**), **-át**, *v. tr.* I, to approach, to bring near ; **a se** —, to come near.
apropiér-e, *n. f.*, **-i**, *pl.*, nearness, neighbourhood.
apucá (a), **apúc**, **-át**, *v. tr.* I, to seize, to catch, to grasp, to snatch, to take.
apúne (a), **apú-n**, **-s**, *v. intr.* III, to set (the sun), to go down (the sun).
apús, *n. m.*, **-uri**, *pl.*, sunset, west.
apuseán, **-ă**, *adj.*, western, occidental.
ará (a), **ar**, **-át**, *v. tr.* I, to plough.
Arád, *prop. n. m.*, town.
arám-ă, *n. f.*, copper ; **arắm-uri**, *pl.*, copper objects.
arătá (a), **arắt**, **-át**, *v. tr.* I, to show, to point out ; **a se** —, to appear, to show oneself.
árbor-e, *n. m.*, **-i**, *pl.*, tree.
arc, *n. mix.*, **-uri**, *pl.*, bow ; arch ; arc.
arcatúr-ă, *n. f.*, **-i**, *pl.*, vault, vaulted ceiling.
árde (a), **ard**, **ars**, *v. tr.*, *intr.* III, to burn ; **îmi arde de ceva**, I care for, I am interested in something.
Ardeál, *prop. n. m.*, Transylvania ; **ardeleán**, **-ă**, *adj.*, Transylvanian.
áre, see **aveá** (a).
aréte, see **heréte**.
argát, *n. m.*, **argáţi**, *pl.*, servant.
arge-á, *n. f.*, **-le**, *pl.*, hut dug in the earth for the loom, where peasant women do their weaving, because the atmosphere is not too dry.
Árgeş, *prop. n. m.*, river, locality.
argín-t, *n. m.*, silver ; **-ţi**, *pl.*, silver coins ; **argintát**, **-ă**, *adj.*, silver-grey.
arhitectúr-ă, *n. f.*, **-i**, *pl.*, architecture.
árip-ă (**arípă**), *n. f.*, **-i**, *pl.*, wing.
aritmétic, **-ă**, *adj.*, arithmetical.
árm-ă, *n. f.*, **-e**, *pl.*, weapon ; rifle.

armăsár, *n. m.*, **-i**, *pl.*, stallion.
armát-ă, *n. f.*, **-e**, *pl.*, army.
Armeán, *n. m.*, **Arméni**, *pl.*, **Armeáncă**, *n. f.*, **Arménce**, *pl.*, Armenian; **armen-ésc**, **-eáscă**, *adj.*, Armenian; **armeán**, **-ă**, *adj.*, Armenian.
armoní-e, *n. f.*, **-i**, *pl.*, harmony.
armoni-ós, **oásă**, *adj.*, harmonious.
arom-í (a), **-ésc**, **-ít**, *v. intr.* IV, to be sleepy, to slumber.
árşiţ-ă, *n. f.*, **-e**, *pl.*, heat, glow, warmth.
árt-ă, *n. f.*, **-e**, *pl.*, art.
artícol, *n. mix.*, **-e**, *pl.*, article, paragraph.
artíst, *n. m.*, **artíşti**, *pl.*, artist.
artístic, **-ă**, *adj.*, artistic.
aruncá (a), **arúnc**, **-át**, *v. tr.* I, to throw, to cast; **a se —**, *intr.*, to rush.
aşá, *adv.*, so, thus; in such a manner.
asált, *n. mix.*, **-uri**, *pl.*, assault.
ascultá (a), **ascúlt**, **-át**, *v. tr.* I, to listen; to obey (see 6. 7).
ascultă-tór, **-toáre**, *adj.*, obedient.
ascúnselea, see **de-ascúnselea**.
ascunzăt-oáre, *n. f.*, **-óri**, *pl.*, hiding place.
ascuţí-t, **-tă**, *adj.*, **-ţi**, **-te**, *pl.*, sharp.
aseáră, *adv.*, last night.
asemăná (a), **aseámăn**, **asemănát**, *v. tr.* I, to compare, to liken; **a se —**, to resemble, to be like.
asemăn-áre, *n. f.*, **-ắri**, *pl.*, comparison, resemblance, likeness.
asémenea, *adj.*, *adv.*, such, like; too, also.
aşezá (a), *v. tr.* I; **aşéz**, **-át**, to set, to put, to place, to situate; **a se —**, *intr.*, to sit.
aşez-áre, *n. f.*, **-ắri**, *pl.*, settlement; position.
asfinţít, *n. mix.*, **-uri**, *pl.*, sunset.
asimil-á (a), **-éz**, **-át**, *v. tr.* I, to assimilate; **asimil-áre**, *n. f.*, **-ắri**, *pl.*, assimilation.
asociáţi-e (**asociaţiún-e**), *n. f.*, **-i**, *pl.*, association, society, union.
aspiraţiún-e, *n. f.*, **-i**, *pl.*, aspiration.
áspr-u, **-ă**, *adj.*, **-i**, **-e**, *pl.*, severe, shaggy, rough; ragged.
ăst, **ástă**, **ásta**, *pron.*, this (see 5. 6. a).
ástă dátă, *adv.*, this time.
astâmpăr-áre, *n. f.*, **-ắri**, *pl.*, repose, relay.
ástăzi, **ázi**, *adv.*, to-day.
aşteptá (a), **aştépt**, **-át**, *v. tr.*, *intr.* I, to wait, to expect.
aştérne (a), **aştérn**, **-út**, *v. tr.* III, to strew, to scatter, to spread.
aşternút, *n. mix.*, **-uri**, *pl.*, bedding, bed-clothes.
ástfel, *adv.*, thus, so, this way.
astup-á (a), **astúp**, **-át**, *v. tr.* I, to fill, to stuff, to stop.
asúpra, *prep.*, against, upon; relating to.
asvârlí (a), **asvấrl**, **-ít**, *v. tr.* IV, to throw, to cast; **a se —**, to jump.
atacá (a), **atác**, **-át**, *v. tr.* I., to attack.
atáre, *adj.*, *dem. pron.*, such (see 5. 6. e).
atất (**atấta**), *adv.*, so; *adj.*, see 5. 9; *conj.*, see 8. 4. i.
aténţi-e, *n. f.*, **-i**, *pl.*, attention.
atínge (a), **atíng**, **atíns**, *v. tr.* III, to touch; to reach; to list.
aţint-í (a), **-ésc**, **-ít**, *v. tr.* IV, to fix, to aim; to stare at.
atrácţi-e, *n. f.*, **-i**, *pl.*, attraction, attractiveness.
atráge (a), **atrag**, **atras**, *v. tr.* III, to attract, to allure.
atúnci, **atúncea**, *adv.*, then.
au, see **avea** (a); **au**=**sau**, or (see 8. 4. g).

auditív, **-ă**, *adj.*, **-i**, **-e**, *pl.*, auditive.
Áugust (**Augúst**), *n. m.*, August.
áur, *n. m.*, gold.
Áustria, *n. f.*, Austria; **austri-ác**, **-ácă**, *adj.*, **-éci**, **-éce**, *pl.*, Austrian.
autór, *n. m.*, **-i**, *pl.*, author.
autorit-áte, *n. f.*, **-ắţi**, *pl.*, authority, power.
auzí (**a**), *v.* IV, **aúd**, **auzít**, *v. tr.* IV, to hear.
avans-á (**a**), **-éz**, **-át**, *v. intr.* I, to advance, to progress; to pay in advance.
avânt, *n. mix.*, **-uri**, *pl.*, elevation, soar; flight.
aveá (**a**), **am**, **avút**, *v. aux.*, *tr.* II, to have.
Ável, *prop. n.*, Abel.
avér-e, *n. f.*, **-i**, *pl.*, fortune, property, wealth.
ázi, *adv.*, to-day.
azúr, *n. mix.*, **-uri**, *pl.*, azure.
azvârlí, see **asvârlí** (**a**).

B

ba, *neg.*, no, not at all (see 7. 6).
báb-ă, *n. f.*, **-e**, *pl.*, old woman.
Bacắu, *prop. n. m.* (town).
báci, *n. m.*, **báci**, *pl.*, chief shepherd.
bacíl, *n. m.*, **-i**, *pl.*, bacillus.
báde, *n. m.*, with article : **bádea**, term of friendly respect, used when addressing an alderman, an elder brother.
bădíţ-ă, *n. m. dim.*, **-i**, *pl.*, from bade.
băgá (**a**), **bag**, **băgát**, *v. tr.* I, to put in, to introduce, to thrust; **a — de seamă**, to pay attention.
bagáj, *n. mix.*, **-e**, *pl.*, luggage.
băiát, *n. m.*, **băiéţi**, *pl.*, boy.
báie, *n. f.*, **bắi**, *pl.*, bath; bathing-tub; bathe.
băieţándr-u, *n. m.*, **-i**, *pl.*, youth, boy.
bălărí-e, *n. f.*, **-i**, *pl.*, weed; heath.
baláur, *n. m.*, **-i**, *pl.*, dragon.
Balcíc, *prop. n. m.* (locality).
báltă, *n. f.*, **bắlţi**, *pl.*, pool, marsh, swamp.
baltág, *n. mix.*, **-e**, *pl.*, hatchet, axe for fighting, stick with hatchet.
ban, *n. m.*, coin; **-i**, *pl.*, money.
báncă, *n. f.*, **bănci**, *pl.*, bank; bench (seat).
bând, *gerund*, see **bea**.
bântu-í (**a**), **-ésc**, **-ít**, *v. intr.* IV, to damage, to infest.
bănuí (**a**), **-ésc**, **-t**, *v. tr.* IV, to suspect, to mistrust.
Bărăgán, *prop. n.*, the plain on the lower Danube south of Brăila.
bará-t, **-tă**, *adj.*, **-ţi**, **-te**, *pl.*, crossed (cheque).
bárbă, *n. f.*, **bắrbi**, *pl.*, beard.
bărbá-t, *n. m.*, **-ţi**, *pl.*, man, husband.
bărbăt-ésc, **-eáscă**, *adj.*, **-éşti**, *pl.*, manly (of a), man.
bărbí-e, *n. f.*, **-i**, *pl.*, chin.
bárcă, *n. f.*, **bắrci**, *pl.*, boat.
bârlóg, *n. mix.*, **bârlóguri** (**bârloáge**), *pl.*, den (of a bear).
Bấrsa, *prop. n. f.*, region in Southern Transylvania; **Bârsán**, *n.*, *adj.*, from the Bârsa-region.
Basarábia, *prop. n. f.* (province).
basmá, *n. f.*, **-ua**, *art.*, **-le**, *pl.*, kerchief.
băţ, *n. m.*, **béţe**, *pl.*, stick.
bătáie, *n. f.*, **bătắi**, *pl.*, fight, beating; shooting (of a rifle); range.
bătătúr-ă, *n. f.*, **-i**, *pl.*, court, courtyard.

báte (a), bat, bătút, *v. tr.* III, to beat; **a-şi bate joc,** to make fun (see 6. 4. b, 6. 7).

batíst-ă, *n. f.*, **-e,** *pl.*, handkerchief.

bâtlán, *n. m.*, **-i,** *pl.*, heron.

bătrấn, -ă, *adj.*, *n.*, **-i, -e,** *pl.*, old man, old woman.

bătrân-ésc, -eáscă, *adj.*, **-éşti,** *pl.*, old.

bătrânéţe, *n. f. pl.*, old age.

băutúr-ă, *n. f.*, **-i,** *pl.*, drink.

beá (a), -u, băút, *v. tr.* II, to drink (see 6. 3. c).

behăí (a), -ésc, -ít, *v. intr.* IV, to bleat, to baa.

beleá, *n. f.*, **beléle,** *pl.*, misfortune, calamity; inconvenience, embarrassment.

belşúg, *n. mix.*, **-uri,** *pl.*, abundance, riches.

bére, *n. f.* (**beri,** *pl.*), beer.

berechét, *n. mix.*, **-e,** *pl.*, abundance, plenty; *adv.* abundantly.

beregát-ă, *n. f.*, **-e,** *pl.*, throat, jugular.

bernevéci, *n. m. pl.*, woollen trousers of coarse homespun cloth worn by peasants.

beţiş-ór, *n. mix.*, **-oáre,** *pl.*, twig, stick.

bézn-ă, *n. f.*, **-e,** *pl.* (pitch) darkness.

Bicáz, *prop. n. m.* (river, defile).

biét, biátă, *adj.*, **biéţi, biéte,** *pl.*, poor.

bilét, *n. mix.*, **-e,** *pl.*, ticket, billet.

bíne, *adv.*, *n. m.*, well; good; see **deabínelea,** *adv.*; **binişór,** *adv.*, pretty well.

binecuvânt-á (a), -éz, -át, *v. tr.* I, to bless.

binecuvânt-áre, *n. f.*, **-ări,** *pl.*, blessing, benediction.

binefăcăt-ór, -oáre, *adj.*, **-óri, -oáre,** *pl.*, beneficent.

biróu, *n. mix.*, **-ri,** *pl.*, office, desk.

biru-í (a), -iésc, -ít, *v. tr.*, *intr.* IV, to defeat, to win the victory.

biséric-ă, *n. f.*, **-i,** *pl.*, church.

biseric-ésc, -eáscă, *adj.*, **éşti,** *pl.*, ecclesiastical, of the church.

Bizánţ, *prop. n. m.*, Byzantium; **bizantín, -ă,** *adj.*, **-ni, -e,** *pl.*, Byzantine.

blajín, -ă, *adj.*, **-i, -e,** *pl.*, mild, meek.

blánă, *n. f.*, **blănuri,** *pl.*, fur, fur coat; **blăni,** *pl.*, planks.

blanchét, *n. mix.*, **-e,** *pl.* (telegraphic), telegram form.

blân-d, -ă, *adj.*, **-zi, -de,** *pl.*, tame, gentle, mild; **blândéţ-ă,** *n. f.*, **-e,** *pl.*, meekness, kindness, mildness.

blăstămá (a) (blestemá), blắstăm, -át, *v. tr.* I, to curse.

blon-d, -dă, *adj.*, **-zi, -de,** *pl.*, fair, light.

boáb-ă, *n. f.*, **-e,** *pl.*, berry.

bo-álă, *n. f.*, **-li (-ále),** *pl.*, illness.

bogá-t, -tă, *adj.*, *n.*, **-ţi, -te,** *pl.*, rich, wealthy.

bogăţí-e, *n. f.*, **-i,** *pl.*, riches, wealth; abundance.

Bogdán, *prop. n.* (name).

boiér, *n. m.*, **-i.,** *pl.*, nobleman, boyar.

bojbăí (a), -ésc, -t, *v. intr.* IV, to grope, to feel.

bolésn-ă, *n. f.*, **-e,** *pl.*, disease, pestilence.

bolnáv, -ă, *adj.*, **-i, -e,** *pl.*, ill, sick; **bolnăv-iór, -ioáră,** *adj. dim.*, ill.

bolován, *n. m*, **-i,** *pl.*, boulder.

bóltă, *n. f.*, **bolţi, bolte,** *pl.*, vault, dome.

boltí-t, tă, *adj.*, **-ţi, -te,** *pl.*, vaulted, arched, curved.

borangíc, see **burangíc.**

Bórcea, Bórca, *prop. n. f.* (locality).
bord, *n. mix.*, **-uri,** *pl.*, deck (of a ship); flap (of a hat).
bór-tă, *n. f.*, **-ţi,** *pl.*, hole.
bot, *n. mix.*, **-uri,** *pl.*, snout, muzzle; mouth; point.
bó-u, *n. m.*, **-i,** *pl.*, ox.
bouléţ, *n. m.*, **-i,** *pl.*, bullock.
bra-d, *n. m.*, **-zi,** *pl.*, fir-tree, silver-fir, Norway spruce (*abies pectinata*); **brad (roşu),** pine, fir (*pinus*).
brădét, *n. mix.* (**-e,** *pl.*), thicket of fir-trees.
Brăíla, *prop. n. f.* (town).
brânci, *n. f. pl.*, push; **pe —,** on all fours.
brấnză, *n. f.*, cheese; **brânzéturi,** *pl.*, kinds of cheese.
Braşóv, *prop. n. m.* (town).
braţ, *n. mix.*, **-e,** *pl.*, arm.
brấ-u, *n. mix.*, **-ie, -ne,** *pl.*, belt; girdle; waistband.
brázd-ă, *n. f.*, **-e,** *pl.*, furrow.
bre, *interj.*, see 9. 2.
Brén(n)er-ul, *prop. n. m.*, the Brenner.
Británia, *prop. n. f.*, Britain.
broáscă, *n. f.*, **broáşte,** *pl.*, frog; lock.
brúm-ă, *n. f.*, **-i,** *pl.*, hoar frost, rime.
brusc, -ă, *adj.*, **brúşti, brúşte,** *pl.*, harsh, rough.
bucălát, -ă (confused with **bucălắu, -láie**), *adj.*, chubby, chub-faced (of children).
bucă-lắu, -láie, *adj.*, **-lắi, -láie,** *pl.*, with black mouth (of sheep).
bucátă, *n. f.*, **bucắţi,** *pl.*, piece, lump; **bucate,** *pl.*, dish, food.
bucăţ-ícă, *n. f.*, **-éle,** *pl.*, little bit.
Bucégi, *prop. n. m.* (mountains).
buchér, *n.*, *adj.*, **-i, -e,** *pl.*, pedant, ignorant.
Bucovína, *prop. n. f.* (province).
Bucuréşti, *m. pl.*, Bucharest.
bucurí-e, *n. f.*, **-i,** *pl.*, joy.
bucur-ós, -oásă, *adj.*, **-óşi, -oáse,** *pl.*, glad, cheerful.
buimăc-eálă, *n. f.*, **-éli,** *pl.*, giddiness, stupefaction.
bulboác-ă, *n. f.*, **-e,** *pl.*, whirlpool.
búlgăre (búlgăr), *n. m.*, **-i,** *pl.*, clod.
bumbác, *n. m.*, cotton.
bun, -ă, *adj.*, **-i, -e,** *pl.*, good.
bunăt-áte, *n. f.*, **-ắţi,** *pl.*, goodness.
buníc, *n. m.*, **-i,** *pl.*, grandfather.
buníc-ă, *n. f.*, **-i (bunele),** *pl.*, grandmother.
burangíc, *n. mix.*, **-uri,** *pl.*, flock-silk, floss-silk.
burui-ánă, *n. f.*, **-éni,** *pl.*, weed.
búşile (de á), *adv.*, on all fours.
búti-e, *n. f.*, **-i,** *pl.*, barrel, tun.
butúc, *n. m.*, **-i,** *pl.*, log, block, stump.
buturúg-ă, *n. f.*, **-i,** *pl.*, log.
búz-ă, *n. f.*, **-e,** *pl.*, lip.
buzunár, *n. mix.*, **-e,** *pl.*, pocket.

C

ca, *adv.*, like, as.
că, *conj.*, that.
cabinét, *n. mix.*, **-e,** *pl.*, cabinet.
căci, *conj.*, because.
căciúl-ă, *n. f.*, **-i,** *pl.*, fur cap.
cădeá (a), *cad*, **căzút,** *v. intr.* II, to fall; **a se —,** to be suitable, to become (see 6. 4. **c**).
cafe-á, *n. f.*, **caféle,** *pl.*, coffee.
cấin-e (cấne), *n. m.*, **-i,** *pl.*, dog.
caí-s, *n. m.*, **-şi,** *pl.*, apricot-tree.
caís-ă, *n. f.*, **-e,** *pl.*, apricot.
ca-l, *n. m.*, **-i,** *pl.*, horse.
căláre, *adj.*, **călắri,** *pl.*, on horseback.
călătór, *n. m.*, **-i,** *pl.*, traveller; **călă-tór, -toáre,** *adj.*, **-tóri, -toáre,** *pl.*, wandering.

călător-í (a), **-ésc**, **-ít**, *v. intr.* IV, to travel, to journey.
călătorí-e, *n. f.*, **-i**, *pl.*, journey.
călắ-u, *n. m.*, **-i**, *pl.*, headsman, executioner.
călăúz-ă, *n. m., f.*, **-e**, *pl.*, guide.
călăuz-í, (a), **-ésc**, **-ít**, to guide, to lead.
călcá (a), **calc**, **călcát**, *v. tr., intr.*, to tread, to walk upon, to step.
cálcul, *n. mix.*, **-e**, *pl.*, calculation.
cal-d, **-dă**, *adj.*, **-zi**, **-de**, *pl.*, warm (see 6. 4. **c**); **căldúr-ă**, *n. f.*, **-i**, *pl.*, heat, warmth.
căldur-ós, **-oásă**, *adj.*, **-óşi**, **-oáse**, *pl.*, warm.
cále, *n. f.*, **căi**, *pl.*, way; journey; avenue; **a găsi cu cale**, to think fit, to approve of.
Călimáni, *prop. n. m. pl.* (mountain group).
Calístru, *prop. n. m.* (name).
căluşél, *n. m.*, **căluşéi**, *pl.*, little horse.
cam, *adv.*, nearly, about; a little.
cămáşă, *n. f.*, **căméşi** (**cămắşi**), *pl.*, shirt.
cámer-ă, *n. f.*, **-e**, *pl.*, room, chamber.
cămeş-ói, *n. m.*, **oáie**, *pl.*, large shirt; woman's embroidered chemise.
cămín, *n. mix.*, **-uri**, *pl.*, hearth; home, house; hostel.
câmp, *n. mix., m.*, **-uri** (**-i**), *pl.*, field.
câmpí-e, *n. f.*, **-i**, *pl.*, field, plain.
când, *adv.*, when; **pe când**, while; *conj.*, see 8. 4. **i**.
cândvá, *adv.*, at any time.
cắnep-ă, *n. f.*, hemp; **-i** (**-e**), *pl.*, hemp-fields.
cânt, *n. mix.*, **-uri**, *pl.*, canto (part of a poem).
cântá (a), **cânt**, **-át**, *v. tr., intr.* I, to sing, to play.
cântăr-í (a), **-ésc**, **-ít**, *v. tr.* IV, to weigh, to balance.
cấntec, *n. mix.*, **-e**, *pl.*, song.
cant-ón, *n. mix.*, **-oáne**, *pl.*, canton, district; house of a roadman or of a railwayman built near the road or near the railway line.
cap, *n. mix.*, **-ete**, *pl.*, head; **capi**, *pl.*, leaders; **capuri**, *pl.*, promontories, end (see 2. 9. **a**).
cápăt, *n. mix.*, **cápete**, *pl.*, end; term.
căpătá (a), **cápăt**, **căpătát**, *v. tr.* I, to receive, to obtain.
căpeténi-e, *n. f.*, **-i**, *pl.*, head, chief, commander; **de căpetenie**, principal.
capitál-ă, *n. f.*, **-e**, *pl.*, capital.
capítol, *n. mix.*, **-e**, *pl.*, chapter.
cápr-ă, *n. f.*, **-e**, *pl.*, goat; **capră sălbatecă**, wild goat, chamois.
căprioár-ă, *n. f.*, **-e**, *pl.*, roe (animal).
căpşún-ă, *n. f.*, **-i** (**-e**), *pl.*, garden strawberry.
căptuş-í (a), **-ésc**, **-ít**, *v. tr.* IV, to catch; to line; to lay on.
car, *n. mix.*, **-e**, *pl.*, cart.
cărăbăn-í (a), **-ésc**, **-ít**, *v. tr.* IV, to carry, to pack; **a se —**, to pack off.
carabín-ă, *n. f.*, **-e**, *pl.*, carabine.
característic, **-ă**, *adj.*, **-i**, **-e**, *pl.*, characteristic.
Caraimán, *prop. n. m.* (mountain).
carấmb, *n. m.*, **-i**, *pl.*, leg of a boot.
Caranfíl, *prop. n.* (surname).
căr-áre, *n. f.*, **-ări**, *pl.*, footway, path.
cărbún-e, *n. m.*, **-i**, *pl.*, coal.
cârd, *n. mix.*, **-uri**, *pl.*, herd, flock; crowd.

cáre, *pron.*, who, which, what (see 5. 7, 5. 8).
carevá, *indef. pron.*, someone (see 5. 9).
cấrjă (cấrje), *n. f.*, **-i**, *pl.*, stick, crutch.
cấrm-ă, *n. f.*, **-i (-e)**, *pl.*, rudder; guidance, management.
cárne, *n. f.*, meat; **cắrnuri**, *pl.*, kinds of meat.
Carpáţi, *n. m. pl.*, Carpathians.
carpatín, -ă, *adj.*, **-i, -e**, *pl.*, Carpathian.
Carst, *prop. n. m.*, Dinaric Alps; Karst.
cárte, *n. f.*, **cắrţi**, *pl.*, book; **cárte poştálă**, postcard.
cărt-icícă, *n. f.*, **-icéle**, *pl.*, little book.
cấrtiţ-ă, *n. f.*, **-e**, *pl.*, mole.
cărturár, *n. m.*, **-i**, *pl.*, scholar, learned man.
cărúţ-ă, *n. f.*, **-e**, *pl.*, cart, car.
căruţáş, *n. m.*, **-i**, *pl.*, carter, carman.
cás-ă, *n. f.*, **-e**, *pl.*, house; **cassă (casă)**, pay-office; safe.
căsător-í (o), **-ésc, -ít**, *v. tr.* IV, to marry, to wed; **a se —**, to marry, to get married.
caşicấnd, *conj.*, as if.
casiér, *n. m.*, **-i**, *pl.*, cashier.
casierí-e, *n. f.*, **-i**, *pl.*, pay-office, cash-desk.
cásn-ă, *n. f.*, **-e**, *pl.*, toil; torture.
castán, *n. m.*, **-i**, *pl.*, chestnut-tree; **castán-ă**, *n. f.*, **-e**, *pl.*, chestnut.
castaní-u, -e, *adj.*, **-i**, *pl.*, brown.
câştíg, *n. mix.*, **-uri**, *pl.*, gain, profit.
câştigá (a), **câştíg, -át**, *v. tr.* I, to win, to gain, to earn.
cât, *adv.*, how much (see 5. 7. **b**); **cât pe ce**, *adv.*, nearly; *conj.*, see 8. 4. **i**.
cắtá (a), see **căutá (a)**.
cấte, *adv.*, **cấte trei**, in threes; **cấteşi trei**, all three together.
catedrál-ă, *n. f.*, **-e**, *pl.*, cathedral.
cấteşi cinci, *num.*, all five.
caţi=**cauţi**, see **căuta (a)**.
câţivá, câtevá, *indef. pron. pl.*, a few (see 5. 9).
catolicísm, *n. mix.* (**-e**, *pl.*), catholicism.
cắtre, *prep.*, towards, to, against.
Catrína, *prop. n. f.*, Catherine.
câtvá, câtăvá, *adj.*, *indef. pron.*, some (see 5. 9).
căúş, *n. mix.*, **-e**, *pl.*, wooden scoop (measure).
căutá (a), **cáut, căutát**, *v. tr.*, *intr.* I, to look, to look for, to care for, to look after, to seek.
cáuz-ă, *n. f.*, **-e**, *pl.*, cause; **din cauza**, because.
cazác, *n. m.*, **-i**, *pl.*, Cossack; **căzăcé-l**, *n. m.*, **-i**, *pl.*, little Cossack.
Cazáne, *prop. n. f. pl.* (rocks).
ce, *pron.*, what (see 5. 7; 5. 8); **din ce în ce**, *adv.*, more and more; **cât pe ce**, *adv.*, nearly; **de ce**, why; *corr. conj.*, see 8. 4. **i**.
Ceahlău, *prop. n. m.* (mountain).
ceáră, *n. f.*, **céruri**, *pl.*, wax.
ceártă, *n. f.*, **cérturi**, *pl.*, quarrel, dispute.
ceás, *n. mix.*, **-uri**, *pl.*, hour; watch; **ceasórnic**, *n. mix.*, **ceasoárnice**, *pl.*, watch, clock.
ceáţă, *n. f.*, **céţe (céţi, céţuri)**, *pl.*, mist, fog.
cec, *n. mix.*, **-uri**, *pl.*, cheque.
Cehoslovácia, *n. f.*, Czechoslovakia.
cel, *m.*, **cea**, *f. pron.*, that (see 5. 6. **b**; 5. 8).
célălalt, céllalt, célalt, *dem. pron. m.*, the other (see 5. 6. **c**).
centrál, -ă, *adj.*, **-i, -e**, *pl.*, central.

céntr-u, *n. mix.*, **-e**, *pl.*, centre, middle.
cenúş-e (**-ă**), *n. f.*, **-i**, *pl.*, ashes.
cenuşí-u, **-e**, *adj.*, **-i**, *pl.*, ashen-grey.
cer(i), *n. mix.*, **-uri**, *pl.*, sky, heaven; **cer-ésc**, **-eáscă**, *adj.*, **-eşti**, *pl.*, heavenly.
cerb, *n. m.*, **-i**, *pl.*, stag, hart.
cerc, *n. mix.*, **-uri**, *pl.*, circle.
cercá (**a**), see **încercá** (**a**).
cercet-á (**a**), **-éz**, **-át**, *v. tr.* I, to inquire, to ask, to interrogate, to question.
cercetătór, **-toáre**, *adj.*, *n.*, **-tóri**, **-toáre**, *pl.*, searcher, investigator.
cerdác, *n. mix.*, **-uri** (**-e**), *pl.*, balcony.
cereál-ă, *n. f.*, **-e**, *pl.*, cereal.
cérer-e, *n. f.*, **-i**, *pl.*, demand, request; solicitation.
Cérna, *prop. n. f.* (river).
Cernăúţi, *prop. n. m. pl.* (town).
cerneálă, *n. f.*, **cernéluri**, *pl.*, ink.
cerş-í (**a**), **-ésc**, **-ít**, *v. tr.* IV, to beg, to ask for alms.
certá (**a**), **cert**, **-át**, *v. tr.* I, to scold; to rebuke, to reprimand; **a se —**, to quarrel.
céstlalt, **ceástălaltă**, *dem. pron.*, this other (see 5. 6. **c**).
cet-áte, *n. f.*, **-ắţi**, *pl.*, city; fortress, stronghold.
Cetátea Álbă, *prop. n. f.* (town), Akerman.
cetí (**cití**) (**a**), **cet-ésc**, **-ít**, *v. tr.* IV, to read.
cetitór, *adj.*, *n. m.*, **-i**, *pl.*, reader.
cetitoáre, *adj.*, *n. f.*, **cetitoáre**, *pl.*, reader.
cevá, *indef. pron.*, something (see 5. 9).
chébe (**ghébă**), *n. f.*, **chéburi**, *pl.*, long cloak of homespun woollen cloth worn by peasants.
chefuí (**a**), **-ésc**, **-ít**, *v. tr.*, *intr.* IV, **chefăluí** (**a**), **-ésc**, **-ít**, *v. tr.*, *intr.* IV, to feast, to revel.
chéi, *n. mix.*, **-uri**, *pl.*, quay, wharf.
chéie, *n. f.*, **chéi**, *pl.*, key.
chélner, *n. m.*, **-i**, *pl.*, waiter; **chelneríţă**, *n. f.*, **-e**, *pl.*, waitress.
cheltuí (**a**), **-ésc**, **-ít**, *v. tr.* IV, to spend; **cheltui-tór**, **-toáre**, *adj.*, *n.*, lavisher, prodigal.
chemá (**chiemá**) (**a**), **ch(i)em**, **ch(i)emát**, *v. tr.* I, to call.
chemáre, *n. f.*, **chemắri**, *pl.*, call, appeal, summons.
chestiún-e (**chésti-e**), *n. f.*, **-i**, *pl.*, question, problem.
chiág, *n. mix.*, **-uri**, *pl.*, rennet.
chiár, *adv.*, even.
chibrít, *n. mix.*, **-uri**, *pl.*, match.
chihlimbár, *n. mix.*, **-e**, *pl.*, amber.
chilográm, *n. mix.*, **-e**, *pl.*, kilogram.
chilométr-u, *n. m.*, **-i**, *pl.*, kilometre.
chimír, *n. mix.*, **-e**, *pl.*, girdle, leather belt for keeping money in.
chin, *n. mix.*, **-uri**, *pl.*, torture, pain.
chinuí (**a**), **-ésc**, **-ít**, *v. tr.* IV, to torture, to torment; **a se —**, to torture oneself.
chior, **chioáră**, *adj.*, **chiori**, **chioáre**, *pl.*, blind.
chioríş, *adv.*, asquint.
chip, *n. mix.*, **-uri**, *pl.*, image, figure, form, model, manner.
chitánţ-ă, *n. f.*, **-e**, *pl.*, receipt, discharge, acquittance.
chit-í (**a**), **-ésc**, **-ít**, *v. tr.*, *intr.* IV, to ponder, to reflect; to hit upon; **a se —**, to ponder.
chíuă (*dial.*), see **píuă**.
Christós, **Hristós**, Christ.

ci, *conj.*, but, yes.
cianúră, *n. f.*, cyanide.
ciasórnic, see **ceas.**
cínci, *num.*, five.
cíncilea (al), *m.*, **cíncia (a)**, *f.*, the fifth.
cincím-e, *n. f.*, **-i**, *pl.*, fifth (part).
cíne, *pron.*, who (see 5. 7, 5. 8).
cinevá, *indef. pron.*, somebody (see 5. 9).
cingăt-oáre, *n. f.*, **-óri**, *pl.*, belt, girdle.
cinst-í (a), **-ésc**, **-ít**, *v. tr.* IV, to honour, to respect.
cinstít, **-ă**, *adj.*, **cinstí-ţi**, **-te**, *pl.*, honest, honourable, fair.
cioáră, *n. m.*, **cióri**, *pl.*, crow.
cioáreci, *n. m. pl.*, woollen peasant trousers.
cioát-ă, *n. f.*, **-e**, *pl.*, log, stump.
ciobán, *n. m.*, **-i**, *pl.*, shepherd.
ciobăné-l, *n. m.*, **-i**, *pl.*, little shepherd.
ciobăn-ésc, **-eáscă**, *adj.*, **-éşti**, *pl.*, pastoral, shepherd's.
cioc, *n. mix.*, **-uri**, *pl.*, beak, bill, nib.
ciocârlí-e, *n. f.*, **-i**, *pl.*, lark.
ciocuIéţ, *n. mix.*, **-e**, *pl.*, little beak.
ciopl-í (a), **-ésc**, **-ít**, *v. tr.* IV, to cut, to sculpture, to hew.
ciórb-ă, *n. f.*, **-e**, *pl.*, sour soup.
ciorchín-ă, *n. f.*, **-i (-e)**, *pl.*, bunch, cluster.
cir-eádă, *n. f.*, **-ézi**, *pl.*, herd.
cireáşă, *n. f.*, **ciréşe**, *pl.*, cherry.
ciréş, *n. m.*, **-i**, *pl.*, cherry-tree.
citáre, *n. f.*, **citări**, *pl.*, quotation; summons.
ciúdă, *n. f.*, anger, vexation; **ciudat**, **-ă**, *adj.*, **ciudaţi**, **-te**, *pl.*, strange.
ciúm-ă, *n. f.*, **-e**, *pl.*, plague.
cízm-ă, *n. f.*, **-e**, *pl.*, boot.
clăd-í (a), **-ésc**, **-ít**, *v. tr.* IV, to construct, to build.
clădír-e, *n. f.*, **-i**, *pl.*, building.
cláp-ă, *n. f.*, **-e**, *pl.*, key (mus.); valve.
clar, **-ă**, *adj.*, **-i**, **-e**, *pl.*, clear, distinct; evident; bright.
clás-ă, *n. f.*, **-e**, *pl.*, class, rank, schoolroom.
clătína (a), **clátin**, **clătinát**, *v. tr.* I, to shake; to agitate; **a se —**, to stagger, to totter.
cléşte, *n. f. pl.*, pincers.
clién-t, *n. m.*, **-ţi**, *pl.*, customer, client.
clíp-ă, *n. f.*, **-e**, *pl.*, instant, moment.
clip-í (a), **-ésc**, **-ít**, *v. intr.* IV, to twinkle, to wink.
cloc-í (a), **-ésc**, **-ít**, *v. tr.* IV, to incubate, to brood.
clocot-í (a), **-ésc**, **-ít**, *v. intr.* IV, to boil, to bubble; **clocoti-tór**, **-toáre**, *adj.*, **-tóri**, **-tóare**, *pl.*, boiling.
clópot, *n. mix.*, **-e**, *pl.*, bell.
Cluj, *prop. n. m.* (town).
coáce (a), **coc**, **copt**, *v. tr.* III, to bake; **a se —**, to ripen, to grow ripe.
coádă, *n. f.*, **cózi (coáde)**, *pl.*, tail; handle.
coalíţi-e, *n. f.*, **-i.**, *pl.*, coalition.
coaliz-á (a), **-éz**, **-át**, to league; **coalizát**, **-ă**, *adj.*, **coalizá-ţi**, **-te**, *pl.*, co-allied.
coám-ă, *n. f.*, **-e**, *pl.*, mane.
coás-ă, *n. f.*, **-e**, *pl.*, scythe.
coáse (a), **cos**, **cusút**, *v. tr.* III, to sew.
coást-ă, *n. f.*, **-e**, *pl.*, rib; coast; hill-slope.
coborí (a), see **scoborí (a)**.
coceán, *n. m.*, **cocéni**, *pl.*, stump, stalk.
cocoán-ă (cucoánă), *n. f.*, **-e**, *pl.*, lady, mistress.
cocór (cucór), *n. m.*, **-i**, *pl.*, crane; **cucoáră**, *n. f.*, **-e**, *pl.*, crane.

cocóș, *n. m.*, **-i**, *pl.*, cock.
cocóș de múnte, *n. m.*, **-i**, *pl.*, mountain-cock, wood-grouse, woodcock (*Tetrao urogallus*).
cocoșé-l, *n. m.*, **-i**, *pl.*, cockerel.
cocostârc, *n. m.*, **-i**, *pl.*, stork.
códr-u, *n. m.*, **-i**, *pl.*, forest.
cóf-ă, *n. f.*, **-e**, *pl.*, wooden jug (pitcher) for fetching water; **cofíț-ă**, *n. f. dim.*, **-e**, *pl.* small wooden jug.
coféturi, *f. pl.*, sugar-plums.
cogémite (cogeámite), *adv.*, big, high and mighty, enormous.
cojóc, *n. mix.*, **cojoáce**, *pl.*, fur coat, sheep-pelt.
colabor-á (a), **-éz**, **-át**, *v. intr.* I, to collaborate.
colíb-ă, *n. f.*, **-e**, *pl.*, hut, shed.
colilí-e, *n. f.*, **-i**, *pl.*, feather-grass (*Stipa pennata*), spike, spikenard (*Nardus strictus*).
colind-á (a), **-éz**, **-át**, *v. intr.* I, to sing carols (at Christmas going from house to house), to stroll about.
coló, *adv.* = **acólo**.
coloné-l, *n. m.*, **-i**, *pl.*, colonel.
colț, *n. mix.*, **-uri**, *pl.*, corner.
colțur-ós, **-oásă**, *adj.*, **-óși**, **-oáse**, *pl.*, angular.
cománd-ă, *n. f.*, **-e**, *pl.*, command, order.
comandá (a), **cománd**, **-át**, *v. tr.*, *intr.* I, to command, to order.
comandán-t, *n. m.*, **-ți**, *pl.*, commander, commandant.
comíte (a), **comít**, **comís**, *v. tr.* III, to commit, to intrust.
com-oáră, *n. f.*, **-óri**, *pl.*, treasure.
compáct, **-ă**, *adj.*, **compácți**, **-te**, *pl.*, compact, dense.
compáni-e, *n. f.*, **-i**, *pl.*, company, society.
compar-á (a), **compár**, **-át**, *v. tr.* I, to compare.
compartimént, *n. mix.*, **-e**, *pl.*, compartment.
común-ă, *n. f.*, **-e**, *pl.*, common, borough, parish.
comunit-áte, *n. f.*, **-ăți**, *pl.*, community.
conác, *n. mix.*, **-e**, *pl.*, manor-house; inn.
concért, *n. mix.*, **-e**, *pl.*, concert.
concís, **-ă**, *adj.*, **concí-și**, **-se**, *pl.*, concise.
concurén-t, *n. m.*, **-ți**, *pl.*, rival, competitor.
condamná (a), *v. tr.* I, **condámn**, **-át**, to condemn, to sentence, to doom.
condéi, *n. mix.*, **-e**, *pl.*, pen, quill.
Condréni, *prop. n. m. pl.* (locality).
condúce (a), **condúc**, **condús**, *v. tr.* III, to lead, to guide; to drive (a mechanical vehicle).
conductór, *n. m.*, **-i**, *pl.*, conductor.
conferínț-ă, *n. f.*, **-e**, *pl.*, lecture, conference.
conservá (a), **consérv (-éz)**, **-át**, *v. tr.* I, to conserve, to preserve; **conserváre**, *n. f.*, conservation.
Constantín, *prop. n.*, Constantin.
consultá (a), **consúlt (-éz)**, **-át**, *v. tr.* I, to consult.
consultáți-e, *n. f.*, **-i**, *pl.*, consult, consultation.
cont, *n. mix.*, **-uri**, *pl.*, account, calculation.
contábil, *n. m.*, **-i**, *pl.*, accountant.
contemporán, **-ă**, *adj.*, **-i**, **-e**, *pl.*, contemporary.
continuá (a), **continuéz (contínui)**, **continuát**, *v. tr.* I, to continue, to go on.
contrást, *n. mix.*, **-e**, *pl.*, contrast.
contribuí (a), **-ésc**, **-ít**, *v. intr.* IV, to contribute.

convingă-tór, -toáre, *adj.*, **-tóri, -toáre,** *pl.*, convincing.

convínge (a), convín-g, -s, *v. tr.* III, to convince, to persuade.

convínger-e, *n. f.*, **-i,** *pl.*, conviction.

convorbír-e, *n. f.*, **-i,** *pl.*, conversation; — **telefónică** (telephone) call.

convúlsi-e, *n. f.*, **-i,** *pl.*, convulsion.

copác (copáci), *n. m.*, **-i,** *pl.*, tree (not fruit bearing).

Copenhága, *prop. n. f.*, Copenhagen.

cópi-e, *n. f.*, **-i,** *pl.*, copy, transcript.

copí-l, *n. m.*, **-i,** *pl.*, child; **copilărí-e,** *n. f.*, **-i,** *pl.*, childhood; **copíl-ă,** *n. f.*, **-e,** *pl.*, girl.

copt, coáptă, *adj.*, **cópţi, coápte,** *pl.*, ripe; baked (see **coace (a)**).

corábie, *n. f.*, **corăbii,** *pl.*, ship, boat, vessel.

corb, *n. m.*, **-i,** *pl.*, raven.

corespunzăt-ór, -oáre, *adj.*, **-óri, -oáre,** *pl.*, corresponding, suitable.

coridór, *n. mix.*, **coridoáre,** *pl.*, corridor, gallery.

corn, *n. mix.*, **coárne,** *pl.*, horn; **cornuri,** *pl.*, roll of bread; **coárnele plúgului,** plough handle.

Cornăţél, *prop. n. m.* (place).

cornút, -ă, *adj.*, horned.

corp, *n. mix.*, **-uri,** *pl.*, body.

cort, *n. mix.*, **-uri,** *pl.*, tent.

cost-á (a), -éz, -át, *v. intr.*, to cost.

Costáche<Constantín, *prop. n.* (name).

costíş-ă, *n. f.*, **-e,** *pl.*, slope; declivity.

costíţ-ă, *n. f.*, **-e,** *pl.*, cutlet, chop.

costúm, *n. mix.*, **-e,** *pl.*, costume, dress.

cot, *n. mix.*, **coáte,** *pl.*, elbow.

cotéţ, *n. mix.*, **-e,** *pl.*, poultry-house; pigsty.

cot-í (a), -ésc, -ít, *v. intr.* IV, to wheel aside, to turn up.

cotig-í (a), -ésc, -ít, *v. intr.* IV, to wring, to shift and turn, to run in zigzag.

cotitúr-ă, *n. f.*, **-i,** *pl.*, bend, bending; turning-point.

Cotnári, *prop. n.* (locality).

cotrop-í (a), -ésc, -ít, *v. tr.* IV, to invade.

covérg-ă, *n. f.*, **-i,** *pl.*, arbour, sheltering roof.

cov-ór, *n. mix.*, **-oáre,** *pl.*, carpet.

crac, *n. m.* (**crácă,** *n. f.*), **-i,** *pl.*, branch, arm; leg, thigh.

Crăciún, *n. m.* (**-uri,** *pl.*), Christmas.

crái, *n. m.*, **crái,** *pl.* (*archaic*), king.

crăi-ásă, *n. f.*, **-ése,** *pl.*, queen.

Craióva, *prop. n. f.* (town).

crâmpéi, *n. mix.*, **-e,** *pl.*, fragment, piece.

crăpá (a) (crepá), crăp, -át, *v. tr., intr.*, to split; to burst; to crack; to chink.

creángă, *n. f.*, **créngi,** *pl.*, branch, bough.

credin-cíos, -cioásă, *adj.*, faithful, loyal.

credínţ-ă, *n. f.*, **-e,** *pl.*, faith, loyalty.

crédit, *n. mix.*, **-e,** *pl.*, credit, trust.

crei-ón, *n. mix.*, **-oáne,** *pl.*, pencil.

crepá (a), see **crăpá (a).**

crescăt-ór, -oáre, *n., adj.*, **-óri, -oáre,** *pl.*, breeder.

créşte (a), cresc, crescút, *v. tr., intr.* III, to grow, to increase, to rise.

créştet, *n. mix.*, **-e,** *pl.*, summit, top; vertex.

creştín, *n. m.*, **-i**, *pl.*, Christian.
creţ, creáţă, *adj.*, curled; **creţ**, *n. m.*, **-i**, *pl.* (**-uri**, *pl. f.*), curl.
crím-ă, *n. f.*, **-e**, *pl.*, crime.
Criméa, *prop. n. f.*, Crimea.
crin, *n. m.*, **-i**, *pl.*, lily.
Crişul Répede, *prop. n. m.* (river).
críţă, *n. f.*, steal.
crív-ăţ, *n. mix.*, **-eţe**, *pl.*, north wind, Boreas.
cronológic, -ă, *adj.*, **-i, -e**, *pl.*, chronological.
crúc-e, *n. f.*, **-i**, *pl.*, cross.
crucíş, *adv.*, crosswise.
crud, -ă, *adj.*, **crúzi, crúde**, *pl.*, raw, unripe; crude; cruel.
cu, *prep.*, with.
cuadrúpl-u, -ă, *adj.*, **-i, -e**, *pl.*, fourfold.
cuc, *n. m.*, **-i**, *pl.*, cuckoo.
cucer-í (**a**), **-ésc, -ít**, *v. tr.* IV, to conquer, to subdue; **cucerír-e**, *n. f.*, **-i**, *pl.*, conquest.
cucór, see **cocór**.
cucóş, see **cocóş**.
cuculéţ, *n. m. dim.*, **-i**, *pl.*, little cuckoo.
cúget, *n. mix.*, **-e**, *pl.*, thought.
cúi, *n. mix.*, **-e**, *pl.*, nail.
cúib, *n. mix.*, **-uri**, *pl.*, nest.
cuib-á (**a**), **-éz, -át**, *v. intr.* I, to nest.
cuibár, *n. mix.*, **-e**, *pl.*, nest; nest-egg.
culcá (**a**), **culc, -át**, to put to bed; to lay down; **a se —**, to go to bed.
culc-áre, *n. f.*, **-ări**, *pl.*, going to bed; lying down.
culegătór, *n. m.*, **-i**, *pl.*, compositor (printer).
cúlm-e, *n. f.*, **-i**, *pl.*, summit, peak.
culoáre, *n. f.*, **culóri**, *pl.*, colour.
cultivá (**a**), **cultív** (**-éz**), **-át**, *v. tr.* I, to cultivate.
cultúr-ă, *n. f.*, **-i**, *pl.*, culture.
culturál, -ă, *adj.*, **-i, -e**, *pl.*, cultural.
cum, *adv.*, how, as; **cum că**, *conj.*, that; *corr. conj.*, see 8. 4. i.
cum-ắtră, *n. f.*, **-étre**, *pl.*, godmother (in relation to the child's parents).
cumắtr-u, *n. m.*, **-i** (**cumétri**), *pl.*, godfather (in relation to the child's parents).
cumínte, *adj.*, **cumínţi**, *pl.*, intelligent, clever; wise, reasonable.
cumná-t, *n. m.*, **-ţi**, *pl.*, brother-in-law; **cumnát-ă**, *n. f.*, **-e**, *pl.*, sister-in-law.
cúmpănă, *n. f.*, **cúmpene**, *pl.*, scale; balance, equilibrium.
cumpărá (**a**), *v. tr.* I, **cúmpăr, -át**, to buy.
cumpătát, -ă, *adj.*, **-ţi, -te**, *pl.*, moderate, temperate.
cumplít, -tă, *adj.*, **-ţi, -te**, *pl.*, terrible, heavy.
cumvá, *adv.*, somehow.
cunoáşte (**a**), **cunósc, -út**, *v. tr.* III, to know.
cunoscú-t, -tă, *adj.*, *n.*, **-ţi, -te**, *pl.*, known; *n.*, acquaintance.
cunoştínţ-ă, *n. f.*, **-e**, *pl.*, knowledge, acquaintance.
cunún-ă, *n. f.*, **-i**, *pl.*, wreath.
cupól-ă, *n. f.*, **-e**, *pl.*, vault, arch, cupola.
cuprínde (**a**), **cuprínd, cupríns**, *v. tr.* III, to comprise, to contain; to take; to embrace.
cuprinzăt-ór, -oáre, *adj.*, **-óri, -oáre**, *pl.*, comprising; succinct.
cup-tór, *n. mix.*, **-toáre**, *pl.*, oven; furnace.
curắnd (**în**), *adv.*, soon, immediately.

curá-t, -tă, *adj.*, **-ţi, -te,** *pl.*, clean, clear, pure, neat; **cură-ţél, cură-ţícă,** *dim. adj.*, **-ţéi, -ţéle,** *pl.*, clean, neat.
cúrc-ă, *n. f.*, **-i,** *pl.*, turkey-hen.
curcán, *n. f.*, **-i,** *pl.*, turkey-cock.
curént, *n. mix.*, **-e,** *pl.*, current, stream; draught; *adj.*, running, usual.
cúrge (a), curg, curs, *v. intr.* III, to flow, to run; to leak.
curi-ós, -oásă, *adj.*, **-óşi, -oáse,** *pl.*, curious, inquisitive.
curmezíş (în), *adv.*, across; **de-a-curmezíşul drumului,** across the road.
curs, *n. mix.*, **-uri,** *pl.*, course; flow; rate.
cúr-te, *n. f.*, **-ţi,** *pl.*, courtyard, court; palace.
cúşm-ă, *n. f.*, **-e,** *pl.*, fur cap.
cusút, see **coase.**
cutáre, *adj.*, *indef. pron.*, so-and-so (see 5. 9).
cutí-e, *n. f.*, **-i,** *pl.*, box, case.
cuţít, *n. m.*, **-e,** knife.
cutreerá (a), cutréer, -át, *v. tr.* I, to travel over, to wander through.
cutremurá (a), cutrémur, -át, *v. tr.* I, to shake, to quake, to tremble; **a se —,** to shiver, to tremble.
cuvânt, *n. mix.*, **cuvínte,** *pl.*, word.
cuvení (a se), se cuvíne, s'a cuvenít, *v. intr.* IV, to be decent, to be due, to become (see 6. 4. **c**).
cuvení-t, -tă, *adj.*, **-ţi, -te,** *pl.*, due.
cuviinci-ós, -oásă, *adj.*, **-óşi, -oáse,** *pl.*, decent, suitable, becoming.
cuviínţ-ă, *n. f.*, **-e,** *pl.*, decency, becomingness; **buna —,** good manners.

D

da, *adv.*, yes.
da=dar, but, however.
da (a), -u, -t, *v. tr.* I, to give.
d-a (d'a), de va=dacă va.
Dac, *n. m.*, **-i,** *pl.*, Dacian.
dácă, *conj.*, if (see 8. 4. i).
Dácia, *prop. n. f.*, Dacia.
dăinuí (a), -ésc, -t, *v. intr.* IV, to last.
dájdi-e, *n. f.*, **dắjdii,** *pl.*, tax, impost.
d'ân (*dial.*)=**din.**
dắns-ul, -a, *pers. pron.*, see 5. 1. **a.**
dar, *n. mix*, **-uri,** *pl.*, gift.
dar, *conj.*, *adv.*, but, however.
dắr-ă, *n. f.*, **-e,** *pl.*, trace, track; wake (of a ship); line.
dăru-í (a), -ésc, -ít, *v. tr.* IV, to make a present, to give.
dáscăl (Mold. **dáscal**), *n. m.*, **-i,** *pl.*, church singer; teacher.
dát-ă, *n. f.*, **-e,** *pl.*, date.
dat-á (a), -éz, -át, *v. tr.*, *intr.* I, to date.
dator-á (a), -éz, -át, *v. tr.* I, to owe.
datorí-e, *n. f.*, **-i,** *pl.*, duty, obligation, debt.
de, *prep.*, of, from, about; *conj.*, if.
deabiá, see **abiá.**
deabínelea (dealbínelea), *adv.*, quite.
de-a-dréptul, *adv.*, straightaway, directly, outright.
deál, *n. mix.*, **-uri,** *pl.*, hill, hillock.
de ál de, see 14. 2, note 2.
Deálu (Mănăstírea), *prop. n. m.* (locality).
Deálu Máre, *prop. n. m.* (locality).
de-a-lúngul, *prep.*, along.
de-andoásele, *adv.*, back to front, contrariwise.
deasúpra, *prep.*, over, above.

decât, *adv.*, than, as.
decé, *adv.*, why, wherefore.
Decémvrie, **Decémbrie**, *n. m.*, December.
déci, *conj.*, then, consequently.
decoratív, **-ă**, *adj.*, **-i**, **-e**, *pl.*, ornamental, decorative.
dedesúbtul, *prep.*, beneath, under; **dedesúbt**, *adv.*
dedúce (a), **dedúc**, **dedús**, *v. tr., intr.* III, to deduct, to infer, to deduce, to conclude.
déget, *n. mix.*, **-e**, *pl.*, finger.
degrábă, *adv.*, soon.
déla, *prep.*, from.
delicá-t, **-tă**, *adj.*, **-ţi**, **-te**, *pl.*, delicate, dainty, nice.
délt-ă, *n. f.*, **-e**, *pl.*, delta.
demâncáre, *n. f.*=**mâncáre**, *n. f.*, **mâncắri**, food, eating.
demnitáte, *n. f.*, **demnitắţi**, *pl.*, dignity.
demúlt, *adv.*, long time ago.
deoarecé, *conj.*, as, because, for.
deodátă, *adv.*, suddenly.
deopotrívă, *adv.*, equally, similarly.
deosebír-e, *n. f.*, **-i**, *pl.*, difference, distinction.
depărt-á (a), **-éz**, **-át**, *v. tr.* I, to remove; **a se —**, to go away.
depărt-áre, *n. f.*, **-ắri**, *pl.*, remoteness, distance, removal.
depárte, *adv.*, far.
deplín, **-ă**, *adj.*, **-i**, **-e**, *pl.*, entire.
depozitár, *n. m.*, **-i**, *pl.*; **depozitár-ă**, *n. f.*, **-e**, *pl.*, depository; trustee; keeper.
deprínde (a), **deprínd**, **depríns**, *v. intr.* III, to learn, to accustom; **a se —**, to get used.
depúne (a), **depú-n**, **-s**, *v. tr.* III, to depose, to deposit.
depúner-e, *n. f.*, **-i**, *pl.*, deposition, deposit.

des, **deásă**, *adj.*, **déşi**, **dése**, *pl.*, dense, solid, compact, close.
desăvârşí-t, **-tă**, *adj.*, **-ţi**, **-te**, *pl.*, complete, perfect.
desbiná (a), **desbín**, **-át**, *v. tr.* I, to disunite.
deschizătúr-ă, *n. f.*, **-i**, *pl.*, opening.
descleşt-á (a), **-éz**, **-át**, *v. tr.* I, to loosen.
descoperí (a), **descópăr**, **descoperít**, *v. tr.* IV, to uncover, to reveal, to discover.
descúlţ, **-ă**, *adj.*, **-i**, **-e**, *pl.*, barefoot.
descurajáre, *n. f.*, **-ắri**, *pl.*, despondency, despair.
desemn-á (**desená**) (a), **-éz**, **-át**, *v. tr.* I, to draw, to sketch; to design.
déseori, *adv.*, see **adéseori**.
deşért, **deşártă**, *adj.*, **deşérţi**, **deşérte**, *pl.*, empty, vacant; desert, waste; **în —**, in vain.
desfătá (a), **desfắt** (**desfătéz**), **-át**, *v. tr.* I, to amuse, to delight; **a se —**, to amuse oneself.
desfăt-áre, *n. f.*, **-ắri**, *pl.*, delight.
deşí, *conj.*, although, though (see 8. 4. i).
desíme, *n. f.*, **-i**, *pl.*, thicket, thickness, density.
desíş, *n. mix.*, **-uri**, *pl.*, thicket.
deslănţuí (a), **-ésc**, **-t**, *v. tr.* IV, to unchain.
desluş-í (a), **-ésc**, **-ít**, *v. tr.* IV, to clear, to explain, to unravel, to see dimly; **deslușí-t**, **-tă**, *adj.* **-ţi**, **-te**, *pl.*, clear.
desmierdá (a), **desmiérd**, **-át**, *v. tr.* I, to caress.
desnădăjduí (a), **-ésc**, **-ít**, *v. tr., intr.* IV, to despair, to despond.
desnădéjd-e, *n. f.*, **-i**, *pl.*, despair.
desnaţionalis-áre, *n. f.*, **-ắri**, *pl.*, denationalisation.

despărţí (a), **despárt** (**despărţésc**), **despărţít**, *v. tr.* IV, to separate, to disunite; **despărţit-ór, -oáre**, *adj.*, **-óri, -oáre**, *pl.*, separating.
desperá (a), **despér** (**-éz**), **-át**, *v. intr.* I, to despair; **desperá-t, -tă**, *adj.*, **-ţi, -e**, *pl.*, hopeless, desperate; **desper-áre**, *n. f.*, **-ări**, *pl.*, despair.
despicá (a), **despíc, -át**, *v. tr.* I, to cleave, to split.
déspre, *prep.*, about, for.
despreţui-tór, -toáre, *adj.*, **-tóri, -toáre**, *pl.*, scornful, contemptuous.
destăinuí (a), **-ésc, -t**, *v. tr.* IV, to divulge, to reveal.
deştépt, deşteáptă, *adj.*, **deştépţi, deştépte**, *pl.*, intelligent.
deşteptá (a), **deştépt, -át**, *v. tr.* I, to awake.
destrăm-á (a), **destrám, -át**, *v. tr.* I, to ravel out, to unweave.
destúl, -ă, *adj.*, **destúi, destúle**, *pl.*, sufficient, enough.
desvoltá (a), **desvólt, -át**, *v. tr.* I, to develop, to unfold; **desvolt-áre**, *n. f.*, **ări**, *pl.*, development, evolution.
devále, *adv.*, downward(s).
deveni (a), **devín, devenít**, *v. intr.* IV, to become, to grow.
devíz-ă, *n. f.*, **-e**, *pl.*, device, motto; money.
diafán, -ă, *adj.*, **-i, -e**, *pl.*, transparent.
diávol, *n. m.*, **-i**, *pl.*, devil.
dicţionár, *n. mix.*, **-e**, *pl.*, dictionary.
diferí-t, -tă, *adj.*, **-ţi, -te**, *pl.*, different, various.
diháni-e, *n. f.*, **dihănii**, *pl.*, creature, monster.
dimin-eáţă, *n. f.*, **-éţi**, *pl.*, morning.
din, *prep.*, from, out, of.
dinadíns, *adv.*, purposely; **cu tot dinadínsul**, *adv.*, quite purposely.
dinaíntea, *prep.*, before.
díncolo de, *prep.*, beyond, over.
dinioárea, *adv.*, see **adineoárea**.
dínspre, *prep.*, from the direction of.
dín-te, *n. m.*, **-ţi**, *pl.*, tooth.
díntre, *prep.*, between, from, among (see 8. 3, note 1).
díntr'o=**din o**; **dintr'odátă**, *adv.*, suddenly, all at once.
díntru, *prep.*, from, out, of (see 8. 3, note 1).
diréc-t, -tă, *adj.*, **-ţi, -te**, *pl.*, direct.
directór, *n. m.*, **-i**, *pl.*, director, manager.
discré-t, -tă, *adj.*, **-ţi, -te**, *pl.*, discreet.
diseáră, *adv.*, to-night (the coming evening).
dişelá (a), **dişél, -át**, *v. tr.* I, to break a horse's back, to cripple.
dispăreá (a) (**dispáre**), **dispár, dispărút**, *v. intr.* II (III), to disappear.
distánţ-ă, *n. f.*, **-e**, *pl.*, distance.
distínc-t, -tă, *adj.*, **-ţi, -te**, *pl.*, distinct.
doámn-ă, *n. f.*, **-e**, *pl.*, mistress, lady.
doáră (**doár**), *adv.*, certainly, of course; **într'o doáră**, *adv.*, at a venture, taking a risk, on the off-chance; **fară doár şi poáte**, *adv.*, without doubt, without fail (see 12. 3, note).
dobând-í (a), **-ésc, -ít**, *v. tr.* IV, to acquire, to purchase.
dobi-tóc, *n. mix.*, **-toáce**, *pl.*, cattle, animal; fool.
Dobrógea, *prop. n. f.*, Dobrudzha; **dobrogeán, -eánă**, *adj.*, **-éni, -éne**, *pl.*, of, from Dobrudzha.

Dobromír, *prop. n. m.* (name).
dóctor, *n. m.*, **-i**, *pl.*, doctor.
documént, *n. mix.*, **-e**, *pl.*, document.
dói, *m.*, **dóuă**, *f. num.*, two.
dóilea (**al**), *m.*, **dóua** (**a**), *f.*, the second.
doím-e, *n. f.*, **-i**, *pl.*, duality.
dóin-ă, *n. f.*, **-e**, *pl.*, a lyric folk-song, folk-poem.
dolár, *n. m.*, **-i**, *pl.*, dollar.
dolín-ă, *n. f.*, **-e**, *pl.*, vale, valley.
doméstic, **-ă**, *adj.*, **-i**, **-e**, *pl.*, domestic.
dominán-t, **-tă**, *adj.*, **-ţi**, **-te**, *pl.*, prevailing.
domir-í (**a se**) (**dumirí**), **mă domirésc**, **-ít**, *v. intr.* IV, to comprehend clearly, to become fully aware of; **nedomirít**, **-ă**, *adj.*, doubtful, hesitating.
domn, *n. m.*, **-i**, *pl.*, master, gentleman, mister.
domn-ésc, **-eáscă**, *adj.*, **-éşti**, *pl.*, of the gentleman, lordly.
domn-í (**a**), **-ésc**, **-ít**, *v. intr.* IV, to rule.
domnía ta, **dumneatá**, **domnía voástră**, **dumneavoástră**, you (see 5. 4).
domní-e, *n. f.*, **-i**, ruling, domination.
domnişór, *n. m.*, **-i**, *pl.*, young gentleman; master.
domnitór, *n. m.*, **-i**, *pl.*, ruler, prince.
dom-ól, **-oálă**, *adj.*, **-ói**, **-oále**, *pl.*, soft, slow.
dóniţ-ă, *n. f.*, **-i** (**-e**), *pl.*, bucket.
dor, *n. mix.*, **-uri**, *pl.*, ardent desire, longing (see 6. 4. **c**).
dor-í (**a**), **-ésc**, **-ít**, *v. tr.* IV, to wish, to desire.
dormí (**a**), **dorm**, **-ít**, *v. intr.* IV, to sleep.
dormi-tór, *n. mix.*, **-toáre**, *pl.*, bedroom.
Dórna, *prop. n.* (locality, river).
dos, *n. mix.*, **-uri**, *pl.*, back; **în dósul cásei**, at the back of the house.
dóua (**a**), see **dóilea**.
dóuă, see **dói**.
doved-í (**a**), **-ésc**, **-ít**, *v. tr.* IV, to prove, to demonstrate; to overcome.
drac, *n. m.*, **-i**, *pl.*, devil.
drag, **-ă**, *adj.*, **-i** (**-e**), *pl.*, dear, beloved.
Drăgăşáni, *prop. n. m. pl.* (locality).
drágoste, *n. f.* (**drágoste**, *pl.*), love.
drăgúţ, **-ă**, *adj.*, **-i**, **-e**, *pl.*, quaint, sweet.
dram, *n. mix.*, **-uri** (**-e**), *pl.*, the smallest weight measure, gram.
drept, *n. mix.*, **-uri**, *pl.*, right, law.
drept, **dreáptă**, *adj.*, **drépţi**, **-te**, *pl.*, straight, direct, right; **de-a-dréptul**, *adv.*, straightaway.
dreptáte, *n. f.*, **dreptắţi**, *pl.*, justice, right.
drójdi-e, *n. f.*, **-i**, *pl.*, yeast, lees, dregs.
drópi-e, *n. f.*, **-i**, *pl.*, bustard.
dropiói, *n. m.*, **dropiói**, *pl.*, he-bustard.
drug, *n. m.*, **-i**, *pl.*, wooden or iron bar.
drum, *n. mix.*, **-uri**, *pl.*, road, journey.
drumeág, *n. mix.*, **-uri** (**drumége**), *pl.*, way, path, lane.
druméţ, *n. m.*, **-i**, *pl.*, traveller.
d-sa, see 5. 4.
d-ta, see 5. 4.
dubl-á (**a**), **-éz**, **-át**, *v. tr.* I, to double.
dúbl-u, **-ă**, *adj.*, **-i**, **-e**, *pl.*, double, twofold.
dúc-e, *n. m.*, **-i**, *pl.*, duke.
dúce (**a**), **duc**, **dus**, *v. tr.* III, to carry, to lead; **a se —**, to go away.

duh, *n. mix.* (*archaic*), **-uri**, *pl.*, spirit, soul; wit.
dui-ós, -oásă, *adj.*, **-óşi, -oáse**, *pl.*, sad, tender, sorrowful.
dúlc-e, *adj.*, **-i**, *pl.*, sweet.
dulceáţă, *n. f.*, **dulcéţuri (dulcéţi)**, *pl.*, preserve, sweetness, jam.
dumeatá, **dumeavoástră**, you (see 5. 4).
dumínecă, *n. f.*, Sunday.
Dumínica-Mare, *n. f.*, Whit-Sunday.
dumirí (a), see **domirí (a)**.
dumitále=**domníei tale**.
Dumnezeu, *n. m.*, God; **dumneze-ésc, -iáscă**, *adj.*, **-éşti**, *pl.*, of God, divine.
Dúnărea, *n. f.*, the Danube; **dunăr-eán, -eană**, *adj.*, **-éni, -éne**, *pl.*, of the Danube.
dúng-ă, *n. f.*, **-i**, *pl.*, stripe; brim, border; line.
dúpă, *prep.*, after; **dúpă cum**, *adv.*, as, so.
durá (a), -éz, -át, *v. intr.* I, to last, to dure, to continue.
dureá (a) (dor), durút, *v. intr.* II, to feel pain (see 6. 4. **d**).
durér-e, *n. f.*, **-i**, *pl.*, pain, sorrow, ache.
duşmán, *n. m.*, **-i**, *pl.*, enemy, foe.
duşmăn-ós, -oásă, *adj.*, hostile.

E

e, *3rd sing. pres.*, is.
ea, *pron.*, she (see 5. 1. **a**).
echipamént, *n. mix.*, **-e**, *pl.*, equipment.
edíţi-e, *n. f.*, **-i**, *pl.*, edition.
eféct, *n. mix.*, **-e**, *pl.*, effect, consequence; performance.
éften, see **iéften**.
Egípt. *prop. n. m.*, Egypt.
ei, *pers. pron.*, they; to her (see 5. 1. **a**); **ei!** *interj.*, eh!
el, *pers. pron.*, he (see 5. 1. **a**).
éle, *pers. pron. f.*, they (see 5. 1. **a**).
elegán-t, -tă, *adj.*, **-ţi, -te**, *pl.*, elegant, smart; fashionable.
elemént, *n. mix.*, **-e**, *pl.*, element.
elév, *n. m.*, **-i**, *pl.*, schoolboy, disciple.
elév-ă, *n. f.*, **-e**, *pl.*, schoolgirl.
eliber-á (a), -éz, -át, *v. tr.* I, to deliver, to free.
Elvéţia, *prop. n. f.*, Switzerland; **elveţi-án, -ánă**, *adj.*, **-éni, -éne**, *pl.*, Swiss.
energí-e, *n. f.*, **-i**, *pl.*, energy.
Englé-z, *n. m.*, **-ji (-zi)**, *pl.*, Englishman; **englez, -ă**, *adj.*, **-ji (-zi), -ze**, *pl.*, English; **englez-ésc, -eáscă**, *adj.*, **-éşti**, *pl.*, English.
Englitéra, *prop. n. f.*, England.
epíscop, *n. m.*, **-i**, *pl.*, bishop; **episcopál, -ă**, *adj.*, **-i, -e**, *pl.*, episcopal.
époc-ă, *n. f.*, **-i (-e)**, *pl.*, epoch, period, era.
épur-e, *n. m.*, **-i**, *pl.*, hare; **epur-ésc, -eáscă**, *adj.*, **-éşti**, *pl.*, (of) hare.
equátor (ecvátor), *n. m.*, equator.
ér-ă, *n. f.*, **-e**, *pl.*, era.
erá (el, ea), *impf. 3rd. sing.*, was being, used to be (he, she).
erés, *n. mix.*, **-uri**, *pl.*, superstition, myth.
eréte, see **heréte**.
eró-u, *n. m.*, **-i**, *pl.*, hero.
erudít, -ă, *adj.*, *n.*, learned man, scholar.
erúncă, see **ierúncă**.
escúrsie, see **excúrsie**.
esenţiál, -ă, *adj.*, **-i, -e**, *pl.*, essential.
eşí (a), see **ieşí (a)**.
est, *n. m.*, East.
éste (el, ea), *3rd sing. pres.* is (he, she).
etáj, *n. mix.*, **-e**, *pl.*, floor.

etérn, -ă, *adj.*, **-i, -e**, *pl.*, eternal.
eterogén, -ă, *adj.*, **-i, -e**, *pl.*, see **ambigen**.
etimológic, -ă, *adj.*, **-i, -e**, *pl.*, etymological.
éu, *pers. pron.*, I.
eufoní-e, *n. f.*, **-i**, *pl.*, euphony.
Európa, *prop. n. f.*, Europe; **europe-án, -ánă**, *adj.*, **-ni, -ne**, *pl.*, European.
ev, *n. mix.*, **-uri**, *pl.*, age; **evul-mediu**, Middle Ages.
evad-á (a), -éz, -át, *v. intr.* I, to escape.
eveniménț, *n. mix.*, **-e**, *pl.*, event, incident.
evocá (a), evóc, -át, *v. tr.* I, to evoke, to call forth.
exámen, *n. mix.*, **-e**, *pl.*, examination, test.
exclamáţi-e, *n. f.*, **-i**, *pl.*, exclamation.
exclusív, -ă, *adj.*, **-i, -e**, *pl.*, exclusive.
excúrsi-e, *n. f.*, **-i**, *pl.*, excursion.
executá (a), execút, -át, *v. tr.* I, to execute, to perform.
exémpl-u, *n. mix.*, **-e**, *pl.*, example.
existá (a), exíst, -át, *v. intr.* I, to exist, to be.
expedi-á (a), -éz, -át, *v. tr.* I, to send off, to forward.
explicá (a), explíc, -át, *v. tr.* I, to explain, to interpret.
expresiún-e, *n. f.*, **-i**, *pl.*, expression, expressiveness.
exprimá (a), exprím, -át, *v. tr.* I, to express.
expúne (a), expún, expús, *v. tr.* III, to expose, to display; **a se —**, to risk, to venture.
exteri-ór, -oáră, *adj.*, **-óri, -oáre**, *pl.*, exterior, external; *n. mix.*, **-óruri**, *pl.*, exterior, outside.
extérn, -ă, *adj.*, **-i, -e**, *pl.*, external, exterior.

F

fă, *imp.*, see **face (a)**.
fábric-ă, *n. f.*, **-i**, *pl.*, fabric, factory.
fáce (a), fac, făcút, *v. tr.* III, to make, to do; **se fáce zíua**, it dawns, it grows (morning), twilight (see 6. 4. e).
fácl-ă, *n. f.*, **-e**, *pl.*, torch.
făclí-e, *n. f.*, **-i**, *pl.*, torch, candle.
fag, *n. m.*, **-i**, *pl.*, beech-tree.
făgăduí (a), -ésc, -t, *v. tr.* IV, to promise.
făgădui-álă, *n. f.*, **-éli**, *pl.*, promise.
Făgăráş, *prop. n. m.* (mountain, town); **făgărăş-án, -ánă**, *adj.*, **-éni, -éne**, *pl.*
făín-ă, *n. f.*, **-uri, -i (-e)**, *pl.*, flour.
fálnic, -ă, *adj.*, **-i, -e**, *pl.*, proud, haughty.
famíli-e, *n. f.*, **-i**, *pl.*, family.
fân, *n. mix.*, **-uri**, *pl.*, hay.
fânáţ, *n. mix.*, **fânéţe**, *pl.*, hay-field.
fântấn-ă, *n. f.*, **-i (-e)**, *pl.*, well, fountain, spring.
fantásm-ă, *n. f.*, **-e**, *pl.*, phantasm, phantom.
fapt, *n. mix.*, **-e**, *pl.*, act; matter; **în fapt de seáră**, when it gets dark.
fápt-ă, *n. f.*, **-e**, *pl.*, deed, act, action.
făptuí (a), -ésc, -t, *v. tr.* IV, to commit, to effect, to do.
fără, *prep.*, without.
fărâmiţá (a), see **firimiţá (a)**.
farmací-e, *n. f.*, **-i**, *pl.*, pharmacy, apothecary, chemist.
fármec, *n. mix.*, **-e**, *pl.*, charm, spell, enchantment.
fasán, *n. m.*, **-i**, *pl.*, pheasant.
făşiít (făşâít), *n. mix.*, **-uri**, *pl.*, rustle.

Făt Frumós, *prop. n.*, Prince Charming of Rumanian fairy tales.
fátă, *n. f.*, **féte**, *pl.*, girl, lass.
fáţă, *n. f.*, **féţe**, *pl.*, face; **fáţă de pérină**, pillow-case.
faţád-ă, *n. f.*, **-e**, *pl.*, frontage, façade.
făţíş, *adv.*, openly.
Februárie, **Február**, *n. m.*, February.
feciór, *n. m.*, **-i**, *pl.*, son, lad.
feerí-e, *n. f.*, **-i**, *pl.*, fairyland scene; **feéric**, **-ă**, *adj.*, **-i**, **-e**, *pl.*, fairylike.
fel, *n. mix.*, **-uri**, *pl.*, kind, sort; **de fel**, *adv.*, not at all; **fel de fel**, *adv.*, all kind of, various.
felinár, *n. mix.*, **-e**, *pl.*, lantern.
feméi-e, *n. f.*, **-a**, *art.*, **feméi**, *pl.*, woman.
ferchezuí (a), **-ésc**, **-ít**, *v. tr.* IV, to dress up.
fer-eástră, *n. f.*, **-éstre**, *pl.*, window.
fer-í (a), **-ésc**, **-ít**, *v. intr.* IV, to avoid; **a se** —, *v. intr. refl.* (see 6. 7).
fericír-e, *n. f.*, **-i**, *pl.*, happiness, prosperity.
ferici-t, **-tă**, *adj.*, **-ţi**, **-te**, *pl.*, happy.
fermecá (a), **férmec**, **-át**, *v. tr.* I, to charm, to enchant; **fermecăt-ór**, **-oáre**, *adj.*, **-óri**, **-oáre**, *pl.*, enchanting, charming; *n.*, magician, sorcerer.
feróce, *adj.*, **feróci**, **feróce**, *pl.*, fierce, wild.
feţişoár-ă, *n. f. dim.*, **-e**, *pl.*, little face.
fetíţ-ă, *n. f.*, **-e**, *pl.*, girl.
fi (a), **sunt** (**sânt**), **fost**, *aux. v.*, to be (see 6. 1).
fiár-ă, *n. f.*, **-e**, *pl.*, beast.
ficá-t, *n. m.*, **-ţi**, *pl.*, liver.
fíe, *imp.*, let it be; *conj.* (see 8. 4. i).
fiecáre, *indef. pron.*, everyone, each (see 5. 9).
fiecé, *indef. pron.*, everything (see 5. 9).
fiecíne, *indef. pron.*, everyone.
fiér, *n. m.*, iron.
fiérbe (a), **fierb**, **fiert**, *v. tr.*, *intr.* III, to boil.
fierbín-te, *adj.*, **-ţi**, *pl.*, hot.
fiére, *n. f.*, **-i**, *pl.*, gall, bile.
fíe-si (see p. 248)=**fiicei sale**.
figúr-ă, *n. f.*, **-i**, *pl.*, figure, form, shape; image.
fíic-ă (**fícă**), *n. f.*, **-e**, *pl.*, daughter.
fiínd, *gerund*, being.
fiíndcă, *conj.*, because.
fiínţ-ă, *n. f.*, **-e**, *pl.*, being, existence.
filosofí-e, *n. f.*, **-i**, *pl.*, philosophy.
finí (a), **fin-ésc**, **-ít**, *v. tr.* IV, to finish.
fior-ós, **-oásă**, *adj.*, **-óşi**, **-oáse**, *pl.*, frightful.
fir, *n. mix.*, **-e**, *pl.*, thread; morsel.
fír-e, *n. f.*, **-i**, *pl.*, nature, temper, disposition.
fir-ésc, **-éască**, *adj.*, **-éşti**, *pl.*, natural.
firimiţ-á (a) (**fărâmiţá**), **-éz**, **-át**, *v. tr.* I, to crumb, to crumble.
fí-u, *n. m.*, **-i**, *pl.*, son.
fixá (a), **-éz**, **-át**, *v. tr.* I, to fix; to stare at.
flácără, *n. f.*, **flắcări**, *pl.*, flame.
flăcắ-u, *n. m.*, **-i**, *pl.*, lad.
flămấn-d, **-dă**, *adj.*, **-zi**, **-de**, *pl.*, hungry.
flamíng, *n. m.*, **-i**, *pl.*, flamingo.
flegmátic, **-ă**, *adj.*, **-i**, **-e**, *pl.*, phlegmatic.
floáre, *n. f.*, **flóri**, *pl.*, flower.
Floárea, *prop. n. f.* (name).
floric-ícă, *n. f.*, **-éle**, *pl.*, little flower.

flueráș, *n. mix.*, **-e**, *pl.*, shepherd's flute, pipe.
flúvi-u, *n. mix.*, **-i**, *pl.*, river.
foáie, *n. f.*, **fói**, *pl.*, leaf.
foáme, *n. f.*, hunger (see 6. 4. **c**).
foámete, *n. f.*, famine.
foárte, *adv.*, very.
foc, *n. mix.*, **-uri**, *pl.*, fire.
Focșáni, *prop. n. pl.* (town).
fol-ós, *n. mix.*, **-oáse**, *pl.*, utility; usefulness; profit.
folosi-tór, **-toáre**, *adj.*, **-tóri**, **toáre**, *pl.*, useful, profitable.
fonologí-e, *n. f.*, phonology.
forfot-í (**a**), **-ésc**, **-ít**, *v. intr.* IV, to boil; to crawl (with), to crowd.
fórmă, *n. f.*, **-e**, *pl.*, form.
form-á (**a**), **-éz**, **-át**, *v. intr.*, *tr.* I, to form, to model.
formúl-ă, *n. f.*, **-e**, *pl.*, formula, formule.
fórț-ă, *n. f.*, **-e**, *pl.*, force, power.
fortificá (**a**), **fortífic**, **-át**, *v. tr.* I, to fortify.
fóșnet, *n. mix.*, **-e**, *pl.*, rustle, noise.
fost, see **fi** (**a**).
fotográfic, **-ă**, *adj.*, **-i**, **-e**, *pl.*, photographic.
frágă, *n. f.*, **-e** (**-i**), *pl.*, wild strawberry.
frăgezím-e, *n. f.*, **-i**, *pl.*, tenderness, delicacy.
fragmént, *n. mix.*, **-e**, *pl.*, fragment.
francá (**a**), **franchéz**, **francát**, *v. tr.* I, to pay the postage.
francéz, **-ă**, *adj.*, **-i** (**-ji**), **-e**, *pl.*, French.
frânghí-e, *n. f.* (**frấnghie**), **-i**, *pl.*, rope, cord.
Fránța, *prop. n. f.*, France.
Franțuz, *prop. n. m.*, see **francez**.
franțuz-ésc, **-eáscă**, *adj.*, **-éști**, *pl.*, French.
frásin, *n. m.*, **-i**, *pl.*, ash-tree.
frá-te, *n. m.*, **-ți**, *pl.*, brother; **frăț-ésc**, **-eáscă**, *adj.*, **-éști**, *pl.* brotherly.
freámăt, *n. mix.*, **frémete**, *pl.*, rustling noise.
frecúș, *n. mix.*, **-uri**, *pl.*, chafing, rubbing.
frésco (**al**), *adj.*, fresco (in).
fríc-ă, *n. f.*, **-i**, *pl.*, fear, fright (see 6. 4. **c**).
frig, *n. mix.*, cold, frost; **fríguri**, *pl.*, fever (see 6. 4. **c**).
fríge (**a**), **frig**, **fript**, *v. tr.* III, to burn, to roast, to fry; **a se —**, to burn oneself.
frigur-ós, **-oásă**, *adj.*, **-óși**, **-oáse**, *pl.*, chilly, cold.
fript, see **frige** (**a**).
friptúr-ă, *n. f.*, **-i**, *pl.*, roast, roast-meat.
fruct, *n. mix.*, **-e**, *pl.*, fruit, fruitage; product.
frum-ós, *adj. m.*, **-oásă**, *f.*, **-óși**, **-oáse**, *pl.*, beautiful, nice, pretty.
frumuș-él, **-ícă**, *adj.*, **-éi**, **-éle**, *pl.*, pretty, nice.
frumuséț-ă (**-e**), *n. f.*, **-i**, *pl.*, beauty.
fruntáș, **-e**, *adj.*, *n.*, **-i**, **-e**, *pl.*, leading man, notable; lance-corporal.
frún-te, *n. f.*, **-ți**, *pl.*, forehead; front, forepart.
frúnz-ă, *n. f.*, **-e**, *pl.*, leaf.
fudúl, **-ă**, *adj.*, **fudúi**, **fudúle**, *pl.*, proud.
fúg-ă, *n. f.*, **-i**, *pl.*, flight.
fu-gí (**a**), **fug**, **-gít**, *v. intr.* IV, to run away, to flee.
fulg, *n. m.*, **-i**, *pl.*, down; flock; flake.
fulgerá (**a**), **fúlger**, **-át**, *v. tr.*, *intr.* I, there is lightning; to fulminate.
fum, *n. mix.*, smoke; **-uri**, *pl.*, snobbery.

fumurí-u, **-e**, *adj.*, **-i**. *pl.*, smoke-grey.
fund, *n. mix.*, **-uri**, *pl.*, bottom, ground.
fundamentál, **-ă**, *adj.*, **-i**, **-e**, *pl.*, fundamental, basic.
furá (**a**), **fur**, **-át**, *v. tr.* I, to steal.
fúrc-ă, *n. f.*, **-i**, *pl.*, pitchfork; distaff.
fúri-e (**furíe**), *n. f.*, **-i**, *pl.*, fury, rage; **furi-ós**, **-oásă**, *adj.*, **-óşi**, **-oáse**, *pl.*, furious, raging.
furíş (**pe**), *adv.*, furtively, stealthily.
furiş-á (**a se**), **mă** —, **-éz**, **-át**, *v. intr.* I, to steal in, to sneak, to creep.
furníc-ă, *n. f.*, **-i**, *pl.*, ant.
furnis-á (**a**), **-éz**, **-át**, *v. tr.* I, to supply, to deliver.
furtún-ă, *n. f.*, **-i**, *pl.*, storm, gale.

G

găín-ă, *n. f.*, **-i**, *pl.*, hen.
Galáţi, *prop. n. m. pl.* (town).
gálben, **-ă**, *adj.*, **-i**, **-e**, *pl.*, yellow.
găl-eátă, *n. f.*, **-éţi**, *pl.*, bucket, pail.
gălúşcă, *n. f.*, **gălúşti**, *pl.*, dumpling; stuffed cabbage.
gând, *n. mix.*, **-uri**, *pl.*, thought.
gând-í (**a**), *v. tr.*, *intr.* IV, **-ésc**, **-ít**, to think; **gândír-e**, *n. f.*, **-i**, *pl.*, thinking; **gândit-ór**, **-oáre**, *adj.*, **-óri**, **-oáre**, *pl.*, pensive, thoughtful.
gáră, *n. f.*, **gări**, *pl.*, station.
gârbov-í (**a se**), **mă** —, **-ésc**, **-ít**, *v. intr.* IV, to stoop, to grow round-shouldered.
gard, *n. mix.*, **-uri**, *pl.*, fence, hedge, inclosure.
gârl-ă, *n. f.*, **-e**, *pl.*, river, brook.
gâscă, *n. f.*, **gâşte**, **gâşti**, *pl.*, goose.
găs-í (**a**), **-ésc**, **-ít**, *v. tr.* IV, to find, to obtain, ; **a se** —, to be found, to meet, to find oneself.
gât, *n. mix.*, **-uri**, *pl.*, neck.
gáta, *adj.*, *adv.*, ready.
găt-í (**a**), **-ésc**, **-ít**, *v. tr.* IV, to make ready; to adorn; to cook; **a se** —, to dress oneself up.
găur-í (**a**), **-ésc**, **-ít**, *v. tr.* IV, to make a hole, to bore, to pierce.
gaz, *n. mix*, **-e**, *pl.*, gas; **gaz metan**, methane gas.
gázd-ă, *n. f.*, *m.*, **-e**, *pl.*, landlady, landlord; hostess.
geám, *n. mix.*, **-uri**, *pl.*, pane, window-pane.
geánă, *n. f.*, **géne**, *pl.*, eyelash.
generál, **-ă**, *adj.*, **-i**, **-e**, *pl.*, general, universal.
generál, *n. m.*, **-i**, *pl.*, general.
genunchér, *n. mix.*, **-e**, *pl.*, coat reaching to the knees.
genúnchi, *n. m.*, **genúnchi**, *pl.* (**genunche**, *pl. f.*), knee.
Georgián, *n. m.*, **Georgiéni**, *pl.*, Georgian; **georgi-án**, **-ánă**, *adj.*, **-éni**, **-éne**, *pl.*, Georgian.
ger, *n. mix.*, **-uri**, *pl.*, cold, frost.
gesticul-á (**a**), **-éz**, **-át**, *v. intr.* I, to gesticulate.
gheátă, *n. f.*, **ghéte**, *pl.*, shoe.
Gheórghe, **Geórge**, *prop. n.*, George.
ghiár-ă, *n. f.*, **-e**, *pl.*, claw, clutch.
ghiáţă, *n. f.*, **ghiéţuri** (**ghiéţe**), ice.
ghic-í (**a**), **-ésc**, **-ít**, *v. tr.* IV, to guess, to divine.
ghici-toáre, *n. f.*, **-tóri**, *pl.*, riddle, puzzle; wise woman, fortune-teller.
ghileméte, **ghileméle**, *n. f. pl.*, inverted commas.
ghintuí-t, **-tă**, *adj.*, **-ţi**, **-te**, *pl.*, rifled.
ghiocé-l, *n. m.*, **-i**, *pl.*, snowdrop.
ghişé-u, *n. mix.*, **-ie**, *pl.*, counter.
gig, see **vig**.

gíner-e, *n. m.*, **-i**, *pl.*, son-in-law.
giránt, *n. m.*, **giránţi**, *pl.*, endorser, guarantor.
glas, *n. mix.*, **-uri**, *pl.*, voice.
gloáb-ă, *n. f.*, **-e**, *pl.*, jade; tit; punishment.
glonţ, *n. mix.*, **gloánţe**, *pl.*, bullet.
glori-ós, **-oásă**, *adj.*, **-óşi**, **-oáse**, *pl.*, glorious.
glúm-ă, *n. f.*, **-e**, *pl.*, joke (see **şagă**).
goán-ă, *n. f.*, **-e**, *pl.*, flight, speed; pursuit; coursing.
gogóş-ă, *n. f.*, **-i**, *pl.*, cocoon.
gol, **goálă**, *adj.*, **goi**, **goále**, *pl.*, naked; empty; bare; **gol**, *n. mix.*, **-uri**, *pl.*, emptiness, vacuum.
goláş, **-ă** (**-e**), *adj.*, **-i**, **-e**, *pl.*, naked, unfeathered, bald.
golf, *n. mix.*, **-uri**, *pl.*, gulf.
Golgóta, *prop. n. f.*, Golgotha.
gon-í (**a**), **-ésc**, **-ít**, *v. tr.* IV, to chase, to expel, to thrust out.
gorún, *n. m.*, **-i**, *pl.*, rowan-tree, oak.
grábă, *n. f.*, haste, hurry, speed.
grăbí-t, **-tă**, *adj.*, **-ţi**, **-te**, *pl.*, hasty, in a hurry.
grábnic, **-ă**, *adj.*, **-i**, **-e**, *pl.*, urgent, speedy.
grad, *n. mix.*, **-e**, *pl.*, degree.
grădín-ă, *n. f.*, **-i**, *pl.*, garden.
gram, *n. mix.*, **-e**, *pl.*, gram.
grămádă, *n. f.*, **grămézi**, *pl.*, heap, pile, amassment; **grămăd-í** (**a**), **-ésc**, **-ít**, *v. tr.* IV, to heap, to collect; **a se** —, to throng.
grămăgioár-ă, *n. f.*, **-e**, *pl.*, little heap.
grânár, *n. mix.*, **-e**, *pl.*, granary.
grâne, *n. f. pl.*, cereal, grain (see **grâu**).
grătár, *n. mix.*, **-e**, *pl.*, grille, roaster.

K*

gratificá (**a**), **gratífic**, **-át**, *v. tr.* I, to confer, to bestow.
grâ-u, *n. mix.*, wheat, **-ie**, *pl.*, wheatfields; **-ne**, *pl.*, cereals.
grăúnte, *n. mix.*, **grăunţe**, *pl.*, grain.
grav, **-ă**, *adj.*, grave, serious, weighty.
gravit-áte, *n. f.*, **-ăţi**, *pl.*, gravity.
gravúr-ă, *n. f.*, **-i**, *pl.* engraving.
grecésc, **greceáscă**, *adj.*, Greek.
Grécia, *prop. n. f.*, Greece.
gréer, *n. m.*, **-i**, *pl.*, cricket.
gre-ói, **-oáie**, *adj.*, **-ói**, **-oáie**, *pl.*, awkward, heavy, unwieldy.
greşálă, *n. f.*, **greşéli** (*arch.* **greşále**), *pl.*, fault, error; trespass.
greş-í (**a**), **-ésc**, **-ít**, *v. intr.*, *tr.* IV, to err, to commit a fault, to mistake.
gré-u, **-a**, *adj.*, **-i**, **-le**, *pl.*; **cu greu**, hardly.
greutáte, *n. f.*, **greutăţi**, *pl.*, weight, difficulty.
gríj-e (**-ă**), *n. f.*, **-i**, *pl.*, task, worry.
Grivéi, *prop. n. m.* (name of a dog).
groápă, *n. f.*, **grópi**, *pl.*, ditch, grave, trench.
groázā, *n. f.*, terror, horror, fright; (great multitude).
groáznic, **-ă**, *adj.*, **-i**, **-e**, *pl.*, dreadful, terrific.
gros, **groásă**, *adj.*, **gróşi**, **groáse**, *pl.*, thick, corpulent.
grozáv, **-ă**, *adj.*, **-i**, **-e**, *pl.*, terrible.
grumáz, *n. mix.*, **-uri**, *pl.* (also **grumáji**), nape, neck.
gun-ói, *n. mix.*, **-oáie**, *pl.*, dunghill; filth, dirt.
gúr-ă, *n. f.*, **-i**, *pl.*, mouth.
gustá (**a**), **gust**, **-át**, *v. tr.*, *intr.* I, to taste, to eat.

H

ha! *interj.*, ah!
hac, *n. m.*, **a da de** —, to get the better of, to find remedy for.
hái! háide! háidem! *interj.*, come! up! (see 9. 2.)
haín, -ă, *adj.*, **-i, -e**, *pl.*, faithless; hateful; odious.
haín-ă, *n. f.*, **-e**, *pl.*, coat, clothes, dress.
haít, *n. mix.*, **-uri**, *pl.*, sluice, flood-gates.
hamál, *n. m.*, **-i**, *pl.*, porter.
han, *n. mix.*, **-uri**, *pl.*, inn.
hargát, see **argát**.
hârsí (a se), mă hârsésc, hârsít, *v. intr.* IV, to be stingy; **hârsit, -ă**, *adj.*, avaricious, stingy, niggardly.
hârtí-e, *n. f.*, **-i**, *pl.*, paper.
hat, *n. mix.*, **-uri**, border separating two fields.
haţ! *interj.*, from the verb **înhăţá (a), înhắţ, -át**, *v. tr.* I, to seize, to catch up.
hăul-í (a), ésc, -ít, *v. intr.* IV, to yell, to yodel.
heréte (aréte, eréte), *n. m.*, **heréţi**, *pl.*, hawk (*Astur, Falco palumbarius*).
heruvím (cheruvím), *n. m.*, **-i**, *pl.*, cherub.
hiát, *n. mix.*, **-e**, *pl.*, hiatus.
hid-ós, -oásă, *adj.*, **-óşi, -oáse**, *pl.*, hideous, horrible.
hodorog-í (a), -ésc, -ít, *v. intr.* IV, to rattle, to rumble.
hóhot, *n. mix.*, **-e**, *pl.*, **de râs**, loud laughter; — **de plâns**, loud lament.
holb-á (a), -éz, -át, *v. tr.* I, to open wide the eyes, to stare; **a se** —, to stare, to gaze.
hór-ă, *n. f.*, **-i**, *pl.*, a dance.
hotár, *n. mix.*, **-e**, *pl.*, frontier.
hotăr-í (a), -ăsc -ít, *v. tr.* IV, to decide; to determine; to sentence; **a se** —, to decide; to determine; to resolve.
hotărír-e, *n. f.*, **-i**, *pl.*, decision, resolution, verdict.
hotél, *n. mix.*, **-uri**, *pl.*, hotel.
Hotín, *prop. n. m.* (town).
hráná, *n. f.*, **hrăní**, *pl.*, food.
hrăn-í (a), -ésc, -ít, *v. tr.* IV, to feed, to nourish; **a se** —, *intr.*, to live upon.
hulúb, *n. m.*, **-i**, *pl.*, pigeon, dove; **hulubíţ-ă**, *n. f.*, **-e**, *pl.*, she-pigeon, she-dove.
Humór (Mănăstirea), *prop. n. m.* (locality).
Humuleşte-án, *prop. n. m.*, **-éni**, *pl.*, inhabitant of Humuleşti (village).
Hurmuzáche, *prop. n.* (surname).

I

i, -i, *pers. pron.*, to him, to her, them (see 5. 1. **a**); *aux. v.*, is (see 6. 1. **a**).
I=ei! *interj.* (see p. 247).
ia! *interj.*, lake, let.
iácă, see **iátă**.
iad, *n. mix.*, **-uri**, *pl.*, hell, inferno.
Ianuárie, *n. m.*, January.
iáp-ă, *n. f.*, **iépe**, *pl.*, mare.
iar (iáră, iárăş), *adv.*, again; *conj.*, and, but, whereas.
iárb-ă, *n, f.*. **iérburi**, *pl.*, plants; **iérbi**, *pl.*, grass fields.
iarmar-óc, *n. mix.*, **-oáce**, *pl.*, fair, market.
iárnă, *n. f.*, **iérni**, *pl.*, winter.
Iáşi, *n. m. pl.*, Jassy.
iátă! *interj.*, behold! that is! here is!
iáu, see **luá (a)**.
iaúrt, *n. mix.*, **-uri**, *pl.*, yogurt.
icoán-ă, *n. f.*, **-e**, *pl.*, icon, image.
ie-d, *n. m.*, **-zi**, *pl.*, kid, young goat.

iéften, -ă, *adj.*, cheap.
iépure, see **épure**.
iéri, *adv.*, yesterday.
iérta (a), **iért, -át**, *v. tr.* I, to forgive.
iert-áre, *n. f.*, **-ări**, *pl.*, pardon, forgiveness.
ierúnc-ă (**irúncă, erúncă**), *n. f.*, **-i**, *pl.*, hazel-hen, heath-cock, heath-pout (*Tetrao bonasia*).
Ileána, *prop. n.*, Helen.
ilustráţi-e, *n. f.*, **-i**, *pl.*, illustration.
imágin-e, *n. f.*, **-i**, *pl.*, image; picture.
imediá-t, -tă, *adj.*, **-ţi, -te**, *pl.*, immediate.
imén-s, -să, *adj.*, **-şi, -se**, *pl.*, immense.
imit-á (a), **-éz** (**imít**), **-át**, *v. tr.* I, to imitate.
impéri-u, *n. mix.*, **-i**, *pl.*, empire.
importán-t, -tă, *adj.*, **-ţi, -te**, *pl.*, important.
imprési-e, *n. f.*, **-i**, *pl.*, impression.
in, *n. mix.*, **-uri**, *pl.*, flax.
inamíc, inimíc, *n. m.*, **-i**, *pl.*, enemy.
independén-t, -tă, *adj.*, **-ţi, -te**, *pl.*, independent.
indiscré-t, -tă, *adj.*, **-ţi, -te**, *pl.*, indiscreet.
inél, *n. mix.*, **-e**, *pl.*, ring.
infernál, -ă, *adj.*, **-i, -e**, *pl.*, infernal, hellish.
influénţ-ă, *n. f.*, **-e**, *pl.*, influence.
informáţi-e, *n. f.*, **-i**, *pl.*, information, inquiry.
ingeni-ós, -oásă, *adj.*, **-óşi, -oáse**, *pl.*, ingenious.
ínim-ă, *n. f.*, **-i** (**-e**), *pl.*, heart.
innavigábil, inavigábil, -ă, *adj.*, **-i, -e**, *pl.*, unnavigable.
inovat-ór, -oáre, *adj.*, **-óri, -oáre**, *pl.*, innovative.
insistá (a), **insíst, -át**, *v. intr.* I, to insist.
instínct, *n. mix.*, **-e**, *pl.*, instinct.
instruí (a), **-ésc, -t**, *v. tr.* IV, to instruct.
instrumént, *n. mix.*, **-e**, *pl.*, instrument, tool.
ínsul-ă, *n. f.*, **-e**, *pl.*, island.
inteligén-t, -tă, *adj.*, **-ţi, -te**, *pl.*, intelligent.
inténţi-e, *n. f.*, **-i**, *pl.*, intention, design, purpose.
interés, *n. mix.*, **-e**, *pl.*, interest, concern.
interi-ór, -oáră, *adj.*, **-óri, -oáre**, *pl.*, interior, inside; inner, inward.
interníst, *n. m.*, **interníşti**, *pl.*, specialist for internal diseases.
intrá (a), **íntr-u, -át**, *v. intr.* I, to enter, to go in.
intráre, *n. f.*, **-ări**, *pl.*, entrance; entering; admission.
introdúce (a), **introdúc, introdús**, *v. tr.* III, to introduce.
introdúcer-e, *n. f.*, **-i**, *pl.*, introduction.
invási-e (**invázie**), *n. f.*, **-i**, *pl.*, invasion.
invitá (a), **invít, -át**, *v. tr.* I, to invite.
Ión, Ioán, *prop. n.*, John.
Iordăchél, *dim.* from **Iordáche**, *prop. n. m.* (name).
Iordán, *prop. n.*, Jordan.
Iorgován, *prop. n. m.* (name).
iortomán, see **ortomán**.
Irác, *prop. n. m.*, Iraq.
ireproşábil, -ă, *adj.*, **-i, -e**, *pl.*, blameless, irreproachable.
Irlánda, *prop. n. f.*, Ireland.
irúncă, see **ierúncă**.
isbấn-dă, *n. f.*, **-zi**, *pl.*, success, victory.
isbí (a), see **izbi** (a).
isbucn-í (**izbucní**) (a), **-ésc, -ít**, *v. intr.* IV, to break out, to break loose, to burst into.

iscusí-t, -tă, *adj.*, **-ţi, -te,** *pl.*, skilful, subtle.
isprăv-í (a), -ésc, -ít, *v. tr.* IV, to end, to finish.
ístlalt, (ístalalt), *dem. pron.*, this other (see 5. 6. **c**).
istóric, *n. m.*, **-i,** *pl.*, historian.
istóri-e, *n. f.*, **-i,** *pl.*, history.
istoris-í (a), -ésc, -ít, *v. tr.* IV, to relate, to tell, to recount.
istov-í (a), -ésc, -ít, *v. tr.* IV, to exhaust.
Ístria, *prop. n. f.*, Istria; **istri-án, -ánă,** *adj.*, **-éni, -éne,** *pl.*, Istrian.
isvór, see **izvór.**
Itália, *prop. n. f.*, Italy; **Italián,** *prop. n. m.*, **Italiéni,** *pl.*, Italian.
iţári, *n. m. pl.*, white peasant woollen breeches.
iub-í (a), ésc, -ít, *v. tr.* IV, to love.
iubi-tór, -toáre, *adj.*, **-tóri, -toáre,** *pl.*, loving.
Iúlie, *n. m.*, July.
Iúnie, *n. m.*, June.
iú-te, *adj.*, **-ţi,** *pl.*, quick.
iuţ-eálă, *n. f.*, **-éli,** *pl.*, quickness, swiftness, celerity.
iví (a se), mă iv-ésc, -ít, *v. intr.* IV, to appear, to rise; **ivír-e,** *n. f.*, **-i,** *pl.*, appearance.
iveálă, *n. f.*, **iveli,** *pl.*, appearance.
izbándă, see **isbándă.**
izb-í (a), -ésc, -ít, *v. tr.* IV, to hit, to strike; **izbi-tor, -toare,** *adj.*, **-tóri, -toáre,** *pl.*, striking.
izvór, *n. mix.*, **izvoáre,** *pl.*, source, well, spring.

Î

îi, *pers. pron.*, to him, to her; them (see 5. 1. **a**).
îl, *pers. pron.*, him (see 5. 1. **a**).
îmbătá (a), îmbắt, -át, *v. tr.* I, to make tipsy, to intoxicate; **a se —,** to get drunk; **îmbătă-tór, -toáre,** *adj.*, **-tóri, -toáre,** *pl.*, intoxicating.
îmbătrân-í (a), -ésc, -ít, *v. intr.* IV, to grow old.
îmbrăcá (a), îmbrác, îmbrăcát, *v. tr.* I, to dress; **a se —,** to dress oneself.
îmbrăcămín-te, *n. f.*, **-ţi,** *pl.*, clothing, dress, clothes.
îmbrăţiş-á (a), -éz, -át, *v. tr.* I, to embrace, to hug; to comprise.
îmbucá (a) (înbucá), îmbúc, -át, *v. tr.*, *intr.* I, to mouth, to swallow.
îmbuib-á (a se), mă îmbuibéz, -át, *v. intr.* I, to gorge oneself.
îmi, *pers. pron.*, to me (see 5. 1. **a**).
împăcá (a), împác, împăcát, *v. tr.* I, to reconcile.
împăc-áre, *n. f.*, **-ắri,** *pl.*, reconciliation, reconcilement.
împânz-í (a), -ésc, -ít, *v. tr.* IV, to cover; to cloak.
împărá-t, *n. m.*, **-ţi,** *pl.*, emperor.
împărăt-eásă, *n. f.*, **-ése,** *pl.*, empress.
împărăt-ésc, -eáscă, *adj.*, **-éşti,** *pl.* imperial.
împărăţí-e, *n. f.*, **-i,** *pl.*, empire.
împărţí (a), împárt (împărţésc), împărţít, *v. tr.* IV, to divide, to distribute, to share.
împărţír-e, *n. f.*, **-i,** *pl.* division.
împărţí-t, -tă, *adj.*, **-ţi, -te,** *pl.*, divided.
împătrí-t, -tă, *adj.*, **-ţi, -te,** *pl.*, fourfold.
împiedecá (a), împiédec, -át, *v. tr.* I, to hinder, to impede; to fetter (a horse); **a se —,** to stumble.
împínge (a), împíng, împíns, *v. tr.* III, to push, to shove, to thrust.
împlin-í (a), -ésc, -ít, *v. tr.* IV, to accomplish, to fulfil; to execute; **a se —,** to come to an end.

împodob-í (a), **-ésc**, **-ít**, *v. tr.* IV, to adorn, to decorate.

împotríva, *prep.*, against.

împrăşti-á (a), **împrắştiu**, **-át**, *v. tr.* II, to disperse, to scatter, to spread.

împreájma, **în preájma**, *prep.*, against, towards.

împrejmuí (a), **-ésc**, **-ít**, *v. tr.* IV, to enclose; to surround.

împrejúr, *adv.*, round, around; **împrejúrul cásei**, round the house.

împrejur-áre, *n. f.*, **-ắri**, circumstance.

împrejurím-e, *n. f.*, **-i**, *pl.*, environs, surroundings.

împresurá (a), **imprésur** (**imprésor**), **-át**, *v. tr.* I, to surround, to invest (a fortification).

împreuná (a), **împréun** (**-éz**), **-át**, *v. tr.* I, to join, to unite.

împreúnă, *adv.*, together.

împroşcá (a), **împróşc**, **-át**, *v. tr.* I, to sprinkle.

împrumút, *n. mix.*, **-uri**, *pl.*, loan, borrowing.

împrumutá (o), **împrumút**, **-át**, *v. tr.* I, to lend, to borrow, to loan.

împuşcá (a), **împúşc**, **-át**, *v. tr.* I, to shoot; **împuşc-áre**, *n. f.*, **-ắri**, *pl.*, shooting.

împuşcătúr-ă, *n. f.*, **-i**, *pl.*, shooting, discharge.

în, *prep.*, in.

înăbuşí (a) (**înnăbuşí**), **înắbuş** (**-ésc**), **-ít**, *v. tr.* IV, to stifle, to smother, to suffocate.

înadíns, *adv.*, purposely, intentionally.

înaint-á (a), **-éz**, **-át**, *v. intr.* I, to advance, to proceed.

înaínte (**-a**), *adv.*, *prep.*, before, in front of, forward, ahead; **înainte de**, *conj.*, before.

înál-t, **-tă**, *adj.*, **-ţi**, **-te**, *pl.*, high, tall.

înălţá (a), **înálţ**, **-át**, *v. tr.* I, to raise, to erect; to lift; **a se** —, to mount, to ascend; to rise up.

înălţím-e, *n. f.*, **-i**, *pl.*, height.

înapói, *adv.*, back.

înarm-á (a), **-éz**, **-át**, *v. tr.* I, to arm.

íncă, *adv.*, still, yet, again.

încâlc-í (a), **-ésc**, **-ít**, *v. tr.* IV, to entangle; **a se** —, to get entangled.

încălecá (a), **încálec**, **încălecát**, *v. tr.* I, to mount on horseback, to bestride, to ride.

încălţá (a), **încálţ**, **încălţát**, *v. tr.* I, to put on shoes; **a se** —, to put on one's shoes.

încălz-í (a), **-ésc**, **-ít**, *v. tr.*, to warm, to heat.

încântá (a), **încắnt**, **-át**, *v. tr.* I, to charm, to enchant, to ravish.

încânt-áre, *n. f.*, **-ắri**, *pl.*, enchantment, delight, ravishing.

încăpeá (a) (**încápe**), **încáp**, **încăpút**, *v. intr.* II (III), to hold, to comprise, to take in.

încărcá (a), **încárc**, **încărcát**, *v. tr.* I, to charge, to load, to burden.

încârj-í (a se), **-ésc**, **-ít**, *v. intr.* IV, to crook oneself, to get hooked.

încắt. *conj.*, that, so that.

începút, *n. mix.*, **-uri**, *pl.*, beginning.

încercá (a), **încérc**, **-át**, *v. tr.* I, to try, to attempt.

încercuí (a), **-ésc**, **-ít**, *v. tr.* IV, to encircle, to surround.

încét, **înceátă**, *adj.*, slow, soft, low; **încetinél**, *adv. dim.*, slowly; **încetişór**, *adv. dim.*, slowly.

încet-á (a), **-éz, -át,** *v. intr.*, to cease, to stop, to discontinue.
înceten-í (**încetin-á**) (a), **-ésc** (**-éz**), **-ít** (**-át**), *v. tr.* IV (I), to slow down.
încheiér-e, *n. f.*, **-i,** *pl.*, conclusion, end.
încheiá (a), **închéi, -át,** *v. tr.* I, to close, to end, to finish ; **a se** —, to button.
închiegá (a), **închiég, -át,** *v. tr.* I, to curdle ; **a se** —, *intr.*, to curdle.
închiná (a), **închín, -át,** *v. tr.* I, to dedicate, to consecrate ; to toast ; **a se** —, *intr.*, to incline, to salute, to make the sign of the cross.
închinăciún-e, *n. f.*, **-i,** *pl.*, worship ; prayer ; salutation.
închipuí (a-şi), **-ésc, -t,** *v. tr.* IV, to imagine.
închis-oáre, *n. f.*, **-óri,** *pl.*, prison.
încincí-t, -tă, *adj.*, **-ţi, -te,** *pl.*, fivefold.
încoáce, *adv.*, here, hither, this way (also temporal : since).
încolăc-í (a), **-ésc, -ít,** *v. tr.* IV, to wind, to twist, to roll up ; **a se** —, *intr.*, *refl.*, to twist.
încólo, *adv.*, thither, that way, there.
încord-á (a), **-éz, -át,** *v. tr.* I, to stretch, to strain ; **a se** —, *intr.*, *refl.*, to stretch oneself.
încorpor-á (a), **-éz, -át,** *v. tr.* I, to embody, to incorporate.
încotró, *adv.*, *conj.*, whither.
încovoiá (a), **încovói, -át,** *v. tr.* I, to bend, to curve.
încréder-e, *n. f.*, **-i,** *pl.*, confidence, trust.
încremen-í (a), **-ésc, -ít,** *v. intr.* IV, to be stupefied, to be petrified, to be turned into stone.
încuiá (a), **încúi, -át,** *v. tr.* I, to lock up.
încunjurá (a) (**înconjurá**), **încunjór** (**încúnjur**), **-át,** *v. tr.* I, to surround, to enclose, to invest, to go round, to avoid.
încurcá (a), **încúrc, -át,** *v. tr.* I, to entangle, to embroil ; **a se** —, to get entangled.
îndărắt, *adv.*, back, behind.
îndărắtnic, -ă, *adj.*, **-i, -e,** *pl.*, stubborn, obstinate.
îndátă, *adv.*, soon, immediately ; **îndátăce,** *conj.*, as soon as.
îndeléte (pe), *adv.*, slowly, tranquilly.
îndelungá-t, -tă, *adj.*, **-ţi, -te,** *pl.*, long, protracted ; **îndelúng,** *adv.*, long time.
îndemná (a), **îndémn, -át,** *v. tr.* I, to instigate, to incite.
îndepart-á (a), **-éz, -át,** *v. tr.* I, to remove, to drive away.
îndoí (a), **-ésc, -t,** *v. tr.* IV, to double ; to fold ; to bend ; **a se** —, to doubt ; to bend.
îndoí-t, -tă, *adj.*, **-ţi, -te,** *pl.*, twofold.
îndrăzn-í (a), **-ésc, -ít,** *v. tr.*, *intr.*, to dare, to venture ; **îndrăzneálă,** *n. f.*, **-éli,** *pl.*, boldness, audacity.
îndreptá (a), **îndrépt** (**-éz**), **-át,** *v. tr.* I, to direct ; to straighten ; to correct.
îndreptăţ-í (a), **-ésc, -ít,** *v. tr.* IV, to entitle, to authorize.
îndrugá (a), **îndrúg, -át,** *v. tr.*, *intr.*, to speak indistinctly.
îndurá (a se), **mă îndúr, îndurát,** *v. intr.* I, to commiserate, to pity.
înebun-í (a), **-ésc, -ít,** *v. tr.*, *intr.* IV, to get mad.
înecá (a), **înéc, -át,** *v. tr.* I, to drown ; **a se** —, *v. intr.*, to drown oneself ; to be choked, to suffocate.
înfăţiş-áre, *n. f.*, **-ắri,** *pl.*, appearance, presentation.

înfierbântá (a), **înfierbânt** (**-éz**), **-át**, *v. tr.* I, to heat; to excite.

înfíge (a), **înfíg**, **înfípt**, *v. tr.* III, to thrust, to stick.

înfioră-tór, **-toáre**, *adj.*, **-tóri**, **-toáre**, *pl.*, frightful, horrible.

înflăcăr-á (a), **-éz**, **-át**, *v. tr.* I, to inflame, to kindle.

înflor-í, **-ésc**, **-ít**, *v. intr.* IV, to flourish, to blossom; **înflorír-e**, *n. f.*, **-i**, *pl.*, flourishing; **înflorí-t**, **-tă**, *adj.*, **-ţi**, **-te**, *pl.*, in flower; with flowers embroidered.

înfrânge (a), **înfrâng**, **înfrânt**, *v. tr.* III, to defeat, to overcome.

înfrăţ-í (a se), **-ésc**, **-ít**, *v. refl.* IV, to fraternize, to join together like brothers.

înfrăţír-e, *n. f.*, **-i**, *pl.*, brotherhood, fraternization.

înfricoş-á (a), **-éz**, **-át**, *v. tr.* I, to frighten; **înfricoşá-t**, **-tă**, *adj.*, **-ţi**, **-te**, *pl.*, frightful.

înfrúnt, *n. m.* (**înfruntáre**, *n. f.*), insult, outrage.

înfruntá (a), **înfrúnt**, **-át**, *v. tr.* I, to affront, to defy.

înfuri-á (a), **-éz**, **-át**, *v. tr.* II, to make furious; **a se —**, to become furious.

îngân-á (a), **-éz**, **-át**, to stammer, to murmur; **a se —**, to mock; to meet.

înger, *n. m.*, **-i**, *pl.*, angel.

îngheţ-á (a), (**înghieţá**) **înghéţ**, **-át**, *v. tr.*, *intr.* I, to freeze, to congeal.

înghiţ-í (a), **-ésc** (**înghít**), **-ít**, *v. tr.* IV, to swallow, to devour.

îngrij-í, **-ésc**, **-ít**, *v. tr.* IV, to attend, to take care of; **îngrijí-t**, **-tă**, *adj.*, **-ţi**, **-te**, *pl.*, careful, clean; troubled, anxious (= **îngrijorat**).

îngrijír-e, *n. f.*, **-i**, *pl.*, care, keeping; uneasiness (= **îngrijoráre**).

îngropá (a), **îngróp**, **-át**, *v. tr.* I, to bury, to inter.

îngroz-í (a se), **-ésc**, **-ít**, *v. intr.* IV, to be terrified, to be horrified.

îngú-st, **-ă**, *adj.*, **-şti**, **-ste**, *pl.*, narrow, close, strait.

înjunghi-á (a), **-éz**, **-át**, *v. tr.* I, to stab, to poinard.

înlăúntru, *adv.*, inside, inward.

înmagazin-á (a), **-éz**, **-át**, *v. tr.* I, to store.

înmân-á, **-éz**, **-át**, *v. tr.* I, to hand over, to deliver.

înmiít, **-ă**, *adj.*, *num.*, thousandfold.

înmulţ-í (a), **-ésc**, **-ít**, *v. tr.* IV, to multiply; **a se —**, *intr.*, *refl.*

înmulţír-e, *n. f.*, **-i**, *pl.*, multiplication.

înmulţí-t, **-tă**, *adj.*, **-ţi**, **-te**, *pl.*, multiplied.

înnăbuşít, see **înăbuşi**.

înnált, see **înált**.

înnapoí, see **înapoí**.

înnecát, see **înecá**.

înopt-á (**înnoptá**) (a), **-éz**, **-át**, *v. intr.* I, to become dark, to stay overnight; **a se —**, *v. intr.*, to become night (see 6. 4. e).

înoptí-t, **-tă**, *adj.*, **-ţi**, **-te**, *pl.*, eightfold.

înrâurír-e, *n. f.*, **-i**, *pl.*, influence.

însă, *conj.*, but, however.

însânger-á (a), **-éz**, **-át**, *v. tr.*, *intr.*, to bleed.

însemná (a), **însémn** (**-éz**), **-át**, *v. tr.*, *intr.* I, to mark; to note, to mean, to signify; **însemná-t**, **-tă**, *adj.*, **-ţi**, **-te**, *pl.*, important, considerable.

însenin-á (a), **-éz**, **-át**, *v. tr.* I, to make serene; **a se —**, to clear up.

înşeptí-t, -tă, *adj., num.*, **-ţi, -te,** *pl.*, sevenfold.

înserá (a), -éz, -át, *v. intr.* I, to become evening; **a se —,** to become evening; **însereáză,** night falls (see 6. 4. e); **pe înseráte,** *adv.*, towards evening.

înser-áre, *n. f.*, **-ări,** *pl.*, nightfall.

înseráte (pe), *adv.*, in the dusk (see 19. 8. d).

înşesí-t, -tă, *adj., num.*, **-ţi, -te,** *pl.*, sixfold.

înşfăcá (a), înşfác, înşfăcát, *v. tr.* I, to grasp.

însoţí (a), -ésc, -ít, *v. tr.* IV, to accompany; to unite.

ínspre, *prep.*, to, towards.

însufl-á (a), -u, -át, *v. tr.* I, to inspire, to suggest.

ínsumi, ínsămi, *pers. pron.*, myself (see 5. 2).

însurá (a), însór, însurát, *v. tr.* I, to marry; **a se —,** *v. intr., refl.*, to get married (about a male).

însur-í (a), -ésc, -ít, *v. intr.* IV, to become grey.

însutít, -ă, *adj., num.*, hundredfold.

întâi, -a, *num., adj.*, first; **întâiul întâia,** *with art.*, the first; **întâii, întâiele,** *pl.*; **întâi,** *adv.*, first.

întâln-í (a), -ésc, -ít, *v. tr.* IV, to meet.

întâlnír-e, *n. f.*, **-i,** *pl.*, meeting, rencounter, appointment.

întâmpl-á (a se), -u, -át, *v. intr.* I, to happen, to chance.

întâmpl-áre, *n. f.*, **-ări,** *pl.*, adventure, happening, case.

întârzi-á (a), -éz (întârziu), -át, *v. intr.* II, to be too late; *v. tr.*, to delay.

înţelége (a), înţelé-g, -s, *v. tr.* III, to understand.

înţelepciún-e, *n. f.*, **-i,** *pl.*, wisdom.

înţel-épt, -eáptă, *adj.*, **-épţi, -epte,** *pl.*, wise.

înţelés, *n. mix.*, **-uri,** *pl.*, meaning, sense, signification.

întemeiér-e, *n. f.*, **-i,** *pl.*, foundation.

înţepen-í (a), -ésc, -ít, *v. tr., intr.* IV, to fix; to stiffen, to get stiff.

întín-de (a), întín-d, -s, *v. tr.* III, to stretch, to extend; **a se —,** *intr.*, to stretch.

întínder-e, *n. f.*, **-i,** *pl.*, extension.

întiner-í (a), -ésc, -ít, *v. tr., intr.* IV, to make young again; to grow young again.

întoárce (a), întór-c, -s, *v. tr.* III, to turn; **a se —,** to return, to come back; **a întoarce ceasul,** to wind up the watch.

întócmai, *adv.*, exactly (the same).

într'adíns, *adv.*, purposely, truly, really.

într'ánsa=întru (d)ánsa, in it (see 8. 3, note 1).

íntre, *prep.*, between (see 8. 3, note 1).

întrebá (a), întréb, -át, *v. tr.* I, to ask, to demand.

întreb-áre, *n. f.*, **-ări,** *pl.*, question.

întré-g, -ágă, *adj.*, **-gi, -ge,** *pl.*, whole.

întreí-t, -tă, *adj., num.*, **-ţi, -te,** *pl.*, threefold, treble, triple.

întreoláltă, *adv.*, each other, between them.

întreprínder-e, *n. f.*, **-i,** *pl.*, enterprise, undertaking; attempt.

întrerúper-e, *n. f.*, **-i,** *pl.*, interruption.

întrist-á (a), -éz, -át, *v. tr.* I, to grieve, to afflict; **a se —,** to become sad.

ĭntru, *prep.*, in (see 8. 3, note 1).
întrucât, *adv.*, *conj.*, as far as, inasmuch.
ĭntr'un, ĭntr'o=în un, în o (see 8. 3, note 1).
întunecá (a), întúnec, -át, *v. tr.*, to become dark, to make dark, to darken, to eclipse (see 6. 4. e).
întunérec, *n. mix.* (**-uri**, *pl.*), darkness.
înturná (a), întórn, înturnát, *v. tr.* I, to turn; **a se** —, to turn away.
învăluí (a), -ésc (învắlui), -it, *v. tr.* IV, to wrap, to envelop; **a se** —, to increase, to swell.
învârtí (a), învấrt (învârtésc), -ít, *v. tr.* IV, to turn round, to revolve, to whirl; **a se** —, to turn, to go round, to toss.
învăţá (a), învắţ, -át, *v. tr.*, *intr.* I, to teach, to learn; **a se** —, to get accustomed.
învăţá-t, -tă, *adj.*, *n.*, **-ţi, -te**, *pl.*, scholar; learned, trained.
învăţătór, *n. m.*, **-i**, *pl.*, teacher (primary school).
învăţătoáre, *n. f.*, **învăţătoáre**, *pl.*, teacher (primary school).
învech-í (a se), mă, -ésc, -ít, *v. intr.* IV, to become old.
învel-í (a), -ésc, -ít, *v. tr.* IV, to envelop, to wrap up.
înverz-í (a), -ésc, -ít, *v. intr.* IV, to grow green.
învi-á (a), -éz, -át, *v. tr.*, *intr.* I, to resuscitate; to raise from the dead.
învingătór, *n. m.*, **-i**, *pl.*, victor, conqueror; *adj.*, victorious.
învínge (a), învíng, -s, *v. tr.* III, to defeat, to conquer, to vanquish.
învinuí (a), -ésc, -t, *v. tr.* IV, to accuse, to incriminate, to charge.
învolbur-áre, *n. f.*, **-ắri**, *pl.*, whirlwind; tornado, vortex.
învrăjb-í (a), -ésc, -ít, *v. tr.* IV, to set at variance; **a se** —, to bear enmity.
înzecí-t, -tă, *adj.*, *num.*, **-ţi, -te**, *pl.*, tenfold.
îşi, *refl. pron.* (see 5. 3).
îţi, *pers. pron.*, to thou (see 5. 1. **a**).

J

jále, *n. f.*, **jéli**, *pl.*, affliction, sadness, mourning.
jálnic, -ă, *adj.*, mournful.
jâlţ (jilţ), *n. mix.*, **-uri**, *pl.*, armchair, easy-chair.
Jára, *prop. n. f.* (locality).
jefuí (a), -ésc, -t, *v. tr.* IV, to plunder, to pillage, to rob.
jel-í (a), -ésc, -ít, *v. tr.*, *intr.* IV, to mourn.
jeţ, see **jâlţ**.
jilétc-ă, *n. f.*, **-i**, *pl.*, vest, waistcoat.
jilţ, see **jâlţ**.
jívin-ă, *n. f.*, **-e**, *pl.*, creature, being, animal.
joc, *n. mix.*, **-uri**, *pl.*, play, game; dance; **în joc**, at stake; **a-şi bate joc de cineva**, to mock, to make mock of somebody.
jói, *n.*, Thursday.
jórdi-e, *n. f.*, **-i**, *pl.*, rod, switch, stick.
jos, joásă, *adj.*, **jóşi, joáse**, *pl.*, low; **din jos de**, *prep.*, down; *adv.*, down; **pe jos**, *adv.*, on foot; low.
jucá (a), joc, jucát, *v. intr.* I, to dance; **a se** —, to play.
jucăúş, -ă (-e), *adj.*, *n.*, **-i, -e**, *pl.*, dancing; dancer.
judecá (a), júdec, -át, *v. tr.* I, to judge.

judec-átă, *n. f.*, **-ắţi**, *pl.*, judgment, lawsuit, process.
judéţ, *n. mix.*, **-e**, *pl.*, district.
Judéţul din úrmă, Last Judgment.
jug, *n. mix.*, **-uri**, *pl.*, yoke.
jumătáte, *n. f.*, **jumătắţi**, *pl.*, half.
júnghi, *n. mix.*, **-uri**, *pl.*, shooting pain; dagger, poinard.
junghi-á (**a**), **-éz**, **-át**, *v. tr.* II, to stab.
jupuí (**o**), **-ésc** (**jupói**), **-ít**, *v. tr.* IV, to flay, to skin.
jurá (**a**), **jur**, **-át**, *v. intr.* I, to swear, to take an oath.
júrul, see **împrejúr**; **în jurul casei**, round the house; **în jur**, *adv.*, round.

K

Kogălniceánu, *prop. n.* (surname).

L

l, *pers. pron.*, him (see 5. 1. **a**).
la, *prep.*, in, at, by, to.
la (**a**), **láu**, **lăút**, *v. tr.* I, to wash (the head) (see 6. 3. **f**).
láb-ă, *n. f.*, **-e**, *pl.*, paw; claw.
lac, *n. mix.*, **-uri**, *pl.*, lake, pool.
lăcáş, *n. mix.*, **-e** (**-uri**), *pl.*, see **locaş**.
lăcomí-e, *n. f.*, **-i**, *pl.*, greediness; covetousness.
lácrim-ă, *n. f.*, **-i** (**-e**), *pl.*, tear.
lăcrim-á (**lăcrămá**) (**a**), **-éz**, **-át**, *v. intr.* I, to shed tears, to weep.
lăcúst-ă, *n. f.*, **-e**, *pl.*, locust, grasshopper.
ládă, *n. f.*, **lăzi**, *pl.*, trunk, chest, box.
láic, *n. m.*, **-i**, *pl.*, layman.
lăicér (**laicér**), *n. mix.*, **-e**, *pl.*, narrow long carpet.
láiţă, see **láviţă**.
lămur-í (**a**), **-ésc**, **-ít**, *v. tr.* IV, to purify; to elucidate, to explain; **a se —**, to clear up, to understand; **lămurír-e**, *n. f.*, **-i**, *pl.*, explanation.
lan, *n. mix.*, **-uri**, *pl.* (large) field, plain.
lấnă, *n. f.*, **lânéţe**, *pl.* (washed) wools; **lấnuri**, *pl.*, pieces of wool.
lấngă, *prep.*, beside, by, near, at, next to.
lanţ, *n. mix.*, **-uri**, chain.
lápte, *n. m.*, milk.
larg, **-ă**, *adj.*, **-i**, *pl.*, broad, wide, large.
laringológ, *n. m.*, **-i**, *pl.*, ear and throat specialist.
laş, *adj.*, *n. m.*, **-ă** (**-e**), *f.*, **-i**, *m. pl.*, **-e**, *f.*, coward.
lăsá (**a**), **las**, **lăsát**, *v. tr.* I, to leave, to let, to allow; **a se —**, to relinquish, to cease.
lăstár (**vlăstár**), *n. mix.*, **-e**, *pl.*, offshoot, young shoot; wood.
la-t, **-tă**, *adj.*, **-ţi**, **-te**, *pl.*, broad, large, wide.
latín, **-ă**, *adj.*, Latin.
latitúdin-e, *n. f.*, **-i**, *pl.*, latitude.
lătrá (**a**), **látru**, **lătrát**, *v. intr.* I, to bark.
látur-e, *n. f.*, **lắturi** (**láturi**), *pl.*, side; **în lături**, *adv.*, sideways, sidewise.
lấu, **láie**, *adj.*, **lắi**, *pl. m.*, *f.*, grey, grizzly.
láud-ă, *n. f.*, **-e**, *pl.*, praise.
lăudá (**a**), **láud**, **lăudát**, *v. tr.* I, to praise.
lăutár, *n. m.*, **-i**, *pl.*, fiddler.
láviţ-ă (**laiţă**), *n. f.*, **-e**, *pl.*, wooden bench.
le, *pers. pron.*, to them (see 5. 1. **a**).
leác, *n. mix.*, **-uri**, *pl.*, remedy, cure.
leácă (**o**), a little.

leáfă, *n. f.*, **léfuri**, *pl.*, salary.
lébăd-ă (**lébedă**), *n. f.*, **-e**, *pl.*, swan.
lécţi-e, *n. f.*, **-i**, *pl.*, lesson.
lectúr-ă, *n. f.*, **-i**, *pl.*, reading, reading material.
lecuí (**a**), **-ésc**, **-ít**, *v. tr.* IV, to cure, to heal.
legá (**a**), **leg**, **-át**, *v. tr.* I, to lie, to bind; **a se —**, to enter into alliance.
legăná (**a**), **légăn**, **-át**, *v. tr.* I, to rock; swing.
legătúr-ă, *n. f.*, **-i**, *pl.*, connexion, junction.
lége, *n. f.*, **-i**, *pl.*, low, religious faith.
legénd-ă, *n. f.*, **-e**, *pl.*, legend.
legúm-ă, *n. f.*, **-e**, *pl.*, vegetable.
léle, *n. f.*, **léli**, *pl.*, term of friendly respect, used when addressing an older woman, an elder sister.
lemn, *n. mix.*, **-e**, *pl.*, wood.
léne, *n. f.*, laziness, sloth, idleness.
léneş, **-ă** (**-e**), *adj.*, **-i**, **-e**, *pl.*, lazy, idle.
leneví (**a se**), **mă lenevésc**, **lenevít**, *v. intr.* IV, to be lazy, to be idle (see 6. 4).
len-t, **-tă**, *adj.*, **-ţi**, **-te**, *pl.*, slow, tardy.
leopár-d, *n. m.*, **-zi**, *pl.*, leopard.
leş-ésc, **-eáscă**, *adj.*, **-éşti**, *pl.* (*archaic*), Polish.
lésne, *adv.*, easily.
lé-u, *n. m.*, **-i**, *pl.*, lion; coin.
li, *pers. pron.*, to them (see 5. 1. a).
líber, **-ă**, *adj.*, **-i**, **-e**, *pl.*, free; vacant, disengaged.
liberál, **-ă**, *adj.*, **-i**, **-e**, *pl.*, liberal.
libert-áte, *n. f.*, **-ăţi**, *pl.*, liberty, freedom.
librărí-e, *n. f.*, **-i**, *pl.*, bookshop.
licărír-e, *n. f.*, **-i**, *pl.*, glimmer.
líchi-d (**lichíd**), **-dă**, *adj.*, **-zi**, **-de**, *pl.*, liquid.
límb-ă, *n. f.*, **-i**, *pl.*, tongue, language.
límit-ă, *n. f.*, **-e**, *pl.*, limit, boundary.
límpe-de, *adj.*, **-zi**, *pl.*, clear.
lin, **-ă**, *adj.*, **-i**, **-e**, *pl.*, soft, slow, mild.
língur-ă, *n. f.*, **-i**, *pl.*, spoon; **linguríţ-ă**, *n. f.*, **-e**, *pl.*, teaspoon.
línişt-e, *n. f.*, **-i**, *pl.*, tranquillity, quietness; peace; silence.
linişti-t, **-tă**, *adj.*, **-ţi**, **-te**, *pl.*, quiet, tranquil.
liniúţă, *n. f.*, **-e**, *pl.*, dash.
lip-í (**a**), **-ésc**, **-ít**, *v. tr.* IV, to stick up; to gum, to glue.
lípsă, *n. f.*, **lípsuri**, **lípse**, *pl.*, lack, need, want, deficiency.
lipsí (**a**), **-ésc**, **-ít**, *v. intr.* IV, to be absent, to want.
lír-ă, *n. f.*, **-e**, *pl.*, lyre.
lír-ă, *n. f.*, **-e**, *pl.*, **sterlínă**, *adj.*, pound.
líst-ă, *n. f.*, **-e**, *pl.*, list, roll; **lístă de mâncare**, menu, bill of fare.
líter-ă, *n. f.*, **-e**, *pl.*, letter, type, character.
literár, **-ă**, *adj.*, literary.
literá-t, *n. m.*, **-ţi**, *pl.*, man of letters.
literatúr-ă, *n. f.*, **-i**, *pl.*, literature.
lítr-u, *n. m.*, **-i**, *pl.*, litter.
liturgí-e, *n. f.*, **-i**, *pl.*, liturgy.
livádă, *n. f.*, **livézi**, *pl.*, meadow; fruit garden, orchard.
loc, *n. mix.*, **-uri**, *pl.*, place, room; **de loc**, *adv.*, not at all.
locáş (**lăcáş**), *n. mix.*, **-uri** (**-e**), *pl.*, dwelling, home, house, residence.
locuínţ-ă, *n. f.*, **-e**, *pl.*, habitation, lodging, residence.
locuit-ór, *n. m.*, **-i**, *pl.*, inhabitant, resident.

lógică, *n. f.*, logic.
Lóndra, *n. f.*, London.
lor, *pers. pron.*, to them (see 5. 1. **a**; *poss. pron.*, see 5. 5).
lord, *n. m.*, **lorzi**, *pl.*, lord.
lótr-u, *n. m.*, **-i**, *pl.*, thief.
luá (**a**), **iáu**, **luát**, *v. tr.* I, to take (see 6. 3. **c**); (**a se**) **lua dúpă cineva**, to go after somebody, to pursue.
luceáf-ăr, *n. m.*, **lucéferi**, *pl.*, morning star, day-star, Venus.
lucí-u, **-e**, *adj.*, **-i**, *pl.*, smooth, sleek.
lúci-u, *n. mix.*, **-uri**, *pl.*, shine, glimmer, glitter.
lucr-á (**a**), **-éz**, **-át**, *v. tr.*, *intr.* I, to work; **lucr-áre**, *n. f.*, **-ắri**, *pl.*, work, action.
lucrăt-ór, **-oáre**, *n.*, *adj.*, **-óri**, **-oáre**, *pl.*, worker, workman; working.
lúcr-u, *n. mix.*, **-uri**, *pl.*, thing; work.
Lúdovic, *prop. n. m.*, Louis.
lúi, *pers. pron.*, to him (see 5. 1. **a**; *poss. pron.*, see 5. 5).
lule-á, *n. f.*, **-le**, *pl.*, tobacco-pipe.
lumăn-áre, *n. f.*, **-ắri**, *pl.*, candle; **lumănă-rícă**, *n. f.*, **-réle**, *pl.*, small candle.
lúm-e, *n. f.*, **-i**, *pl.*, world.
lumín-ă, *n. f.*, **-i**, *pl.*, light.
lumin-á (**a**), **-éz**, **-át**, *v. tr.* I, to illuminate, to light; **a se —**, to begin to break, to dawn; to enlighten each other.
luminiş, *n. mix.*, **-uri**, *pl.*, clearing in a forest.
lún-ă, *n. f.*, **-i**, *pl.*, moon; month.
lúnc-ă, *n. f.*, **-i**, *pl.*, meadow, mead.
lunecá (**a**), **lúnec**, **-át**, *v. intr.* I, to glide, to slide.
lunec-ós, **-oásă**, *adj.*, **-óşi**, **-oáse**, *pl.*, slippery.
lung, *adj. m.*, **-ă**, *f.*, **-i**, *pl.*, long; see **dealungul**, *adv.*
lúni, *n.*, Monday.
lúntr-e, *n. f.*, **-i**, *pl.*, boat.
lup, *n. m.*, **-i**, *pl.*, wolf.
lúpt-ă, *n. f.*, **-e**, *pl.*, battle, struggle, combat, fight.
luptá (**a**), **lupt**, **-át**, *v. intr.* I, to fight, to struggle, to combat.

M

mă, *pers. pron.*, me (see 5. 1. **a**).
măcár, *adv.*, at least; **— că**, *conj.*, although; **— să**, even if.
Macedónia, *prop. n. f.*
maéstru, *n. m.*, **maéştri**, *pl.*, maestro.
măgár, *n. m.*, **-i**, *pl.*, ass, donkey.
mắgur-ă, *n. f.*, **-i**, *pl.*, mountain, hill; **Măgura**, *prop. n. f.* (mountain).
mâhnír-e, *n. f.*, **-i**, *pl.*, sadness, affliction, sorrow.
máhní-t, *adj. m.*, **-tă**, *f.*, **-ţi**, **-te**, *pl.*, sad.
mái, *adv.*, more; nearly.
Mái, *n. m.*, May.
mắi! *interj.*, see 9. 2.
máic-ă, *n. f.*, **-i**, *pl.*, mother; nun; **măicúţ-ă**, *n. f.*, **-e**, *f. dim.*, little mother.
mắine (**mắne**), *adv.*, to-morrow.
majes-tós, **-toásă**, *adj.*, **-tóşi**, **-toáse**, *pl.*, majestic.
mal, *n. mix.*, **-uri**, *pl.*, bank of the river, shore, coast.
mám-ă, *n. f.*, **-e**, *pl.*, mother.
mămălíg-ă, *n. f.*, **-i**, *pl.*, maize-flour, porridge.
mamíc-ă, *n. f. dim.*, **-e**, *pl.*, mummy.
mắn-ă, *n. f.*, **-i**, **mâini**, *pl.*, hand.
mâná (**a**), **mân**, **-át**, *v. tr.* I, to drive; to incite.
mănăstír-e, *n. f.*, **-i**, *pl.*, monastery, convent.

Mănăstírea Neámţului, *prop. n. f.* (locality).

mâncá, mănânc, mâncát, *v. tr.* I, to eat (see 6. 3. **f**; 6. 4. **c**).

mâncáre, *n. f.*, **mâncắri (mâncắruri)**, food, meal, eating.

mandát, *n. mix.*, **-e**, *pl.*, mandate, commission; **mandát poştál**, postal order.

mândrí-e, *n. f.*, **-i**, *pl.*, pride, haughtiness.

mấndr-u, -ă, *adj.*, **-i, -e**, *pl.*, proud; beautiful; *n.*, sweetheart.

mấne, see **mâíne**.

mângâiá (a), mấngâi, -át, *v. tr.* II, to console, to comfort, to caress; **mângâíer-e**, *n. f.*, **-i**, *pl.*, consolation, caress; **mângâie-tór, -toáre**, *adj.*, **-tóri, -toáre**, *pl.*, caressing, consoling.

mâni-á (a), -u, -át, *v. tr.* II, to irritate; **a se —**, *intr.*, to get angry.

manifest-áre, *n. f.*, **-ắri**, *pl.*, manifestation.

mâni-ós, -oásă, *adj.*, **-óşi, -oáse**, *pl.*, angry, wrathful.

Mânjoálă, *prop. n.* (surname).

manóper-ă, *n. f.*, **-e**, *pl.*, manoeuvre, trick.

măn-ós, -oásă, *adj.*, **-óşi, -oáse**, *pl.*, fertile, rich.

mântu-í (a), -ésc, -ít, *v. tr.* IV, to save, to redeem.

manuál, *n. mix.*, **-e**, *pl.*, handbook, guide; **manuál, -ă**, *adj.*, **-i, -e**, *pl.*, manual.

manuscrís, *n. mix.*, **-e**, *pl.*, manuscript.

mân-z, *n. m.*, **-ji**, *pl.*, foal.

măr, *n. mix.*, **mére**, *pl.*, apple; **măr**, *n. m.*, **méri**, *pl.*, apple-trees.

máre, *n. f.*, **mắri**, *pl.*, sea.

már-e, *adj.*, **-i**, *pl.*, great, big.

măréţ, măreáţă, *adj.*, **-i, -e**, *pl.*, magnificent, grandiose, sumptuous.

márfă, *n. f.*, **mắrfuri**, *pl.*, goods, merchandise.

Marghioála, *prop. n. f.* (name).

mărg-ícă (mărge-á), *n. f.*, **-éle**, *pl.*, bead.

márgin-e, *n. f.*, **-i**, *pl.*, border; rim; edge; margin.

mắri! *interj.*, behold!

măr-í (a), -ésc, -ít, *v. tr.* IV, to increase, to magnify, to aggrandize; **mărír-e**, *n. f.*, **-i**, *pl.*, greatness; glory; enlargement.

măric-él, -ícă, *adj.*, **-éi, -éle**, *pl.*, fairly big.

Măría Ta, *n. f.*, Your Highness Majesty.

Marín, *prop. n. m.* (name).

Marioára, *prop. n. f. dim.*, from María.

mărítá (a), mărít, -át, *v. tr.* I, to marry; **a se —**, *v. refl.*, to get married (about a female).

mármor-ă, *n. f.*, **-e**, *pl.*, marble.

márţi, *n.*, Tuesday.

Mártie, Mart, *n. m.*, March.

mârţoág-ă, *n. f.*, **-e**, *pl.*, jade, tit, old mare.

mărturis-í (a), -ésc, -ít, *v. tr.* IV, to confess, to witness.

mărún-t, -tă, *adj.*, **-ţi, -te**, *pl.*, small, thin; **mărunte**, *f. pl.*, change (money).

másă, *n. f.*, **mése**, *pl.*, table.

másă, *n. f.*, **máse**, *pl.*, mass.

mắ-sa=**máma sa.**

mắ-si=**mámei sále.**

măse-á, *n. f.*, **-le**, *pl.*, molar tooth.

maşinalicéşte, *adv.*, mechanically.

masív, *n. mix.*, **-uri**, *pl.*, group of mountains; **masív, -ă**, *adj.*, **-i, -e**, *pl.*, massive.

maslín-ă, *n. f.*, **-e**, *pl.*, olive.

măsúr-ă, *n. f.*, **-i**, *pl.*, measure.

măsurá (a), **măsór, măsurát,** *v. tr.* I, to measure.
măt-ásă, *n. f.*, **-ắsuri,** *pl.*, silk.
matéri-e, *n. f.*, **-i,** *pl.*, matter; materials; **matérii príme,** raw materials.
mătúş-ă (**mătúşe**), *n. f.*, **-i,** *pl.*, peasant woman; aunt.
mauzolé-u (**mausoléu**), *n. mix.*, **-e** (**-uri**), *pl.*, mausoleum.
Mediáş, *prop. n. m.* (locality).
medicamént, *n. mix.*, **-e,** *pl.*, medicine, medicament.
médi-u, *n. mix.*, **-i,** *pl.*, medium; **médi-u, -e,** *adj.*, **-i,** *pl.*, medium; **médi-e,** *n. f.*, **-i,** *pl.*, average, medium.
megiéş, -ă (**-e**), *adj.*, *n.*, **-i, -e,** *pl.*, neighbour.
melc, *n. m.*, **-i,** *pl.*, snail.
meréu, *adv.*, continually, always, steadily.
mérge (a), **merg, mers,** *v. intr.* III, to go.
merínde, *n. f. pl.*, provisions (of food).
mesteác-ăn, *n. m.*, **mestéceni,** *pl.*, birch-tree.
méşter, *n. m.*, **-i,** *pl.*, master, skilled worker.
meşteşúg, *n. mix.*, **-uri,** *pl.*, handicraft, trade.
métr-u, *n. m.*, **-i,** *pl.*, meter.
méu, *poss. pron.*, mine, my (see 5. 5).
mi, *pers. pron.*, to me (see 5. 1. a).
miáză-noápte, *n. f.*, north.
miáză-zí, *n. f.*, south; **zíua-miáză-máre,** *adv.*, at noon.
mic, -ă, *adj.*, **-i,** *pl.*, small.
micşor-á (a), **-éz, -át,** *v. tr.* I, to diminish, to decrease.
micşun-ícă (**micşuneá**), *n. f.*, **-éle,** *pl.*, violet; gillyflower.
micúţ, -ă, *adj.*, *dim.* **-i, -e,** *pl.*, little, small, wee.
míe, *pers. pron.*, to me (see 5. 1. a).
mí-e, *num.*, *n. f.*, **-i,** *pl.*, thousand.
mié-l, *n. m.*, **-i,** *pl.*, lamb.
miércuri, *n.* Wednesday.
miére, *n. f.*, honey; **mier-ós, -oásă,** *adj.*, **-óşi, -oáse,** *pl.*, sweet (like honey).
miérl-ă, *n. f.*, **-e,** *pl.*, blackbird.
mierós, see **miére.**
miéz, *n. m.*, middle, midst; **miézul de pấine,** the soft inner bread; **miézul nópţii,** midnight; **miézul zílei,** midday.
migdál, *n. m.*, **-i,** *pl.*, almond-tree; **migdál-ă,** *n. f.*, **-e,** *pl.*, almond.
Mihái, *prop. n.*, Michael.
miím-e, *n. f.*, **-i,** *pl.*, thousandth.
míjloc (**mijlóc**), *n. mix.*, middle, means; **mijloáce,** *pl.*, means, way.
míl-ă, *n. f.*, **-e,** pity; mile.
Mílcov, *prop. n. m.* (river).
miliárd, *n. mix.*, **-e,** *pl.*, milliard, billion (thousand millions).
milimétr-u, *n. m.*, **-i,** *pl.*, millimetre.
mili-ón, *num.*, *n. mix.*, **-oáne,** *pl.*, million.
milu-í (a), **-iésc, -ít,** *v. tr.* IV, to accord pity, to give alms.
minarét, *n. mix.*, **-e,** *pl.*, minaret.
mincin-ós (**minciunós**), **-oásă,** *adj.*, **-óşi, -oáse,** *pl.*, lying, false.
mincíun-ă, *n. f.*, **-i.** *pl.*, lie.
míne (pe), *pers. pron.*, me (see 5. 1. a).
minerál, *n. mix.*, **-e,** *pl.*, mineral; **minerál, -ă,** *adj.*, **-li, -le,** *pl.*, mineral.
minístru, *n. m.*, **miníştri,** *pl.*, minister.
minór, -ă, *adj.*, **-i, -e,** *pl.*, minor; under age.
minorit-áte, *n. f.*, **-ắţi,** *pl.*, minority.
mín-te, *n. f.*, **-ţi,** *pl.*, mind, intelligence.

minteán, *n. mix.*, **minténe**, *pl.*, short sheepskin coat, with or without sleeves.
minún-e, *n. f.*, **-i**, *pl.*, miracle.
minút-ă, *n. f.*, **-e**, *pl.*, minute.
mioáră, *n. f.*, **mióri**, *pl.*, young sheep.
mioríţ-ă, *n. f.*, **-e**, *pl.*, young sheep.
mirá (a se), **mă mir**, **-át**, *v. intr.* I, to wonder; **mir-áre**, *n. f.*, **-ări**, *pl.*, astonishment, wonder.
mír-e, *n. m.*, **-i**, *pl.*, bridegroom.
mir-eásă, *n. f.*, **-ése**, *pl.*, bride.
mir-eázm-ă (**mireásmă**), *n. f.*, **-ézme**, *pl.*, scent, smell.
mírişt-e, *n. f.*, **-i**, *pl.*, stubble field.
mirosí (a), **mirós**, **-ít**, *v. tr.*, *intr.* IV, to smell; **mirosi-tór**, **-toáre**, *adj.*, fragrant, odorous.
mişcá, (a) mişc, **-át**, *v. tr.*, *intr.* I, to move.
mişc-áre, *n. f.*, **-ări**, *pl.*, movement, motion; agitation.
misteri-ós, **-oásă**, *adj.*, **-óşi**, **-oáse**, *pl.*, mysterious.
mistréţ, *n. m.*, **-i**, *pl.*, boar.
mitit-él, **-ícă**, *adj.*, **-éi**, **-éle**, *pl.*, little, tiny, small.
mitropolí-t, *n. m.*, **-ţi**, *pl.*, metropolitan.
mláştin-ă, *n. f.*, **-i (-e)**, *pl.*, marsh, bog, fen, morass, pool.
moále, *adj.*, **mói**, *pl.*, soft.
moáră, *n. f.*, **móri**, *pl.*, mill.
moár-te, *n. f.* (**-ţi**, *pl.*), death.
mód-ă, *n. f.*, **-e**, *pl.*, fashion.
modél, *n. mix.*, **-e**, *pl.*, model, pattern.
modérn, **-ă**, *adj.*, modern; fashionable.
moh-ór, *n. mix.*, **-oáre**, *pl.*, wild millet.
mólcum, **-ă**, *adj.*, **-i**, **-e**, *pl.*, silent, quiet.
Moldóva, *prop. n. f.*, Moldavia; **Moldoveán**, *n. m.*, **-că**, *n. f.*, Moldavian; **moldoven-ésc**, **-eáscă**, *adj.*, **-éşti**, *pl.*, Moldavian.
molíd, *n. m.*, **molízi**, *pl.*, see **molíft**.
molíft (**molíd**), *n. m.*, **-ţi**, *pl.*, pine-tree (*picea excelsa*).
momént, *n. mix.*, **-e**, *pl.*, moment, instant.
mondiál, **-ă**, *adj.*, **-i**, **-e**, *pl.*, worldly.
monéd-ă, *n. f.*, **-e (monézi)**, *pl.*, money, coin.
mormânt, *n. mix.*, **mormínte**, tomb.
mort, **moártă**, *adj.*, **mórţi**, **moárte**, *pl.*, dead.
mortăciún-e, *n. f.*, **-i**, *pl.*, carcass; dead body.
moş, *n. m.*, **-i**, *pl.*, old man; grandfather; uncle.
Moséla, *prop. n. f.*, Moselle.
moşí-e, *n. f.*, **-i**, *pl.*, estate, landed property.
moşn-eág, *n. m.*, **-égi**, *pl.*, old man.
mos-ór, *n. mix.*, **-oáre**, *pl.*, bobbin, spool.
moşorói (**muşurói**), *n. mix.*, **moşoroáie**, *pl.*, hill; — **de cârtiţe**, mole-cast, mole-hill.
moşten-í, **(a)**, **-ésc**, **-ít**, *v. tr.* IV, to heir, to inherit.
Mótrul, *prop. n.*, river tributary of Jiul in Oltenia.
movíl-ă, *n. f.*, **-e**, *pl.*, hillock, mound.
Moviléşti, *prop. n. m. pl.*, family Movila, Moldavian dynasty.
mreánă, *n. f.*, **mréne**, *pl.*, barbel fish (*Barbus fluviatilis*).
múget, *n. mix.*, **-e**, *pl.*, roar, bellowing.
mug-í (a), **-ésc**, **-ít**, *v. intr.* IV, to low, to bellow, to roar.

muiér-e, *n. f.*, **-i**, *pl.*, woman, wife; female.
mul-t, -tă, *adj.*, **-ţi, -te**, *pl.*, much, many; **cu atât mai mult**, so much the more.
mulţămí (a), see **mulţumí (a)**.
mulţămít-ă (mulţumítă), *n. f.*, **-e**, *pl.*, thanks, gratitude.
mulţím-e, *n. f.*, **-i**, *pl.*, crowd; multitude.
mulţumí (a), -ésc, -ít, *v. intr.* IV, to thank, to reward; **mulţumít, -ă**, *adj.*, **-ţi, -te**, *pl.*, satisfied, content.
múmă, see **mámă**.
múnc-ă, *n. f.*, **-i**, *pl.*, work, labour, toil.
munc-í (a), -ésc, -ít, *v. intr.*, *tr.*, to toil.
munci-tór, -toáre, *adj.*, *n.*, **-tóri, -toáre**, *pl.*, laborious; worker.
mún-te, *n. m.*, **-ţi**, *pl.*, mountain.
Munténia, *n. f.*, Walachia.
Múnţii Apuséni, *prop. n. m. pl.*, Western Alps (in Transylvania).
múr-ă, *n. f.*, **-e (-i)**, *pl.*, blackberry.
murál, -ă, *adj.*, **-i, -e**, *pl.*, mural, wall.
Múreş, *prop. n. m.* (river).
murí (a), -mor, murít, *v. intr.* IV, to die.
murit-ór, -oáre, *adj.*, **-óri, -oáre**, *pl.*, mortal.
múscă, *n. f.*, **múşte**, *pl.*, fly.
muşcătúr-ă, *n. f.*, **-i**, *pl.*, bite, biting.
mustáţă, *n. f.*, **mustăţi**, *pl.*, moustache.
mustăcioár-ă, *n. f. dim.*, **-e**, *pl.*, little moustache.
mustr-á (a), -éz, -át, *v. tr.* I, to scold, to rebuke, to reprimand.
muşurói, see **moşorói**.
mu-t, -tă, *adj.*, **-ţi, -te**, *pl.*, dumb, mute.
muzé-u, *n. mix.*, **-e**, *pl.*, museum.

N

na! *interj.*, take! here is for you!
năcăjí (a), see **necăjí (a)**.
nădéjd-e, *n. f.*, **-i**, *pl.*, hope.
nădúh (nădúf), *n. mix.*, **-uri**, *pl.*, sultriness.
nahláp, *n. m.*, **-i**, *pl.*, wave.
nált, -ă, *adj.*, see **înalt**.
n'am = nu am.
năpástă, *n. f.*, **năpăşti**, *pl.*, accusation (of an innocent), crimination.
năprásnic, -ă, *adj.*, **-i, -e**, *pl.*, terrible; sudden; monstrous.
năráv, *n. mix.*, **-uri**, *pl.*, bad habit.
nas, *n. mix.*, **-uri**, *pl.*, nose.
naş, *n. m.*, **-i**, *pl.*, sponsor (at wedding and christening).
năsdrăván, -ă, *adj.*, **-i, -e**, *pl.*, uncanny, with magic powers.
náşe (náşă), *n. f.*, **náşe**, *pl.*, lady sponsor (at wedding and christening).
náşte (a), nasc, născút, *v. tr.* III, to bear, to bring forth; **a se —**, to be born.
náşter-e, *n. f.*, **-i**, *pl.*, birth.
nástur-e, *n. m.*, **-i**, *pl.*, button.
naţionál, -ă, *adj.*, **-i, -e**, *pl.*, national.
năúc, -ă, *adj.*, **-i, -e**, *pl.*, stupid.
năválă, *n. f.*, **năvăli**, *pl.*, assault, attack; incursion; aggression.
ne, *pers. pron.*, us (see 5. 1. **a**).
Neácşul, *prop. n. m.* (surname).
Neágra, *prop. n. f.*, tributary of Dorna river.
neám, *n. mix.*, **-uri**, *pl.*, nation; generation; race; kinsman.
Neámţ, *prop. n. m.*, **Némţi**, *pl.*, German.

neapărát, *adv.*, indispensably, absolutely, unconditionally.
neastâmpărá-t, -tă, *adj.*, **-ţi, -te**, *pl.*, restless, turbulent, unruly.
neaşteptá-t, -tă, *adj.*, **-ţi, -te**, *pl.*, unexpected; **pe neaşteptáte**, *adv.*, unexpectedly.
neatârn-áre, *n. f.*, **-ắri**, *pl.*, independence.
nebún, -ă, *adj.*, *n.*, **-i, -e**, *pl.*, mad; lunatic.
nebuná-tec (-tic), -ă, *adj.*, **-i, -e**, *pl.*, foolish.
nebuní-e, *n. f.*, **-i**, *pl.*, madness, folly, insanity.
necăj-í (năcăjí) (a), -ésc, -ít, *v. tr.* IV, to anger, to grieve, to vex; **a se —**, *intr.*, to be vexed.
necáz, *n. mix.*, **-uri**, *pl.*, misery, need; trouble; sufferance.
necesár, -ă, *adj.*, **-i, -e**, *pl.*, necessary.
neclintí-t, -tă, *adj.*, **-ţi, -te**, *pl.*, unshaken, fix.
necreză-tór, -toáre, *adj.*, **-tóri, -toáre**, *pl.*, unbelieving.
nedrept-áte, *n. f.*, **-ắţi**, *pl.*, injustice.
nedumirít, see **domiri (a)**.
nefavorábil, -ă, *adj.*, **-i, -e**, *pl.*, unfavourable.
neghín-ă, *n. f.*, **-e**, *pl.*, darnel.
négur-ă, *n. f.*, **-i**, *pl.*, mist, fog.
negustór, *n. m.*, **-i**, *pl.*, merchant; purchaser.
negustorí-e, *n. f.*, **-i**, *pl.*, trading, commerce.
neguţătór, *n. m.*, **-i**, *pl.*, merchant; purchaser.
negreşít, *adv.*, certainly.
négr-u, neágră, *adj.*, **-i, -e**, *pl.*, black.
nelegiuí-t, -tă, *adj.*, **-ţi, -te**, *pl.*, outrageous; impious, wicked.
némai = nu mai, no more.
nemărginí-t, -tă, *adj.*, **-ţi, -te**, *pl.*, unlimited.
nemérnic, -ă, *adj.*, *n.*, **-i, -e**, *pl.*, worthless, wretched; base, mean.
nemijlocí-t, -ă, *adj.*, **-ţi, -te**, *pl.*, immediate, direct.
nemil-ós, -oásă, *adj.*, **-óşi, -oáse**, *pl.*, merciless.
nemişcá-t, -tă, *adj.*, **-ţi, -te**, *pl.*, unmoved; motionless.
nénea, *n. m.*, the elder brother; the uncle.
nenorocír-e, *n. f.*, **-i**, *pl.*, unhappiness, misfortune, disaster.
nenorocí-t, -tă, *adj.*, **-ţi, -te**, *pl.*, unhappy, unfortunate.
neobicinuí-t, -tă, *adj.*, **-ţi, -te**, *pl.*, unaccustomed.
neóm, *n. m.*, inhuman creature.
nepăsă-tór, -toáre, *adj.*, **-tóri, -toáre**, *pl.*, careless, unconcerned.
neputínţ-ă, *n. f.*, **-e**, *pl.*, inability, powerlessness; **cu —**, impossible.
nerăbd-áre, *n. f.*, **-ắri**, *pl.*, impatience.
nerăsufláte (pe), see **răsufla (a)**.
neseri-ós, -oásă, *adj.*, **-óşi, -oáse**, *pl.*, not serious.
nesimţít, see **simţí (a)**.
nestatórnic, -ă, *adj.*, **-i, -e**, *pl.*, instable, unstable.
neţărmurí-t, -tă, *adj.*, **-ţi, -te**, *pl.*, endless, unlimited.
néted, -ă, *adj.*, **nétezi, nétede**, *pl.*, smooth, neat.
netez-í, (a) -ésc, -ít, *v. tr.* IV, to smooth, to polish.
neturbur-áre, *n. f.*, **-ắri**, *pl.*, calm, tranquillity.
neuit-áre, *n. f.*, **-ắri**, *pl.*, remembrance.
neútr-u, -ă, *adj.*, **-i, -e**, *pl.*, neuter, neutral.
nevástă, *n. f.*, **nevéste**, *pl.*, young woman, spouse, wife.

nevinová-t, -tă, *adj.*, **-ţi, -te**, *pl.*, innocent, guiltless.
nevói-e, *n. f.*, **-a**, *art.*, **nevói**, *pl.*, need, necessity, misery.
nicăíri, *adv.*, nowhere.
níci, *conj.*, neither; **níci de cum**, *adv.*, not at all; **níci . . . níci**, neither . . . nor; **níci chiár**, not even.
niciodátă (**níci odátă**), *adv.*, never.
niciúnul, *indef. pron.*, no one (see 5. 9).
Niculáe, Nicolái, *prop. n.*, Nicholas.
Nil, *prop. n. m.*, Nile.
níme, nímeni, *indef. pron.*, nobody (see 5. 9).
nimer-í, -ésc, -ít, *v. tr.* IV, to strike, to hit, to locate, to find.
nimíc (**-ă, -a**), *indef. pron.*, nothing (see 5. 9).
nínge (**a**), **ning, nins**, *v. intr.* III, to fall snow.
nins-oáre, *n. f.*, **-óri**, *pl.*, snowing, snowfall.
niscái, niscáiva, *indef. pron.*, some, something (see 5. 9).
niscarevá, *indef. pron.*, someone (see 5. 9).
nisíp, *n. mix.*, **-uri**, *pl.*, sand.
nisip-ós, -oásă, *adj.*, **-óşi, -oáse**, *pl.*, sandy.
níşte, *indef. pron.*, some (see 5. 9).
Nístrul, *prop. n. m.*, Dniester.
noápte, *n. f.*, **nópţi**, *pl.*, night.
noáten, *n. m.*, **-i**, *pl.*, one-year-old sheep; yearling.
nóbil, -ă, *adj.*, *n.*, **-i, -e**, *pl.*, noble, great; nobleman.
nod, *n. mix.*, **-uri**, *pl.*, knot.
Noémvrie, Noémbrie, *n. m.*, November.
nói, *pers. pron.*, we (see 5. 1. **a**).
nor (**nóur**), *n. m.*, **-i**, *pl.*, cloud.
nóră, *n. f.*, **nuróri**, *pl.*, daughter-in-law.
Nord, *n. m.*, North.
Nord-Vest, *n. m.*, North-West.
normál, -ă, *adj.*, **-i, -e**, *pl.*, normal.
noróc, *n. mix.*, **noroáce**, *pl.*, luck, good fortune, chance; **noroc-ós, -oásă**, *adj.*, **-óşi, -oáse**, *pl.*, lucky, fortunate.
noród, *n. mix.*, **noroáde**, *pl.*, people, nation.
nor-ói, *n. mix.*, **-oáie**, *pl.*, mud, mire.
nóstru, noástră, *poss. pron.*, our (see 5. 5).
nót-ă, *n. f.*, **-e**, *pl.*, note; remark; mark.
noţiún-e, *n. f.*, **-i**, *pl.*, idea, notion, conception.
nóu, -ă, *adj.*, **nói** (**nóue, nóuă**), *pl.*, new.
nóuă, *num.*, nine; *pers. pron.*, to us (see 5. 1. **a**).
nóulea (**al**), **nóua** (**a**), *ord. num.*, the ninth.
nóur, see **nor**.
Novác, *prop. n. m.* (person).
nu, *neg.*, no, not.
nuánţ-ă, *n. f.*, **-e**, *pl.*, shade.
nuc, *n. m.*, **-i**, *pl.*, walnut-tree; **núc-ă**, *n. f.*, **-i**, *pl.*, walnut.
nui-á, *n. f.*, **-éle**, *pl.*, rod, twig.
númai, *adv.*, only, but (see 8. 4. **i**).
núm-ăr, *n. mix.*, **-ere**, *pl.*, number; copy (of a newspaper).
numărá (**a**), **númăr, -át**, *v. tr.* I, to count.
núme, *n. mix.*, **núme**, *pl.*, name.
numerár, *n. m.*, ready cash.
num-í (**a**), *v. tr.* IV, **-ésc, -ít**, to name, to call; **a se numí**, *intr.*, to be called.
nún-tă, *n. f.*, **-ţi**, *pl.*, wedding.
nuntáş, *n. m.*, **-i**, *pl.*, wedding guest.

O

o, *pers. pron.*, her (see 5. 1. a).
oácheş, -ă (-e), *adj.*, **-i, -e**, *pl.*, dark, brown.
oáie, *n. f.*, **ói**, *pl.*, sheep.
oáră, *n. f. sg.*, in **întâia oáră**, *num.*, the first time; see **óri**.
oáre? *conj.*, isn't? indeed? (see 8. 4. g).
oarecáre, *indef. pron.*, someone, a certain (see 5. 9).
oarecé, *indef. pron.*, something (see 5. 9).
oáspe, *n. m.*, **-ţi**, *pl.*, guest.
oáz-ă, *n. f.*, **-e**, *pl.*, oasis.
obicéi, *n. mix.*, **-uri**, *pl.*, custom, use, rite.
obiéct, *n. mix.*, **-e**, *pl.*, object, thing, article.
oblăduír-e, *n. f.*, **-i**, *pl.*, rule, reign.
obligá (a), oblíg, -át, *v. tr.* I, to oblige, to compel.
obos-éală (obosálă), *n. f.*, **-éli**, *pl.*, fatigue, tiredness.
obrá-z, *n. m.*, **-ji**, *pl.*, cheek.
obráznic, -ă, *adj.*, **-i, -e**, *pl.*, shameless, cheeky.
óbşti-e (óbşte), *n. f.*, **-i**, *pl.*, community, commune.
ocá, *n. f.*, **-le**, *pl.*, capacity and weight measure, 4-8 lb.
oceán, *n. mix.*, **-e**, *pl.*, ocean.
ochelári, *n. m. pl.*, spectacles, glasses.
óchi (u), *n. m.*, **óchi**, *pl.*, eye.
ochişór, *n. m.*, **-i**, *pl.*, little eye.
ócn-ă, *n. f.*, **-e**, *pl.*, salt-mine; forced labour in salt-mines.
ocól, *n. mix.*, **ocoále**, *pl.*, enclosure; district; turning round.
ocroti-tór, -toáre, *adj.*, *n.*, **-tóri, -toáre**, *pl.*, protecting, protector.
Octómvrie, Octómbrie, *n. m.*, October.
ocup-á (a), ocúp, -át, *v. tr.* I, to occupy; to employ.
odátă, *adv.*, *num.*, once, one time; once (upon a time); **odátă ce**, *adv.*, once, since.
odíhn-ă, *n. f.*, **-e**, *pl.*, rest.
odihn-í (a), -ésc, -ít, *v. tr.* IV, to rest; **a se —**, *v. intr.*, to rest, to repose.
odinioáră, *adv.*, once, formerly.
oficiál, -ă, *adj.*, **-i, -e**, *pl.*, official.
ofíci-u, *n. mix.*, **-i**, *pl.*, office, function, service.
ofilí (a se), ofil-ésc, -ít, *v. intr.* IV, to wither, to fade away.
oghiál (ogheál) (*dial.*), *n. mix.*, **-uri**, *pl.*, quilt.
oglín-dă, *n. f.*, **-zi**, *pl.*, mirror, looking-glass.
oglind-í (a), -ésc, -ít, *v. tr.* IV, to reflect; **a se —**, to reflect one's image in a mirror.
oglingioár-ă, *n. f.*, **-e**, *pl.*, small mirror.
ogór, *n. mix.*, **ogoáre**, *pl.*, (cultivated) field.
ográdă, *n. f.*, **ográzi**, *pl.*, enclosure, courtyard.
ói! *interj.* = **ei** (see 9. 2).
olói, *n. mix.* (*dial.*), **-uri**, *pl.* = **uléi**, (vegetable) oil.
Olt, *prop. n. m.* (river).
Olténia, *prop. n. f.* (province).
om, *n. m.*, **oámeni**, *pl.*, man, human being.
omen-ésc, -eáscă, *adj.*, **-éşti**, *pl.*, human.
omení-e, *n. f.*, **-i**, *pl.*, decency, honour, honesty.
omór, *n. mix.*, **-uri**, *pl.*, murder, homicide.
omorî́ (a), omór, -ît, *v. tr.* IV, to kill, to murder.
onoáre, *n. f.*, honour.
onorár, *n. mix.*, **-e**, *pl.*, honorary; fee; salary.

opáiţ, *n. mix.*, **-e**, primitive tallow lamp used by peasants.
opál, *n. mix.*, **-e**, *pl.*, opal.
ópcin-ă, *n. f.*, **-e** (**-i**), *pl.*, ridge of a mountain.
óper-ă, *n. f.*, **-e**, *pl.*, work ; opera.
operáţi-e, *n. f.*, **-i**, *pl.*, operation (surgical) ; **operaţiún-e**, *n. f.*, **-i**, *pl.*, operation.
opínc-ă, *n. f.*, **-i**, *pl.*, peasant sandal.
opr-í (**a**), **-ésc**, **-ít**, *v. tr.* IV, to stop ; **a se** —, *v. intr.*
opt, *num.*, eight.
optimí-st, **-stă**, *adj.*, *n.*, **-şti**, **-ste**, *pl.*, optimistic ; optimist.
óptulea (**al**), *m.*, **ópta** (**a**), *f.*, the eighth.
opú-s, **-să**, *adj.*, **-şi**, **-se**, *pl.*, opposite ; contrary.
ór-ă, *n. f.*, **-e**, *pl.*, hour.
Orádea-Máre, *prop. n. f.* (town).
oráş, *n. mix.*, **-e**, *pl.*, town.
orb, **oárbă**, *adj.*, **órbi**, **oárbe**, *pl.*, blind.
orbéşte, *adv.*, blindly.
oréz, *n. m.*, rice.
organisáţi-e, *n. f.*, **-i**, *pl.*, organization.
óri, *n. f. pl.*, in **de două ori**, *num.*, twice ; *conj.*, or (see 8. 4. **a**, **i**).
oricắnd, *adv.*, any time.
oricáre, **orişicáre**, *indef. pron.*, whoever (see 5. 9).
oricắt, *indef. pron.*, *adv.*, however much (see 5. 9).
oricé, **orişicé**, *indef. pron.*, whatever (see 5. 9).
oricíne, **orişicíne**, *indef. pron.*, whoever (see 5. 9).
oricúm, *conj.*, anyhow, however ; *adv.*, in whatever manner.
oriént, *n. mix.* (**-uri**, *pl.*), East, Orient.
originál, **-ă**, *adj.*, original.
orígin-e, *n. f.*, **-i**, *pl.*, origin, source.
oriúnde, *adv.*, *conj.*, wherever.
orizónt, *n. mix.*, **-uri**, *pl.*, horizon.
ortodó-x, **-xă**, *adj.*, **-cşi**, **-xe**, *pl.*, orthodox.
ortodoxísm, *n. mix.*, **-e**, *pl.*, orthodoxy.
ortomán (**iortomán**), **-ă**, *adj.*, *n.*, **-i**, **-e**, *pl.*, brave, valiant.
os, *n. mix.*, **oáse**, *pl.*, bone.
osắnd-ă, *n. f.*, **-e**, *pl.*, condemnation, punishment.
osând-í (**a**), **-ésc**, **-ít**, *v. tr.* IV, to condemn, to sentence.
Óslea, *prop. n. f.* (mountain).
ospắţ, *n. mix.*, **ospéţe**, *pl.*, feast, entertainment.
ospăt-á (**a**), **-éz**, **-át**, *v. tr.*, *intr.* I, to host, to entertain, to treat; to feast.
osten-í (**a**), **-ésc**, **-ít**, *v. tr.* IV, to tire, to fatigue ; **a se** —, *intr. refl.*, to get tired.
oştír-e, *n. f.*, **-i**, *pl.*, army, host.
ostróv, *n. mix.*, **ostroáve**, *pl.*, isle (in a river).
otráv-ă, *n. f.*, **-uri**, *pl.*, poison, venom.
otrăv-í (**a**), **-ésc**, **-ít**, *v. tr.* IV, to poison.
óu, *n. mix.*, **-ă** (**-e**), egg.
ouá (**a**), **óu**, **ouát**, *v. tr.*, *intr.* I, to lay eggs ; **a se** —, *intr.*

P

păcát, *n. mix.*, **-e**, *pl.*, sin.
páce, *n. f.*, **păci**, *pl.*, peace.
pachét, *n. mix.*, **-e**, *pl.*, parcel.
paciént, *n. m.*, **paciénţi**, *pl.*, patient.
pădurár, *n. m.*, **-i**, *pl.*, wood-keeper, forester, forest-ranger, gamekeeper.
pădúr-e, *n. f.*, **-i**, *pl.*, wood, forest.
pădur-ós, **-oásă**, *adj.*, **-óşi**, **-oáse**, *pl.*, woody, wooded.

pâgub-ă, *n. f.*, **-e**, *pl.*, loss, harm.
păgub-í (**a**), **-ésc**, **-ít**, *v. tr.*, *intr.*, to lose.
păhár, *n. mix.*, **-e**, *pl.*, cup, goblet.
pái, *n. mix.*, **-e**, *pl.*, straw; **acoperit cu paie**, thatched.
păi=**apói**.
pấin-e (**pấne**), *n. f.*, **-i**, *pl.*, bread, loaf.
pájişt-e, *n. f.*, **-i**, *pl.*, lawn, grass plot.
paláncă, *n. f.*, **palănci**, *pl.*, **a face palancă**, to lay (flat), lodge (the corn).
pălărí-e, *n. f.*, **-i**, *pl.*, hat.
palát, *n. mix.*, **-e**, *pl.*, palace.
pâlc, *n. mix.*, **-uri**, *pl.*, crowd, troupe, band.
păl-í (**a**), **-ésc**, **-ít**, *v. tr.*, *intr.* IV, to hit (*dial.*); to become pale.
pálmă, *n. f.*, **pálme** (**pălmi**), *pl.*, palm, hand (measure).
páltin, *n. m.*, **-i**, *pl.*, plane-tree.
păltináş, *n. m. dim.*, **-i**, *pl.*, maple-tree (*Acer pseudo-platanus*).
pămấnt, *n. mix.*, **-uri**, *pl.*, earth, soil, land.
pánă, *n. f.*, **páne**, *pl.*, motor-defect, puncture.
pánă, *n. f.*, **péne**, *pl.*, feather.
pấnă, *adv.*, **pấnă la**, *prep.*, till, until, to; **până ce**, *adv.*, until.
pấnd-ă, *n. f.* (**-e**, *pl.*), watch, wait, ambuscade.
pând-í (**a**), **-ésc**, **-ít**, *v. tr.* IV, to watch, to be in wait for.
pấne, see **pâine**.
pângăr-í (**a**), **-ésc**, **-ít**, *v. tr.* IV, to desecrate; to pollute; to soil.
pantalóni, *n. m. pl.*, trousers.
pấntece, *n. mix.* (**pấntece**, *pl.*), belly; abdomen.
pấnur-ă, *n. f.*, **-i**, *pl.*, wool cloth produced by the peasants; fine wool prepared for spinning.
pấnză, *n. f.*, linen; **pânzéturi**, *pl.*, kinds of linen; **pấnze**, *pl.*, sails.
Páp-ă, *n. m.*, **-i**, *pl.*, Pope.
pápură, *n. f.*, rush.
păr, *n. m.*, **péri**, *pl.*, hair; pear-tree.
pará, *n. f.*, **-ua**, *art.*, **-le**, *pl.*, coin, money.
páră, *n. f.*, **pére**, *pl.*, pear.
parábol-ă, *n. f.*, **-e**, *pl.*, parable; parabola.
pârâí (**a**), **-ésc**, **-t**, *v. intr.* IV, to crackle, to crepitate.
parantéz-ă, *n. f.*, **-e**, *pl.*, bracket.
părăs-í (**a**), **-ésc**, **-ít**, *v. tr.* IV, to abandon, to leave.
pârấu, **pârấu**, **părấu**, *n. mix.*, **pâráie**, *pl.*, brook, stream.
pârăuáş, *n. mix.*, **-e**, *pl.*, small stream.
parc, *n. mix.*, **-uri**, *pl.*, park.
párcă, *conj.*, as if.
pár'că=**parcă**.
pârcăláb, *n. m.*, **-i**, *pl.*, prefect; governor; commander of a fortification.
păreá (**a**), **par**, **părút**, *v. intr.* II, to seem, to appear (see 6. 4. **c**).
paréch-e (**peréche**), *n. f.*, **-i**, *pl.*, pair, couple.
părér-e, *n. f.*, **-i**, *pl.*, opinion.
păré-te (**peré-te**), *n. m.*, **-ţi**, *pl.*, wall.
părín-te, *n. m.*, **-ţi**, *pl.*, parent; priest.
París, *prop. n. m.*, Paris (town).
pârl-í (**a**), **-ésc**, **-ít**, *v. tr.* IV, to singe, to sear; **pârlitúr-ă**, *n. f.*, **-i**, *pl.*, singeing.
pârlóg, *n. m.* (**pârloágă**, *n. f.*) (**pârlóguri**, *pl.*), **pârloáge**, *pl.*, fallow ground, untilled ground.
párte, *n. f.*, **părţi**, *pl.*, part, share, deal, portion.
părtic-ícă, *n. f.*, **-éle**, *pl.*, small part.

pas, *n. m.*, **páşi**, *pl.*, step, pace; defile; **pásuri**, *pl.*, defiles.
păsá (a), **pas**, **păsát**, *v. intr.* I; **îmi pásă**, I care for, I am concerned.
pásăre (**pásere**), *n. f.* **păsări** (**pásări, páseri**), *pl.*, bird.
păsăr-ícă, *n. f.*, **-éle**, *pl.*, little bird.
păscăt-oáre, *n. f.*, **-óri**, *pl.*, pasture, pasturage.
păş-í (a), **-ésc**, **-ít**, *v. intr.* IV, to pace, to go slowly.
Páşti, *n. f. pl.*, **Páşte**, *n. m. sg.*, Easter.
păstr-á (a), **-éz**, **-át**, *v. tr.* I, to preserve, to keep, to save.
păstrav, *n. m.*, **-i**, *pl.*, trout.
pat, *n. mix.*, **-uri**, *pl.*, bed.
păt-á (a), **-éz**, **-át**, *v. tr.* I, to spot, to stain.
pátă, *n. f.*, **péte**, *pl.*, stain, spot.
păţ-í (a), **-ésc**, **-ít**, *v. intr.* IV, to endure; to meet with; to experience.
pătrár, *n. mix.*, **-e**, *pl.*, quarter.
patriarcál (**patriarhál**), **-ă**, *adj.*, **-i**, **-e**, *pl.*, patriarchal.
pátri-e, *n. f.*, **-i**, *pl.*, fatherland, country.
pătrím-e, *n. f.*, **-i**, *pl.*, fourth.
patriotísm, *n. mix.*, **-e**, *pl.*, patriotism.
patrón, *n. m.*, **-i**, *pl.*, master, owner, defender, protector.
pátru, *num.*, four.
pátrulea (**al**), *m.* **pátra** (**a**), *f.*, the fourth.
pătrúnde (a), **pătrúnd**, **pătrúns**, *v. intr.* III, to penetrate, to pierce; to permeate; to enter into.
páuz-ă, *n. f.*, **-e**, *pl.*, pause; suspension.
pázǎ, *n. f.*, watching, ward, guard.
păz-í (a), **-ésc**, **-ít**, *v. tr.* IV, to guard, to watch; **a se —**, *intr.*, to be on one's guard.
pe, *prep.*, on, upon, over.
peánă, *n. f.*, **péne**, *pl.*, feather (see **pánă**).
peír-e, *n. f.*, **-i**, *pl.*, ruin, disaster.
peisáj, *n. mix.*, **-e**, *pl.*, landscape.
péla, *prep.*, at, about.
pelicán, *n. m.*, **-i**, *pl.*, pelican.
pelín, *n. m.*, wormwood, absinthium (*Artemisia absinthium*).
pe'ndeléte, *adv.*, see **îndelete**.
pens, *n. m.*, **pénşi**, *pl.*, penny.
péntru, *prep.*, for, on account of, for the sake of; to, towards.
pentrucă, *conj.*, because, since.
pentrucé, *adv.*, why, what for.
pépen-e, *n. m.*, **-i**, *pl.*, melon; (*dial.* Mold.), cucumber.
peréche, see **păréche**.
peréte, see **păréte**.
pergamént, *n. mix.*, **-e**, *pl.*, parchment.
perí (a), see **pierí** (a).
péri-e, *n. f.*, **-i**, *pl.*, brush.
perişór, *n. m. dim.*, **-i**, *pl.* (little) hair.
pérn-ă (**périnǎ**), *n. f.*, **-e**, *pl.*, pillow, cushion.
persián, **-ă**, *adj.*, **persiéni**, **persiéne** (**persiáne**), *pl.*, Persian.
personál, **-ă**, *adj.*, **-i**, **-e**, *pl.*, personal, in person; *n. m.*, staff; slow train.
perspectív-ă, *n. f.*, **-e**, *pl.*, perspective, prospect, view, vista.
pescár, *n. m.*, **-i**, *pl.*, fisher.
péste, *prep.*, over, on, upon, above.
péşt-e, *n. m.*, **-i**, *pl.*, fish.
péşter-ă, *n. f.*, **-e**, *pl.*, grotto, burrow.
pétec, *n. mix.*, **-e**, *pl.*, patch, bit, morsel.
Pétrea, *prop. n.*, Peter.

petréc-e (a), petréc, -út, *v. intr., tr.*, to pass; to amuse oneself; to accompany; **a se** —, to happen.
petról, *n. m.*, oil (mineral), paraffin oil.
piáţă, *n. f.*, **piéţe,** *pl.*, market, public place.
piátră, *m. f.*, **piétre,** *pl.*, stone.
pic! *interj.*, drip!
picá (a), pic, -át, *v. intr.* I, to drop, to fall; to die (of cattle).
picătúr-ă, *n. f.*, **-i,** *pl.*, drop.
piciór, *n. mix.*, **picioáre,** *pl.*, foot.
pictúr-ă, *n. f.*, **-i,** *pl.*, picture, painting.
picurá (a), pícur, -át, *v. tr., intr.* I, to drop, to trickle down; to drizzle.
piéle, *n. f.*, **piéi,** *pl.*, skin, hide; fur.
piépt, *n. mix.*, **-uri,** *pl.*, breast, chest, bosom.
pieptăná (a), piéptăn, -át, *v. tr.* I, to comb.
piépten-e, *n. m.*, **-i,** *pl.*, comb.
piérde (a), piérd, -út, *v. tr.* III, to lose.
pierí (a), piér, -ít, *v. intr.* IV, to perish; to die; to disappear.
piés-ă, *n. f.*, **-e,** *pl.*, piece, play.
piet-áte, *n. f.*, **-ắţi,** *pl.*, piety.
pietr-ós, -oásă, *adj.*, **-óşi, -oáse,** *pl.*, stony.
píld-ă, *n. f.*, **-e,** *pl.*, example; parabola.
p'în (*dial.*)=**prin.**
pipăí (a), -ésc, -ít, *v. tr.* IV, to touch, to feel, to grope.
Pirineí, *prop. n. m. pl.*, Pyrenees.
pirot-eálă, *n. f.*, **-éli,** *pl.*, doze, slumber.
pisíc-ă, *n. f.*, **-i,** *pl.*, cat.
pitíc, *n. m.*, **-i,** *pl.*, dwarf.
pitpalác! *interj.* (quail-call, cry of the quail).
pitulá (a se), mă pituléz, pitulát, *v. intr.* I, to hide, to conceal.
pitul-í (a se), mă pitulésc, -ít, *v. intr.* IV, to hide, to conceal oneself.
píu-ă, *n. m.*, **-e,** *pl.*, fulling-mill; mortar; cloth-mill.
plac, *n.*, pleasure, liking; **dúpă búnul plac,** the own way.
plăceá (a), plac, plăcút, *v. intr.* II, to please, to like (see 6. 4. **c**).
plăcú-t, -tă, *adj.*, **-ţi, -te,** *pl.*, agreeable, pleasant.
plăcér-e, *n. f.*, **-i,** *pl.*, pleasure, joy.
plai, *n. mix.*, **-uri,** *pl.*, highland, plain mountain ridge, flat terrain for pasture in the mountains.
plấnge (a), plâng, plâns, *v. tr., intr.* III, to cry, to weep; to lament; **a se** —, to complain.
plátă, *n. f.*, **plắţi,** *pl.*, payment, pay.
plăt-í (a), -ésc, -ít, *v. tr., intr.* IV, to pay.
platóu, *n. mix.*, **-ri,** *pl.*, plateau.
plăvíţ, -ă, *adj.*, straw-coloured, fair, light-coloured.
pleátă, *n. f.*, **pléte,** *pl.*, plait, hair.
plecá (a), plec, plecát, *v. tr., intr.* I, to go, to depart, to set out; to bow, to low, to bend; **a se** —, *intr. refl.*
Pleş, *prop. n. m.* (mountain).
plesn-í (a), -ésc, -ít, *v. tr., intr.* IV, to burst, to crack, to split.
plet-ós, -oásă, *adj.*, **-óşi, -oáse,** *pl.*, long-haired; **sálcie pletoásă,** weeping willow.
plimbá (a), plimb, -át, *v. tr.* I, to take for a walk, to lead about; **a se** —, to walk about.
plimbáre, *n. f.*, **plimbắri,** *pl.*, walk, promenade.
plin, -ă, *adj.*, **-i, -e,** *pl.*, full.

plin-áer, open-air.
ploáie, *n. f.*, **plói**, *pl.*, rain.
plop, *n. m.*, **-i**, *pl.*, poplar.
plug, *n. mix.*, **-uri**, plough.
plumb, *n. m.*, lead; **plúmbi**, *pl.*, bullets.
plus, *adv.*, plus.
plút-ă, *n. f.*, **-e**, *pl.*, raft; cork; poplar-tree (*populus alba v. pyramidalis*).
plutáş, *n. m.*, **-i**, *pl.*, raftsman.
plut-í (a), **-ésc**, **-ít**, *v. intr.* IV, to float, to swim.
poál-ă, *n. f.*, **-e**, *pl.*, lap; flap of a coat; **poálele múnţilor**, foot of the mountain.
poártă, *n. f.*, **pórţi**, *pl.*, gate.
poáte, *adv.*, perhaps.
pócnet, *n. nix*, **-e**, *pl.*, crack, clap.
pod, *n. mix.*, **-uri**, *pl.*, bridge.
pode-álă, *n. f.*, **-éle**, *pl.*, floor.
podgóri-e, *n. f.*, **-i**, *pl.*, vineyard.
podíş, *n. mix.*, **-uri**, *pl.*, plateau, highland.
podoáb-ă, *n. f.*, **-e**, *pl.*, ornament, decoration, attire.
poesí-e, *n. f.*, **-i**, *pl.*, poem, poetry.
poé-t, *n. m.*, **-ţi**, *pl.*, poet.
póft-ă, *n. f.*, **-e**, *pl.*, desire.
poft-í (a), **-ésc**, **-ít**, *v. tr.* IV, to wish for, to desire; to invite.
poiánă, *n. f.*, **poiéni (poiéne)**, *pl.*, clearing.
pol, *n. mix.*, **-uri**, *pl.*, pole (North, etc.); **póli**, *pl.*, sovereign (coin).
polár, **-ă**, *adj.*, **-i**, **-e**, *pl.*, polar.
polimár-i (pălimár), *n. mix.*, **-e**, *pl.*, gallery, balcony.
polítică, *n. f.*, **-i**, *pl.*, politics, policy; **polític**, **-ă**, *adj.*, **-i**, **-e**, *pl.*, political.
póliţ-ă, *n. f.*, **-e**, *pl.*, bill of exchange; shelf.
Polónia, *n. f.*, Poland.
pom, *n. m.*, **-i**, *pl.*, tree (fruit-bearing).
pománă, *n. f.*, **poméni**, *pl.*, alms; charity.
póp-ă, *n. m.*, **-i**, *pl.*, priest.
po-pór, *n. mix.*, **-poáre**, *pl.*, people, folk.
popul-á (a), **-éz**, **-át**, *v. tr.* I, to populate, to people.
populár, **-ă**, *adj.*, **-i**, **-e**, *pl.*, popular, of the people; **cântec** —, folk-story.
populáţi-e, *n. f.*, **-i**, *pl.*, population.
popuş-ói, *n. mix.*, maize; **-oáie**, *pl.*, maize fields.
porc, *n. m.*, **-i**, *pl.*, pig.
porcán, *n. m.*, **-i**, *pl.*, pig, hog.
poroncí (a), see **poruncí (a)**.
port, *n. mix.*, **-uri**, *pl.*, dress, wear; harbour, port.
portrét, *n. mix.*, **-e**, *pl.*, portrait, picture.
Portugália, *prop. n. f.*, Portugal.
Portughéz, *prop. n. m.*, **-i**, *pl.*, Portuguese.
porúmb, *n. m.*, maize, sweet-corn; **porúmb**, *n. m.*, **-i**, *pl.*, pigeon, dove.
porunc-í (a), **-ésc**, **-ít**, *v. intr.* IV, to order, to command.
posíbil, **-ă**, *adj.*, **-i**, **-e**, *pl.*, possible.
posomorí-t, **-tă**, *adj.*, **-ţi**, **-te**, *pl.*, sulky, sullen.
póşt-ă, *n. f.*, **-e**, *pl.*, post office.
potcov-í (a), **-ésc**, **-ít**, *v. tr.* IV, to shoe (a horse).
potol-í (a), **-ésc**, **-ít**, *v. tr.* IV, to calm, to appease, to quench.
potrívă, *n. f.*, conformity, equality; **de o** —, equally.
potriv-í (a), **-ésc**, **-ít**, to fit to, to adapt; to arrange, to equal; **a se** —, to fit, to be equal.
potriví-t, **-tă**, *adj.*, **-ţi**, **-te**, *pl.*, suitable, equal.
pováră, *n. f.*, **povéri**, *pl.*, load, burden.

povăţuí (a), -ésc, -t, *v. tr., intr.* IV, to give advice, to counsel, to lead.
pové-ste, *n. f.*, **-şti**, *pl.*, tale, fairy tale, story.
povest-í (a), -ésc, -ít, *v. tr.* IV, to tell, to narrate, to relate.
pozíţi-e, *n. f.*, **-i**, *pl.*, position, situation.
prád-ă, *n. f.*, **prăzi**, *pl.*, prey; booty, plunder.
prag, *n. mix.*, **-uri**, *pl.*, threshold, door-sill.
Práhova, *prop. n.* (river).
prăjín-ă, *n. f.*, **-i**, *pl.*, perch, pole; measure of approximately 6-7 m.
prânz, *n. mix.*, **-uri**, noon; lunch.
prăpădéni-e, *n. f.*, **-i**, *pl.*, disaster, extermination.
prăpăd-í (a), -ésc, -it, *v. tr.* IV, to lose; to ruin, to destroy; **a se —**, to perish.
prăpăsti-ós, -oásă, *adj.*, **-óşi, -oáse**, *pl.*, steep, with precipices.
prăvălí-e, *n. f.*, **-i**, *pl.*, shop, store.
preá, *adv.*, too; very.
preájm-ă, *n. f.*, (environs), see **în preájma, împreájma**.
precúm, *adv.*, *conj.*, as, so as.
predomin-á (a), predomín(-éz), -át, *v. tr., intr.* I, to predominate, to prevail.
predoslóvi-e, *n. f.*, **-i**, *pl.* (*archaic*), preface.
prefáce (a), prefác, prefăcút, *v. tr.* III, to transform, to remake; to alter; **a se —**, to feign, to disguise oneself; **prefácer-e**, *n. f.*, **-i**, *pl.*, transformation, change, alteration.
preferá (a), prefér, -át, *v. tr.* I, to prefer.
pregăt-í (a), -ésc, -ít, *v. tr.* IV, to prepare, to make ready.
prelárg, -ă, *adj.*, *n.*, **-i**, *pl.*, wide, broad; wideness, extension.
prelung-í (a), -ésc, -ít, *v. tr.* IV, to prolong, to protract; to lengthen; **prelúng, -ă**, *adj.*, **-i**, *pl.*, long, protracted.
prémi-u, *n. mix.*, **-i**, *pl.*, reward, recompense.
préo-t (preót), *n. m.*, **-ţi**, *pl.*, priest.
prépeliţ-ă (prepelíţă), *n. f.*, **-e**, *pl.*, quail (*Perdrix coturnix*).
prepúne (a), prepún, prepús, *v. tr.* III, to suspect, presuppose.
présur-ă, *n. f.*, **-i**, *pl.*, yellow-hammer, bunting (*Emberiza citrinella*).
preţ, *n. mix.*, **-uri**, *pl.*, price.
pretá (a se), mă pret-éz, -át, *v. intr.* I, to engage in.
preţi-ós, -oásă, *adj.*, **-óşi, -oáse** *pl.*, precious, costly.
pretutíndeni, *adv.*, everywhere.
prevesti-tór, -toáre, *adj.*, *n.*, **-tóri, -toáre**, *pl.*, foreteller.
prezént, -ă, *adj.*, **-ţi, -te**, *pl.*, present.
pribeág, -ă, *adj.*, **pribég-i, -e**, *pl.*, homeless, refugee.
pribegír-e, *n. f.*, **-i**, *pl.*, wondering.
pricépe (a), pricép, -út, *v. tr., intr.* III, to understand, to conceive; **a se —**, to be skilful in, to be aware of; **pricepú-t, -tă**, *adj.*, **-ţi, -te**, *pl.*, skilled, intelligent.
prícin-ă (pricínă), *n. f.*, **-i**, *pl.*, cause, reason; quarrel, dispute.
priélnic, -ă, *adj.*, **-i, -e**, *pl.*, favourable.
priéten, *n. m.*, **-i**, *pl.*, friend.
priéten-ă, *n. f.*, **-e**, *pl.*, lady friend.
primár, *n. m.*, **-i**, *pl.*, mayor, burgomaster; *adj.*, primary.

primăv-áră, *n. f.*, **-éri**, *pl.*, spring.
priméjdi-e, *n. f.*, **-i**, *pl.*, danger.
prim-í (a), **-ésc**, **-ít**, *v. tr.* IV, to receive, to get, to obtain.
primitív, **-ă**, *adj.*, **-i**, **-e**, *pl.*, primitive, native.
prímul, *m.*, **príma**, *f.*, **prímii**, **prímele**, *pl.*, *num.*, *adj.*, the first.
prin, *prep.*, through, across.
principál, **-ă**, *adj.*, **-i**, **-e**, *pl.*, principal, chief.
principát, *n. mix.*, **-e**, *pl.*, principality.
prínde (a), **prin-d**, **-s**, *v. tr.* III, to catch.
prinprejúr, *adv.*, around; **prinprejúrul**, *prep.*, round.
príntre, *prep.*, among, between, amongst (see 8. 3, note 1).
príntru, *prep.*, through, by (see 8. 3, note 1).
prip-í (a), **-ésc**, **-ít**, *v. tr.* IV, to hasten; **a se —**, to haste, to speed, to hurry.
prisós, *n. mix.*, **-uri**, *pl.*, surplus, abundance; **de —**, *adv.*, superfluous, in vain.
prísp-ă, *n. f.*, **-e**, *pl.*, earthen bench round a peasant house.
privélişt-e, *n. f.*, **-i**, *pl.*, view, sight, vista.
priv-í (a), **-ésc**, **-ít**, *v. intr.* IV, to regard, to look, to view; **mă privéşte**, it is my business; **nu mă privéşte**, I don't care.
privír-e, *n. f.*, **-i**, *pl.*, look, view.
privighit-oáre, *n. f.*, **-óri**, *pl.*, nightingale.
probábil, **-ă**, *adj.*, **-i**, **-e**, *pl.*, probable.
problém-ă, *n. f.*, **-e**, *pl.*, problem.
procedé-u, *n. mix.*, **-ie**, *pl.*, proceeding, procedure.
procént, *n. mix.*, **-e**, *pl.*, percentage, interest.
procés, *n. mix.*, **-e**, *pl.*, process, lawsuit, action.
proclamá (a), **proclám**, **-át**, *v. tr.* I, to proclaim.
Procóv, *prop. n. m.* (hermitage).
procurá (a), **procúr**, **-át**, *v. tr.* I, to procure, to provide.
prodúce (a), **prodúc**, **prodús**, *v. tr.* III, to produce, to yield.
profesór, *n. m.*, **-i**, *pl.*, professor.
profíl, *n. mix.*, **-uri**, *pl.*, profile, side-face.
profil-á (a), **-éz**, **-át**, *v. tr.* I, to profile.
progrés, *n. mix.*, **-e**, *pl.*, progress.
prohód, *n. mix.*, **-uri**, *pl.*, burial, funeral.
promíte (a), **promít**, **promís**, *v. tr.* III, to promise.
promov-á (a), **-éz**, **-át**, *v. tr.* I, to promote.
propietár, *n. m.*, **-i**, *pl.*, proprietor, landlord.
propórţi-e, *n. f.*, **-i**, *pl.*, proportion.
propozíţi-e (propoziţiún-e), *n. f.*, **-i**, *pl.*, proposition; proposal; promise.
própri-u, **-e**, *adj.*, **-i**, *pl.*, proper; own.
pros-óp, *n. mix.*, **-oápe**, *pl.*, towel.
prost, **proástă**, *adj.*, **próşti**, **proáste**, *pl.*, stupid; common, ordinary; **prostím-e**, *n. f.*, **-i**, *pl.*, populace, mob, rabble; **prostí-e**, *n. f.*, **-i**, *pl.*, stupidity, nonsense.
provení (a), **provín**, **provenít**, *v. intr.* IV, to proceed, to arise from, to originate from.
provínci-e, *n. f.*, **-i**, *pl.*, province.
prun, *n. m.*, **-i**, *pl.*, plum-tree; **prún-ă**, *n. f.*, **-e**, *pl.*, plum.
prundíş, *n. mix.*, **-uri**, *pl.*, gravel.
Prut, *n. m.*, Pruth.
psihológic, **-ă**, *adj.*, **-i**, **-e**, *pl.*, psychological.

puf, *n. mix.* (**-uri**, *pl.*), down.
puh-ói, *n. mix.*, **-oáie**, *pl.*, inundation, rushing and roaring waters.
púi(u), *n. m.*, **pui**, *pl.*, chicken; young animal.
puls, *n. mix.*, **-uri**, *pl.*, pulse.
punct, *n. mix.*, **-e**, *pl.*, point, dot, full stop.
púne (a), **pun**, **pus**, *v. tr.* III, to put, to lay, to place.
púnte, *n. f.*, **púnţi**, *pl.*, bridge (small); deck (of a ship).
purcé-l, *n. m.*, **-i**, *pl.*, young pig, farrow.
púrice, *n. m.*, **-i**, *pl.*, flea.
purit-áte, *n. f.*, **-ắţi**, *pl.*, purity, clearness.
purtá (a), **port**, **purtát**, *v. tr.* I, to wear, to carry; **a se purta**, to behave.
purt-áre, *n. f.*, **-ắri**, *pl.*, behaviour.
púş-că, *n. f.*, **-ti**, *pl.*, gun, rifle.
puşcáş, *n. m.*, **-i**, *pl.*, shooter, fusilier.
pustíu, *n. mix.*, **-ri**, *pl.*, desert, wilderness; **pustí-u**, **-e**, *adj.*, **-i**, *pl.*, desert; **pustí-e**, *n. f.*, **-i**, *pl.*, wilderness; **pustiet-áte**, *n. f.*, **-ắţi**, *pl.*, wilderness.
puteá (a), **pot**, **putút**, *v. intr.*, to be able (may, can); **a se** —, to be possible.
putér-e, *n. f.*, **-i**, *pl.*, strength, power, force.
puţín, **-ă**, *adj.*, **-i**, **-e**, *pl.*, little, few; **puţintél**, **puţintícă**, *adj. dim.*, *adv.*, a little.
putinéi, *n. m.*, **putinícă**, *n. f.*, **putinéle**, *pl.*, small barrel.

R

răbdá (a), **răbd (rabd)**, **-át**, *v. tr.*, *intr.*, to endure, to suffer, to bear.

răbdár-e, *n. f.*, **răbdắri**, *pl.*, patience, endurance, sufferance.
răc-í (a), **-ésc**, **-ít**, *v. tr.*, *intr.* IV, to cool, to chill; to catch a cold.
răcoáre, *n. f.*, **răcóri**, *pl.*, freshness, coolness.
răcor-í (a), **-ésc**, **-ít**, *v. tr.* IV, to refresh, to cool; **a se** —, to get cold; to take fresh air.
răcor-ós, **-oásă**, *adj.*, refreshing, fresh; coolly.
rădăcín-ă, *n. f.*, **-i**, *pl.*, root.
rấde (a), **râd**, **râs**, *v. tr.* III, to laugh (see 6. 7).
rădicá (a) (ridicá, râdicá), **rădíc**, **-át**, *v. tr.* I, to lift; to elevate, to erect; to pick up; **rădic-áre (râdicáre)**, *n. f.*, **-ắri**, *pl.*, lifting, raising.
răgáz, *n. mix.*, **-uri**, *pl.*, rest, respite, delay.
răguş-í (a), **-ésc**, **-ít**, *v. intr.* IV, to become hoarse; **răguşí-t**, **-tă**, *adj.*, **-ţi**, **-te**, *pl.*, hoarse.
rái, *n. mix.* (**-uri**, *pl.*), paradise, heaven.
rămás, *n. mix.*, remaining; **a-şi luá rămás bun**, to take leave, to wish farewell.
rámur-ă, *n. f.*, **-i**, *pl.*, branch, twig, bough.
rămure-á, *n. f.*, **-le**, *pl.*, little branch, twig, bough.
rând, *n. mix.*, **-uri**, *pl.*, row, line; succession; **un rând de haine**, a suit of clothes; **de-a rândul**, in succession.
rândun-ícă (rânduneá), *n. f.*, **-éle (-íci)**, *pl.*, swallow.
răn-í (a), **-ésc**, **-ít**, *v. tr.* IV, to wound; to injure.
răpaus-á (a) (răposá), **-éz**, **-át**, *v. intr.* I, to decease, to die.
răpezí (a), see **repezí (a)**.

răp-í (a), **-ésc**, **-ít**, *v. tr.* IV, to ravish, to plunder, to take away.
rapórt, *n. mix.*, report ; **rapoárte**, *pl.*, reports ; **rapórturi**, *pl.*, relations.
răposát, see **răpắusat**, late (deceased).
Rarắu, *prop. n. m.* (mountain).
răr-í (a), **-ésc**, **-ít**, *v. tr.* IV, to rarefy ; **a se** —, to get rare.
ras, **-ă**, *adj.*, **ráşi**, **ráse**, *pl.*, shaved ; flat ; **în rásul** (*prep.*) **pămắntului**, touching the earth (see 8. 3).
râs, *n. mix.*, **-uri**, *pl.*, laughing, laughter.
râ-s, *n. m.*, **-şi**, *pl.*, lynx.
răsărí (a), **răsár**, **răsărít**, *v. intr.* IV, to germinate, to shoot ; to rise (the sun), to dawn.
răsărít, *n. m.*, **-uri**, *pl.*, sunrising, east.
răsărit-eán, **-eánă**, *adj.*, **-éni**, **-éne**, *pl.*, Eastern.
răsbáte (a), **răsbát**, **răsbătút**, *v. intr.*, *tr.* III, to penetrate ; to traverse.
răsbói (**răzbóiu**), *n. mix.*, **-boáie**, *pl.*, war.
răsbuná (a), **răsbún**, **-át**, *v. tr.*, to revenge ; **a se** —, *intr.*, to take revenge for.
răsfirá (a), see **resfirá** (a).
răsgâiá (a), see **răzgâiá** (a).
răsînţelége (a), **răsînţelég**, **răsînţelés**, *v. tr.* III, to quite understand, to understand very well.
răsl-éţ, **-eáţă**, *adj.*, **-éţi**, **-éţe**, *pl.*, dispersed ; asunder ; scarce.
râşn-í (a), **-ésc**, **-ít**, *v. tr.* IV, to grind in a handmill.
râşniţ-ă, **-e**, *n. f.*, handmill.
răsplăt-í, **-ésc**, **-ít**, *v. tr.* IV, to recompense, to reward.
răspúnde (a), **răspún-d**, **-s**, *v. intr.* III, to answer, to reply.
răspúnder-e, *n. f.*, **-i**, *pl.*, responsibility.
răspúns, *n. mix.*, **-uri**, *pl.*, answer, reply.
răsputér-e, *n. f.*, **-i**, *pl.* (all) power, force, strength.
răst-í (a se), **mă răstésc**, **-ít**, *v. intr.* IV, to speak roughly, to snub someone.
răsturná (a), **răstórn**, **răsturnát**, *v. tr.* I, to overthrow.
răsuc-í (a), **-ésc**, **-ít**, *v. tr.* IV, to twist, to twine ; **a se** —, to turn.
răsufl-á (a), **-u**, **-át**, *v. intr.* I, to breathe, to respire, to inhale ; **răsufl-áre**, *n. f.*, **-ắri**, *pl.*, breath, respiration.
răsuná (a), **răsún**, **-át**, *v. intr.* I, to sound, to resound.
ráţ-ă, *n. f.*, **-e** (**réţe**), *pl.*, duck.
rătăc-í (a), **-ésc**, **-ít**, *v. intr.* IV, to err ; to go astray ; to stroll.
raţionál, **-ă**, *adj.*, **-i**, **-e**, *pl.*, rational, reasonable.
rắu, **reá**, *adj.*, **rắi**, **réle**, *pl.*, bad, wicked.
rắu, *n. mix.*, **-ri**, *pl.*, river.
râuléţ, *n. mix.*, **-e**, *pl.*, brook, stream.
răutăci-ós, **-oásă**, *adj.*, **-óşi**, **-oáse**, *pl.*, wicked, malicious.
răut-áte, *n. f.*, **ắţi**, *pl.*, wickedness.
ráz-ă, *n. f.*, **-e**, *pl.*, beam, ray ; radius.
răzắş (**răzéş**), *n. m.*, **-i**, *pl.*, possessor of a freehold estate ; yeoman ; free peasant.
răzbói (u), see **răsbói**.
răzbuná (a), see **răsbuna** (a).
răzgâi-á (a), **-éz**, **-át**, *v. tr.* II, to spoil, wheedle.
răzim-á (**răzemá**, **rezemá**), **rázim**, **-át**, *v. tr.* I, to lean, to prop up, to support.
răzléţ, see **răsléţ**.

reácţi-e, *n. f.*, **-i**, *pl.*, reaction.
reamint-í (a), **-ésc**, **-ít**, *v. tr.* IV, to remind; **a-şi — ceva**, to remember something.
réce, *adj.*, **-i**, *pl.*, cold, cool.
recét-ă, *n. f.*, **-e**, *pl.*, prescription.
recipís-ă, *n. f.*, **-e**, *pl.*, receipt.
recomandá (a), **recománd**, **-át**, *v. tr.* I, to recommend; to register (a letter).
recomandáţi-e, *n. f.*, **-i**, *pl.*, recommendation, introduction.
reconstructív, **-ă**, *adj.*, **-i**, **-e**, *pl.*, reconstructive.
reconstruí (a), **-ésc**, **-ít**, *v. tr.* IV, to reconstruct, to rebuild.
recrut-á (a), **-éz**, **-át**, *v. tr.* I, to recruit.
recunoáşte (a), **recunósc**, **recunoscút**, *v. tr.* III, to recognize; to reconnoitre.
recunoscă-tór, **-toáre**, *adj.*, **-tóri**, **-toáre**, *pl.*, grateful, thankful.
redá (a), **redáu**, **redát**, *v. tr.* I, to render, to give back, to return; to represent.
reflect-á (a), **-éz**, **-át**, *v. tr.*, *intr.* I, to reflect; to think; **a se —**, to reflect.
refugi-á (a se), **mă —**, **-éz**, **-át**, to take refuge.
refugiá-t, *n. m.*, **-ţi**, *pl.*, refugee.
regál, **-ă**, *adj.*, **-i**, **-e**, *pl.*, royal, kinglike.
regát, *n. mix.*, **-e**, *pl.*, kingdom, realm.
rég-e, *n. m.*, **-i**, *pl.*, king.
regént-ă, *n. f.*, **-e**, *pl.*, regent-woman.
reg-ésc, **-eáscă**, *adj.*, **-éşti**, *pl.*, royal, kinglike, of the king.
regín-ă, *n. f.*, **-e**, *pl.*, queen.
regiún-e, *n. f.*, **-i**, *pl.*, region.
regulá-t, **-tă**, *adj.*, **-ţi**, **-te**, *pl.*, regular.
remarcábil, **-ă**, *adj.*, **-i**, **-e**, *pl.*, remarkable.
Renáşter-e, *n. f.* (**-i**, *pl.*), Renaissance.
rentábil, **-ă**, *adj.*, **-i**, **-e**, *pl.*, remunerative.
renumí-t, **-tă**, *adj.*, **-ţi**, **-te**, *pl.*, famous, renowned.
renunţá (a), **renúnţ**, **-át**, *v. tr.* I, to renounce, to give up.
répe-de, *adj.*, **-zi**, *pl.*, fast, speedy, swift.
repetá (a), **repét**, **-át**, *v. tr.* I, to repeat.
repezí (a), **repắd**, **repezít**, *v. tr.* IV, to precipitate, to push, to hurry; **a se —**, to bounce, to rush into.
repeziciún-e, *n. f.*, **-i**, *pl.*, rapidity, celerity, speed.
resfirá (a), **resfír**, **-át**, *v. tr.* I, to scatter, to spread, to disperse.
respect-á (a), **respéct -(éz)**, **-át**, *v. tr.* I, to respect.
rest, *n. mix.*, **-uri**, *pl.*, rest, remains; scraps; remnant; change (money).
restauránt, *n. mix.*, **-e**, restaurant.
resté-u, *n. mix.*, **-ie**, *pl.*, stick, cane, cudgel.
retráge (a), **retrá-g**, **-s**, *v. tr.* III, to withdraw, to retire; **a se —**, *v. intr.*
revedér-e, *n. f.*, **-i**, *pl.*, seeing again, meeting after a separation.
revení (a), **revín**, **revenít**, *v. intr.* IV, to come back, to resume.
rezắş, see **răzắş**.
rezemá (a), see **răzimá (a)**.
rezerv-á (a), **-éz**, **-át**, *v. tr.* I, to reserve.
rezolvá (a) (resolvá), **rezólv**, **-át**, *v. tr.* I, to solve, to resolve.
rítmic, **-ă**, *adj.*, **-i**, **-e**, *pl.*, rhythmical.
roátă, *n. f.*, **róţi**, **roáte**, *pl.*, wheel.
rob, *n. m.*, **-i**, *pl.*, slave.

rob-í (a), -ésc, -ít, *v. tr.* IV, to enslave.
rod, *n. mix.,* **-uri (roáde),** *pl.,* fruit, product.
rod-í (a), -ésc, -it, *v. intr.* IV, to bear fruit.
rodit-ór, -oáre, *adj.,* **-óri, -oáre,** *pl.,* fertile, fruitful.
Ródna, *prop. n. f.* (locality).
rogojín-ă, *n. f.,* **-i (-e),** *pl.,* mat, rush-mat, straw-plat.
Róma, *prop. n. f.,* Rome.
Róman, *prop. n. m.* (town).
román, -ă, *adj.,* **-i, -e,** *pl.,* Roman.
Romấn, *n. m.,* **-i,** *pl.,* Rumanian.
romấn, -ă, *adj.,* **-i, -e,** *pl.,* Rumanian.
român-ésc, -eáscă, *adj.,* **-éşti,** *pl.,* Rumanian.
Romînía, *n. f.,* Rumania.
románic, -ă, *adj.,* **-i, -e,** *pl.,* Romanic, Romance.
románţ-ă, *n. f.,* **-e,** *pl.,* romance.
rópot, *n. mix.,* **-e,** *pl.,* rattle; tramp; trotting (of horses).
rost, *n. mix.,* **-uri,** *pl.,* sense, meaning; speech.
róşu (roş), *adj. m.,* **róşie (róşe),** *f.,* **róşi (róşii),** *pl.,* red.
rotúnd, -ă, *adj.,* **rotún-zi, -de,** *pl.,* round.
róuă, *n. f.,* dew.
rubín, *n. mix.,* **-e,** *pl.,* ruby.
rúd-ă, *n. f.,* **-e,** *pl.,* kin, relation, relative.
rugá (a), rog, rugát, *v. tr.* I, to ask; **a se** —, to say prayers (see 6. 4. **a**), to ask.
rugămín-te, *n. f.,* **-ţi,** *pl.,* demand, request.
rugín-ă, *n. f.,* **-i,** *pl.,* rust.
ruín-ă, *n. f.,* **-e (-i),** *pl.,* ruin.
rup-t, -tă, *adj.,* **-ţi, -te,** *pl.,* broken, torn; **în rúptul cáp-ului,** at any price.
ruşin-á, (a), -éz, -át, *v. tr.* I, to shame; **a se** —, to be ashamed, to shame (see 6. 4. **c**).
ruşín-e. *n. f.,* **-i,** *pl.,* shame; shyness; **mi-i** —, I am ashamed.
ruşin-ós, -oásă, *adj.,* shameful; shy.
Ruxándra, *prop. n. f.* (name).

S

-s, see **sunt.**
să, *conj.* (used to form the subjunctive mood).
sac, *n. m.,* **-i,** *pl.,* sack, bag.
săcá (secá), săc, -át, *v. tr., intr.* I, to dry up, to drain.
sacrificá (a), sacrífic, -át, *v. tr.* I, to sacrifice.
săge-átă, *n. f.,* **săgéţi,** *pl.,* arrow.
sálă, *n. f.,* **săli,** *pl.,* hall, room.
sălbătăcí-e, *n. f.,* **-i,** *pl.,* wildness, savageness, ferocity.
sălbátec, -ă, *adj.,* **-i, -e,** *pl.,* wild.
salcấm, *n. m.,* **-i,** *pl.,* acacia.
sálci-e, *n. f.,* **sălcii,** *pl.,* willow-tree.
salt, *n. mix.,* **-uri,** *pl.,* leap, spring.
săltá (a), salt, săltát, *v. tr., intr.* I, to spring, to jump.
salutá (a), salút, -át, *v. tr.* I, to greet, to salute.
salut-áre, *n. f.,* **-ări,** *pl.,* salutation, greeting, regard.
salv-á (a), -éz, -át, *v. tr.* I, to save; to deliver.
sámă, see **seámă.**
sămănă (a), sámăn, -át, *v. tr.* I, to sow.
sămănător, *n. m.,* **-i,** *pl.,* sower.
sămấnţă, *n. f.,* **semínţe (semínţi),** *pl.,* seed.
sấmbătă, *n. f.,* Saturday.
sấmbur-e, *n. m.,* **-i,** *pl.,* stone (of a fruit), kernel.
sân, *n. mix.,* **-uri,** *pl.,* bosom.
sănătáte, *n. f.,* health.

sanatóri-u, *n. mix.*, **-i**, *pl.*, nursing home.
sănă-tós, **-toásă**, *adj.*, **-tóşi**, **-toáse**, *pl.*, healthy, sound, wholesome.
sanctuár, *n. mix.*, **-e**, *pl.*, sanctuary.
Sándi, *prop. n. dim.*, Alexander.
sắnge, *n. m.*, blood.
sânger-á (a), **-éz**, **-át**, *v. tr.*, *intr.*, to let blood; to bleed; see **însângerá**.
sânger-ós, **-oásă**, *adj.*, bloody.
sáni-e, *n. f.*, **sắnii**, *pl.*, sledge, sleigh.
sânt, see **sunt**.
sáp-ă, *n. f.*, **-e**, *pl.*, hoe, mattock.
săpá (a), **sap**, **săpát**, *v. tr.* I, to dig.
săptămắn-ă, *n. f.*, **-i**, *pl.*, week.
sáră, see **seáră**.
sărác, **-ă**, *adj.*, *n.*, **-i**, **-e**, *pl.*, poor.
sărăcí-e, *n. f.*, **-i**, *pl.*, poverty, misery, want.
Sârb, *prop. n. m.*, **-i**, *pl.*, Serb; **sârb-ésc**, **-eáscă**, *adj.*, **éşti**, *pl.*, Serbian; **sârb**, **-ă**, *adj.*, **-i**, **-e**, *pl.*
sárcin-ă, *n. f.*, **-i**, *pl.*, burden, charge, weight.
sărdác, *n. mix.*, **-e**, *pl.*, short peasant coat of coarse wool cloth reaching to the hips.
sáre, *n. f.*, salt; **sắruri**, *pl.*, mineral salts.
sărí (a), **sar**, **sărít**, *v. intr.* IV, to jump.
săritúr-ă, *n. f.*, **-i**, *pl.*, leap, jump, skip, spring.
sărmán, **-ă**, *adj.*, **-i**, **-e**, *pl.*, poor.
sărutá (a), **sărút**, **-át**, *v. tr.* I, to kiss, to hug.
Sas, *prop. n. m.*, Saxon.
sat, *n. mix.*, **-e**, *pl.*, village.
satisfácţi-e, *n. f.*, **-i**, *pl.*, satisfaction, gratification.
sătú-l, **-lă**, *adj.*, **-i**, **-le**, *pl.*, satiated, full.
sáu, *conj.*, or (see 8. 4. i).
sắu, *n. m.*, tallow; **sắu**, *poss. pron.*, his (see 5. 5).
saván-t, **-tă**, *adj.*, *n.*, **-ţi**, **-te**, *pl.*, learned, erudite; student.
sbáte (a se), **sbat**, **sbătút**, to strive, to sprawl, to flounder.
sbor, see **zbor**.
sbuciumá (a), **sbúcium**, **-át**, *v. tr.* I, to trouble, to agitate; **a se —**, *v. intr.*, *refl.*
sbur-á (zburá) (a), **sbór**, **-át**, *v. intr.* I, to fly.
scădeá (a) (scáde), **scad**, **scăzút**, *v. tr.*, *intr.* II (III), to lower, to reduce; to decrease; to subtract; to sink.
scadén-t, **-tă**, *adj.*, **-ţi**, **-te**, *pl.*, due (to pay).
scădér-e, *n. f.*, **-i**, *pl.*, subtraction.
scăldá (a), **scald**, **scăldát**, *v. tr.* I, to bathe; **a se —**, to bathe.
scăldát, *n. mix.*, bathing.
scandál, *n. mix.*, **-uri**, *pl.*, scandal.
scắndur-ă, *n. f.*, **-i**, *pl.*, board, plank.
scăpá (a), **scap**, **scăpát**, *v. intr.* I, to escape; to get rid of; to let fall, to drop.
scăp-áre, *n. f.*, **-ắri**, *pl.*, salvation.
scáră, *n. f.*, **scắri**, *pl.*, ladder; staircase; scale.
scârb-ós, **-oásă**, *adj.*, **-óşi**, **-oáse**, *pl.*, disgusting, repugnant, nauseous.
scărpiná (a), **scárpin**, **scărpinát**, *v. tr.* I, to scratch, to scrape.
scârşní (a), see **scrâşni (a)**.
scârţâí (a), **scắrţâi (-ésc)**, **-ít**, to creak.
scatí-u, *n. m.*, **-i**, *pl.*, siskin, greenfinch, aberdevine (*Fringilla spinus*).
scáun, *n. mix.*, **-e**, *pl.*, chair.

scăunél, *n. mix.*, **-e**, *pl.*, little chair, footstool.
scén-ă, *n. f.*, **-e**, *pl.*, scene, stage; scenery.
schi-lód, **-loádă**, *adj.*, **-lózi**, **-loáde**, *pl.*, invalid, crippled, maimed.
schimbá (a), **schimb**, **-át**, *v. tr.* I, to change.
schit, *n. mix.*, **-uri**, *pl.*, hermitage.
scoár-ță, *n. f.*, **-țe**, *pl.* (**scorț**, *n. mix.*, **-uri**, *pl.*), carpet; bark; cover (of a book).
scoáte (a), **scot**, **scos**, *v. tr.* III, to take out, to draw, to remove.
scobori (a), **scobór**, **-ít**, *v. tr.*, *intr.* IV, to descend, to bring down; to go down, to come down.
scop, *n. mix.*, **-uri**, *pl.*, purpose, intention, aim.
Scóția, *prop. n. f.*, Scotland.
scrâșn-í (a), **-ésc**, **-ít**, *v. intr.* IV, to grind, to gnash one's teeth.
scrí-e (a), **-u**, **-s**, *v. tr.*, *intr.* III, to write (see 6. 3. **f**).
scris, *n. mix.*, **-uri**, *pl.*, writing.
scris-oáre, *n. f.*, **-óri**, *pl.*, letter, epistle.
sculá (a), **scol**, **sculát**, *v. tr.* I, to awake, to rouse; **a se** —, to rise, to awake, to get up, to stand up.
scump, **-ă**, *adj.*, **-i**, **-e**, *pl.*, dear, expensive; avaricious.
scúrge (a), **scurg**, **scurs**, *v. tr.* III, to drain, to drop; **a se** —, to run out, to flow, to slip away.
scur-t, **-tă**, *adj.*, **-ți**, **-te**, *pl.*, short.
scuturá (a), **scútur**, **-át**, *v. tr.* I, to shake; to toss; **a se** —, *v. intr.*, *refl.*
sdrávăn, see **zdrávăn**.
sdrob-í (a), **-ésc**, **-ít**, *v. tr.* IV, to crush, to crash, to mince.
se, *refl. pron.*, himself, herself, themselves (see 5. 3).
seámă (sámă), *n. f.*, attention; **de búnă seámă**, *adv.*, surely, for certain; **a luá seáma**, to pay attention; **a da seáma**, to be responsible.
seáră, *n. f.*, **séri**, *pl.*, evening.
secá (a), see **săcá (a)**.
secár-ă (săcáră), *n. f.*, rye; **-i**, *pl.*, rye-fields.
secerá (a), **sécer**, **-át**, *v. tr.* I, to reap, to harvest, to cut cereals; **secerát**, *n. mix.*, **-uri**, *pl.*, reaping, cutting of cereals.
secerătór, *n. m.*, **-i**, *pl.*, reaper, harvester.
sécer-e, *n. f.*, **-i**, *pl.*, sickle.
sécol, *n. mix.*, **-e**, *pl.*, century.
seculár, **-ă**, *adj.*, **-i**, **-e**, *pl.*, secular; worldly.
secúr-e, *n. f.*, **-i**, *pl.*, axe, hatchet.
a semăná (a sămăná), **seámăn**, **semănát**, *v. intr.* I, to be alike; to sow (see **sămăna**).
semănătór, see **sămănătór**.
semn, *n. mix.*, **-e**, *pl.*, mark, sign; **pe sémne**, *adv.*, as it seems, apparently.
semn-á (a), **-éz**, **-át**, *v. tr.*, *intr.* I, to sign, to subscribe.
senín, **-ă**, *adj.*, **-i**, **-e**, *pl.*, clear, serene.
sentinél-ă, *n. m.*, **-e**, *pl.*, sentry.
Septémvrie, **Septémbrie**, *n. m.*, September.
serb-áre, *n. f.*, **-ări**, *pl.*, feast, festivity.
séri-e, *n. f.*, **-i**, *pl.*, series.
seri-ós, **-oásă**, *adj.*, **-óși**, **-oáse**, *pl.*, serious.
servíci-u, *n. mix.*, **-i**, *pl.*, service; employment.
servitór, *n. m.*, **-i**, *pl.*, man-servant.
servitoáre, *n. f.*, **servitoáre**, *pl.*, maid, servant.
séte, *n. f.*, thirst (see 6. 4. **c**).
Sevástopol, *prop. n. m.* (town).

sfânt, -ă, *n.*, *adj.*, **sfín-ţi, -te**, *pl.*, saint; holy.
sfârş-í (a), **-ésc, -ít**, *v. tr.*, *intr.*, to end, to finish.
sfârşit. *n. mix.*, **-uri**, *pl.*, end; **în sfârşít**, at last, on the whole.
sfăşiá (a), **sfắşi-u, -át**, *v. tr.* I, to tear to pieces; **sfâşie-tór, -toáre**, *adj.*, **-tóri, -toáre**, *pl.*, heartbreaking.
sfat, *n. mix.*, **-uri**, *pl.*, advice, counsel.
sfătuí (a), **-ésc, -ít**, *v. tr.* IV, to counsel, to advise; **a se —**, to deliberate, to take advice.
sfert, *n. mix.*, **-uri**, *pl.*, quarter.
sfii (a se), **mă sfiésc, sfiít**, *refl. v.* IV, to be timid, to be meek (see 6. 4); **sfiálă**, *n. f.*, **sfiéli**, *pl.*, timidity, shyness, diffidence.
sfinţ-í (a), **-ésc, -ít**, *v. tr.* IV, to consecrate.
sgârcí-t, -tă, *adj.*, **-ţi, -te**, *pl.*, avaricious, covetous, stingy.
sgómot (**zgómot**), *n. mix.*, **-e**, *pl.*, noise; **sgomot-ós, -oásă**, *adj.*, **-óşi, -oáse**, *pl.*, noisy.
sgribulí (a se), see **zgribulí (a se)**.
Sibíu, *n. m.* (town).
sicrí-u, *n. mix.*, **-e**, *pl.*, coffin.
síe, *refl. pron.*, see 5. 3.
sieálă, see **sfii (a se)**, **sfiálă**.
síeşi, *refl. pron.*, see 5. 3.
sigil-á (a), **-éz, -át**, *v. tr.* I, to seal.
sihástr-u, *n. m.*, **-i**, *pl.*, hermit, solitarian.
sil-í (a), **-ésc, -ít**, *v. tr.* IV, to force, to compel; **a se —**, *v. refl.*, to force to, to endeavour.
silit-ór, -oáre, *adj.*, **-óri, -oáre**, *pl.*, diligent, industrious, assiduous.
silogísm, *n. mix.*, **-e**, *pl.*, syllogism.
símpl-u, -ă, *adj.*, **-i, -e**, *pl.*, simple.
simţ, *n. mix.*, **-uri**, *pl.*, sense, instinct.
simţ-í (a), **-ésc** (**simt**), **-ít**, *v. tr.*, *intr.* IV, to feel; **pe nesimţíte**, *adv.*, insensibly.
simţír-e, *n. f.*, **-i**, *pl.*, sensibly, feeling.
síncer, -ă, *adj.*, **-i, -e**, *pl.*, sincere.
síne, *refl. pron.*, see 5. 3.
síngur, -ă, *adj.*, **-i, -e**, *pl.*, alone, single.
singurátec, *adj.*, **-ă**, *f.*, **-i, -e**, *pl.*, lonely, solitary.
sintáx-ă, *n. f.*, **-e**, *pl.*, syntax.
sinucíde (**a se**), **mă sinucíd, sinucís**, *v. refl.* III, to commit suicide.
Sirét, *prop. n. m.* (river and town).
slab, -ă, *adj.*, **-i, -e**, *pl.*, weak, feeble, powerless; meagre, lean.
slăb-í (a), **-ésc, -ít**, *v. intr.* IV, to grow lean; to slacken; *tr.*, to let alone.
Slátina, *prop. n. f.* (locality).
Slav, *n. m.*, **-i**, *pl.*, Slav.
slávă, *n. f.*, **slắvi**, *pl.*, glory, magnificence; height.
slăví-t, -tă, *adj.*, **-ţi, -te**, *pl.*, glorious.
slavón, -ă, *adj.*, **-i, -e**, *pl.*, Slavonic.
slóbo-d, -dă, *adj.*, **-zi, -de**, *pl.*, free.
sloboz-í (a), **-ésc, -ít**, *v. tr.* IV, to deliver, to free.
slúg-ă, *n. m.*, *f.*, **-i**, *pl.*, servant.
slújb-ă, *n. f.*, **-e**, *pl.*, service; divine service, liturgy.
smaráld, *n. mix.*, **-e**, *pl.*, emerald.
smoc, *n. mix.*, **-uri**, *pl.*, tuft, bunch, bundle.
smochín, *n. m.*, **-i**, *pl.*, fig-tree; **smochín-ă**, *n. f.*, **-e**, *pl.*, fig.
smucí (a), **smuc-ésc, -ít**, *v. tr.* IV, to wrest, to snatch; **a se —**, *v. refl.*, to tear oneself away.

smúlge (a), **smulg**, **smuls**, *v. tr.* III, to pluck up, to root up; to wrest.
snop, *n. m.*, **-i**, *pl.*, sheaf.
snoáv-ă, *n. f.*, **-e**, *pl.*, anecdote.
soácr-ă, *n. f.*, **-e**, *pl.*, mother-in-law.
soáre, *n. m.*, **sóri**, *pl.*, sun.
soárt-ă, *n. f.*, fate, destiny.
sób-ă, *n. f.*, **-e**, *pl.*, stove.
soc, *n. m.*, **-i**, *pl.*, elder-tree.
sociál, **-ă**, *adj.*, **-i**, **-e**, *pl.*, social.
socot-í (a), **-ésc**, **-ít**, *v. tr.*, *intr.*, to count, to number, to calculate; to account, to reckon; to judge; **socot-eálă**, *n. f.*, **-éli**, *pl.*, account; calculation, bill, judgment.
sócr-u, *n. m.*, **-i**, *pl.*, father-in-law.
soldát, *n. m.*, **soldáţi**, *pl.*, soldier.
solémn, **-ă**, *adj.*, **-i**, **-e**, *pl.*, solemn.
sólz, *n. m.*, **-i**, *pl.*, scale.
Sómeş, *prop. n. m.* (river).
somn, *n. m.*, sleep.
somnor-ós, **-oásă**, *adj.*, **-óşi**, **-oáse**, *pl.*, sleepy.
somptu-ós, **-oásă**, *adj.*, **-óşi**, **-oáse**, *pl.*, sumptuous, magnificent, splendid.
sóră, *n. f.*, **suróri**, *pl.*, sister.
sorb-í (a), **-ésc**, **-ít**, *v. tr.* IV, to sip, to sup; to suck in; **sorbír-e**, *n. f.*, **-i**, *pl.*, sip.
Sorént (o), *prop. n. m.*, Sorento.
sosí (a), **sos-ésc**, **-ít**, *v. intr.* IV, to arrive, to come to.
soţ, *n. m.*, **-i**, *pl.*, husband; companion, comrade.
soţí-e, *n. f.*, **-i**, *pl.*, wife.
spaím-ă, *n. f.*, **-e**, *pl.*, fright, terror.
spăl-á, **spăl**, **-át**, *v. tr.* I, to wash.
Spánia, *prop. n. f.*, Spain; **Spaniól**, *prop. n. m.*, **-i**, *pl.*, Spaniard.
spasm, *n. mix.*, **-e** (**-uri**), *pl.*, spasm.
spáte, *n. mix.* (**spáte**, *pl.*), back; shoulder.
spáţi-u, *n. mix.*, **-i**, *pl.*, space, room.
speciál, **-ă**, *adj.*, **-i**, **-e**, *pl.*, special, particular.
specialíst, *n. m.*, **specialíşti**, *pl.*, specialist.
sperá (a), **sper**, **-át**, *v. intr.* I, to hope.
speriá (**spăriá**) (a), **spéri-u**, **-át**, *v. tr.* II, to frighten.
spic, *n. mix.*, **-e**, *pl.*, ear, spike.
spin, *n. m.*, **-i**, *pl.*, thorn, prickle.
spintecătúr-ă, *n. f.*, **-i**, *pl.*, split, slit, cut.
spitál, *n. mix.*, **-e**, *pl.*, hospital.
spor-í (a), **-ésc**, **-ít**, *v. tr.*, *intr.* IV, to advance, to increase, to have success, to be efficient.
spórnic, **-ă**, *adj.*, **-i**, **-e**, *pl.*, increasing; productive.
sport, *n. mix.*, **-uri**, *pl.*, sport.
sprânc-eánă, *n. f.*, **-éne**, *pl.*, eyebrow.
spre, *prep.*, to, towards.
sprijin-í (a), **-ésc**, **-ít**, *v. tr.* IV, to prop, to support, to help.
sprínten, **-ă**, *adj.*, **-i**, **-e**, *pl.*, brisk, agile; **sprintei-ór**, **-oáră**, *adj. dim.*, **-óri**, **-oáre**, *pl.*, agile, quick.
spulberá (a), **spúlber**, **-át**, *v. tr.* I, to scatter, to disperse; to whirl; **spúlber**, *n. m.*, dust, powder.
spúm-ă, *n. f.*, **-e**, *pl.*, foam, scum; lather.
spúne (a), **spun**, **spus**, *v. tr.* III, to say, to tell.
spurcá (a), **spurc**, **-át**, *v. tr.* I, to soil, to desecrate, to profane.
sta (a), **-u**, **-t**, *v. intr.* I, to stay (see 6. 3. b).

stabil-í (a), **-ésc**, **-ít**, *v. tr.* IV, to establish, to settle.
stấn-ă, *n. f.*, **-i**, *pl.*, sheepfold, sheep-cot.
stấnc-ă, *n. f.*, **-i**, *pl.*, rock.
stânc-ós, **-oásă**, *adj.*, **-óşi**, **-oáse**, *pl.*, rocky.
stâng, **-ă**, *adj.*, **-i**, *pl.*, left.
stấnge (a), see **stínge** (a).
stăpấn, *n. m.*, **-i**, *pl.*, master; **stăpấnă**, *n. f.*, **-e**, *pl.*
stăpân-í (a), **-ésc**, **-ít**, *v. tr.* IV, to dominate, to rule; to hold, to possess.
stăpânír-e, *n. f.*, **-i**, *pl.*, domination; rule, government; possession.
stáre, *n. f.*, **-stări**, *pl.*, state, condition; **a fi în —**, to be able.
stárost-e, *n. m.*, **-i**, *pl.*, provost, foreman of a corporation, elder, senior.
stăruínţ-ă, *n. f.*, **-e**, *pl.*, insistence, perseverance.
stârv, *n. mix.*, **-uri**, *pl.*, carcass, carrion.
stat, *n. mix.*, **-e**, *pl.*, state.
staţiún-e, *n. f.*, **-i**, *pl.*, station; **staţiúne balneáră**, spa.
statúr-ă, *n. f.*, **-i**, *pl.*, stature.
stávil-ă, *n. f.*, **-e**, *pl.*, dam, sluice; sluice-gate, dyke.
ste-á, *n. f.*, **-le**, *pl.*, star.
stej-ár, *n. m.*, **-éri**, *pl.*, oak-tree.
stép-ă, *n. f.*, **-e**, *pl.*, steppe.
stícl-ă, *n. f.*, **-e**, *pl.*, glass.
sticlé-te, *n. m.*, **-ţi**, *pl.*, thistle-finch (*Fringilla carduelis*).
stil, *n. mix.*, **-uri**, *pl.*, style.
stimá-t, **-tă**, *adj.*, **-ţi**, **-te**, *pl.*, esteemed.
stínge (a), **sting**, **stins**, *v. tr.* III, to extinguish, to quench, to blow out (a candle); **a se —**, to die.
stínger-e, *n. f.*, **-i**, *pl.*, extinction, disappearance.
stoárce (a), **storc**, **stors**, *v. tr.* III, to squeeze, to press; to exploit.
stol, *n. mix.*, **-uri**, *pl.*, flight (of birds); cluster, crowd.
stólnic, *n. m.*, **-i**, *pl.*, chamberlain.
stomác, *n. mix.*, **-uri**, *pl.*, stomach.
străbáte (a), **străbát**, **străbătút**, *v. tr.* III, to penetrate, to pass through; to travel over.
strá-dă, *n. f.*, **strằzi** (**stráde**), *pl.*, street.
strái, *n. mix.*, **-e**, *pl.*, cloth, coat, dress.
străín, **-ă**, *adj.*, *n.*, **-i**, **-e**, *pl.*, foreigner, alien.
străinătáte, *n. f.*, **străinătằţi**, *pl.*, abroad, foreign country.
străluc-í (a), **-ésc**, **-ít**, *v. intr.* IV, to shine, to glare, to glitter, to brighten.
strălucí-t, **-tă**, *adj.*, **-ţi**, **-te**, *pl.*, resplendent, brilliant, lustrous.
strălucit-ór, **-oáre**, *adj.*, **-óri**, **-oáre**, *pl.*, shining, resplendent, glittering.
strâmb, **-ă**, *adj.*, **-i**, **-e**, *pl.*, crooked, curved.
strămóş, *n. m.*, **-i**, *pl.*, great-grandfather; ancestor.
strâmt-oáre, *n. f.*, **-óri**, *pl.*, narrowness, pass, defile, strait.
strângă-tór, **-toáre**, *adj.*, *n.*, **-tóri**, **toáre**, *pl.*, sparing, saving.
străpúnge (a), **străpúng**, **străpúns**, *v. tr.* III, to pierce through.
străşnic, **-ă**, *adj.*, **-i**, **-e**, *pl.*, terrible.
străvéch-i, **-e**, *adj.*, **-i**, *pl.*, very old, primeval.
stréch-e, (**stréchi-e**), *n. f.*, **-ii** (**-i**), *pl.*, horse-fly.
strecurá (a), **strecór**, **strecurát**, *v. tr.* I, to filter, to strain; **a se —**, *v. intr.*, to slip.
stréin, see **străín**.

stricá (a), stric, -át, *v. tr.* I, to break, to spoil.
strict, -ă, *adj.*, severe, strict.
strígăt, *n. mix.*, **-e,** *pl.*, shout, cry, shriek.
strop, *n. m.*, **-i,** *pl.*, drop.
strúgur-e, *n. m.*, **-i,** *pl.*, grapes.
strúng-ă, *n. f.*, **-i,** *pl.*, narrow passage in a sheepfold where sheep are milked.
studén-t, *n. m.*, **-ţi,** *pl.*, student, undergraduate.
studént-ă, *n. f.*, **-e,** *pl.*, girl-student.
stúdiu, *n. mix.*, **stúdii,** *pl.*, study.
sturz, *n. m.*, **-i,** *pl.*, thrush.
sub (subt, supt), *prep.*, under, beneath, below.
subiéct, *n. mix.*, **-e,** *pl.*, subject.
subţír-e, *adj.*, **-i,** *pl.*, thin, fine.
succés, *n. mix.*, **-e,** *pl.*, success.
Suceáva, *prop. n. f.* (river and town).
Sucevíţa, *prop. n. f.* (locality).
Sud, *n. m.*, South.
Sud-Est, *n. m.*, South-East.
sud-oáre, *n. f.*, **-óri,** *pl.*, sweat, perspiration.
suferí (a), súfăr, suferít, *v. tr.*, *intr.* IV, to suffer, to endure, to tolerate; **suferínţ-ă,** *n. f.*, **-e,** *pl.*, suffering, pain.
sufl-á (a), súflu, -át, *v. intr.* I, to breathe, to blow.
sufl-áre, *n. f.*, **ắri,** *pl.*, breath.
súflet, *n. mix.*, **-e,** *pl.*, soul.
sufragí-u, *n. m.*, **-i,** *pl.*, butler.
sugésti-e, *n. f.*, **-i,** *pl.*, suggestion.
suhát, *n. mix.*, **-uri,** *pl.*, pasture-ground for horses and cattle.
suí, (a), -súi, -t, *v. intr.*, *tr.* IV, to climb; **a se —,** to climb.
sulemení-t, -tă, *adj.*, **-ţi, -te,** *pl.*, rouged, painted, flaked.
súliţ-ă, *n. f.*, **-e,** *pl.*, lance, pike.
sumán, *n. mix.*, **-e,** *pl.*, peasant coat made of coarse woollen cloth; woollen cloth.
suná (a), sun, -át, *v. intr.* I, to sound; to ring (the bell), to toll.
súnet, *n. mix.*, **-e,** *pl.*, sound.
sunt, sânt, îs, -s, *pres. 3rd pl.*, they are.
súp-ă, *n. f.*, **-e,** *pl.*, soup.
supăr-á (a), súpăr, -át, *v. tr.* I, to make angry, to vex, to irritate; to disturb; **a se —,** to get angry.
supăr-áre, *n. f.*, **-ắri,** *pl.*, grief, affliction, trouble.
superi-ór, -oáră, *adj.*, **-óri, -oáre,** *pl.*, superior, upper, better.
suprém, -ă, *adj.*, **-i, -e,** *pl.*, supreme.
sur, -ă, *adj.*, **-i, -e,** *pl.*, grey.
surấde (a), surấd, surấs, *v. intr.* III, to smile.
surprinzăt-ór, -oáre, *adj.*, **-óri, -oáre,** *pl.*, surprising.
surtúc, *n. mix.*, **-e,** *pl.*, coat.
surugí-u, *n. m.*, **-i,** *pl.*, stage-coach driver, postillion.
surzéni-e, *n. f.* (**-i,** *pl.*), deafness.
sus, *adv.*, above, upstairs; **în súsul ápei,** upstream.
suspensiún-e, *n. f.*, **-i,** *pl.*, suspension.
suspiná (a), suspín, -át, to sigh.
sút-ă, *num.*, *n. f.*, **-e,** *pl.*, hundred.
sutím-e, *n. f.*, **-i,** *pl.*, hundredth.
svârcol-í (a se), mă —, -ésc, -ít, *v. intr.* IV, to twist, to writhe.
svârlí (a), svârl, -ít, *v. tr.* IV, to throw (see **asvârli**).
svon, *n. mix.*, **-uri,** *pl.*, sound; rumour; talk.

Ş

şacál, *n. m.*, **-i,** *pl.*, jackal.
şágă, *n. f.*, **şégi,** *pl.*, joke, jest, pleasantry.

şále, *n. f. pl.*, small of the back.
şanţ, *n. mix.*, **-uri**, *pl.*, ditch, moat, trench.
şápte (şépte), *num.*, seven.
şáptelea (al), *m.* **şáptea (a)**, *f.*, the seventh.
şárpe, *n. m.*, **şérpi**, *pl.*, snake, serpent.
Şárul, *prop. n.* (mountain).
Şárul (*m.*), **Dórnei** (*f.*), *prop. n.*, hamlet forming part of Vatra Dornei town.
şáse (şése), *num.*, six.
şáselea (al), *m.*, **şása (a)**, *f.*, the sixth.
şátră, *n. f.*, **şétre**, *pl.*, tent, gipsy-camp.
şcoálă, *n. f.*, **şcóli**, **şcoále**, *pl.*, school.
şeá, *n. f.*, **şéle**, *pl.*, saddle.
şedeá (a), **şed**, **şezút**, *v. intr.* II, to sit; **a se —**, *v. intr.*, to suit (see 6. 4. **c**).
şépte, see **şápte**.
şérpe, see **şárpe**.
şerpuí (a), **-ésc**, **-t**, *v. intr.* IV, to wind (like a serpent).
şes, *n. mix.*, **-uri**, plain, level, flat.
şesím-e, *n. f.*, **-i**, *pl.*, sixth.
şi, *conj.*, and (see 8. 4. **i**); *refl. pron.*, see 5. 3.
şíling, *n. m.*, **-i**, *pl.*, shilling.
şirét, **şireátă**, *adj.*, **şiréţi**, **şiréte**, *pl.*, sly, cunning.
şoápt-ă, *n. f.*, **-e**, *pl.*, whispering, whisper.
şoárec-e, *n. m.*, **-i**, *pl.*, mouse.
şofér, *n. m.*, **-i**, driver.
şóim, *n. m.*, **-i**, *pl.*, falcon.
şopârl-ă, *n. f.*, **-e**, *pl.*, lizard.
şos-eá, *n. f.*, **-éle**, *pl.*, high-road, causeway.
Ştéfan, *prop. n.*, Stephen.
ştérge (a), **şterg**, **şters**, *v. tr.* III, to wipe; to rub; to efface.
ştergár, *n. mix.*, **-e**, *pl.*, towel.
ştí (-e) (a), **ştíu**, **ştiút**, *v. tr.* IV, to know (see 6. 3. **f**).
ştír-e, *n. f.*, **-i**, *pl.*, news, announcement.
şuerá (a), **şúer**, **-át**, *v. intr.* I, to whistle, to hiss, to fizzle.
şúet, *n. mix.*, **-e**, *pl.*, rustling noise.
şumuióg, *n. mix.*, **şumuioáge**, *pl.*, straw-bundle.
şupur-í (a se), **mă şupurésc**, **-ít**, *v. intr.* IV, to steal away, to sneak.

T

tabiét, *n. mix.*, **-e (-uri)**, *pl.*, habit, practice, (concerning eating, drinking, sleeping).
tablóu, *n. mix.*, **-ri**, *pl.*, picture, painting.
tăceá (a), **tac**, **tăcút**, *v. intr.* II, to be silent.
tăcér-e, *n. f.*, **-i**, *pl.*, silence.
tact, *n. mix.*, **-e**, *pl.*, tact; measure, time.
tăiá (a), **tái**, **tăiát**, *v. tr.* I, to cut (see 6. 3. **f**).
táin-ă, *n. f.*, **-e**, *pl.*, secret, mystery; **táinic**, **-ă**, *adj.*, secret.
talént, *n. mix.*, **-e**, *pl.*, talent, faculty.
tâlhár, *n. m.*, **-i**, *pl.*, thief.
tălmăc-í (a), **-ésc**, **-ít**, *v. tr.* IV, to translate, to explain.
Tămădăi-án, *prop. n. m.*, **-éni**, *pl.*, inhabitants of Tămădăieni.
tămâi-á (a), **-éz**, **-át**, *v. tr.*, *intr.* II, to (burn) incense.
tâmpl-ă, *n. f.*, **-e**, *pl.*, temple of the head.
tânăr, **-ă**, *n.*, *adj.*, **tíner-i**, **-e**, *pl.*, youth, young.
tânjálă, *n. f.*, **tânjéli**, *pl.*, plough-shaft, pole.
târâí (a), **-ésc**, **-ít**, see **târî (a)**.

tărấţe, *n. f. pl.*, bran.
târcól, *n. mix.*, **târcoále**, *pl.*, round; **a da târcoale**, to go round, to approach stealthily.
tár-e, *adj.*, **-i**, *pl.*, strong; *adv.*, very.
târg, *n. mix.*, **-uri**, *pl.*, market, town.
Tấrgu-Frumós, *prop. n. m.* (town).
Târgóvişte, *prop. n. f.* (town).
târí (a), **târấsc**, **târít**, *v. tr.* IV, to drag; **a se —**, *v. intr.*, to crawl.
târíş, *adv.*, crawling.
Târnáva (**Tấrnava**), *prop. n. f.* (river).
târzí-u, **-e**, *adj.*, **-i**, *pl.*, late; **târzíu**, *adv.*
tá-tă, *n. m.*, **-ţi**, *pl.*, father; **Tátăl**, *n. m.*, the Heavenly Father (see 2. 4. **d**).
tắu, *m.*, **ta**, *f.*, *poss. pron.*, thine (see 5. 5).
táur, *n. m.*, **-i**, *pl.*, bull.
táx-ă, *n. f.*, **-e**, *pl.*, fee, tax, rate, duty.
te, *pers. pron.*, thee, you (see 5. 1. **a**).
teácă, *n. f.*, **téci**, *pl.*, sheath; case.
teátr-u, *n. mix.*, **-e**, *pl.*, theatre.
téi (u), *n. m.*, **téi**, *pl.*, lime-tree.
telefón, *n. mix.*, **telefoáne**, *pl.*, telephone; **telefon-á (a)**, **-éz**, **-át**, *v. intr.* I, to telephone; **telefónic**, **-ă**, *adj.*, **-i**, **-e**, *pl.*, telephonic.
telegrám-ă, *n. f.*, **-e**, *pl.*, telegram; **telegrafi-á (a)**, **-éz**, **-át**, *v. intr.* II, to cable.
téme (a se), **mă tem**, **temút**, *v. intr.* III, to be afraid of, to fear (see 6. 4. **a**, 6. 7).
temperamént, *n. mix.*, **-e**, *pl.*, temper, nature.
temperatúr-ă, *n. f.*, **-i**, *pl.*, temperature.
tenacitáte, *n. f.*, tenacity.
teríbil, **-ă**, *adj.*, **-i**, **-e**, *pl.*, terrible, dreadful.
teritóri-u, *n. mix.*, **-i**, *pl.*, territory.
términ, *n. m.*, **-i**, *pl.*, term, expression.
tífl-ă, *n. f.*, **-e**, *pl.*, gesture of contempt made with open fingers against somebody's face.
tígr-u, *n. m.*, **-i**, *pl.*, tiger.
tíhnă (**tícnă**), *n. f.*, tranquillity, comfort, rest.
tímbr-u, *n. m.*, **-e**, *pl.*, stamp.
timp, *n. mix.*, **-uri**, *pl.*, time.
tíne, *pers. pron. acc.*, thee (see 5. 1. **a**).
tineréţe, *n. f. pl.* (**tineréţea**, *art. n. f. sing.*), youth.
tirán, *n. m.*, **-i**, *pl.*, tyrant.
Tísa, *prop. n. f.*, Tisa, Theis.
títlu, *n. mix.*, **-uri**, *pl.*, title.
toác-ă, *n. f.*, **-e**, *pl.*, a board hammered with wooden mallet sounded alone or together with the church bells at certain ceremonies of the Orthodox Church; **pe la toácă**, *adv.*, when the vesper-bell sounds.
toárce (a), **torc**, **tors**, *v. tr.* III, to spin.
tócmai, *adv.*, just, exactly; **tocmai din**, as far as from.
tolăn-í (a se), **mă tolănésc**, **tolănít**, *v. intr.* IV, to lie down at full length, to stretch.
tólb-ă, *n. f.*, **-e**, *pl.*, quiver.
ton, *n. m.*, **-uri**, *pl.*, tune, note, voice.
tón-ă, *n. f.*, **-e**, *pl.*, ton.
top-í (a), **-ésc**, **-ít**, *v. tr.* IV, to melt.
top-ór, *n. mix.*, **-oáre**, *pl.*, axe, hatchet.
tórb-ă, *n. f.*, **-e**, *pl.*, bag.
torént, *n. mix.*, **-e**, *pl.*, torrent, stream.

tot, *m.*, **toátă**, *f.*, *adj.*, *pron.*, entire, whole; every, each; **tótul**, everything; **tot**, *adv.* (see 5. 9).
totdeúna, *adv.*, always.
tótuş (i), *conj.*, nevertheless, however (see 8. 4. **c**, **i**).
továrăş, *n. m.*, **-i**, *pl.*, partner, associate, companion.
tovărăşí-e, *n. f.*, **-i**, *pl.*, companionship, partnership, association.
trăd-á (**a**), **-éz**, **-át**, *v. tr.* I, to betray.
tradiţionál, **-ă**, *adj.*, **-i**, **-e**, *pl.*, traditional.
trăgăn-á (**a**), **-éz**, **-át**, *v. tr.*, *intr.* I, to delay, to defer, to postpone.
trăgătór, *n. m.*, **-i**, *pl.*, shooter; trigger.
tráge (**a**), **trag**, **tras**, *v. tr.* III, to pull; to fire a gun, to shoot.
trăí (**a**), **-ésc**, **-ít**, *v.intr.* IV, to live.
Traián, *prop. n.*, Trajan.
tramvái, *n. mix.*, **-e**, *pl.*, tramcar.
trandafirí-u, **-e**, *adj.*, **-i**, *pl.*, rosy.
trândav, **-ă**, *adj.*, **-i**, **-e**, *pl.*, lazy, idle, indolent.
transformá (**a**), **transfórm**, **-át**, *v. tr.* I, to transform.
transilvăn-eán, **-eánă**, *adj.*, **-éni**, **-éne**, *pl.*, Transylvanian.
Transilvánia, *prop. n. f.*, Transylvania.
trânt-í (**a**), **-ésc**, **-ít**, *v. tr.* IV, to throw down; to bang; **a se** —, *v. intr.*, *refl.*, to throw oneself.
trăsătúr-ă, *n. f.*, **-i**, *pl.*, stroke, line; feature.
trăsnet, *n. mix.*, **-e**, *pl.*, thunder, bolt.
trăsúr-ă, *n. f.*, **-i**, *pl.*, vehicle; **trăsúră de uníre**, hyphen.
treábă, *n. f.*, **tréburi**, **trébi**, *pl.*, business; **de treábă**, decent, good.
tre-áz, *adj. m.*, **-áză**, *f.*, **-ji**, *m.*, **-ze**, *f. pl.*, awake; sober.
trebuí (**a**), **-ésc**, **-ít**, *v. intr.* IV, to be obliged; **trébuie**, must (general form used for every person in the present tense, see 6. 4. **c**).
trebuşoár-ă, *n. f.*, **-e**, *pl.*, little business, work, affair.
trecăt-ór, **-oáre**, *adj.*, *n.*, **-óri**, **-oáre**, *pl.*, transient, temporary; passer-by; **trecăt-oáre**, *n. f.*, **-óri**, *pl.*, pass, defile.
tréce (**a**), **trec**, **-út**, *v. intr.* III, to pass; **trécer-e**, *n. f.*, **-i**, *pl.*, passing, passage.
trecút, *n. mix.*, **-uri**, *pl.*, past.
tréi, *num.*, three.
tréilea (**al**), *m.*, **tréia** (**a**), *f.*, the third.
treím-e, *n. f.*, **-i**, *pl.*, trinity.
tremurá (**a**), **trémur**, **-át**, *v. intr.* I, to tremble, to shake.
tren, *n. mix.*, **-uri**, *pl.*, train.
trésti-e, *n. f.*, **-i**, *pl.*, reed.
trez-í (**a**), **-ésc**, **-ít**, *v. tr.* IV, to awaken; **a se** —, to wake; to get sober.
trib, *n. mix.*, **-uri**, *pl.*, tribe.
trípl-u, **-ă**, *adj.*, **-i**, **-e**, *pl.*, threefold, treble.
trist, **-ă**, *adj.*, **tríşti**, **tríste**, *pl.*, sad, triste.
tristéţe, *n. f.*, **-i**, *pl.*, sadness.
triúmf, *n. mix.*, **-uri**, *pl.*, triumph.
triúnghi, *n. mix.*, **-uri**, *pl.*, triangle.
tropă-í (**a**), **-ésc**, **-ít**, *v. intr.* IV, to trot, to make noise (going).
trúd-ă, *n. f.*, (**-e** *pl.*), work, trouble.
trúnchi, *n. mix.*, **-uri**, *pl.*, stem, trunk, stump, block.
trup, *n. mix.*, **-uri**, *pl.*, body.
trúp-ă, *n. f.*, troupe, company; **-e**, *pl.*, troops.
tu, *pers. pron.*, thou (see 5. 1).

tufíş, *n. mix.*, **-uri**, *pl.*, thicket.
tulburá (**turburá**) (**a**), **túlbur**, **-át**, *v. tr.* I, to trouble ; to agitate ; **a se** —, to be disturbed.
tulpín-ă, *n. f.*, **-e** (**-i**), *pl.*, trunk, stem, stalk.
turb-á (**a**), **-éz**, **-át**, *v. intr.* I, to be in a rage, to be mad.
Turc, *n. m.*, **-i**, *pl.*, Turk ; **turcésc**, **-ceáscă**, *adj.*, **-éşti**, *pl.*, Turkish.
turíst, *n. m.*, **turíşti**, *pl.*, tourist.
túrm-ă, *n. f.*, **-e**, *pl.*, flock, herd.
turn, *n. mix.*, **-uri**, *pl.*, tower, steeple.
turná (**a**), **torn**, **turnát**, *v. tr.* I, to pour.
Túrnu-Severín, *prop. n.* (town).
tuscínci, *num.*, all five.
tuş-í (**a**), **-ésc**, **-ít**, *v. intr.* IV, cough.
tuspátru, *num.*, all four.
tusşáse, *num.*, all six.
tustré-i, *m.*, **-le**, *f.*, all three.

Ţ

ţanc, *n. mix.*, **-uri**, *pl.*, agreed measure ; aim ; steep rock.
ţânţár (**ţinţár**), *n. m.*, **-i**, *pl.*, mosquito, gnat.
ţap, *n. m.*, **-i**, *pl.*, he-goat.
ţápăn (**ţeápăn**), **-ă**, *adj.*, **ţépeni**, **ţépene**, *pl.*, stiff, rigid.
ţáră, *n. f.*, **ţări**, *pl.*, country.
Ţára Gálilor, *prop. n. f.*, Wales.
Ţára Româneáscă, *n. f.*, Walachia.
ţărán, *n. m.*, **-i**, *pl.*, peasant ; **ţărăním-e**, *n. f.*, **-i**, *pl.*, peasantry.
ţărm, *n. mix.*, **-uri**, *pl.*, coast, shore, bank.
ţeápăn, see **ţápăn**.
ţeávă, *n. f.*, **ţévi**, *pl.*, tube, pipe.
ţel, *n. mix.*, **-uri**, *pl.*, aim, intention, design ; aim-sight.
ţi, *pers. pron.*, to thou (see 5. 1. **a**).
ţíe, *pers. pron.*, to thou (see 5. 1. **a**).
ţigán, *n. m.*, **-i**, *pl.*, Gipsy.
ţiínd = **ţinấnd**.
ţin-eá (**a**), **ţin**, **-út**, *v. tr.* II, to hold.
ţínt-ă, *n. f.*, **-e**, *pl.*, tack, nail ; mark, aim ; target ; *adv.*, straightly.
ţinţár, see **ţânţár**.
ţinút, *n. mix.*, **-uri**, *pl.*, region, country, province.
ţipá (**a**), **ţip**, **-át**, *v. intr.* I, to shriek, to squeal, to scream, to cry ; **ţípăt**, *n. mix.*, **ţípete**, *pl.*, cry, shriek.
ţúic-ă, *n. f.*, **-i**, *pl.*, plum-brandy.

U

ucenic, *n. m.*, **-i**, *pl.*, apprentice ; disciple, apostle.
ucíde (**a**), **ucíd**, **ucís**, *v. tr.* III, to kill, to murder.
ucígă-l = **să-l ucidă** (see 6. 2. **a**, *E*).
ucigáş, *n. m.*, **-i**, *pl.*, assassin, murderer.
udá (**a**), **ud**, **-át**, *v. tr.* I, to water, to wet, to moisten ; **udătúr-ă**, *n. f.*, **-i**, *pl.*, watering, drink.
uimír-e, *n. f.*, **-i**, *pl.*, astonishment.
uitá (**a**), **uit**, **-át**, *v. tr.* I, to forget ; **a se — la ceva**, to look at something.
ulc-ícă, *n. f.*, **-éle**, *pl.*, earthenware mug.
ulm, *n. m.*, **-i**, *pl.*, elm.
úmăr, *n. m.*, **úmeri**, *pl.* (**úmere**, *pl. f.*, Mold. and Trans.), shoulder.
umbl-á (**a**), *v.* I., **úmblu**, **-át**, to walk.
úmbr-ă, *n. f.*, **-e**, *pl.*, shade, shadow.

úmed, -ă, *adj.*, **úmezi, úmede,** *pl.*, damp, moist.
umez-eálă, *n. f.*, **-éli,** *pl.*, moisture, humidity, dampness.
umfl, -á (a), úmflu, -át, *v. tr.* I, to swell up; to inflate, to blow.
un, *m.*, **o,** *f.*, *indef. art.*, a, an; **únu (l), un,** *m.*, **úna, o,** *f.*, *num.*, one (see 2. 1; 4. 1; 5. 9); **tot una,** *adv.*, all the same, indifferently; **într'úna,** *adv.*, continually.
unchiáş, *n. m.*, **-i (unchiéşi),** *pl.*, old man; *dial.*, uncle.
únd-ă, *n. f.*, **-e,** *pl.*, wave.
únde, *adv.*, where.
undevá, *adv.*, somewhere.
únge (a), un-g, -s, *v. tr.* III, to oil, to grease; to anoint.
unghiulár, -ă, *adj.*, **-i, -e,** *pl.*, angular, cornered.
Ungur-eán, *n. m.*, **-éni,** *pl.*, Transylvanian (which was under Hungarian rule).
un-í (a), -ésc, -ít, *v. tr.* IV, to unite, to join together; **a se —,** *v. intr.*, to unite.
uníc (únic), -ă, *adj.*, **-i, -e,** *pl.*, only, alone, unparalleled.
ún-ii, -ele, *indef. pron. pl.*, some (see 5. 9).
unim-e, *s. f.*, **-i,** *pl.*, one, unit (of the series: tens, hundreds, etc.).
unifórm, -ă, *adj.*, **-i, -e,** *pl.*, uniform; **unifórm-ă,** *n. f.*, **-e,** *pl.*, uniform.
unír-e, *n. f.*, **-i,** *pl.*, union.
universit-áte, *n. f.*, **-ắţi,** *pl.*, university.
ún'se (see p. 246)=**unde se.**
únu (l), see **un.**
ur-á (a), -éz, -át, *v. tr.* I, to wish luck, to congratulate.
urâciúne, see **uriciúne.**
urcá (a se), urc, -át, *v. intr.* I, to climb, to mount; to rise.
uréch-e, *n. f.*, **-i,** *pl.*, ear.
urgí-e, *n. f.*, **-i,** *pl.*, fury, rage, wrath.
urî́ (a), urắsc, urî́t, *v. tr.* IV, to hate; **urî-t, -tă,** *adj.*, **-ţi, -te,** *pl.*, ugly; **mi se urăşte cu ceva,** I am tired of something.
uriáş, -ă, *adj.*, *n.*, **-i, -e,** *pl.*, giant.
uricún-e (urâciúne), *n. f.*, **-i,** *pl.*, ugliness.
úrm-ă, *n. f.*, **-e,** *pl.*, track, trace, vestige; **în urmă,** *adv.*, behind, late; **cel din urmă,** the last.
urm-á (a), -éz, -át, *v. tr.*, *intr.* I, to follow, to proceed, to continue.
urm-áre, *n. f.*, **-ắri,** *pl.*, consequence, sequel; continuation.
urmăr-í (a), -ésc, -ít, *v. tr.* IV, to pursue, to chase; to prosecute.
următ-ór, -oáre, *adj.*, **-óri, -oáre,** *pl.*, following, next.
urn-í (a), -ésc, -ít, *v. tr.* IV, to move, to remove.
ur-s, *n. m.*, **-şi,** *pl.*, bear.
ursoáic-ă, *n. f.*, **-e,** *pl.*, she-bear.
urz-eálă, *n. f.*, **-éli,** *pl.*, foundation; creation, beginning; woof, weft.
uscá (a), usúc, uscát, *v. tr.* I, to dry; **a se —,** *v. intr.*, to dry, to get dry (see 6. 3. **f**).
uscăţív, -ă, *adj.*, **-i, -e,** *pl.*, meagre, lean, lank.
úş-e (úşă), *n. f.*, **-i,** *pl.*, door.
uşór, uşoáră, *adj.*, **-i, uşoáre,** *pl.*, easy, light, not heavy.
usturói, *n. mix.* (**usturoáie,** *pl.*), garlic.
uşur-á (a), -éz, -át, *v. tr.* I, to ease, to lighten.
uşur-él, -ícă, *adj.*, **-éi, -éle,** *pl.*, fairly light.
uşurínţ-ă, *n. f.*, **-e,** *pl.*, ease, facility, easiness.

V

vă, *pers. pron. dat., acc.*, to you, you (see 5. 1. a).
vácă, *n. f.*, **vaci**, *pl.*, cow.
vacánţ-ă, *n. f.*, **-e**, *pl.*, vacancy; holidays.
vad, *n. mix.*, **-uri**, *pl.*, ford.
văd-í (a), **-ésc**, **-ít**, *v. tr.* IV, to divulge, to denounce; **a se** —, to appear; **vădí-t**, **-tă**, *adj.*, **-ţi**, **-te**, *pl.*, manifest, evident.
vádr-ă, *n. f.*, **védre**, *pl.*, bucket, old measure of about 14 litres.
vắduv-ă, *n. f.*, **-e**, *pl.*, widow.
vagabón-d, **-dă**, *adj.*, **-zi**, **-de**, *pl.*, vagabond, vagrant.
vag-ón, *n. mix.*, **-oáne**, *pl.*, wagon, railway carriage.
vái! *interj.*, woe.
val, *n. mix.*, **-uri**, *pl.*, wave; wall, rampart.
Valáhiea (*archaic*), see **Ţăra-Românească**=**Muntenia**.
vâlc-eá, *n. f.*, **-éle**, *pl.*, valley.
vále, *n. f.*, **văi**, *pl.*, valley; **la vale**, down.
vắlnic, *n. mix.*, **-e**, *pl.*, apronlike skirt of coloured woollen cloth.
val-oáre, *n. f.*, **-óri**, *pl.*, value, worth, price.
vălurél, *n. mix. dim.*, **-e**, *pl.*, small wave.
valút-ă, *n. f.*, **-e**, *pl.*, money.
van (în), *adv.*, in vain.
vắnă, *n. f.*, **víne**, *pl.*, vein; **a şedéa pe víne**, to lie squat.
vân-á (a), **-éz**, **-át**, *v. tr.* I, to hunt.
vânát, *n. mix.* (**-uri**, *pl.*), game, venison; hunting.
vânătór, *n. m.*, **-i**, *pl.*, hunter.
vânăt-oáre, *n. f.*, **-óri**, *pl.*, hunting.
vânător-ésc, **-eáscă**, *adj.*, **-éşti**, *pl.*, hunting.
vânt, *n. mix.*, **-uri**, *pl.*, wind.
vânz-áre, *n. f.*, **-ări**, *pl.*, sale.
văr, *n. m.*, **véri**, *pl.*, cousin.
váră, *n. f.*, **véri**, *pl.*, summer; **la váră**, *adv.*, next summer; **vára**, *adv.*, in summer.
váră, *n. f.*, **vére**, *pl.*, girl-cousin.
vărátec, **-ă**, *adj.*, **-i**, **-e**, *pl.*, (of the) summer.
vârí (a), **vâr**, **-ít**, *v. tr.* IV, to put into, to press in; **a se** —, to go in, to enter forcibly.
vari-á (a), **-éz**, **-at**, *v. tr.* II, to vary, to alter.
variet-áte, *n. f.*, **-ắţi**, *pl.*, variety.
vârf, *n. mix.*, **-uri**, *pl.*, peak, point, top.
vărs-á (a), **vărs**, **-át**, *v. tr.* I, to shed, to spill.
vắrst-ă, *n. f.*, **-e**, *pl.*, age.
vârtéj, *n. mix.*, **-uri** (**-e**), *pl.*, whirlwind; vortex.
vâr-tós, **-toásă**, *adj.*, **-tóşi**, **-toáse**, *pl.*, hard; strong, stable.
văruí (a), **-ésc**, **-ít**, *v. tr.* IV, to whitewash, to lime.
vas, *n. mix.*, **-e**, *pl.*, vase, vessel.
Vasilíu, *prop. n.* (surname).
Vaslúi, *prop. n. m.* (river, locality).
vátră, *n. f.*, **vétre**, *pl.*, hearth; open fire.
Vátra Moldovíţei, *prop. n. f.* (locality).
văzdúh, *n. mix.*, **-uri**, *pl.*, air, ether.
veác, *n. mix.*, **-uri**, *pl.*, generation, life; century.
véchi (u), **véche**, *adj.*, **véchi**, *pl.*, old (of things), ancient.
vecí-e, *n. f.*, **-i**, *pl.*, eternity; **în véci**, *adv.*, eternally.
vecín, *n. m.*, **-i**, *pl.*, neighbour.
vecín-ă, *n. f.*, **-e**, *pl.*, neighbour (woman).
vedeá (a), **văd**, **văzút**, *v. tr.*, *intr.* II, to see; **vedér-e**, *n. f.*, **-i**, *pl.*, eyesight, sight, view.

vedéni-e, *n. f.*, **-i**, *pl.*, vision, apparition.
vegetál-ă, *n. f.*, **-e**, *pl.*, plant.
véghe, *n. f.*, **-i**, *pl.*, watching, watch.
vegh-eá (a), **-éz**, **-át**, *v. tr.*, *intr.* II, to wake, to watch.
vení (a), **vin**, **venít**, *v. intr.* IV, to come.
venín, *n. mix.*, **-uri**, *pl.*, poison.
vérde, *adj.*, **vérzi**, *pl.*, green.
verde-áță, *n. f.*, **-țuri (-țe)**, *pl.*, verdure, green; greens.
vers, *n. mix.*, **-uri**, *pl.*, verse.
verzúi, **-e**, *adj.*, greenish.
vésel, **-ă**, *adj.*, **-i**, **-e**, *pl.*, merry, joyful.
véșnic, **-ă**, *adj.*, **-i**, **-e**, *pl.*, eternal.
Vest, *n. m.*, West.
véste, *n. f.*, **véști**, *pl.*, news.
vest-í (a), **-ésc**, **-ít**, *v. tr.* IV, to announce, to inform.
vézi, see **vedea (a)**.
vi, *pers. pron. dat.*, to you (see 5. 1. **a**).
viáță, *n. f.*, **viéți (viéțe)**, *pl.*, life.
vicl-eán, **-eánă**, *adj.*, **-éni**, **-éne**, *pl.*, cunning, sly.
viclen-í (a), **-ésc**, **-ít**, *v. tr.* IV, to deceive, to cheat.
victóri-e, *n. f.*, **-i**, *pl.*, victory; **victori-ós**, **-oásă**, *adj.*, **-óși**, **-oáse**, *pl.*, victorious.
ví-e, *n. f.*, **-i**, *pl.*, vine, vineyard.
Viéna, *n. f.*, Vienna.
viérm-e, *n. m.*, **-i**, *pl.*, worm.
viérs, see **vers**.
viésp-e, *n. f.*, **-i**, *pl.*, wasp.
viețui-toáre, *n. f.*, **-tóri**, *pl.*, being, living.
vifor-ós, **-oásă**, *adj.*, stormy, tempestuous.
vig (gig), *n. mix.*, **-uri**, *pl.*, web, piece.
vii-tór, **-toáre**, *adj.*, **-tóri**, **-toáre**, *pl.*, future, next; *n. m.*, future.
vin, *n. mix.*, **-uri**, *pl.*, wine.
víne, see **veni (a)**.
víneri, *n. f.*, Friday; **Víneria Máre**, Good Friday.
vinová-t, **-tă**, *adj.*, **-ți**, **-te**, *pl.*, guilty.
violé-t, **-tă**, *adj.*, **-ți**, **-te**, *pl.*, violet (colour).
vior-ícă, *n. f.*, **-éle**, *pl.*, violet.
vipí-e, *n. f.*, **-i**, *pl.* (Wal., Olt.), the most intensive part of an action, culmination point; extreme heat.
vírgulă, *n. f.*, **-e**, *pl.*, comma.
vis-á (a), **-éz**, **-át**, *v. tr.* I, to dream; **a se** —, to dream about oneself; **vis**, *n. mix.*, **-uri**, *pl.*, dream.
vis-áre, *n. f.*, **-ări**, *pl.*, dreaming.
víscol, *n. mix.*, **-e**, *pl.*, snowstorm, tempest.
visuní-e, *n. f.*, **-i**, *pl.*, see **vizuínă**.
vít-ă, *n. f.*, **-e**, *pl.*, cattle.
víț-ă, *n. f.*, **-e**, *pl.*, root; vine.
vit-eáz, **-eáză**, *adj.*, *n.*, **-éji**, **-éze**, *pl.*, brave, valiant, hero.
vitej-ésc, **-eáscă**, *adj.*, **-éști**, *pl.*, heroic, valiant, brave.
Vítus, **Veit**, *prop. n. m.*
ví-u, **-e**, *adj.*, **-i**, *pl.*, alive.
vízit-ă (vísită), *n. f.*, **-e**, *pl.*, visit, call.
vizuín-ă, *n. f.*, **-i**, *pl.*, den.
vlădíc-ă, *n. m.*, **-i**, *pl.*, bishop.
vlăstár, see **lăstár**.
vóce, *n. f.*, **-i**, *pl.*, voice.
Vódă, see **voevód**.
voevód, *n. m.*, **voevózi**, *pl.*, ruling Prince.
vói, *pers. pron.*, you (see 5. 1. **a**).
voí (a), **voiésc (vói)**, **voít**, to will (see 6. 1; 6. 3. **d**), to wish.
vóie, *n. f.*, permission, allowance; will; disposition.
voinínc, **-ă**, *adj.*, **-i**, **-e**, *pl.*, strong (physically), brave, valiant; buxom; **voinic-ésc**, **-eáscă**, *adj.*, **-éști**, *pl.*, brave.

voínţ-ă, *n. f.*, **-e**, *pl.*, will.
voi-ós, -oásă, *adj.*, **-óşi, -oáse**, *pl.*, gay, glad.
vórb-ă, *n. f.*, **-e**, *pl.*, word.
vorb-í (a), -ésc, -ít, *v. intr.*, to speak, to talk; **a se —**, to agree upon, to concert.
Voronéţ, *prop. n. m.* (locality).
vóstru, *poss. pron.*, your (see 5. 5).
vóuă, *pers. pron.*, to you (see 5. 1. **a**).
Vovidénie, *prop. n. f.* (locality).
vrábie, *n. f.*, **vrắbii**, *pl.*, sparrow.
vrăjmáş, *n. m.*, **-i**, *pl.*, enemy, foe.
Vrânc-eán, *prop. n. m.*, **-éni**, *pl.*, inhabitant of the region of **Vráncea** in the district of **Pútna**.
vreá (a), vreáu, vrut, *v. tr.*, *intr.* II, to will, to be willing, to wish (see 6. 3. **d**).
vrém-e, *n. f.*, **-i, -uri**, *pl.*, time, weather; **de cu vreme**, *adv.*, in good time; **de vreme**, *adv.*, early; **de vreme ce**, *conj.*, since, because.
vreún, vreó, *indef. pron.*, some, someone (see 5. 9).
vroí (a), see **voí (a)**.
vúiet, *n. mix.*, **-e**, *pl.*, noise.
vúlp-e, *n. f.*, **-i**, *pl.*, fox.
vúltur, *n. m.*, **-i**, *pl.*, eagle.

X

Xenópol, *prop. n.* (surname).

Z

zăbávă, *n. f.*, **zăbắvi**, *pl.*, retardation, enjoyment.
zâmb-í (a), -ésc, -ít, *v. intr.* IV, to smile.
zắmnic (zắmnic), *n. mix.*, **-e**, *pl.*, cellar.
zấn-ă, *n. f.*, **-e**, *pl.*, fairy, fay.
zárе, *n. f.*, **zắri**, *pl.*, horizon.
zăv-ói, *n. mix.*, **-oáie**, *pl.*, thicket on the borders of a river; river forest formed generally of small trees and bushes.
zbor (sbor), *n. mix.*, **-uri**, *pl.*, flight, flying.
zbuciumá (a se), see **sbuciumá (a se)**.
zdráv-ăn, -ănă, *adj.*, **-eni, -ene**, *pl.*, vigorous, strong, stout.
zéce, *num.*, **zéci**, *pl.*, ten.
zécelea (al), *m.*, **zécea (a)**, *f.*, the tenth.
zecím-e, *n. f.*, **-i**, *pl.*, tenth.
zéstre, *n. f.*, dowry, dower; **zestriş-oáră**, *n. f.*, **-oáre**, *pl.*, small dowry.
zé-u, *n. m.*, **-i**, *pl.*, god.
zgribulí (zgriburí, sgribulí) (a se), mă zgribul-ésc, -ít, *v. intr.* IV, to squat, to cower.
zi, *n. f.*, **-le**, *pl.*, day; **zíua**, the day.
ziár, *n. mix.*, **-e**, *pl.*, newspaper, journal, diary.
zíce (a), zic, zis, *v. intr.* III, to say, to tell.
zid, *n. mix.*, **-uri**, *pl.*, wall.
zidár, *n. m.*, **-i**, *pl.*, mason, bricklayer.
zid-í (a), -ésc, -ít, *v. tr.* IV, to build (with stone or brick).
zóri, *n. f. pl.* (*n. m. pl.*), dawn; **în zori**, *adv.*, in the dawn; **în zori de zi**, *adv.*, in the dawn.
zméură, *n. f.*, raspberry.
zugrăv-í (a), -ésc, -ít, *v. tr.* IV, to paint.
zup! *interj.*, down.
zvârr! *interj.*, from **zvârli (a)**.
zvârcolí (a se), see **svârcoli (a se)**.
zvârlí (a), see **svârli (a)**.
zvoní (a), zvon-ésc, -ít, *v. tr.* IV, to announce, to rumour; **a se —**, to rumour.
zvon, see **svon**.